# HENRY OF NAVARRE

**HENRY IV.**
From a contemporary painting in museum at Versailles.

# HENRY OF NAVARRE

AND

## THE HUGUENOTS IN FRANCE

BY

## P. F. WILLERT, M.A.

FELLOW OF EXETER COLLEGE, OXFORD

---

"Truly your great enemy is the Spaniard.' He is naturally so, he is
naturally so throughout—by reason of that enmity that is in him against
whatsoever is of God."—OLIVER CROMWELL.

---

## AMS PRESS
### NEW YORK

Reprinted from the edition of 1893, New York and London
First AMS EDITION published 1971
Manufactured in the United States of America


International Standard Book Number: 0-404-06949-5

Library of Congress Number: 76-149680




AMS PRESS INC.
NEW YORK, N.Y. 10003

# CONTENTS.

CHAPTER                PAGE

I.—THE REFORMATION IN FRANCE—THE WARS OF RELIGION BEFORE THE DEATH OF CONDÉ (1512–1569) . . . . . . I

II.—THE PARENTAGE OF HENRY OF BOURBON—HIS EDUCATION AND MARRIAGE—ST. BARTHOLOMEW—THE PEACE OF ˋMONSIEUR (1555–1576) . . . . . . 44

III.—HENRY OF NAVARRE THE PROTECTOR OF THE CHURCHES (1576–1586) . . . III

IV.—THE THREE HENRYS (1585–1589) . . 149

V.—CAN A HERETIC BE KING OF FRANCE? (1589–1592) . . . . . . 183

VI.—THE KING GOES TO MASS, AND ENTERS PARIS (1592–1595) . . . . . . 247

VII.—OPEN WAR WITH SPAIN—PEACE WITH FOREIGN AND DOMESTIC ENEMIES—THE EDICT OF NANTES (1595–1598) . . . . 292

VIII.—THE REORGANISATION OF THE MONARCHY (1598–1610) .40337. . . . 347

IX —THE DIVORCE AND SECOND MARRIAGE OF THE KING (1598–1601) . . . . 378

iii

| CHAPTER | PAGE |
|---|---|
| X.—WAR WITH SAVOY — SPANISH INTRIGUES—CONSPIRACIES OF BIRON AND THE ENTRAGUES (1599–1609) . . . . | 399 |
| XI.—COMPLICATIONS IN GERMANY — PREPARATIONS FOR WAR—ASSASSINATION OF THE KING (1609–1610) . . . . . | 428 |

GENEALOGICAL TABLES

| | | |
|---|---|---|
| HOUSE OF LORRAINE . . . *facing page* | | 464 |
| HOUSE OF BOURBON-VENDÔME . . " " | | 465 |

INDEX . . . . . . . . 465

# ILLUSTRATIONS.

PAGE

PORTRAIT OF HENRY IV. FROM A CONTEMPORARY
PAINTING IN MUSEUM AT VERSAILLES, *Frontispiece*

PORTRAIT OF ADMIRAL COLIGNY . . . . 60

MEDAL OF CHARLES IX. STRUCK TO COMMEMORATE
THE MASSACRE OF ST. BARTHOLOMEW . . 78

MEDAL OF GREGORY XIII. STRUCK TO COMMEMORATE
THE MASSACRE OF ST. BARTHOLOMEW . . 78

PORTRAIT OF HENRY III. . . . . . 92

PORTRAIT OF CHARLES IX. FROM THE PAINTING
BY F. CLOUET . . . . . . . 100

PORTRAIT OF CATHERINE DE' MEDICI . . . 146

FAC-SIMILE OF THE WRITING OF HENRY IV. . . 152

PORTRAIT OF DUKE HENRY OF GUISE. FROM THE
PAINTING BY F. CLOUET . . . . 170

PORTRAIT OF HENRY IV. . . . . . 216

ENTRANCE OF HENRY IV. INTO PARIS (BY THE
NEW GATE). FROM A CONTEMPORARY EN-
GRAVING OF A PAINTING BY N. BOLLERY . 282

EXIT OF THE SPANIARDS FROM PARIS (BY THE
ST. DENIS GATE). FROM A CONTEMPORARY
ENGRAVING . . . . . . . 284

PORTRAIT OF MARGARET OF VALOIS . . . 380

PORTRAIT OF MARY OF MEDICI. FROM THE
PAINTING BY F. PORBUS IN PRADO MUSEUM
IN MADRID . . . . . . . 394

DEATH MASK TAKEN FROM FACE OF HENRY IV. . 454

# HENRY OF NAVARRE

## AND THE HUGUENOTS IN FRANCE.

### CHAPTER I.

#### THE REFORMATION IN FRANCE—THE WARS OF RELIGION BEFORE THE DEATH OF CONDÉ.

#### 1512–1569.

RENCH historians, anxious to vindicate in all things the priority of their nation, point out that in 1512, five years before Luther denounced the sale of indulgences, Lefevre, a lecturer on theology and letters at Paris, published a commentary on the Epistles of St. Paul in which he taught the doctrine of justification by faith.

But an isolated theologian might deny the efficacy of good works without danger to the established system, so long as the logical consequences of such doctrine were not pressed vigorously home against the abuses of Rome. Lefevre had nothing of the passionate activity of a successful reformer; his teaching produced little effect till the minds of men were stirred by the great events taking place in Germany.

Lefevre and his friends did little more than give expression to the general desire that the Church should be reformed from within. They were supported by the sympathy of the scholars and men of letters who had long been engaged in a bitter quarrel with the monkish pedants, to whom the system and the maxims of the schoolmen were not less sacred than the cardinal doctrines of the Church.

The false renderings, the spurious documents, the historical frauds and obsolete philosophy, on which the Catholic theologians of the day relied, hardly allowed a learned man to be orthodox.

But these cultivated men had not the fervour and their doctrine lacked the emphasis needed to stir popular enthusiasm; the real impulse to the Reformation in France was given by men of more decided views, who at first, with the exception of Farel, a friend of Lefevre, belonged to a lower class.

The growth of heresy did not escape the notice of the University of Paris, the acknowledged judge and champion of orthodoxy throughout Latin Christendom. In the 14th century the University had interfered in politics with the authority of a Fourth Estate and had lectured kings and princes. In the 15th century at the Councils of Constance and Basle its doctors had been the acknowledged leaders of the Western Church. As if foreseeing the approaching struggle, the faculty of theology, the Sorbonne, as it was called from the name of the College founded by Lewis IX. for the support of the teachers of divinity, appointed a permanent committee to watch over the purity of the faith.

Heresy was in France an offence against the Common Law, and those accused of it were tried before the ordinary courts of justice; but these courts never entered into the question of what constituted heresy, allowing the decision of the Sorbonne to be final on that point. Hence their function seemed to be little more than the punishment of whomsoever the theologians chose to pronounce guilty.

In 1521 the Sorbonne solemnly condemned the doctrines of Luther, declaring that they ought to be extirpated by fire and sword; yet the new sectaries were little molested till after the fatal day of Pavia.

Francis I. was not sorry to have a convenient bugbear wherewith to frighten the clergy. He was also disposed to toleration by more worthy motives, by the influence of his sister Margaret, and by his unfeigned sympathy with letters and culture, the best trait in a character which has been saved from well deserved infamy by the gratitude of the Muses. But when the King was captive in Spain the Regent, his mother, was anxious to secure the co-operation of the Pope and clergy in her efforts for his liberation, and the heretics, who it was said had drawn down the wrath of heaven on their country, had a foretaste of the severities which awaited them. Lewis de Berquin a young man of great promise, a scholar and a courtier, was thrown into prison, al-

though a favourite of the King.   On the return of
Francis, Berquin was released.   Erasmus, whose Col-
loquies had been condemned by the Sorbonne, was
invited to Paris, but preferred to revenge himself on
his opponents by satire from a safe distance.   He
criticised a book published by Beda, the leader of
the bigots of the University, and proved that that
pillar of orthodoxy had been guilty of eighty lies,
three hundred calumnies, forty-seven blasphemies.
Lefevre now in his eightieth year, who had recently
completed his translation of the New Testament
into French, was recalled from Strasburg and appointed tutor of the King's youngest son.   The
hopes of the reforming party ran high.   Zwingli
the most amiable and tolerant of the great fathers
of the Reformation dedicated his book on true and
false religion to the King of France.

But the tide of court favour was already turning :
the influence of Margaret over her brother was in the
wane.   The Chancellor Duprat, who aspired to the
Papacy, and the King's favourite the Constable Anne
of Montmorency, urged the repression of heresy.
Yet Francis hesitated to sanction active persecution
—when an event occurred which at once gave the
preponderance to the fanatical party.

One evening ( June 1, 1528) an image of the Virgin
at a street corner in Paris was thrown down and
mutilated.   The whole town was in an uproar ; the
numerous guilds formed in honour of Our Lady
looked upon the outrage as a personal insult.   The
ignorant mob was infuriated by such sacrilege to their
favourite deity, the better classes were alarmed by

this proof of the audacity of the sectaries, the King was indignant at an act which seemed an abuse of his indulgence and which was likely to provoke disorder. For a whole week there were expiatory processions—processions of the University, of the clergy, of the King and his courtiers. The partisans of persecution triumphed, and Lewis de Berquin was one of their first victims.

Henceforth the history of French Protestantism is that of an oppressed minority, never safe from legal persecution and from public and private violence, except when, from time to time, their own valour and resolution or political expediency obtained for them a partial and precarious respite.

Persecution compelled the French Reformers to become a church militant, yet it may be doubted whether any organisation or discipline would have enabled them to increase their numbers and their influence during the remainder of the reign of Francis I. and that of Henry II., exposed as they were to the rigour of the law and the hatred of the mob, had they not found a leader and an inexpugnable citadel—Calvin and Geneva.

Calvin threw the doctrines of the French Reformers into the most definite and logical form possible—he organised their churches, his personal influence gave unity to their councils.

Under the anagram of Alcuin, Calvin published in 1555, after he had fled from Paris to Basle, a book called *Institution de la Religion Chrétienne* dedicated to Francis I. It professed to be an exposition of the doctrines of the Reformers, and to point out how undeserving they were of persecution, and how untainted by all doctrines dangerous to society. In this book—amplified in later editions—Calvin laid the foundations of the religion of the Huguenots, of the Dutch, of the Scotch, of the Puritans in England and America, in short of the most heroic, the most militant and the most characteristic form of Protestantism.

In the dogmatic part of the treatise Calvin does not originate, he only presses the doctrines of others to their logical conclusions. The fundamental dogma—justification by faith of those elected by grace —is borrowed from Luther and Lefevre. But Calvin draws from their premises the irrefutable conclusion, that those predestined to salvation by the certain foreknowledge of God must of necessity be saved. More original than his dogmatic theology was the combination by Calvin of views about church government far more revolutionary than those of the Lutherans with the High Church doctrine of the independence of the Church and of its authority over the State. "He saw," says a French historian, "the Church among the Lutherans fallen from the control of the Pope to that of the princes, and that the great maxim of Luther, ' Every man is a priest,' was interpreted in practice to mean, ' Every prince is a Pope.' Even in Switzerland, where there were no princes, the magistrates took upon themselves to legislate for the Church, which appeared to be upon the point of becoming wholly merged in the State." Calvin endeavoured to secure her independence and spiritual authority. He insists upon the importance

and power of the ministry, who are to be elected
with the consent and approval of the people, the
pastors presiding over the election.   The Consistory,
the assembly of ministers and elders, must admonish
and censure all breaches of discipline and morality.
The Church, as represented by this assemblage, has
the power of the keys, the right of excommunication
—surely an empty terror to the Elect?   There is no
remission of sins for those who are outside the pale
of Christ's Church, we must therefore beware of
separating ourselves from it, because we may have
been offended by some trifling imperfections.   The
true Church is that in which the Gospels are faithfully and simply preached, in which the sacra-
ments are administered according to the ordinance
of Christ, as interpreted by Calvin, and in which
new articles of faith are not devised; those who
separate themselves from the true Church, like the
Anabaptists, those who adhere to a false church like
the Papists, are alike apostates from the faith and
irrevocably damned.

It might be supposed that a careless despair, or a
self-satisfied and inactive acquiescence in the conviction of personal election would result from rigid
predestinarianism.   But this has not been the case.
No doctrine has proved more capable of nerving
men for great efforts, of sustaining them in moments
of doubt and difficulty and isolation.   The feeling
that we are but the puppets, or the passive instruments of an overruling fate—identified with the
Divine Will—has enabled the soldier to advance
undaunted to a hopeless struggle, the reformer to

attack institutions which have the sanction of centuries, the martyr to believe in his cause amid the
execration of a unanimous crowd.

The Papacy had upheld monarchical principles in
the Church.　Œcumenical councils had asserted
the authority of an hierarchical aristocracy.　The
constitution of Calvinism was representative and
democratic.　It is therefore natural that no other
religious system should have shown itself so favourable to political freedom.　The struggles for liberty
and constitutional government made by the European nations during the 16th and 17th centuries
are unmistakably connected with Calvinism.
In the Netherlands, as in Scotland, the return
of the Protestant exiles who had taken refuge at
Geneva was the signal for resistance to the excesses
of arbitrary power.　The English refugees who fled
from the persecution of Mary Tudor became the
founders of the great Puritan party.　Nowhere—
not even at his own Geneva—were the principles of
Calvin more energetically carried out than in New
England, by the Pilgrim Fathers, the founders of
the freest as well as the greatest republic the world
is ever likely to see.

In France, as elsewhere, the Calvinists were the
opponents of despotism, the champions of popular
government.　That some historians should have
failed to see this must be explained by the accident,
that the prince whom the Huguenots recognised as
their leader, happened to be the claimant of the
throne by indefeasible hereditary right, so that his
and their enemies naturally appealed to the elective

and popular theory of sovereignty; while their alliance with the populace of the big towns gave a spurious air of democracy to these defenders of the Papacy and clients of the Spanish tyrant.

Calvin became the legislator, the acknowledged leader of the French Reformers, yet even Calvin could have effected little without Geneva. That little town, situated on the confines of three nationalities and inhabited by a French-speaking population, was admirably adapted by its position to interpret the teaching of Germany and Switzerland to France. For a hundred years Geneva was the citadel of the Evangelical religion. There were the printing-presses which, as St. Francis de Sales complained, scattered their pestilential produce over all the world; there was the Seminary, where the ministers were trained who preached the Gospel to congregations assembled by stealth on desert mountain or heath, or in towns amid the more dangerous fanaticism of the crowd, whose least hazardous service was to invoke the blessing of heaven while they accompanied their flock into battle. There exiles and pilgrims from every part of Europe met and took council for the common interests of the Cause.

The influence of Calvin and of his doctrines was needed to give the French Reformers the energy and the organisation which enabled them to sustain an unequal and unavoidable conflict; yet that conflict was embittered, the issue enlarged and a compromise made impossible by the extreme and aggressive form assumed by French dissent. The majority of Englishmen who conformed with equal readiness to

the religion by law established under Mary Tudor
or Elizabeth probably saw no essential difference
between a service said in Latin or in English, but
the most careless Gallio could not but perceive
something more than a dissimilarity in forms between the prayers in a Calvinist meeting-house and
the "idolatrous sacrifice" of the Mass.

Francis I. had long shrunk from persecution, but
having once begun he showed no further hesitation.
During the remainder of his reign and the whole of
that of his son Henry II. (1534–1559) the cruelty of
the sufferings inflicted on the Reformers increased
with the number of the victims.   At first they were
strangled and burnt, then burnt alive, then hung in
chains to roast over a slow fire.   It was found that
this last method of prolonging their agony gave
them time to sing their psalms and to pray for their
persecutors from the midst of the flames.   Even the
stupid ferocity of the mob might be touched; it was
therefore ordered that they should be gagged; but
the fire snapped the cords, the gag fell out and the
ejaculations of the half-charred lips excited pity: it
seemed a safer plan to cut out the tongues of the
heretics before they were led to execution.

The Edict of Chateaubriand (1551), taking away all
right of appeal from those convicted of heresy, was
followed by an attempt to introduce an Inquisition
on the model of that of Spain, and when this failed
owing to the opposition of the lawyers, the Edict of
Compiègne (1557) denounced capital punishment
against all who in public or private professed any
heterodox doctrine.

It is a commonplace that persecution avails nothing against the truth—that the true Church springs from the blood of martyrs. Yet the same cause which triumphed over persecution in France was crushed by it in Spain and in the Walloon Netherlands. Was it therefore not the truth? The fact would rather seem to be, that there is no creed, no sect which cannot be extirpated by force. But that it may prevail, persecution must be without respect of persons, universal, continuous, protracted. Not one of these conditions was fulfilled in France. The opinions of the greater nobles and princes, and of those who were their immediate followers, were not too narrowly scanned, nor was the persecution equally severe at all times and in all places. Some governors and judges and not a few of the higher clergy inclined to toleration. Sadolet, Bishop of Carpentras, protected the Vaudois, and Du Châtel of Macon saved for a time Stephen Dolet, the learned friend of Rabelais. "Do you, a Catholic bishop, dare to defend a Lutheran and an atheist?" asked the pitiless Cardinal Tournon. "I am a bishop and I speak like a bishop," was the undaunted reply; "but you—you play the hangman." At the worst the preachers of the Word found a sure refuge at Geneva, in the dominions of the Bourbons and at Montargis, where Renée of France, the Duchess of Ferrara, kept her court.

The cheerful constancy of the French martyrs was admirable. Men, women and children walked to execution singing the psalms of Marot and the Song of Simeon. This boldness confounded their enemies.

Hawkers distributed in every part of the country the books issued from the press of Geneva and which it was a capital offence even to possess. Preachers taught openly in streets and market-places. One of these missionaries of the Gospel was asked when in prison, how it came that he laughed and rejoiced in the prospect of death, although our Saviour in His agony sweated blood and prayed that the cup might pass from Him? Still smiling, he replied, " Christ had taken upon Him all human infirmities and felt the bitterness of death, but I, who by faith possess such a blessing, the assurance of salvation, what can I but rejoice?" Such men died in ecstasy, insensible to the diabolical ingenuity of the punishments inflicted on them. The sight of sufferings thus endured could not be without an effect. More than one judge was stricken to death with horror and remorse; others embraced the faith of their victims. The executioner of Dijon proclaimed his conversion at the foot of the scaffold.

The increasing numbers of their converts and the high position of some among them gave confidence to the Protestants. Delegates from the reformed congregations of France were on their way to Paris to take part in the deliberations of the first national Synod on the very day (April 2, 1559) when the peace of Cateau Cambresis was signed, a peace which was to be the prelude to a vigorous and concerted effort to root out heresy on the part of the kings of France and Spain. The object of the meeting was twofold: first to draw up a detailed profession of faith, which was submitted to Calvin—

there was, he said, little to add, less to correct—
secondly to determine the "ecclesiastical discipline"
of the new Church.  The ministers were to be chosen
by the elders and deacons, but approved by the
whole congregation.  The affairs of each congregation were placed under the control of the Consistory,
a court composed of the pastors, elders and deacons;
more important matters were reserved for the decision of the provincial "colloques" or synods, which
were to meet twice a year, and in which each church
was represented by its pastor and at least one elder.
Above all was the national Synod also composed of
the clergy and of representative laymen.

This organisation was thoroughly representative
and popular, the elected delegates of the congregations, the elders and deacons, preponderated in all
the governing bodies, and all ministers and churches
were declared equal.

The Reformed churches, which although most numerous in the South spread over almost the whole
country, are said at this time to have counted some
400,000 members (1559).  These were of almost all
classes, except perhaps the lowest, although even
among the peasantry there were some martyrs for
the faith.  Coligny truly said that the lowly had
been the first to show the way of salvation to the
rich and powerful; the vast majority of the earliest
converts belonged to the middle classes, the better
educated artisans and traders and to the lower ranks
of the professions; but the upper classes had not
been slow to follow.  Little is proved by Michelet's
assertion that he could find only three men of noble

birth among the lists of victims who perished before 1555, except that the privileged classes escaped the persecution the weight of which fell on their poorer brethren.

The first minister of the Church of Paris, which was founded by a noble, was the son of a rich and dignified magistrate of Dijon; honourable women were among its earliest martyrs. The first converts in Dauphiny were of gentle birth. The Edict of Fontainebleau (1540) speaks of the favour and support received by the heretics from men of rank. In Brittany the nobles welcomed the new teaching which was rejected by the ignorant and superstitious peasantry.

The rapid diffusion of their doctrines among the upper classes and the consciousness of the sympathy and support of men of great position probably gave the Huguenots a boldness remarkable in a small and persecuted minority: but it would be altogether erroneous to imagine that they were an oligarchical faction. The strength of the Protestants always lay among the trading and professional classes and the country gentry. From these classes came the men who were the first to embrace a simpler faith and who clung to it after great nobles, courtiers and statesmen had fallen away. At the Revocation of the Edict of Nantes not many Schombergs and Ruvignys passed the frontiers, but thousands of skilful artisans, frugal tradesmen and honourable merchants.

The most significant, and to the orthodox the most alarming, symptom of the diffusion of the new opinions and of the sympathy with which they were regarded, was that the Parliament of Paris, long the uncompromising opponent of dissent, hesitated to enforce the laws against heresy.

Henry II. determined himself to be present at a general meeting of the members of the various courts of law, at which it was proposed to decide how the laws against heresy should be applied. It was thought that the King's presence would over-awe those who were in favour of toleration. But the most respectable magistrates disdained to conceal their opinions. Anne du Bourg thanked God that his Majesty was present at the decision of a matter which concerned the cause of our Saviour. "It was," he said, "no light thing to condemn those who from the midst of the flames call upon His name. What! Crimes most worthy of death, blasphemy, adultery, horrible sins and perjuries are committed day by day with impunity in the face of heaven, while day by day new tortures are devised for men whose only crime is that by the light of the Scriptures they have discovered the corruptions of the Church of Rome!" "Let us clearly understand," said another judge, "who they are that trouble the Church, lest it should be said, as Elijah cried to King Ahab, 'Thou art he that troublest Israel.'" The indignation of the King exceeded all measure. He ordered Du Bourg and seven others to be at once committed to the Bastille; he swore he would see Du Bourg burn with his own eyes.

But before his vengeance could take effect Henry II. tilting with the Captain of his Guards was killed

by the splinter of a lance. Some bold believer who
had access to the room where the King's body lay,
threw over the corpse a piece of tapestry: Saul falling from his horse on the road to Damascus, as the
terrible words sounded in his ears, " Saul, Saul, why
persecutest thou me ? "

Although the Protestants saw the judgment of
God in the King's death, the more farsighted among
them must have doubted whether that event was
likely to improve their position. Two policies had
divided the councils of Henry II. The Constable
Montmorency had been in favour of alliance with
Spain, an alliance the necessary consequence of
which was the violent suppression of heresy. Montmorency's rivals, the Guises, although not less hostile to the Reformers, were opposed to the Spanish
connection. They wished to support the claims of
their niece Mary Stuart to the English throne, and
dreamt of uniting France, Scotland and England
into a monarchy capable of balancing the Austro-
Spanish power. Thus it came that Philip II. was
compelled to protect the heretic Elizabeth, while
the Guises were placed in the difficult position of
being at once the enemies of Spain and of Protestantism.

The Guises, ignoring the elder branch of their
family, which sought to maintain itself peaceably and
unambitiously in Lorraine, and to provoke as little
as might be the interference of more powerful neighbours, claimed to be the representatives of the
ambitious and unfortunate House of Anjou, from
which they were descended in the female line. Duke

Francis signed his marriage contract " Francis of Anjou "; he obtained from Henry II. when Dauphin a promise of the investiture, or as he preferred to call it the " restitution " of Provence ; he sacrificed, when commanding an army in Italy, the interests of France to some chimerical plan for asserting the old Angevin claim to the Crown of Naples. This baseless assumption was the prelude to bolder flights of ambitious fancy. The time was not far distant when the agents and pamphleteers of the House of Lorraine strove to establish that the Crown of France might more justly be worn by the descendants of Charles the Great than by any member of the usurping House of Capet.

The Duke of Guise had the reputation of a great and popular captain. He had been successful in war, his bravery was undoubted, and he affected magnanimity in success and a soldierly directness of bearing and conduct. The pliant disposition of his brother the Cardinal, his experience in every form of intrigue, maintained the influence of the family at Court, and enabled the Duke to stand aloof from a contest of meanness and duplicity, alien not so much to his real character as to an ostentatious display of chivalrous pride and independence.

The Cardinal of Lorraine was of graceful and commanding presence, gifted with refined and persuasive eloquence, an accomplished scholar and singularly successful in winning the confidence of those with whom he conversed ; but he was as mean-spirited and despondent in adversity as he was arrogant and presumptuous in success, and the lustre of many splendid qualities was dimmed by a sordid avarice unusual in a man of such lofty ambition ; and not to be excused in one who enjoyed the revenues of three archbishoprics, nine bishoprics and numerous other benefices.

The accession of Francis II. threw the whole government of the State into the hands of the Guises. The new King was a sickly boy, weak in body and mind, the slave of his wife Mary Stuart, who was herself ruled by her uncles.

The Cardinal of Lorraine was so elated to find himself in the undisputed control of the royal power that he disdained to conciliate his rivals and enemies. The Princes of the Blood were treated with contempt, the Queen-Mother was neglected, no attempt was made to disarm the hostility of the nobles, who hated the Guises as foreign favourites and upstarts. The Protestants were persecuted with increased severity. All who attended their meetings, all who knew of such meetings and did not at once denounce them, were to be punished by death. Du Bourg was burnt, notwithstanding the urgent intercessions of the Elector Palatine and the Swiss.

The authority of the Guises depended on the frail life of the King ; their power was not firmly enough established to render hopeless the thoughts of resistance which it provoked. These Lotheringians, it was muttered, had usurped the Government ; if the King was himself incapable of ruling he ought to be assisted by the natural advisers of the Crown, the Princes of the Blood, the great officers of state, the representatives of the Three Estates of the Realm.

Calvin persistently inculcated the passive endurance of persecution, and the majority of the ministers of the French Church were his obedient disciples, but it became more and more difficult for them to restrain their flocks.  The early Christians had suffered themselves to be led unresistingly to martyrdom, and had not cared to attempt to reform— except by their prayers and example—a state and a society of which they scarcely felt themselves to be members, and the end of which they believed to be at hand.  There was little of this patient spirit about the Huguenots—as the French Protestants began to be called.*  Those of them who belonged to the middle classes had not yet forgotten the struggles of their ancestors for municipal independence ; the country people had, it is true, been accustomed to oppression, but there were few proselytes among the peasantry, except where, as in Languedoc and the country of the Vaudois, the ground was prepared by older traditions of resistance ; least of all were the Protestant noblemen and gentlemen, whose numbers were rapidly increasing, disposed quietly to submit to persecution.  By what arguments could Calvin restrain them ?  He might appeal to a few isolated texts in the New Testament, but the Huguenots, like the Puritans, considered themselves a chosen people, and could find warrant enough in Holy Writ for smiting the enemies of the Lord.  If any scruple was still felt in resisting a

---

* The derivation of this name is very obscure.   According to the most probable guess it is a corruption of the German, " *Eidgenossen,*" confederates.

lawfully constituted authority, this, it was urged, did
not apply to the tyranny of the Guises. Moreover,
the Protestants were dragged before extraordinary
tribunals unknown to the laws, or hunted down by
riotous mobs. It was afterwards their boast, that
they had patiently submitted so long as they had
been butchered under the forms of law and by
sentence of the established courts.

In the spring of 1560, partly among the Huguenots, partly among those who for public or private
reasons hated the Guises, a plot was formed to seize
the King and to place the Prince of Condé at the
head of the Government. The conspirators failed,
and were cruelly punished. But at an assembly of
notables, which the Cardinal had summoned in his
first alarm, those who were opposed to the policy
of the Government on religious and political grounds
made themselves heard. Marillac, Archbishop of
Vienne, an old diplomatist, insisted that the representatives of the nation ought to take their part in
the government of the country ; the Admiral of
France, Coligny, presented a petition from the
Reformers of Normandy, of which province he was
governor, repudiating all sympathy with the late
conspiracy but demanding toleration.

The Guises believed that the influence of the
Government could secure a subservient majority and
determined to summon the Estates. The Protestants were to be excluded by requiring all members
to subscribe an orthodox confession of faith. All
who refused to do so would not only not be allowed
to take their seats, but would be at once thrown into

prison and punished as heretics without further form of trial.

By these means the Guises trusted to obtain from the States-General such a confirmation of their authority as might effectually silence all objections to its legitimacy.   They were the more confident because the men who would have been the natural leaders of all opposition both religious and political, Antony of Bourbon, King of Navarre, and his brother Lewis, Prince of Condé, had foolishly ventured to Court and placed themselves in their power, and might be punished as accomplices in the conspiracy against the liberty of the King.

The death of Francis II. (December 5, 1560) frustrated all these plans.   The accession of Charles IX., a child barely eleven years old, necessitated the appointment of a Regent.   That Regent could only be the Queen-Mother or the first Prince of the Blood, the King of Navarre.   But the latter had promised Catherine de' Medici as the price of her protection against the Guises, that he would not, in the event of the King's death, press his claim to the Regency, and he now kept his word.   But the council decided that all questions should in the first instance be referred to him, and if his authority carried little weight, this was due rather to his weakness and want of political skill, than to the fact that he did not hold the title of Regent.

The States-General met on December 15, 1560, but under auspices very different from what had been anticipated.   The enemies of the Guises, the Bourbons, Montmorency and Châtillons, were now

in the ascendant in the royal council. Notwithstanding government influence many Protestants
had been elected and were allowed to take their
seats ; a larger number of members belonged to the
moderate party ; and as yet all who were not fanatically orthodox were disposed to sympathise with
the Huguenots, who so far had suffered without
attempting to retaliate on their enemies.

The proceedings of the States-General of 1561
would, had we space, be deserving of our most careful attention, because they show that there was at
that time in France a large party in favour of a
policy of religious, constitutional and administrative
reform, which could it have been adopted might
have changed the whole future of the country and
have saved it from many years, perhaps from centuries,
of war, suffering, despotism and revolution : because
then for the first time we find the great principle of
toleration authoritatively laid down. " It is unreasonable to compel men to do what in their hearts
they consider wrong. . . . for whatever we do
against our conscience is sin."

The Estates would have sold the property of the
Church for the benefit of the King and nation, reformed Religion in accordance with the word of God.
as interpreted by a national council in which both
the clergy and representative laymen should have
sat, limited the royal prerogative by periodical meetings of the representatives of the nation, diminished
the privileges of the nobles, and substituted an elective magistracy for one which, owing to the sale of
offices, was rapidly becoming hereditary.

The demands of the States-General of 1561 are the best evidence of the political tendencies of the majority of the Huguenots and of those moderate men who although opposed or indifferent to changes in doctrine were hostile to the Pope, the King of Spain and the Guises. We may contemplate in them an ideal, compared with which all that Henry IV. was able to effect shrinks into insignificance. But what he attempted was possible, the scheme of the Reformers of 1561 was too complete and consistent to be within the range of practical politics. Changes so great could only have been effected by an overwhelming tide of public opinion, or by an energetic minority controlling the machinery of government. The States-General were not supported by public opinion and many of the measures they proposed excited the violent opposition of all constituted authorities. The Third Estate for the most part represented municipal oligarchies, neither numerous nor popular. The nobility were not organised for united action ; among their natural leaders, the great nobles and princes, there were few who were not mainly actuated by selfish motives, and those few were wanting in political insight. Coligny, pre eminent in character, ability and position, failed to see that a reformed Church was possible only in a reformed State.

Not only did the proposals of the Estates meet with no acceptance, but the dislike with which they were regarded was extended to the religious opinions with which they were believed to be connected.

We may henceforth notice a marked change in the

attitude of the Parliaments, of the higher clergy and of a powerful party at Court, whose enmity to the Huguenots became implacable. The lawyers were indignant at the attempt, if not suggested, at any rate countenanced by the Protestants, to interfere with the number, the emoluments and the tenure of judicial offices, which they had begun to consider the hereditary possessions of their families. They were especially jealous of the interference of the States-General, for they had never regarded the principle of representative government with favour, and had themselves usurped many of the functions which a popular assembly, meeting at regular intervals, would have resumed. Henceforward all but a small minority of the judges were eager to strain the laws against the dissenters and reluctant to apply them in their favour.

It was, as we shall see, only after years of civil war, after full experience of the unpatriotic fanaticism, the anarchy, the selfish and unconstitutional ambition of the League and its leaders, after the weight of their traditional respect for monarchical principles had been thrown into the scale, that a considerable number of the more eminent lawyers joined the moderate or " political " party ; and, even then, a majority in the courts opposed the formal recognition of the principle of toleration.

Hitherto, also, many of the higher clergy, though they had not embraced Calvinism, had been well disposed to some measures of reform, which, freeing them from the interference of the Roman Curia and the avarice of Italian churchmen, might leave them in the enjoyment of their revenues and dignity ; but henceforth, since the Reformers proposed the secularisation of the estates of the Church, they could only be regarded as pestilent heretics.

A proposal to resume the lavish grants of money, crown lands and pensions made to his favourites by Henry II. alarmed and irritated many powerful men, such as the Constable Montmorency and Marshal St. André ; while the fact that the Huguenots should have been able to exercise so great an influence over the election of the members of the Estates, was a confirmation of the alarming reports of the wide diffusion of the new doctrines. Fear stimulated the hatred of their enemies.

A quarter of the inhabitants of France were, it was said, included in the 2,500 reformed congregations. This is certainly an exaggeration, but it is probable that the number of the Protestants was never greater than during the first years of the reign of Charles IX. What that number was we can only guess. The 2,500 congregations may have existed ; but while some of these counted many hundred or even thousand members, others were composed of only the family and retainers of the owner of the manor house in which they met. On the other hand among the townspeople and smaller gentry there must have been numerous believers who had no opportunity of public worship, or but seldom met to partake of the rare ministrations of an itinerant preacher. The most probable estimate is that at the beginning of the wars of religion, the Huguenots with women and children amounted to some

1,500,000 souls out of a population of between fifteen and twenty millions. But in this minority were included about one-fourth of the lesser nobility, the country gentlemen, and a smaller proportion of the great nobles, the majority of the better sort of townspeople in many of the most important towns, such as Caen, Dieppe, Havre, Nantes, La Rochelle, Nîmes, Montpellier, Montauban, Châlons, Mâcon, Lyons, Valence, Limoges and Grenoble, and an important minority in other places, such as Rouen, Orleans, Bordeaux and Toulouse. The Protestants were most numerous in the South-west, in Poitou, in the Marche, Limousin, Angoumois and Perigord, because in those districts, which were the seats of long-established and flourishing manufactures, the middle classes were most prosperous, intelligent and educated.

It is doubtful whether the Catholics were not in a large majority, even where the superior position, intelligence and vigour of the Huguenots gave them the upper hand. Only in some parts of the South-west and of Dauphiny do the bulk of the population appear to have been decidedly hostile to the old religion.

During the course of the Civil War the Protestants came to be more and more concentrated in certain parts of the country, as for instance between the Garonne and the Loire. A scheme for the conversion of this district into a Protestant republic was discussed by the English Council as late as 1625. Where they were not strong enough to hold their own in arms the Huguenots were either compelled to migrate or were butchered and extirpated.

On the first outbreak of hostilities, the Catholics of Toulouse supported by the Parliament massacred or drove into exile 3,000 heretics,—among them a majority of the scholars of the University and nearly all the leading members of the municipality. In Provence, although supported by the Governor, the Count of Tenda, the Protestants could not maintain themselves. The Parliament of Aix began the work of extirpation by sentencing 1,300 heretics to the flames. These are two instances out of many. Thus it was that Protestantism tended to become more and more local in character. Yet from the first it made little way in the North-east, in Picardy and in Champagne, and in the very heart of the country, the Isle de France. It must therefore be allowed that the Reformation took root most readily in those provinces where the traditions of local independence were strongest, or the immediate authority of the Crown most recent, in Gascony, Guienne, Languedoc and Dauphiny.

The Huguenot preachers at first met with considerable success in Paris. Their congregations amounted at times to 50,000 people, but they could not make way against the fanaticism of the mob, the unscrupulous hatred of the clergy, the opposition of the municipality, who dreaded disturbance, and the enmity of Parliament and University. The Protestants, La Noue tells us, were as little a match for their opponents in the capital as a gnat is for an elephant: the novices of the convents and the priests' housekeepers could have driven them out with their broomsticks. Paris indeed was scarcely less than Rome the centre of Catholicism. Her University was the chosen abode of sacred learning, the supreme teacher and judge of orthodox doctrine.  All strangers admired the piety of the Parisians and the many churches which vied with each other in the splendour of their services and filled the air with the peals which rang from the forest of their spires and towers.  The streets were crowded with monks and nuns; a procession was met at every turn, and the passerby who did not do reverence to the Host by kneeling in the filth of the ill-paved lanes was likely to rue his excess of niceness or want of fervour.  The tenants and clients of the monks filled the populous suburbs, which for the most part were the property of the great religious houses, St. Germain des Prés, the Charterhouse on the site of the Luxembourg, St. Victor, the Carmelites in the Faubourg St. Jacques.  The University with its sixty-five colleges was almost a town in itself.  Inside the walls the convents and monasteries were not less numerous, many of them rising like fortresses from the lofty enclosures of their gardens.

Not only were the Huguenots but a small minority of the nation, but that minority itself was composed of two very different classes of men.  There were those whom we may call the French Puritans, men of austere life and firm convictions, who wished to establish throughout France the same rigid discipline which Calvin had introduced at Geneva, and which John Knox was labouring to uphold in Scotland.  There were also those who had embraced the doctrines of the Reformation, not so much from spiritual conviction as from discontent with the abuses of Rome, from love of change, from the influence of the new learning, which had shaken the foundation of old beliefs, or for purely political and social reasons.

The bold attitude of the Reformers in the Estates, the apparent influence at Court of the King of Navarre, who boasted that before the year was out the Gospel should be preached throughout the Kingdom, the conversion of many even of the higher clergy, the Cardinal of Châtillon, the Archbishop of Aix, the Bishops of Uzès, Oleron, Lescars, Chartres and Troyes, were held to be heretics—these were among the signs which convinced many that the Reformation was on the point of triumphing in France. Time-servers like Monluc, Bishop of Va. lence, began to preach the Gospel and to denounce the errors of Rome to crowded congregations of courtiers and nobles, many of whom were glad to show their sympathy with a less superstitious creed by eating meat in Lent, avoiding the confessional and looking forward to a share in the spoils of the Church.

The Queen-Mother appeared not displeased to see her ladies reading the New Testament, singing the psalms of Marot, and practising the "language of Canaan," as they called the biblican cant of the zealous Reformers. Margaret of Valois boasts in her memoirs that her infant orthodoxy stood unshaken in the midst of this rising tide of heresy, in spite of persecution suffered at the hands of her brother, Henry of Anjou, because she would not change her missal for a Calvinist hymn-book.

Indifferent to the principles involved, Catherine de' Medici was watching events, leaving them to determine what her future policy should be.

Thus much at any rate was clear, that it was to her interest that neither party should become so strong as to be indifferent to her support.  Besides she was as much attracted by the intrigues, the constant negotiations, the trickery which a trimming policy entailed, as she was repelled by the dangers of a more decided course.  Machiavelli's heroes, the Castracanis, the Sforzas, the Borgias of Italian history, may be cited to prove that courage and a tortuous policy are not incompatible: their treachery often wears the air of splendid audacity.  Not so the statecraft of the Florentine who so long and so fatally influenced the destinies of France.

The character of Catherine, which has sometimes been called an enigma, would rather appear to have been singularly simple.  A really great statesman must understand the varied passions and motives of men; he will understand them best if he has himself experienced them, if he is indeed " so various as to be, not one, but all mankind's epitome," but he may also understand them, less intimately indeed yet sufficiently, by the force of a powerful and sympathetic imagination.  Catherine had neither passion nor enthusiasm nor virtue.  Revenge and hatred, if not malice and rancour, were as strange to her nature as gratitude and love ; nor had she sufficient imagination to realise how others might be influenced by

emotions of which she herself had no experience.
Hence the defects of her policy, due less to her inability to see that the tricks and devices, which might
have been successful in some petty Italian State, were
ill adapted to the wider stage and different conditions of France, than to the assumption that
others were swayed by the same simple motives of
self-interest as herself.   Thus her schemes generally
ended in failure, though she was a clever, unscrupulous woman with insight and adroitness, full of
energy and restless activity ; as indefatigable in the
pursuit of her ambitious intrigues as she had been,
when younger, in hunting the deer amid the forests
of Vincennes and Touraine.

Since it seemed to the Queen-Mother's interest to
endeavour to keep the peace between the Reformers
and their enemies, lest she should be at the mercy of
the conquerors, she allowed herself to be guided by
the Chancellor L'Hôpital, a sincere advocate of
toleration, and a true patriot, a man, says a contemporary, "who wore the lilies in his heart."

L'Hôpital had shown by his opening address to
the States-General, in which he expatiated on the old
maxim—one faith, one law, one king— that he, a
representative of those moderate men, afterwards
called "politicians," still clung to the Gallican principle of the intimate connection between Church and
State, of the dependence of the unity of the one on
the unity of the other.   A Frenchman and an Eng-
lishman, he said, might, holding the same faith, live
in peace together ; not so two citizens of the same
town who differ in religion.   He dreamt of some

compromise acceptable both to the Huguenots and to the orthodox. But of such a compromise the necessary conditions were, first, mutual toleration, and secondly, a calm discussion of the points at issue. The Chancellor persuaded the Queen-Mother to assent to an edict, known as the Edict of January, by which all breaches of the public peace were strictly forbidden; and toleration promised to the Protestant congregations, provided that they built no new places of worship, restored the churches they had occupied and held no synods without the sanction of the royal council.

But a conference of the most moderate Protestant and Romanist theologians at Poissy disclosed the impossibility of a compromise when the points at issue were fundamental; and the Regent, in return for a large subsidy, promised the clergy to maintain the rights, privileges and orthodoxy of the Catholic Church.

The " Edict of January," although very noteworthy as the first legal recognition obtained by the Reformed Church, was merely an attempt to compel the members of the two religions to live peaceably together under the protection of the law.

It was intended by L'Hôpital to be a temporary expedient, lasting only till some compromise could be effected. It did not go far enough to satisfy the majority of the Huguenots, whose hopes had been raised to an extravagant pitch, while it excited the violent opposition of the Catholics and may be said to have given the signal of civil war. Everywhere the Huguenots were exposed to violence and

insult, and vainly importuned the law courts for
protection and redress. In Paris attempts were made
by the mob to disturb the worship of the Protestants
in the suburbs. Riot and bloodshed followed. The
King's council ordered the townspeople to be disarmed. It was clear, the citizens muttered, that the
Court intended to deliver up the orthodox people of
Paris to the tender mercies of the Prince of Condé
and his armed nobles. Condé was now the acknowledged leader of the Huguenots. His credulous and
vacillating brother, Antony of Navarre, had preferred
the vague and deceitful promises of Spain to his
religion and his party. The baits by which he was
caught give the measure of his capacity. The kingdom of Sardinia and conquests on the African coast,
or the hand of Mary Stuart and the help of Spain
to make good her pretensions to the English Crown:
true he was married and owed his title and the greater
part of his dominions to his wife, but the Pope might
annul his marriage with a heretic.

The first service which Antony of Bourbon did his
new allies was to demand that the Admiral Coligny
should be dismissed from Court. Coligny, who seems
to have dreaded the outbreak of hostilities more than
any other man, and to have foreseen more clearly
the evils of civil war and the dangers of his party,
voluntarily left Paris. Catherine endeavoured to
obtain the simultaneous retirement of the Catholic
leaders. But the Marshal St. André, a man enriched
and powerful by the favour of Henry II., refused to
go to Lyons, the seat of his government, and spoke
of the Queen-Mother in no measured terms. He

3

said, she would but meet with her deserts if she were
tied in a sack and tossed into the river.  The Guises
and their allies agreed to meet in Paris (March, 1562)
and to try conclusions with Condé.  It was clear that
hostilities could not long be averted.

It was important to deprive the Huguenots of the
sympathy and help of the German Lutherans.  No
prince had greater influence among the German
Protestants, by his character and family connections,
than Duke Christopher of Wurtemberg.  The Duke
of Guise and his brother the Cardinal visited him.
They were prodigal of flattery and caresses.  They
listened to the arguments of his theologians and
pronounced them reasonable, nay convincing.  The
Duke said he was a rough soldier and did not profess
to understand such things, but it seemed to him that
he was a Lutheran.  The Cardinal declared that he
would as soon pray in a black gown as a red.  Both
thanked God that they never had and swore that
they never would put any man to death for his
religion's sake.  The first act of the Duke on his
return was, as he passed through St. Nicholas in
Lorraine, to order the execution of an artisan whose
child had been baptised according to the Lutheran
rite !  On reaching Vassy, a small manufacturing
town, whose inhabitants had embraced Calvinism,
he allowed his guards to fire upon a barn in which
they were assembled for their Sunday worship.  The
Protestants tried to barricade the door and a horrid
struggle ensued, if indeed that can be called a struggle in which one side consisted of unarmed towns-
folk encumbered by women and children, the other

of veteran soldiers armed to the teeth. Sixty men, women and children were killed and far more wounded. But the importance of the "Massacre of Vassy," from which we may date the commencement of the wars of religion which were to desolate France for more than a generation, was out of all proportion to the number of victims; far more atrocious scenes of bloodshed had taken place in the South, yet had excited little attention. It was the presence of Guise at this bold violation of the Edict of January, at this defiance of the Huguenots and of the law, which made it so important. The most notable man in the Catholic party had thrown down the gauntlet, would the Protestants dare to pick it up?

The Catholic preachers glorified the slaughter of the heretics. They justified it by the example of Moses who had caused the worshippers of the golden calf to be slain, and of Jehu whose godly zeal had put to the sword two kings and twelve hundred princes, and cast out Queen Jezebel to be eaten by the dogs. The irritation of the Protestants was proportionate to the exultation of their enemies. They sent Beza, the most eminent as well as the most courtly of their divines, to wait upon the Queen and to demand the punishment of the assassins who violated the royal edict. These requests were ardently supported by Condé, who offered to raise 50,000 men to maintain the King's authority. The King of Navarre on the other hand angrily reproached Beza with stirring up civil strife: "Sire," replied the divine, "it is true that it is for the Church of God to receive rather than to give blows, but remember, it is an anvil on which many hammers have been broken."

On March 10, Guise, accompanied by other nobles and escorted by 2,000 men-at-arms, entered Paris. The people hailed him as their deliverer and received him with royal honours. Condé was compelled to leave the city and fell back on Meaux instead of hurrying with the forces at his command to Fontainebleau, whither the Queen-Mother and her children had retired, and thus securing for his party the prestige of the King's name and presence.

Catherine had repeatedly written urging him to protect her, the King and the nation against the men who would overthrow all peace and order. But before the Prince made up his mind to act, the opportunity was gone. The confederates had reached Fontainebleau, and although the Queen-Mother resisted for a few days, and even attempted flight, she was in the end compelled or persuaded to return to Paris.

Condé had perhaps been delayed by the hesitation of Coligny. The Admiral shrank from civil war, he recognised also more clearly than his friends the weakness of his party. His brothers and his wife urged him to join the Prince; for two days he refused to listen to their arguments. The story has often been told how during the night he was aroused by the sobs of his wife : " Husband, I fear lest to be so wise in the wisdom of this world prove folly in God's sight ; you will be the murderer of those whose murder you do not prevent." " Lay your hand on your heart," he replied, " ask yourself whether you are ready to bear failure and defeat, the reproaches of enemies and friends, the condemnation of the many who judge causes by the event, treason, exile, dishonour, nakedness, hunger, and, harder to endure, the hunger of your children, death on the scaffold after seeing your husband suffer. Ponder these thing for three weeks, and then, if you so decide, I will go and perish with you, and with our friends." " The three weeks are already passed," she exclaimed, " let not the blood of the victims of three weeks be upon your head, or I shall be a witness against you before the judgment-seat of God." Next morning the Admiral took horse with his household and his brothers to join the Prince of Condé at Meaux, and the civil war had begun which was to desolate France for forty years.

Was the hesitation of Coligny justified ? Had the Protestants any alternative to an appeal to the sword ? Some writers both at the time and since have maintained that if the Huguenots had continued to submit to persecution with the same patience as in the past, their doctrine would have continued to spread ; that the sight of their sufferings and of their virtues would have converted the less fanatical of their opponents and have softened the hearts of even the most cruel. Undoubtedly the number of Protestants in France diminished after the first civil war ; therefore it is argued the war was the cause of that diminution. But the Great Hound, as the Catholics called the fanatical mob, had been slipped ; before the outbreak of hostilities, the Protestants of the middle classes were being massacred or robbed and driven into exile by their orthodox neighbours. There were more victims in 1562 than ten years later in the year of the Massacre of St. Bartholomew. Soon the nobility would have fared no better. Even the leaders themselves, had they not taken up arms, would have been sacrificed to the jealous ambition cloaked by religious zeal of the Guises and their allies. No patient endurance on the part of the Huguenots would have disarmed their persecutors ; and the time was past when such patient endurance could be expected from them. Here and there they were and felt themselves to be the stronger party. The images and relics of the Papists were an abomination to them ; on these at any rate they could avenge the sufferings of their brethren. But, although with few exceptions they abstained at first from injury to the property or persons of Catholics, the orthodox population resented far more bitterly the disfigurement of a statue of the Virgin, the destruction of the toe bone of St. Crispin, or the thumb nail of St. Athanasius, than an insult to a nun or the assassination of a friar.

Yet, although we hold that the Protestants had no alternative but to fight for their existence, when once they had drawn the sword, all chance of France becoming a Protestant country, if such chance ever existed, was at an end. They were too small a minority to impose their faith on a majority whose fanaticism and zeal were inflamed by the struggle.

At the outset the numerical superiority of the Catholics was to some extent counterbalanced by the organisation of the Protestant churches, which

enabled the Huguenots to act with singular unanimity and concert. They had seized many of the
most important towns before their adversaries had
even begun to take the field. It was also counterbalanced by the fact that the Huguenot minority
was almost entirely composed of the most warlike,
intelligent and industrious classes; that in short
it comprised the very flower of the French people.
The noblest traditions of feudal chivalry, the culture
of the Renaissance, a piety inspired and sustained
by the constant study of the Gospels produced men
in whom the best characteristics of their nation were
combined with a moral elevation, a purity and
dignity of character, " an heroic breath of soul ani-
mated by a simple piety and chastened by a chequered
experience " rarely if ever equalled. By the side of
the Colignys, the La Noues and Du Plessis-Mornays,
the characters of the Eliots, Hampdens and Hutchin-
sons of our own civil wars appear narrow and incom-
plete, and not a few of the rank and file of the party
were worthy of such leaders. But besides their
numerical superiority the Catholics had three great
advantages : the possession of the King's person;
the control of the capital and the sympathy of its
inhabitants ; the command of the financial resources
of the Government and of the clergy.

The contributions of their churches were a precarious resource, insufficient to provide for the
regular payment of the infantry and of the foreign
mercenaries, whom the Protestants were obliged to
employ. The cavalry which formed the strength of
the Huguenot armies was indeed composed almost

entirely of the gentry, who served at their own expense.  It was their poverty which compelled them, armed only with rapier and pistols, to encounter the mailclad lancers of the royal armies.  Few among them could afford the high price of a trained charger, able to carry his own and his rider's armour.  But though, in La Noue's phrase, the Huguenot gentry were better armed with courage than corselets, the lightness of their equipment had its advantages.  It enabled them by the rapidity of their movements to hold their own against the greater numbers of their enemies.  In battle, the cumbrous defensive armour and ponderous lance of the man-at-arms made him a formidable antagonist, but only when he could fight in his own way and on suitable ground.  A more serious disadvantage was the difficulty of enforcing discipline among these well-born volunteers, of inducing them to serve far away from their homes and the impossibility of keeping them together for a long campaign.  The dangers incurred by their families during their absence, the necessity of obtaining further resources, could always be alleged as an excuse for leaving the army.

The leadership of Condé was another source of weakness to the Protestant cause.  Lewis of Bourbon was more sincerely attached to the Reformed Religion than his brother, yet the licence of his life was strangely at variance with Puritan morality.  More than once Calvin had rebuked him for his " mad intrigues," which were not less dangerous to the cause than to his own salvation.  His good nature, his bravery and his chivalry were far from compen-

sating for his political incapacity and recklessness. On most occasions the Prince, much to his
credit, showed due deference to the wisdom and experience of Coligny, his uncle by marriage; yet
there were times when the Admiral must have felt
how greatly the necessity of working in harmony
with such a man, of leading while he appeared to
follow, increased the difficulties of the situation.

We have not space to follow the events of the wars
of religion, except so far as they immediately affected
the fortunes of Henry of Navarre. Nor is it important to remember the terms of treaties and of
edicts of toleration which were never observed, nor
perhaps intended to be observed, or the details of
battles which decided nothing, and to each of which
we might apply the answer of Marshal Vielleville
when asked by Charles IX. who had won the day at
St. Denis (1567). " Neither your Majesty nor the
Prince of Condé, but King Philip of Spain, since as
many gallant gentlemen have fallen on both sides, as
would have sufficed to drive the Spaniards out of
Flanders."

One by one the men fell whose ambition had led
them to provoke the war in the name of Him who
had said that whoso draws the sword shall perish by
the sword; St. André at Dreux, Antony of Bourbon
in the same year before Rouen (1562); in the next
year Francis of Guise by the hand of an assassin;
four years later the Constable Anne of Montmorency at St. Denis.

In the summer of 1568 the Châtillons and the
Prince of Condé escaped almost miraculously an

attempt to seize them in time of peace. A sudden
and unexpected flood of the Loire saved from their
pursuers the little band of women and children who
escorted by barely 150 men had traversed the breadth
of hostile France to gain the sheltering walls of La
Rochelle.

Early in the next year (1569) the Prince and the
Admiral were marching towards the upper Loire to
effect a junction with the Protestants of Languedoc,
when want of discipline brought on an engagement
between the vanguard led by Coligny, and the Catholic army under the command of the Duke of Anjou.
Condé, hearing that the Admiral was attacked by
overwhelming numbers, galloped to his assistance at
the head of his staff and escort. As he was about to
charge, a kick from the horse of his brother-in-law,
the Count of La Rochefoucauld, broke his leg. The
bone protruded through his jack-boot, but he refused
to leave the saddle, and, as he gathered his little
troop around him, exclaimed : " Nobles of France,
this is the moment we have longed for ; remember in
what state Lewis of Bourbon charges for Christ and
his country."

The onslaught of the Prince and his guard broke
through the Catholic ranks, but overwhelmed by
numbers he was at length borne from his horse. He
was unable to rise and had surrendered to a gentleman whom he knew, when the Captain of the Guards
of the Duke of Anjou came up and shot him from
behind, by the command of his master, as was generally believed.

The Battle of Jarnac, so this engagement was called,

was little more than a skirmish, but the death of Condé was an event of importance.

So far as the presence of princes in their army was an answer to those who affected to despise the Huguenots, they did not suffer by Condé's death, for no sooner had the news reached the Queen of Navarre than she hurried to the camp at Cognac with her son and his cousin, the heir of the murdered Prince.

In the presence of the army, the young Prince of Béarn, Henry of Bourbon, swore " on his honour, soul and life " never to abandon the cause, and was hailed as their leader by the acclamations of the soldiery.

The Queen herself solemnly put on her son's armour. The joy of maintaining so just a cause raised him, she said, above his age, and her above her sex.

But, although accompanied by the two young Princes, whom the Catholics mockingly called his pages, Coligny had henceforward the undivided command of the Huguenot army as well as the principal voice in determining the policy of his party.

# CHAPTER II.

THE PARENTAGE OF HENRY OF BOURBON—HIS
EDUCATION AND MARRIAGE—ST. BARTHOL-
OMEW—THE PEACE OF MONSIEUR.

## 1555—1576.

T the beginning of the 16th century the three branches into which the House of Bourbon, descended from Robert of Clermont, sixth son of St. Lewis, had divided, were represented respectively by Peter, Duke of Bourbon, husband of Anne of France, the daughter of Lewis XI., Charles, Count of Montpensier and Charles, Count of Vendôme. The only child of the Duke of Bourbon became the wife of her cousin Montpensier, who with her hand obtained the duchy, but fell childless, a traitor and an exile, leading the army of Charles V. to the sack of Rome. By his death Vendôme became the head of his family and heir to the French throne, should the male lineage of the House of Valois fail. His son Antony of Bourbon was brave and good-natured, showing flashes of generosity and enthusiasm, but unstable and licentious, easily influenced by those around him, as dangerous

and as little to be trusted, said Calvin, as if his fits of zeal had been the calculated hypocrisy of a traitor. Such as he was he obtained the hand of the greatest heiress in France, Jane d'Albret, the daughter of Henry d'Albret, King of Navarre, and Margaret of Angoulême, the sister of Francis I.

The saying of Napoleon, that Africa begins at the Pyrenees, can scarcely fail to occur to the traveller who climbs to the Port de Venasque, or to any other of the high passes, which are little more than notches cut into a continuous wall of mountains, and turns from the green valleys and chestnut-clad slopes of France to the stony mountain ridges which rise on the Spanish side, one behind the other, till they gradually sink into what appears an arid table-land. Here at any rate he must believe Nature herself has set the limits of two nations; yet during the Middle Ages the Pyrenees separated nothing. On the east the counts of Barcelona, afterwards Kings of Aragon, were the lords of wide domains in Languedoc and Provence, which before the 16th century had shrunk to the county of Roussillon. On the west the Kings of Navarre owing fealty to the French Crown for other possessions, ruled from the Ebro to the Adour as sovereign Princes over a territory inhabited by a population mainly Basque in origin.

The marriage of Jane of Navarre with Philip the Fair, in 1285, united for a time the kingdom of Navarre to France. In 1328 her granddaughter, excluded by the Salic law from the French throne, inherited Navarre, which passed by marriage successively to the House of Evreux, Foix and Albret.

In 1512 Ferdinand of Spain conquered all Navarre south of the Pyrenees, on the pretext that John d'Albret, King of Navarre by right of his wife Catherine de Foix, had refused a passage through his dominions to the Spanish troops, and had concluded a treaty with Lewis XII.

The kingdom of Navarre was henceforth reduced to a few square leagues of territory on the French side of the Pyrenees; but its ruler was still a sovereign monarch, who paid homage neither to France nor Spain, while Béarn and the other fiefs of the houses of Foix and Albret supplied the means for keeping up some show of kingly state. It did not therefore seem a wholly disproportionate match when in 1527 Francis I. allowed his sister Margaret to marry Henry d'Albret, the son of John d'Albret and Catherine of Foix. The county of Armagnac, given to her in perpetuity as part of her dower, very conveniently rounded off the possessions of the Kings of Navarre.

Margaret, lively and high-spirited, eagerly interested both in this world and the next, had before been ill matched with the dull and lethargic Duke of Alençon, to whose cowardice at Pavia the defeat of the French and the capture of their King, her hero and her idol, had been ascribed. Her fancy probably fixed on Henry of Albret because he possessed those brilliant qualities in which her late husband had been wanting. He had fought with the same valour as Francis, he had shared his captivity till he made his escape under romantic circumstances, he was chivalrous—as chivalry was then understood—ready-witted and justly popular among his subjects.

The King of Navarre was twelve years younger than his bride, but it was not disparity in years only which made the second marriage of Margaret as little happy as the first. It was more bitter to be the victim of misplaced love than of a match imposed by political necessity. Henry of Albret, who had neither elevation of character nor fixity of purpose, a libertine in an age when what would now be licence was accounted sober and godly living, was not likely to be faithful to a plain and elderly wife, or even considerate in the manner of his infidelity. There may possibly have been faults on both sides. The Queen was an author, a theologian and a poetess ; in short, a most superior woman, accustomed to the homage and flattery of courtiers, scholars and divines. " Madame, you would know too much," her husband is said to have exclaimed with an irritation perhaps pardonable, had it not been emphasised with a box on the Queen's ears. Nor could Margaret's blind devotion to her selfish brother, however amiable a weakness, have been other than an additional element of discomfort in her married life.

Henry of Albret would have been well pleased that his only child Jane should have married Philip of Spain; and since the match would have given the Spanish house a sure title to Navarre and a firm footing on the French side of the Pyrenees it might not have been displeasing to Charles V. But the mere suggestion of such an arrangement was alarming to Francis I., and his sister would not entertain the thought of any

opposition to the King's wish; she would sooner,
she said, see her daughter dead than do him a
disservice.

After the accession of Henry II. (1547) Jane, now
a handsome brunette of seventeen, was among the
gayest of his Court, and the King, haunted like his
father by the fear that Spain might with her hand
obtain the northern slope of the Pyrenees, was well
pleased to see her encourage the addresses of Antony
of Bourbon, a suitor but little approved by her
parents. Their opposition yielded to the royal
will, and the marriage took place at Moulins on
October 20, 1548.

Henry of Bourbon was the last of three sons born
to Jane of Albret and her husband. His little
brothers died in their first infancy. The eldest was
entrusted to the care of a chilly old lady who so
carried into practice her maxim that it was better to
sweat than to shiver, that no breath of air was ever
allowed to reach the hot and stifling rooms where
the unfortunate baby was slowly suffocated in his
swaddling clothes. The next child was dropped by
his nurse and a gentleman who were amusing him, or
themselves, by tossing him in and out of a window.
His hurt might have been cured had it not been concealed by the terrified culprits.

The King of Navarre, anxious for an heir, declared that, since his daughter so little understood
how to look after her children, the next baby must
be born in Béarn, and that he himself would see that
it was properly brought up. Accordingly, although
it was winter, Jane hurried in a fortnight from

Picardy to Pau where, ten days later, Henry of Bourbon came into the world during the night of December 13, 1555.

Jane and her husband had seen with some anxiety the influence gained by his mistresses over the King of Navarre; they feared that his will might not be satisfactory. The Princess hinted to her father that she would like to see it. He replied : " You shall have it to keep, if you will give me in exchange a lusty grandson, and sing when he first sees the light, for I want no whimpering, puling baby!" It has often been told how the bargain was kept. How the King brought to his daughter's room his will in a golden casket, and received in exchange the new-born infant which he wrapped in a fold of his dressing-gown, delighted to see it joyously nod its head and suck its lips when they were rubbed with a clove of garlic and moistened with a drop of Gascon wine. It was perhaps this precocious indulgence which gave the infant a distaste for its natural food. Nurse after nurse was tried, and it was with the eighth that the little Henry was sent to a castle in the mountains of Béarn, where the air was keenest and most bracing, to be brought up according to the directions of his grandfather, under the care of Madame de Miossans, a connection of the Bourbons.

Historians tell us how the King of Navarre insisted that the child should run about barefoot, join in the rough sports of the village lads, and live on the national porridge. Since, however, Henry of Albret died when his grandson was only two years

4

old, we may surmise that this hardening process was scarcely begun during his lifetime.

On the old King's death, his daughter and her husband hurried to take possession of their inheritance, and at once sent for their little son, whom they took with them to the French Court, where their interests required their presence. Henry II. was attracted by the bold prattle of the child and made some proposal that he should be affianced to his daughter Marguerite, his senior by six months. The King also offered to have him educated with his own children, but this Jane refused, and returning to Béarn took her son with her. There he remained till the death of Francis II. (1560), and there we may suppose the education began which helped to make Henry of Navarre, in the phrase of a Protestant writer, " that iron wedge tempered by God, to cleave the hard knot of our calamities." If it was Henry of Albret who determined that his grandson should be no effeminate weakling, but a true moun-taineer, frugal, active and enduring, the Queen of Navarre must at least have the credit of having carried out her father's intention. Nor was the rod spared. " Whip the Dauphin well," wrote Henry IV., " whenever he is naughty. I know by my own experience there is nothing in the world so profitable. I was constantly thrashed when of his age." Graver studies were not neglected. His first tutor was one La Gaucherie, a man of learning who, like the great majority of scholars, had adopted the opinions of the Reformers. He was probably chosen by Antony of Bourbon, at whose invitation " the Ven-

erable Company of the pastors of Geneva " had sent
Theodore Beza (de Bèze) to Nerac, to instruct the
royal family in the doctrine of Calvin (July, 1556).
The convictions of Antony were fleeting and superficial, the deeper nature of his wife was less easily
stirred.    " In your family," wrote a correspondent of
her daughter, " by some reversal of the Salic law,
constancy is the exclusive heritage of the women."
Jane was slow to embrace the faith in defence of
which she afterwards hazarded her possessions, her
children and her life.    Beza wrote that the King of
Navarre showed great devotion.    Every one believed that he thought of nothing but the means
whereby Christ's Kingdom might be advanced, while
the Queen his wife was very cold, fearing to give the
Spanish or French King a pretext for seizing her
dominions, and unwilling to sacrifice the pleasures of
this world.

It was not till 1560 that Jane abjured the errors of
Rome.    " Hearing the news of the imprisonment of
the Prince of Condé and of the plots formed against
her husband, as well as that the Spaniards were preparing to scize by surprise her principality of Béarn
and what she still retained of Navarre, the Queen,
seeing that her trust in man availed nothing, and
touched to the quick by the love of God, had recourse to Him as to her only refuge."    No doubt
she saw the answer to her prayers in the death of
Francis II. and the release of her brother-in-law and
husband.

La Gaucherie, like a more celebrated educator of
the time, Beroalde, taught the dead languages orally,

a method by which surprising results appear sometimes to have been obtained. Henry learnt Latin
sufficiently well for practical purposes; of Greek he
seems only to have known a few tags, which his tutor
made him learn by rote, parrot-fashion. He was
probably not a very apt or patient pupil. His
wonderful physical activity, or rather abnormal rest-
lessness, must have made all sedentary study difficult
and unprofitable. In later years, when after a long
day's hunting his weary attendants could scarcely
stand, he could not rest, but must move about or
dance; even when he was past middle life his subjects wondered how a Prince so constantly in the
saddle or at the tennis court had time for affairs of
state. No wonder that a man who was movement
incarnate could scarce find leisure or patience to read
a book.

All Henry's childhood was not spent in the bracing air of the Pyrenees and in the healthy moral
atmosphere of the more and more Puritan Court of
Nerac or Pau. After the death of Francis II. the
Queen of Navarre, bringing her children with her,
joined her husband at the French Court. We have
already seen how Antony of Bourbon allowed himself to be outwitted by the Queen-Mother and
befooled by the Guises and Spain. Jane, indignant
at the weak inconstancy of her husband, retired to
her hereditary dominions. Antony kept his son
with him, but neither dismissed his Protestant tutor
La Gaucherie, nor even seriously insisted upon his
attending Mass. Probably the recent orthodoxy of
the King of Navarre had no other root than his am-

bition.   Such religious convictions as he may have
possessed remained unchanged.   The heretical education of the Prince of Béarn was however supple-
mented by such instruction as a boy of nine could
obtain at the College of Navarre,* where in a desultory fashion he attended lectures with two other
young Princes, his name-sakes, Henry of Valois and
Henry of Guise.

After Antony of Bourbon had fallen before Rouen
and Condé had been taken prisoner at Dreux (December, 1562), the Queen-Mother, fearing nothing so
much as the growing power of the Guises, was
anxious to conciliate the Huguenots.   She therefore
allowed Jane of Navarre to send for her son.   But it
seemed very important to Catherine and her council
to keep under their control and influence a boy who
was the head of the House of Bourbon, the heir to
vast possessions and who would be a hostage for the
good behaviour of his mother, for she more and more
identified her interests with those of the Huguenot
party.   He was therefore urgently invited to return
to Court in the name of Charles IX., who had now
attained his nominal majority.

The Queen of Navarre did not think it expedient
to disregard the King's wish.   She had been excommunicated by the Pope, and a conspiracy had been
formed to betray her into the power of Philip II.,
who, so it was reported, hoped to merit the special

---

* The College of Navarre, one of the oldest colleges attached to the
University of Paris, founded in 1304 by Jane of Navarre, wife of
Philip the Fair, had at all times been especially distinguished by
royal favour.

favour and indulgence of heaven by an *auto-da-fé*, of which a queen should be the victim, while he trusted to secure the possession of her dominions by the eternal captivity of her children. The French Government had interfered energetically on her behalf at Rome and she might need the same help against Spain. She therefore sent her son once more to a court where he would be beyond her care and exposed to influences which she could not but dread.

The Prince of Béarn accompanied Charles IX. and the Queen-Mother during a long progress through the kingdom (March, 1564, to December, 1565). It is probable that in this wandering court the book-learning of Henry made no great progress, although he is said under the supervision of La Gaucherie to have completed a translation of the Commentaries of Cæsar. But he must have learnt much far more useful to a future ruler of men than Greek and Latin syntax, perhaps also much that had better been unlearnt. For the sharp-eyed, quick-witted and ready-tongued boy of twelve, who appeared, says an eye-witness, several years older than his age, and whom Catherine liked to have about her, for the sake of his bold and lively sallies, must have seen through the thin veil of decorum spread over a court, the ladies of which were allowed at their will to be " votaresses of Dian or of Venus," provided that their intrigues were serviceable, or at least no hindrance, to the policy of their mistress.

But though the knowledge of manners acquired among the courtiers of the Florentine must have been singularly unedifying, a progress through France which lasted nearly two years, must have taught the young Prince better than the care of any tutor to know the provinces, the cities and the men by whose side and against whom he was destined to fight and whom he was afterwards to reunite under his sceptre.

In the course of this progress the Court visited the Queen of Navarre at Nerac, but it was not till Jane had returned this visit in the following year and had again entertained the King and his mother in her Picard county of Marle, that she was allowed to take her son back with her to Béarn. She seems to have been satisfied that by the care of his tutor her boy had escaped the contagion of the Court; for (December, 1566) she wrote to Beza that it was to La Gaucherie that Henry owed "that root of piety, which by God's grace has now been so implanted in his heart by godly precepts, that it already puts forth both branch and fruit."

Henry, now thirteen, had during the latter half of his short life spent most of his time at Court, and, except so far as his studies were directed by his Calvinist tutor, had shared the education of the Valois Princes; but for the next two years he was trained physically, intellectually and morally under the eye of his mother. The hardy education of his childhood was resumed. He was taught to live a frugal and active life, to endure fatigue and privation, to excel not only in riding, fencing and tennis, the universal accomplishments of a gentleman, but also to run and wrestle and to climb the rocks barefoot in pursuit of chamois and bear. La Gaucherie was succeeded in the office of tutor by a more eminent scholar, Florent Chrestien, the pupil of Henry Stephens, the friend of De Thou, a man whose friendship was sought and valued even by Ronsard and Pibrac, whom he had engaged in theological controversy. The Prince of Béarn's scholarship apparently improved under Chrestien's tuition and he became in Scaliger's opinion no bad judge of Latin style, yet it is probable that classical studies were not much insisted on, since the Queen thought it more important that he should know the history of his own and other countries and the languages of Italy and Spain. Chrestien afterwards accompanied his pupil to the camp of the Huguenot army and showed himself as capable of using a sword as a pen in the defence of his religion, no doubt to the advantage of his influence over the Prince.

Michelet fancifully speculates how far Henry of Bourbon's versatility and many-sidedness of character may have been due to the rapid succession of wet-nurses during his infancy. We might more plausibly seek to explain it on the principle of "heredity," and point out that he was the descendant of the Foix, the Graillis and the Albrets, half princes, half adventurers, who pushed their fortunes by love and war, amid the quarrels of more powerful neighbours: that he was the grandson of the mystical and romantic yet alert and cheerful Margaret of Angoulême and of the popularity-loving, affable and jovial but licentious and superficial Henry of Albret; the son of the determined, passionate and religious Queen of Navarre and of the weak and inconstant though physically brave Antony of Bourbon. But it is perhaps more profitable to bear in mind how various were the influences to which the boyhood of Henry was exposed. How useful an education, though dangerous to any strength or depth of moral and religious conviction, it was, that the Prince who was destined to reunite the jarring factions and sects of France, should have been from his earliest youth equally at home in the Tuileries or the Louvre, among the motley crowd of Italian adventurers, intriguing priests, dissolute gallants, ambitious nobles and unscrupulous statesmen, in the little court of Nerac and Pau, the asylum and stronghold of French Protestantism, in the farms and cottages of the Gascon peasantry and in the camps of the Huguenot veterans.

After the battle of Jarnac, Coligny, who had been joined by a powerful body of German auxiliaries, was compelled by the impatience of his followers to besiege Poitiers and afterwards, at Montcontour, to engage with inferior forces the army of the Duke of Anjou. Their superior numbers and a field of battle well suited to the manœuvres of heavy cavalry gave the Papists a victory loudly celebrated throughout Catholic Europe. Yet the results of the victory were unimportant.

Charles IX., jealous of his brother's glory, joined the army, and sat down before St. Jean d'Angely, wasting three months and the lives of 6,000 men. The Admiral, accompanied by the young princes of Béarn and Condé, after throwing strong garrisons into the Protestant towns of Poitou, led the remains of his cavalry into the South, where he was joined by numerous partisans and soon found himself once more at the head of a formidable force.

It was clear that without the help of Spain the Huguenots could not be crushed; but Philip II. was fully occupied by a war with the Turks and with the revolted Moors. He moreover expected as the price of his assistance that the interests and policy of France, if not her independence, should be subordinated to Spanish ambition. If war and persecution implied submission to Spain all Frenchmen, whose love of their country was not extinguished by fanaticism, were necessarily disposed to peace and toleration. Catherine de' Medici, who cared little for the suppression of heresy, thought that too high a price might easily be paid for an object itself of doubtful advantage. It was true that her favourite Anjou was for the moment the Catholic hero, his fresh laurels overshadowed the old glories of the House of Guise, yet at some future time Coligny and his followers, who seemed less formidable since their defeat and the death of Condé, might be needed as a counterpoise to the faction of Lorraine.

The unsuccessful siege of St. Jean d'Angely had disgusted the King with a war which exhausted his resources, interfered with his amusements and ministered only to the aggrandisement of a brother whom he detested. The country generally was weary of a painful and indecisive struggle. The Protestants were anxious to return to their homes and were exhausted by the sacrifices required to maintain so unequal a contest. To none was the civil war more hateful than to the Admiral himself.

His loyalty to the King as a French noble and great officer of his Crown, his patriotism, his inborn love of order, his feelings as a Christian were alike pained by a war against his King, in which Frenchmen destroyed Frenchmen to the profit of their common enemies, which ruined the social order of the country, demoralised his own adherents and was waged on both sides with countless circumstances of horror and atrocity.

In order that the growing inclination of the Court to peace might be confirmed, and to secure more favourable terms, he determined on a movement of ably calculated audacity. Accompanied by the young Bourbon Princes and a small army of veteran cavalry he left Languedoc and moved rapidly on Paris. Acceptable terms were at once offered by Catherine and the King. Greater freedom of worship than had been allowed by previous edicts; the members of the so-called " Reformed " Church to be in every respect on a footing of equality with the Catholics and equally eligible to all civil and military offices; an amnesty for all that had happened during the war. Finally, as a pledge of the sincerity of the Court, four important fortresses were to be placed in the hands of the Huguenot leaders for three years: Montauban in Languedoc, La Charité commanding the Loire, Cognac in Poitou, and La Rochelle on the ocean. It was in vain that Pius V. and Philip II. protested with loud outcries against so iniquitous a peace with the enemies of God and man; the terms were joyfully accepted by the Protestants and ratified at St. Germains by the King (August 8, 1570).

So far from being crushed the Protestants after eight years of civil war had obtained terms which they would have welcomed at the outset. It is true that the same concessions would have meant more had they been granted earlier. The war had shown that the Huguenots were too strong a minority to be subdued by force, but it had also made it impossible for that minority to become a majority. The numbers of the sectaries had been greatly reduced, less by losses in the field than by massacres in the towns.

According to some historians 10,000 had so perished in one year alone (1568). These victims for the most part belonged to the middle classes, to the better sort of townspeople. Many others had been compelled to fly the country. In war, as was natural, the nobles and soldiers became more and more influential; but the great majority of these had little sympathy with the strict morality and discipline of Calvinism. Even at La Rochelle, where the ministers exercised an authority almost as absolute as at Geneva, a spirit of lawlessness had been fostered by the adventures and more than half piratical enterprises of the citizens.

The Italian admirers of the Machiavellian statecraft of Catherine de' Medici, and the Protestants to whom she appeared a monster of dissimulation, represent the treaty of St. Germains as the first of a series of measures devised to lure the Huguenots to destruction. Such was not the opinion of the best informed contemporaries.

Walsingham, the English ambassador, assured

GASPARD DE COLIGNI SEIGNEUR DE CHATILLON
ADMIRAL DE FRANCE.

**ADMIRAL COLIGNY.**

Queen Elizabeth that the peace would last. The King had always been averse to the civil war, the Guises were in disgrace, the favour of the Montmorencys and of the " Politicians " constantly growing. Petrucci, the Florentine envoy, wrote that the King was determined at all costs to avoid future conflicts with the Huguenots. Alava, the Spanish ambassador, told Philip II. that Catherine was the source of all evil, although with her usual oaths and tears she had sworn that her son no longer listened to her advice.

The Queen-Mother, who had been seeking an establishment for her third daughter Margaret, believed that she had reason to complain of Philip II. After the death of his wife Elizabeth the King in reply to a proposal that he should marry her sister suggested that his nephew Sebastian of Portugal would be a more suitable match for the young lady. Long negotiations followed. It was believed that the young King of Portugal, who had romantic visions of combining the saint and the hero, did not wish to marry at all ; he certainly showed no eagerness to marry Margaret of Valois. Catherine thought that Philip II. had not seriously attempted to overcome his nephew's reluctance, and in her irritation lent a ready ear to those who suggested that though little remained of the independent kingdom of Navarre, yet the head of the House of Bourbon, the heir of domains which extended from the Pyrenees to far beyond the Garonne, of the principality of Béarn, of the duchies of Vendôme, Beaumont and Albret, of the counties of Bigorre, Armagnac, Rouergue,

Perigord and Marle, of the viscounties of Marsac and Limoges and of numerous other lordships, the acknowledged leader of a great and martial faction, was no unequal match for the third daughter even of a King of France.

After the conclusion of peace Henry had been sent back to Béarn, while his mother and the Protestant leaders remained at La Rochelle; refusing to separate or to visit the Court till the provisions of the edict had been fully carried out. Towards the end of 1570 Marshal de Cossé, a prominent member of the moderate party was sent to assure the Queen of Navarre that the Government was determined to fulfil its engagements, and at the same time to let it be known that Charles IX. would gladly see Henry of Bourbon a suitor for the hand of his sister. Early in the next year (1571) riotous mobs robbed and massacred the Protestants of Orange and Rouen. The exemplary punishment of these excesses, and the permission to hold a national synod of the Reformed churches at La Rochelle, went far to convince the Huguenots of the good faith of the Court; a conviction which was strengthened by the eagerness with which the King pressed on the negotiations for the marriage of his brother to Queen Elizabeth, and the favourable reception given to Count Lewis of Nassau.

The King and the Queen-Mother repeatedly invited Coligny to Court. His cousin Montmorency urged him to grasp so favourable an opportunity of overthrowing the influence of the Guises.

The well-known story of Coligny's reception at

Blois, how the King embraced him again and again, exclaiming " Now we have you we shall not again let you go," rests on no good evidence.  Charles received the Admiral well, but with no excess of cordiality, while the Queen-Mother and Anjou had taken to their beds the day of his arrival: they were really ill, but the circumstances were so suspicious, that Coligny alarmed by the coolness of his reception was on the point of leaving Blois.  Soon, however, he received abundant proof of royal favour and affection.  His advice constantly prevailed in the King's council, where his supporters now formed the majority.  The royal council was a large body. Some members were summoned by letters patent, while Princes of the Blood, dukes and peers, the great officers of the Crown and knights of the King's orders appear to have had a right to sit *ex-officio*. But of these privileged persons only a small number attended, or were expected to attend, and a change in policy was often marked by one set of members absenting themselves, their place being taken by others who had previously stayed away.  Now the Guises and their most devoted adherents were no longer seen in the council-chamber—there was as it were a change of ministry favourable to the Huguenots and the Politicians.

Meantime (winter of 1571–1572) the negotiations for the marriage of Henry of Navarre and Margaret of Valois continued.  Coligny, now persuaded that the King was sincere, urged Queen Jane to bring her son to Court, to see the young lady and to conduct the treaty in person.

The Queen of Navarre was full of misgivings. She trembled for her son's religion, for his morals; she could not trust the Florentine and the King whose bible was Machiavelli. Her ministers by their contradictory advice distracted her still further; but finally, leaving the Prince at Pau, she accepted the King's invitation. The Court was at Blois, and there also was a papal legate who had been sent to protest against so impious a marriage and to offer once more the hand of the King of Portugal or of an Austrian Prince to Madame Marguerite. But the victory of Lepanto (October 7, 1571) had only increased the King's jealousy and dislike of Spain. All his thoughts, he wrote to his ambassador at Constantinople, were directed to the one object of humbling the power of Philip II.; he was determined to maintain peace in his kingdom and to marry his sister to the Prince of Béarn; in no other way could he avenge himself on his enemies. The legate departed, indignantly refusing the customary gift of plate.

Charles IX. received his " best beloved aunt " with effusive affection. The first interview with Catherine was satisfactory and the Queen of Navarre as she left the room said joyfully " the marriage is settled." But the negotiations did not proceed so smoothly as their beginning promised. Queen Jane dreaded the effect on her son of the corruption she saw around her, she had believed it to be great, but she found it to be greater than she could have conceived. If he were there, she said, nothing short of the signal grace of God could save him.

With prophetic eagerness she begs him to be on

his guard against the attempts that will be made to debauch him in his life and his religion. "It is their object; they do not affect to conceal it." They wish, she said to Walsingham, to keep the Prince at Court to turn him into an atheist. If this happened, what greater calamity could befall him or the Cause?

Catherine accepted the marriage because she trusted to keep her future son-in-law at Court. She hoped that her band of lively maids of honour, her masques and ballets, would prove more attractive than the rough Calvinist soldiers, the tedious theologians, the prayers and improving discourses at Nerac and Pau. If Henry were converted, the Protestants lost the support of the first Prince of the Blood, and of the most powerful vassal of the French Crown; if he remained a Huguenot, his rank secured to him the first place among the sectaries and he might be the means of perplexing their councils and embarrassing the Admiral. Either alternative filled the Queen of Navarre with apprehension. "Pray," she writes to her son, "that this marriage may not be made in God's anger for our punishment." Her letters are full of nervous irritation; she finds it impossible to speak to the King or his sister; she only sees their mother, who treats her with insolent duplicity. "She behaves in such wise, laughing in my face, that you may say my patience surpasses Griselda's; though I burst, I am determined not to lose my temper. I cannot say I lack advice; every one has advice to give me and all different. It is a marvel I can endure the annoyances I suffer. I am dared, insulted and worried. They even make holes in the walls of my room to spy upon me." The poor woman, naturally self-willed and irritable, was all the while suffering from the disease which ended her life a few months later. No wonder that the Florentine envoy thought that her temper was uneven and that she was full of whims and fancies.

In her more hopeful mood she describes Margaret as good-looking though somewhat stout and too tightly laced, and so much painted that it was difficult to see what her face really was, sensible and pleasant-mannered and with great influence over her mother and brothers. At the same time she gives Henry some hints about his behaviour as a suitor. "Do not be afraid of speaking out, for remember that the impression you make at your first coming will determine the esteem in which you will be held. Wear your hair more raised, not in the style of Nerac, but with large locks; I should recommend the last fashion as the one I prefer."

When more despondent, she remembers that the young Princess has been educated in the most corrupt and abominable society, where the women woo the men. She certainly was clever, but that was only another cause for anxiety; if she remained Catholic her prudence and judgment were but additional dangers. Was Henry wiser or more experienced than Solomon, who was misled by his Egyptian wife?

We must allow that Jane showed some insight into the character of her future daughter-in-law, though it is probable that the Princess Margaret, whom she saw shrinking behind her mother, was not more like the Queen of Navarre of later years, in character, than the graceful and lively bright-haired girl, with eyes only too expressive, was like the painted and beruddled woman whose exuberant bulk was made disgusting and ridiculous by vast farthingales, hung round with pockets containing, it was reported, the embalmed hearts of dead lovers, by tightly laced but too scanty bodices stiffened with steel, and large frizzed wigs shorn from the heads of her flock of flaxen-haired footmen.

Margaret of Valois was a clever, even a talented woman. Though her letters would not, as Brantome pretends, have excited the envious despair of Cicero, they are as free from the determination to have a style, the affectation which disfigures so much of the prose of the 16th century, as the letters of Henry IV. himself, and they show a more cultivated literary sense. Even higher praise might be given to the " memoirs," which she wrote with taste and tact to prove herself the victim of circumstances and of the cruel malignity of her brother Henry III. Henry IV. could never read to the end of a serious book, Margaret became so absorbed in what she read, that, fond as she was of the pleasures of the table, she would forget to eat and drink. In practical matters she had clear insight and could give sound advice, nor was she without some good qualities of the heart as well as of the head. She was a constant friend, though a fickle mistress, kind-hearted and charitable; and her good-nature was of a better quality than that of her mother or her husband, since it proceeded neither from insensibility nor indifference. Her gallantry was scandalous in an age of incredible licence. She indulged her love of eating and drinking till her size became so enormous that she could scarcely squeeze through an ordinary doorway. Her taste for music and painting, her extensive use of perfumes seem to show that all her senses imperiously demanded the satisfaction which they largely received.

A disposition not averse to vice had received a detestable education, and she disliked the marriage imposed upon her; it is not therefore surprising that a union which proved both loveless and childless was a curse to bride and bridegroom. The life and character of Henry of Navarre might have been different had he, before his moral sense was blunted by vice, been brought under the influence of a woman he both loved and respected. His subsequent relations with his mistresses showed that his affections, if not his senses, were capable of constancy.

The marriage contract was signed on April 11, 1572. Charles IX. insisted that the wedding should take place in Paris, in order that he might exhibit to the world in the chief city of his kingdom this proof and pledge of his determined love of civil peace.

The ceremony itself had been one of the questions most debated. Jane would not allow her son to countenance by his presence the idolatry of the Mass. It was finally arranged that Henry's uncle the Cardinal of Bourbon should give the nuptial benediction at the door of the Cathedral and then lead the pair to the high altar, but that as soon as the celebration of Mass began, the Prince of Béarn should

say to one of the King's brothers, " My lord, I beg
you to attend Mass for me," and should then, without
leaving the church, retire into one of the side
chapels.

Charles IX. affected to make light of the Pope's
refusal to grant a dispensation.  If the old gentleman persisted, he would take Margot by the hand
and marry her to his cousin in the Protestant meeting-house.

The Queen of Navarre did not live to see the
marriage.  She had been unwell when she came to
Blois; perplexities, vexations of every kind had taken
away sleep and appetite.  All the symptoms of her
illness appear to have been natural, but her death
was generally attributed to the arts of Catherine de'
Medici and her Florentine perfumer.

Henry of Navarre was in Poitou on his way from
Béarn when the news of his mother's death reached
him.  He continued his journey and entered the city
in the first week of August, accompanied by his
cousin Condé and eight hundred gentlemen dressed
in mourning.

The marriage was celebrated on August 18, 1572.
Margaret, accompanied by her mother and brothers,
by the great officers of the Crown and the principal
members of the Court, met the young Prince of
Navarre, who was attended by his cousins the
Prince of Condé and the Count of Soissons, by the
Admiral, the Count of La Rochefoucauld and other
Huguenot nobles, upon a great stage covered with
cloth of gold, erected before the portal of Notre
Dame.  The bride, glittering with the Crown jewels,

was adorned as a queen, with crown and ermine, the train, four yards long, of her blue mantle carried by three princesses.  The bridegroom and his attendants had laid aside their mourning and were dressed in all the gay magnificence which the fashion of the time allowed.

Henry and his Huguenots walked in the nave of the Cathedral, while the bride heard Mass in the quire.  The Admiral noticed hung round the walls the standards he had lost at Montcoutour; soon, he exclaimed, they should be replaced by more glorious trophies won from the common enemy.

The Duke of Anjou organised the feasts in honour of his sister's wedding, questionable and ill-omened revels, in which the King, his brothers, the Bourbon princes and the young nobles of both parties joined, while the older Protestants, witnessed these scenes of sinister and ill-timed debauchery with invincible repugnance.  "As before a storm," says a contemporary," the ocean is seen to heave and mutter, so men's minds appeared to be moved by a prophetic horror and foreboding of the evils so soon to come." The air was heavy with a feeling of disquiet, alarming reports spread on every side, and the pulpits of Paris re-echoed with exhortations to intolerance and bloodshed.

More serious questions than the marriage of the Princess Margaret had divided the councils of the French King during the past year, questions which involved the whole future policy of France and the fate of the Huguenots.

At no period has the connection between the domestic and foreign policy of the states of western Europe been closer than during the sixteenth century. The Protestants in England, in France, in the Low Countries, in northern Germany, were conscious that their interests were the same.

At the beginning of the eighteenth century we find a European league formed to check the preponderance of the House of Bourbon, which, like the power of Philip II. a century and a half earlier, appeared dangerous to the independence of other nations. But resistance to Spain in the name of religious and political liberty meant something very different from resistance to France for the preservation of the balance of power. Spain was at once a domestic and a foreign enemy to the Englishmen who thought like Cecil and Walsingham, to the French Huguenots, to the patriots of the Netherlands; and they had more in common with her enemies, though foreigners, than with countrymen, who were her friends. A check to the policy of Philip II. a defeat of his partisans in one country, reacted upon the balance of parties elsewhere, gave confidence to his opponents, and diminished the authority of his allies. Hence to understand the course of French politics it is often necessary to bear in mind contemporary events in England and in the Netherlands.

The destinies of the three countries were never more closely interwoven than during the time which elapsed between the Peace of St. Germains and the Massacre of St. Bartholomew; indeed, that tremendous catastrophe itself may be said to have been occasioned as much by the vacillation of Elizabeth of England and by the course of events in the Netherlands, as by the jealous and unscrupulous ambition of the Queen-Mother, the party hatred and private vengeance of the Guises and the fanaticism of the Catholic mob.

The all-important question for the Low Countries, for France, and for Europe was : could Charles IX. be induced to take part openly in the struggle against Spain ? This was the stake against which Coligny was willing to set his life. With the assistance of the Politicians, of soldiers who preferred the honour to be gained in fighting against Spain to the questionable triumphs of civil war, the Admiral hoped to carry through his policy,—if possible with the good will of the Queen-Mother, but if that might not be, then, in spite of her opposition.

It was mainly on the English marriage that Coligny relied as the means of winning the support of Catherine. Had Elizabeth been able to make up her mind, had the marriage been concluded, a war with Spain would have followed, and it is probable that "Walsingham and Burghley were right in believing that the course of European history would have been different and the power of the Papacy would have been rolled back in one broad wave across the Alps and the Pyrenees."

But Elizabeth could not make up her mind, and the success of Coligny in establishing his influence over the King became the chief source of his danger. It seemed as if peaceably and by moral means he was about to succeed in doing what physical force had failed to effect at Meaux, when the Huguenots had attempted to seize the young King and to remove him from under the control of his mother. Henceforth therefore her opposition to and hatred of the Admiral became desperate and irreconcilable. Her first object now was by fair means or foul to remove an influence fatal to her own.

In the early summer of 1572, when Holland and Zealand were in arms and the Huguenots pouring over the frontiers of Hainault to the assistance of the rebels, peace or war with Spain meant the predominance of Catherine or of Coligny.

The King's hatred of Spain, his jealousy and suspicion of Anjou, the great personal influence of Coligny, the favour of Teligny, the Admiral's son-in-law, of La Rochefoucauld and other young Huguenot nobles, the obvious advantage of strengthening the royal authority at home by a successful foreign war were thrown into the scale against the authority, confirmed by long habit, of the Queen-Mother, the advice of councillors who from deference to her, from jealousy of her opponents, or from sincere conviction pointed out the danger of entering upon so formidable a struggle without any formal offensive and defensive alliance with England, with an empty treasury and a country exhausted by war and divided by faction. For if the war meant, as it did, the predominance of the Protestants and their friends, those zealous Catholics, and they were many, who preferred their religion to their country would be the best allies of Philip II.

Had the Nassaus and their Huguenot confederates been more successful in the Low Countries it is
possible that Coligny might have prevailed.

More than once it was generally believed that the
King had determined to declare war. But at two
meetings of the council held on August 6th and 9th,
attended by all the officers and ministers of the
crown, a large majority pronounced against a breach
with Spain. Charles IX. yielded to their representations and to the urgent and private expostulations
of his mother, who, says Tavannes in the memoirs
of his father, one of her most intimate and trusted
advisers, threw herself at the King's feet and burst-
ing into tears begged him to allow her to leave the
Court, since after all her labours on his behalf he no
longer had any confidence in her, and abandoned
himself to the councils of his enemies. But even
yet her victory was not assured. On August 10th
Walsingham wrote to Burghley that " though the
Admiral cannot obtain what were requisite and
necessary for the advancement of the cause, yet doth
he obtain somewhat in conference with the King."
Charles IX. in a letter of the same date to his ambassador in England told him that he must exert
himself to induce Elizabeth to help Orange. It was
evident that the frank acceptance by the Queen of
England of the French alliance or any decisive re-
verse to the Spanish arms might again turn the scale
in favour of war and of Coligny.

" The Queen," says Tavannes, " considering that
not only the fortunes of France, but, what touched
her far more nearly, her power and the safety of

Anjou were at stake, resolved with M. d'Anjou and
two other advisers to .compass the death of the Admiral, believing that the whole Huguenot party was
centred in him ; and trusting to remedy all—*i. e.*,
prevent the outbreak of civil war—by the marriage
of her daughter to the King of Navarre and by
throwing the blame of the murder on the Guises, to
the assassination of whose father the Admiral had
been privy."

By making the Guises responsible for her crime,
Catherine trusted, it is said, to obtain an even more
satisfactory result. She expected that the Huguenots would rush to arms and attack the Guises, that
the populace of Paris would seek to protect their
favourites, the leaders of the faction of Lorraine,
and that the Montmorencys and their friends would
support the Huguenots ; whichever side prevailed
would be exhausted by a bloody and obstinate conflict and might be fallen upon and annihilated by the
King's troop's, as disturbers of the public peace !

All the great nobles of France, gathered together
in Paris to celebrate the wedding of the King of
Navarre, would thus be destroyed and the Queen
and the Duke of Anjou left without rivals in the
King's council. Moreover, this great end would be
attained without incurring the odium of the crime ;
it would appear to have been the unavoidable result
of the violence of faction, and would not commit
the Crown to irreconcilable hostility with either the
Catholic or Protestant party.

After the wedding of the King of Navarre, Catherine and Anjou sent for the young Duke of Guise

and his mother to concert measures for the death of the man who, as they pretended and perhaps believed, had encouraged the assassin of Duke Francis. A bravo formerly in the service of Anjou and at that time of the Guises was stationed behind the blinds of a house which the Admiral used to pass on his way to the Louvre. Three days he lay in wait. But when the opportunity came, although his piece was loaded with three balls he only wounded his victim. Coligny at once sent to inform the King of what had happened ; his messenger found Charles IX. playing tennis with Henry of Guise and Teligny ; turning pale and dashing his racquet to the ground he exclaimed with many oaths, " Are we never to have peace ? " and went to his room " with sad and downcast countenance."

Soon the King of Navarre, the Prince of Condé and a crowd of nobles demanded an audience and the King's permission to leave a town where their lives were in danger. Full, apparently, of grief and anger Charles declared he would take such vengeance as should never be forgotten on those who were guilty of the outrage. Nor could his sincerity be doubted when he ordered the gates of the city to be shut to prevent the escape of the would-be assassins, intrusted the inquiry into the crime to an impartially chosen commission, forbade the towns-people to arm or to close their shops, sent a detachment of his guards to protect the Admiral, and offered lodgings to the Huguenot gentlemen near Coligny's house, or in the Louvre.

After dinner Charles came accompanied by his

Court, his mother and his brothers to visit the Admiral, whom he overwhelmed with demonstrations of affection. " My father," he said, " the pain of the wound is yours, but the insult and the wrong are mine," and again he swore with his usual oaths that the guilty should dearly rue their deed. The Queen and Anjou were filled with apprehension and as soon as they had reached the Tuileries sent Gondi, Count of Retz, formerly the King's tutor, and who had still much influence over him, to pacify him.

On the next morning the Protestant nobles deliberated whether they should leave Paris, taking with them the Admiral, wounded as he was; but Coligny and the majority were persuaded of the King's good faith; to fly would be to abandon him to the Guises and to make civil war inevitable. They determined to stay, and Catherine heard that they intended on the next day to present themselves at Court in a body, and to accuse the Duke of Guise of attempting the life of Coligny. It was probable that Henry of Guise would not care to deny his complicity in an act which established his popularity among the mob and the friars, but would excuse himself by saying that he had acted by the authority of the Duke of Anjou, the lieutenant-general of the kingdom. Thus the vengeance of the Protestants and the anger of the King would fall on the Queen-Mother and her favourite son. Catherine felt that she must act, and act at once. Accompanied by Anjou, by Gondi, by Gonzaga, Duke of Nevers, Birago, a Milanese, the unworthy successor of the Chancellor l'Hôpital, and Marshal Tavannes, she requested an audience of the

King. There are three fairly authentic accounts, which agree in the main, of what passed at this interview ; nor is it hard to understand how the half mad King, whose nature had been prepared for crime, whose nobler qualities had been perverted or stunted, was harassed and perplexed and driven into the toils by the infernal art of his advisers. No argument was neglected which might overcome his reluctance, not so much to break his faith, as to sacrifice men for whom he seems to have felt sincere respect or liking.

The dangerous ambition of the Huguenots, their turbulence and previous attacks on the royal authority, the discontent of the Catholics at the favours shown to the heretics, and their determination if the King did not listen to their complaints to form a Holy League under a captain-general of their own, and save the realm in his spite,—all this and much more was urged. For an hour and a half Charles resisted, but stung at length by the imputation that he was too timid to act, he leapt up in a frenzy of passion, cursing everybody and everything: " By God's death since you insist that the Admiral must be killed I consent; but with him every Huguenot in France must perish, that not one may remain to reproach me with his death ; and what you do, see that it be done quickly." So speaking, he rushed like a madman from the room.

When the King's assent had been obtained, the arrangements for the massacre were soon concerted between the Queen-Mother, Anjou, the Guises and the leaders of the Parisian mob. The signal was **to**

MEDAL OF CHARLES IX. STRUCK TO COMMEMORATE THE MASSACRE OF
ST. BARTHOLOMEW.

MEDAL OF GREGORY XIII. STRUCK TO COMMEMORATE THE MASSACRE OF
ST. BARTHOLOMEW.

be given that very night by the bells of the church
nearest to the Louvre.

As the fatal moment approached Charles IX.
attempted to revoke the permission extorted from
him. Even Catherine felt some misgivings, but it
was too late. " We went," so the Duke of Anjou
during a sleepless night told his physician, " we went
to a room in the gate tower of the Louvre, to watch
from a window which looked into the yard the
beginning of the execution. We had not been there
long, and we were considering the consequences of so
great an enterprise, when we suddenly heard the
report of a pistol. I do not know where the shot
was fired, nor whether it hurt any one, but the mere
sound struck us with strange terrors and apprehensions of the great disorders that were then about to
be committed. We suddenly and hastily sent a
gentleman to M. de Guise, bidding him retire to his
house, and to beware of attempting anything against
the Admiral. But our messenger came back, and
said that it was too late, and that the Admiral was
already dead."

Guise himself and the Duke of Angoulême, a
bastard of Henry II., superintended the murder of
Coligny. The guards who were sent by the King
for his protection were the first to fire upon his
retainers. Coligny, hearing the uproar, knew that
his last hour was come. He told the great surgeon
Ambrose Paré, himself a Protestant, and others
who had been watching in his room to escape by the
roof; only one of his attendants, a German, refused
to leave him. The murderers burst open the door

but they were so abashed by the fearless dignity of their victim, that they stood hesitating on the threshold. One only, a foreigner, a Bohemian who was half drunk stepped forward : " Are you the Admiral ? " and with an oath felled him to the ground. The others hacked him with their swords. " Have you finished ? " shouted the Duke of Guise from the courtyard ; " throw him out of the window for us to see with our own eyes." Even yet there seemed to be some life in the body, for a moment it clung to the window bars. The features were crushed and scarcely to be distinguished. Angoulême wiped away the blood from the face, and recognising the Admiral, kicked it as he turned away. When Guise in his turn fell by the assassin's sword and his corpse was spurned by the man he had despised and dared, the accomplice of his present crime, it was remembered that he also had struck the dead hero with his foot.

So perished Admiral Coligny, one of the noblest characters and of the ablest soldiers and statesmen produced by the French Reformation.

Aristotle describes the man of perfect character as slow and deliberate of speech, considerate to his inferiors, but unaccommodating to his equals and haughty to his superiors, little disposed to frequent places where he has to give way to others, more ready to confer than to receive obligations, and with a high and just conceit of his own merits. Devout Christian as he was, the Admiral would have satisfied the pagan philosopher's ideal. But a virtue less proud and austere would not have given him the influence

which he needed to control the excesses, the dis-
cordant aims and councils of his party. The vanity
of the Huguenot nobles yielded to a pride better
founded and more masterful than their own. As
a general, he knew how to effect great results with
small means and was never more formidable than
when defeated.

Coligny was a Puritan by conviction and temperament, but a Puritan of the French Renaissance. His
house of Châtillon sur Loing, where the day began
with prayers, which he himself conducted, contained
choice collections of books and works of art, and
was as hospitable to scholars and artists as the
palace of a Montefeltro or a Medici. The interest
in literature and culture which somewhat redeems
the bestial licence of the French Court in the 16th
century made Calvinism itself more amiable.

" There," said the Elector Palatine, showing the
portrait of his victim to Henry of Anjou, " there is
the most virtuous man and the wisest, and the
greatest captain of Europe, whose children I have
invited to live with me, lest they should be torn in
pieces like their father by those French hounds."

But there is perhaps no greater tribute to the
Admiral's integrity than the praise of Brantôme,
who belonged to the faction of the Guises, yet maintains that no selfish motive led Coligny to draw his
sword, and that had he been less patriotic and less
loyal he would not have perished a victim to his
hatred of civil strife.

The death of the Admiral was the signal for the
slaughter of the Huguenot gentlemen who were

lodged in the neighbourhood.  It was in the Louvre itself that the massacre was most odious, if not most cruel.  The Protestant nobles who were sleeping in the palace had been expressly invited by the King, and were protected by the duty which he owed to them as his guests as well as his subjects, by his honour as a prince and as a gentleman.  One by one they were summoned and cut down by the Swiss guards under the very eyes of the King, who, mad with the excitement of his crime, himself urged on the butchery.  His victims as they fell reproached him with his broken faith.

When day dawned the great bell of the Hôtel de Ville summoned the rabble of the city to complete the slaughter.  On the first·day the massacre was chiefly confined to the Huguenot nobles and their followers.  The municipality and the most respectable citizens begged the King to put an end to the disorders which they said were committed by the princes and nobles of his Court, and by the dregs of the populace.  Charles IX. asked them to assist in quelling the riot which he affected to deplore.  But nothing was done, the bloodshed and horrors of the second and third days outdid the atrocities of the first.  Every evil passion, fanaticism, hate, envy, lust and avarice raged uncontrolled, in a hideous scene of anarchy and carnage.  Catholic tradesmen murdered their Huguenot competitors, needy courtiers hounded on the mob to slaughter their creditors, men were killed for their offices, for their houses, for their wives.  But most horrible perhaps was the ferocity of the mob, of the women and even of the

little children.   A ferocity, which the dregs of Paris
had shown in the civil wars of Armagnac and Burgundy and which they were again to display in 1793.
Women were ripped up, babies spitted on pikes or
dragged to the river by children scarcely older than
themselves.

At the lowest computation 2,000 Protestants perished in Paris, and these men were the flower of the
Huguenot nobility, the most enlightened and energetic of the professional and mercantile classes of
the capital.   It is remarkable that the boldest soldiers and proudest nobles in France allowed themselves to be slaughtered like sheep, so completely
were these men, whom their enemies accused of
plotting to seize the capital and the King's person,
taken by surprise.   Only one man, and he a lawyer,
attempted resistance, barred his doors and kept his
assailants at bay, till his house was stormed by a
company of the royal guards.

The Count of Montgomery, the vidame of Chartres, with other nobles who were lodged in the Faubourg St. Germain, had timely warning and escaped.

The Duke of Guise, suspecting that an attempt
might be made to throw the odium of what had
happened upon his faction, was anxious that his
moderation should contrast with the mad frenzy of
bloodshed into which the King had fallen.   " He is
not," the English envoy wrote to Cecil, " so bloody,
neither did he kill any man himself, but saved divers;
he spake openly that for the Admiral's death he was
glad, for he knew him to be his enemy, but for the
rest the King had put to death such as might do

him very good service." Following the example of
the Guises, other influential Catholics saved some of
the victims who took refuge in their houses. A few
were even protected by the favour of the Court;
among these was the famous potter Bernard Palissy,
who escaped in his workshop in the garden of the
Tuileries, to perish eighteen years later of want and
ill usage in the prisons of the League.

The horrors of Paris were repeated on a smaller
scale, but with not less atrocious circumstances, at
Meaux, Orleans, Angers, Troyes, Bourges, Lyons,
Rouen, Toulouse, Bordeaux and other places. Although not a few of the governors refused to obey
the orders of the Court and the tranquillity of some
provinces was comparatively undisturbed, yet at
least 20,000 victims perished.

The Queen-Mother and her advisers had, it is
said, at first intended that the King of Navarre and
the Prince of Condé should share the fate of the
other Huguenots. But their individual importance
appeared too insignificant, their rank too exalted.
It was not worth while to incur the odium of putting to death the first Prince of the Blood, the husband of the King's sister, in order to guard against
any danger that seemed likely to arise from this
"half-fledged kinglet," who appeared less eager to
share in the councils of his party than in the revels
and debaucheries of his royal brothers.

Margaret of Valois gives in her memoirs an apparently faithful account of the events of the fatal
night of St. Bartholomew, so far as they concerned
herself and her husband. "The Huguenots," she

says, " suspected me because I was a Catholic ; the Catholics, because I had married the King of Navarre. So that I heard nothing of what was going on till the evening, when, as I was sitting on a chest in my mother's room by the side of my sister, the Duchess of Lorraine, whom I saw to be very sad, the Queen-Mother noticed me and told me to go to bed. As I was curtesying to her my sister laid hold of my arm and burst into tears saying, ' For God's sake, sister, don't go.' I was greatly frightened and seeing this the Queen, my mother, spoke very sharply to my sister, and forbade her to say anything to me, adding that, please God, no harm would happen to me, but that, come what might, go I must, lest something should be suspected. I did not hear what was said, but again and very roughly my mother told me to go.

" As soon as I was in my room I threw myself on my knees and prayed God to protect me, though I knew not from what or against whom.

" Meanwhile the king, my husband, had gone to bed and sent word to me to come to him. I found his bed surrounded by thirty or forty Huguenots whom I did not yet know, for I had only been married a few days. All night long they remained talking of what had happened to the Admiral, and determining as soon as day broke to ask for redress against M. de Guise ; and if it were not granted, then to seek it for themselves. As for me the tears of my sister weighed on my mind and I could not sleep for fear of some unknown evil. At dawn, the King, my husband, said he would go and play tennis till

King Charles was awake, having made up his mind to ask him at once to do justice. He then left my room, and his gentlemen with him. Seeing that it was light, and thinking that the danger of which my sister had spoken was passed, and being heavy with drowsiness, I told my nurse to lock the door, so that I might sleep undisturbed. An hour later, when I was fast asleep, some one came beating with hands and feet against the door and shouting ' Navarre, Navarre ! ' My nurse thinking that it was my husband ran to open. It was a gentleman wounded by a sword-thrust in the elbow, and his arm cut by a halberd, who rushed into my room pursued by four archers. Seeking safety, he threw himself on my bed [no doubt a four-poster with curtains out of the comparative privacy of which her husband had talked with his gentlemen]. Feeling this man clutching me, I threw myself into the space between the bed and the wall, where, he still grasping me, we rolled over, both screaming and both equally frightened. Fortunately, the Captain of my Guards, M. de Nançay, came by, who saw me in such plight, that sorry as he was he could not help laughing, but drove the archers out of the room and gave me the life of the poor gentleman, who was still clinging to me, and whom I caused to be tended and nursed in my dressing-room till he was quite cured. While I changed my night-dress, for he had covered me with his blood, M. de Nançay told me what had happened, but assured me that my husband was in the King's room and in no danger. Making me throw on a dressing-gown, he then led me to the room of my sister Madame de Lorraine, which I reached more dead than alive; just as I was going into the ante-room a gentleman trying to escape from the archers who were pursuing him fell stabbed three paces from me. I too fell half fainting into the arms of M. de Nançay and felt as if the same blow had pierced us both."

Meantime the King of Navarre and the Prince of Condé had been summoned to the King's presence. All that had happened, had, he told them, been done by his orders. Henceforward he would tolerate no other religion in his dominions than the Roman Catholic. They had allowed themselves to be made the leaders of his enemies, and their lives were justly forfeit. But, as they were his kinsmen and connec-tions, he would pardon them on condition that they conformed to the church of their ancestors; if not they must prepare to be treated like their friends.

Navarre, surprised and disconcerted by the unex-pected catastrophe, muttered some ambiguous words; Condé more boldly replied, that he was accountable for his religion to God alone. They were then dis-missed with threats of the Bastille or death, should they be obstinate.

After some weeks the cautious and measured re-sistance of Henry and the bolder defiance of Condé alike yielded to their fears. The latter indeed, after he had been once dragged to Mass, was zealous in the observances of his new religion; he was, laughed the courtiers, so busy crossing himself in season and out, that he had no time to notice the love passages between his Princess and Anjou.

Henry's life was now safe, perhaps it had never been seriously threatened, but it would not be easy to imagine a more difficult and dangerous position than that in which he now found himself. The eight hundred gentlemen who had accompanied him to his wedding were slain or fled, there was none near him to warn him or advise, powerless as he appeared in the hands of his mother-in-law. Catherine suggested to her daughter, if the latter may be believed, that a divorce might easily be procured, which would have deprived him of such security as the position of the King's brother-in-law conferred. But Margaret declined to be a party to any such scheme, and, though she had no affection for her husband, appears at this crisis of his fortunes to have played the part of a loyal friend, helping him by her advice to thread his way through the mazes of a Court, than which none was ever more disturbed by unscrupulous intrigue, by mutual hatred and suspicion.

It was indeed a strange stage on which this beardless youth of nineteen, this King, with more nose than kingdom, as the courtiers jested, was called to play his perilous part ; still reeking with the blood of the tragedy just enacted, crowded with a motley crew of cut-throats, courtesans and adventurers, elbowing nobles, ladies and princes, who differed from them little in manners, dress or decency of life.

" In that Court," says an eye-witness, " common sin seemed too near virtue to please, and he was reckoned to show little spirit who was content to be the gallant of but one adulteress." There everything, another contemporary declares, was tolerated, except a decent life and virtuous conversation. There, too, was "hate hard by lust," and the general profligacy was accompanied by a violence of manners such as we cannot easily realise. Flown with insolence and wine, the princes and their minions ranged the streets, insulting the women, beating and wounding inoffensive citizens and engaging in bloody and fatal broils with their rivals in debauchery.

Such was the example set in the highest places. The Kings of France, Poland and Navarre and their attendants, after a hideous orgy which began with a banquet served by naked women, stormed and sacked the house of a gentleman, who had offended Henry of Anjou by refusing to marry his cast-off mistress. Nor did this exploit attract attention as anything out of the common course.

Eight thousand gentlemen were killed in duels during the reign of Henry IV., and probably no fewer during the previous twenty years. The Romans, a moralist complained, left the duel and the point of honour to gladiators and to the dregs of their slaves. Now to be the first to break through the ranks of the enemy, to plant the standard on the breach, to rally a flying squadron, is no proof of courage—courage can only be shown in a quarrel about a dog or hawk or harlot.

To kill an enemy in fair combat was a source of legitimate pride, but it was scarcely reckoned dishonourable to get rid of him by assassination. Writing a few years later, the diarist L'Estoile remarks, that the gentry following the example of the great nobles were beginning to have recourse to assassination instead of to the duel. The annals of one princely house will furnish us with sufficient examples. The Duke of Mayenne killed with his own hand a soldier of fortune who had the assurance to propose to marry his step-daughter, the son of Henry of Guise proved his manhood by stabbing the Captain St. Pol, the Duke of Aumale sought to assassinate the Duke of Épernon, the Count of Chaligny murdered Chicot the Court jester. Maurevert, a hireling bravo of the Guises, who, after failing to assassinate Coligny, killed by treachery a Huguenot gentleman, his benefactor, was made a knight of the order of St. Michael by Charles IX. But nothing perhaps is more significant than that, when Aubigné accuses his admired master Henry IV. of seeking to compass his assassination, either because he had refused to pander to his licentious amours, or, as he would have us believe, from jealousy of his martial renown, he evidently does not suspect that he is bringing a monstrous and improbable charge against the Prince, whom he elsewhere so loudly praises. Even the women were prompt in the use of the dagger. Madame de Châteauneuf, discovering the infidelity of her husband, stabbed him " in right manly fashion " then and there with her own hand. Never have the unbridled ferocity and savage passions of the barbarian shown themselves in closer and more startling contrast to the artificial corruptions and effeminate graces of an apparently decadent society.

The most prominent actors were worthy of the

scene and the drama.   The half frenzied King distrusted all around him, and none more than his
brother Anjou and his mother, by whom he had
allowed himself to be persuaded to sacrifice the one
man who had touched his better nature, and to
exchange his dreams of honourable renown for
eternal infamy.   Charles IX. was capricious, violent,
liable to sudden starts and gusts of passion.   In his
fits of fury, he lost all control over his actions, and
showed in his sports a morbid cruelty and love of
bloodshed.   Yet he was perhaps the best of his
family.   He kept clear in some measure of the
shameless immorality which disgraced so many of
his contemporaries; he had real feeling for music
and poetry; he addressed Ronsard in well known
lines not inferior to anything written by that poet.
He was not incapable of being influenced by noble
motives, or by a noble character, if brought into
contact with it.   We have seen the ascendancy
Coligny obtained over him, and towards the miserable end of his life, he befriended and clung to his
brother-in-law Henry of Navarre, recognising in him
some sparks of generosity, manliness and honour
wanting in his own brothers.

Next to the King, says a satirist, came one who
appeared better skilled to judge of the harlots of the
Court, better composed for love—smooth chin, pale
face, the gestures of a woman, the eye of Sardanapa-
lus; and he goes on to describe how this ambiguous
thing appeared without 'a blush at a Court ball, its
hair full of strings and pearls under an Italian cap,
its smooth face rouged and whitened, the body of

the doublet cut low like a woman's with long sleeves falling to the ground, a painted courtesan rather than a prince—a second Nero, and worse than Nero, fed from his cradle on poisons, secret wiles and treachery. The picture of course is overcharged—even Henry of Valois had some qualities not wholly abject. He was neither a madman like Charles IX. nor an ambitious and meddlesome fool like his younger brother Alençon. He had insight into men and things. He could speak with weight and dignity; he had more than once given proof of personal courage. But the influence of his mother, the evil atmosphere in which he had been brought up, had at an early age encouraged a luxuriant growth of vices and follies which choked his better qualities. He was so entirely without any moral sense, that not only did it seem as if good and evil were indifferent to him, but also as if he had lost all measure of the relative importance of the objects he pursued.

Of the three sons of Henry II., the youngest, Francis Duke of Alençon, was the most contemptible, in ability and even in character; and although, as a contrast to the shameless effeminacy of his brother Anjou, he affected a rough frankness and martial bearing, he was not less false, or less corrupt. If all treachery were banished from earth, said Margaret of Valois of this her favourite brother, he had enough to re-stock the world.

Next in importance to the Princes of the Blood, was the head of the younger branch of the House of Lorraine, the youthful Henry of Guise—courting popularity, affable and splendid, concealing an

HENRY III.

insatiable and unscrupulous ambition under the exterior of a soldier and a man of pleasure.

United in their amusements and debaucheries, these young Princes were divided by their ambition and by the interests of those who had attached themselves to their fortunes.

Catherine de' Medici no doubt was well pleased with the success of her policy. The Admiral, whose influence over the King would have been fatal to her ambition, was dead. Six hundred of the most prominent Huguenot nobles had perished, and a blow had been dealt to their party from which it was believed that it would not readily recover.

The French Court showed a little consistency in the accounts which it gave of the events of the 24th of August. Naturally it did not wish to present the massacre in the same light to Elizabeth and to the Protestant Princes of Germany as to the Pope and Philip of Spain. But the version which on the whole it seemed desirable to have accepted was that the Huguenots had formed a conspiracy against the Crown, that the King had been compelled to take measures to defend himself, but that the excesses committed had proceeded from the hostility of the Houses of Guise and Châtillon, and from the uncontrollable religious zeal of the Parisians.

To Catherine the massacre was merely a domestic incident; she did not intend to allow it to influence the foreign policy of France. What she had objected to had been not the policy which Coligny urged upon the King, but Coligny himself. It is true that she had shrunk from a formal declaration of war against Spain, but she was ready to vie with Queen Elizabeth in helping the rebels and harrying the subjects of a Prince still, in diplomatic phrase, her good friend and ally.

Various circumstances tended to encourage Catherine in the belief that a government so stained with murder and perfidy, execrated by half Europe, could, up to a certain point, adopt as its own and carry on the policy of the Admiral.

At the first report of the blow, the fatal blow as it was supposed, dealt to the Protestant cause in France, Orange advancing to the relief of Mons was driven back into Holland. The rebellion was crushed in the southern provinces, the garrisons and populations which had refused to admit the Spanish troops were exterminated. Holland and Zealand still resisted, but their resistance seemed hopeless unless they could obtain help from no matter what quarter. It was just because her crime had been so fatal to them, that the Nassaus could not refuse the hand which Catherine held out, red though it was with the blood of their brethren.

Nor did Queen Elizabeth venture to break with the French Court, fearing lest it should be driven into an alliance with Spain. The indignation of the English people was indeed deeply stirred, and the Queen gave some satisfaction to their feelings by the theatrical severity of her reception of the French ambassador, when he attempted to justify his Government. Cecil, whose sympathy with the Protestants of the continent was deeper than that of his mistress, ventured to condemn in harsher terms the unexampled infamy of a crime committed in the presence of the King and in violation of his plighted word, but he too felt that even in such a cause, England could not venture to quarrel with her only ally.

It is not probable that Catherine quickly realised how completely her master-stroke had failed in attaining the result she expected in France. The Huguenots were stunned for a space by the violence of the blow. The death of the Admiral and of so many of their leading men threw the organisation of the party out of gear. Many who had joined the Protestants from interested motives abandoned a cause which they considered desperate; others affected to see in this disaster the judgment of heaven, and followed Navarre and Condé to Mass. Nothing but a conviction of the hopelessness of further resistance could have induced La Noue, the Knight without reproach, the Bayard of his party, to become the agent of the murderers of his friends and to undertake the task of persuading La Rochelle to admit a royal garrison.

But friends and enemies were soon to learn that though the effect of the massacre on the Huguenot party was great, it had done little to break their spirit, or even to diminish their power of resistance. Most of the powerful nobles to whom they had looked up as their leaders had been slaughtered, others had conformed to Romanism. After 1572 the popular element predominated in the Huguenot assemblies. The struggle which the Bourbons and the Châtillons had begun was continued by the citizens of La Rochelle and Montauban, of Sancerre

and Nîmes.  But the princes and nobles had only
demanded religious liberty, the townsmen, not content with asking for toleration, required also that
the States-General should be assembled, the political grievances of the country remedied.  The republican tendencies which seem to be the necessary
consequence of Calvinism, began to make themselves felt.  Numerous books and pamphlets poured
from the press, publishing on the housetops, what
hitherto men had scarcely whispered in a friend's
ear, discussing the reciprocal rights of rulers and
subjects, and affirming that if the King sought the
hurt of his people, they were absolved from their
allegiance.  The obedience, so it was now taught, of
the people is conditional on the Prince performing
his engagement, whether implied or explicit, to govern justly and equitably.  No man is born a king,
and it was proved historically that the French monarchy was elective, and that sovereignty was not in
the Crown, but in the people, represented by the
Three Estates.  This natural and lawful sovereignty
of the nation, after lasting eleven centuries, had been
extinguished by the gradual and unconstitutional
encroachments of the kings.  The inapplicability to
the French monarchy of the Imperialist maxims
borrowed by the lawyers from Roman law was
pointed out.  The only possible justification of despotism is the maintenance of order ; the Massacre of
St. Bartholomew had been an appeal to disorder,
licence and anarchy.  The Government had let loose
upon society those destructive passions which it is
its primary function to bridle.  It was thus that the

Protestant publicists forged the weapons afterwards used by the League in their struggle against Henry III. and Henry IV.

The Protestant middle classes in uniting the cause of political liberty and progress with that of their religion showed a truer insight into the needs of their country than was ever attained to by the nobles of their party. It would have proved of inestimable advantage to France had they been able to make their voice heard with more decisive effect. In the mouths of the demagogues of the League, of the hirelings of Spain and of the disciples of the Jesuits, such an appeal to the old constitutional liberties of France, and to the indefeasible sovereignty of the people was a meaningless or hypocritical jargon.

Montauban, Sancerre and La Rochelle set the first example of resistance, refusing to receive the royal garrisons. Towards the end of 1572 a synod held in Béarn drew up a plan for the organisation of the Protestant communities in districts, governed by officers elected by all classes.

The Government determined to attack La Rochelle, in every respect the most important of the Huguenot strongholds, the port by which they communicated with their friends in the Low Countries and England, and which assisted the cause by contributing a considerable share of the wealth acquired by preying on Spanish commerce.

The siege of La Rochelle cost the lives of over 20,000 men and of more than three hundred officers of some distinction. The King of Navarre and the

Prince of Condé were compelled to prove the sincerity of their conversion by serving side by side with the Guises under the Duke of Anjou. But this Prince had meantime been elected King of Poland. The French agents had spared neither lies nor promises. Anjou, they declared, had taken no share in the persecution of the Protestants, which he had always lamented. It was not desirable that the Polish ambassadors, who were on their way to salute their new sovereign, should find him engaged in the siege of a Protestant town. To appear to yield to a diplomatic necessity was less humiliating than to confess the total failure of all efforts to take La Rochelle by treachery or force; and the Court gladly seized the opportunity to offer acceptable terms to the besieged (June 24, 1573).

The lesson taught by the successful resistance of La Rochelle was not thrown away. On the anniversary of the massacre (August 24, 1573), the delegates of the Huguenots of Languedoc and Guienne met and after organising themselves into a kind of federal republic, sent a deputation to communicate their demands to the King : complete toleration and liberty of worship throughout the kingdom ; all law courts to contain an equal number of judges of both religions ; members of the Reformed Church to be released from the payment of tithes ; punishment of the authors of the massacre and restitution of the property of the victims to their heirs ; two fortresses in each province to be placed as security in the hands of the Protestants and garrisoned by them at the King's expense. Catherine exclaimed in indignant amazement, " that if Condé had been alive and in possession of Paris with 70,000 men he would not have asked half so much," yet she did not dare altogether to refuse to entertain the demands of the Reformers—so threatening had become the attitude of the moderate Catholic party, the Politicians. They were disgusted by the misgovernment of Charles IX., the perfidy and cruelty of his mother, the baseness of her Italian favourites. The sufferings of the Huguenots had excited the sympathy of many who did not care to abandon the Established Church, yet were not fanatically attached to its doctrines. A spirit of compromise and toleration was more widely diffused, weariness of the sufferings caused by a struggle in which the atrocities of the Catholics had been avenged by reprisals scarcely less cruel, indignation that such horrors should be perpetrated in the name of religion, experience of the fact that it was possible for two religions to exist side by side in the same state and even in the same town, disposed all humane and moderate men to wish rather to join in seeking to remedy the anarchy and misgovernment under which the country was sinking, than to attempt to restore unity of faith by the sword. Moreover the Montmorencys, the leaders of the moderate party, were aware that the Queen Mother intended their ruin after that of the Bourbons and Châtillons.

The Politicians published a manifesto demanding the reformation of the Government, the assembly of the Estates, and the restoration of the national liberties. The Huguenots began to occupy the fortresses of Poitou. Montgomery, the splinter of whose lance

had killed Henry II., and who, to the disappoint-
ment of Catherine, had escaped on St. Bartholomew's
Day, landed in Normandy with English supplies and
English volunteers.

The Duke of Damville, the second son of the Constable Montmorency, who was governor of Languedoc,
where he ruled with almost sovereign authority,
observed an attitude of friendly neutrality to the
Huguenots of his province and of Guienne.

In Poitou the Huguenots prospered, but in Normandy Montgomery was unable to maintain himself
and was finally compelled to capitulate.

Catherine hurried to tell the King that Montgomery, whom she hated, was a prisoner ; but turning his face to the wall he asked to be left in peace.
Even Protestant historians are moved to pity by
the miserable end of Charles IX. He had again completely fallen under the influence of his mother. On
one point only he had firmly insisted. He compelled
his brother Anjou to leave France (September, 1573),
to take possession of his Polish throne. Notwithstanding his weak health he exhausted himself in
insane revels. He appeared to seek to lose himself
in the wildest physical exertions. His eyes were
sunk, his complexion livid, he was unable to meet
the gaze of those with whom he spoke. In the
autumn of 1573, he was attacked by smallpox, his
health became worse and worse, he often awoke
bathed in his blood, a judgment as it seemed to him
of the carnage to which he had consented. Indeed,
from the first he was tormented by remorse.

Less than a fortnight after the massacre, so Henry

**CHARLES IX.**

From the painting by F. Clouet.

IV. used to tell his friends, Charles IX. sent for him in the middle of the night; the King had started from his bed alarmed by a confused noise of shouts, shrieks and groans, such as had re-echoed through the streets of Paris on that fatal night. Henry of Navarre himself and all who were present heard the turmoil, and officers were sent to discover what new riot had broken out in the city. The streets were empty, all was quiet in Paris, only round the Louvre the air was filled with horrid uproar.

At other times the King was disturbed by black bands of obscene birds, crows and ravens, who obstinately perched on the towers and gables of the palace, and by their importunate cries appeared to call for such another banquet of murdered corpses.

As his death approached, the King was constantly disturbed by fearful visions. He begged God to have mercy on him and on his people. What would become of them? he cried; as for himself, he well knew that he was lost. His last words were that he rejoiced to leave no son behind him, the heir of his kingdom and his crimes.

Queen Catherine showed both spirit and skill in securing the peaceable succession of her favourite son. Fortunately for her the opponents she had most reason to dread were in her power. Montmorency and Cossé the leaders of the Politicians were in the Bastille; Navarre and Alençon prisoners in all but name, watched, wrote the English envoy, by guard upon guard, and even the windows of their rooms grated.     Lincoln Christian College

Condé alone had slipped from her clutches, and

after visiting Geneva, was negotiating with the German Princes and collecting mercenaries at Strasbourg. The news of his brother's death reached Anjou in Poland, where he had already disgusted his subjects by his womanish ways, his evident distaste for their country and customs and his neglect of his public duties. He fled from Cracow with indecent haste in the middle of the night, excusing himself on the ground that the state of France was so disturbed that a week's delay might imperil his succession. Yet instead of taking the shortest road to the French frontier, he preferred to travel by Vienna and through Italy, and wasted two months in luxurious debauchery. Pignerol, the gate of Italy, was restored to the Duke of Savoy, in acknowledgment of his sumptuous hospitality. The Duke at least repaid Henry's generosity by good advice, such as he had already received from the Emperor Maximilian and the Venetian Doge. He urged him to conciliate the Politicians, and to re-establish peace by moderate concessions to the Protestants. He invited Damville to Turin to confer with the King. Damville came and the King tried to persuade his host to allow him to be arrested. Damville was warned to be on his guard, and hastily returning to Languedoc at once formed a closer alliance with the Huguenots.

He was elected protector of the confederates, but was to act by the advice of a council composed of three representatives of each of the districts which adhered to the cause of the Protestants and the allied Catholics. Of these deputies, one was to be a noble and two of the Third Estate ; the majority was thus assured to the representatives of the commons, a decisive proof that the movement was not, as has been often alleged, aristocratic. Yet it must be allowed that the Protestants from henceforth became less and less a national party. In the manifesto which they now published we find for the last time demands for toleration coupled with a clear statement of the reforms necessary for the constitutional development of the monarchy—regular meetings of the States-General, abolition of arbitrary taxation and other securities for public liberty.

Persecution and war had driven the Protestants out of the provinces in which they formed only a small minority of the population ; they stood at bay in Dauphiny, Languedoc, Guienne, Poitou, Auvergne and the lordships under the Pyrenees, districts in which the traditions of provincial independence were most powerful, the sense of national unity weakest. Hence the danger that the great nobles, the heads of families, who had long enjoyed a consideration and authority in their respective provinces scarcely inferior to that of the Crown, such as the La Tour d'Auvergnes in Auvergne, the La Rochefoucaulds in Guienne, the La Tremoilles and Rohans in Poitou, might use the strength of the party for the gratification of their private ambition. But it cannot be too often repeated that the Catholic party, the party of the League, was not in any true sense a more popular party more patriotic, or more concerned for the maintenance of the national liberties and unity than their opponents. One of the main objects of the

Catholic leaders was to convert the governorships of provinces and towns into hereditary offices; yet it was not forgotten that a similar conversion of the counties and duchies of the Carlovingian kingdoms, from offices held during the good-will of the sovereign into hereditary principalities, had produced the disruption of those kingdoms and the feudal anarchy of the 10th and 11th centuries. The numerous towns which joined the League aimed only at recovering the selfish municipal privileges of the Middle Ages. To secure the independence enjoyed by the free towns of Germany, they would have acquiesced in the partition of the monarchy.

Catherine de' Medici was waiting to welcome her son at Bourgoin and they entered Lyons in state together. There the new King proclaimed his intention of subduing by force of arms those who resisted his authority. Refusing to listen to those wiser councillors who pointed to the exhaustion of the country and the emptiness of the treasury, he followed the advice of his mother, who, fearing, if peace were made, the influence of Montmorency and other Moderates, and believing that nothing was impossible to the hero of Jarnac and Montcontour when directed by her councils, had abandoned her habitual caution and was the advocate of a vigorous policy.

But when the money needed to pay the expenses of military operations had been raised by loans from foreign princes, by extortion and by ruinous expedients, it was wasted in senseless profusion by the King, who showed his Catholic zeal not by placing himself at the head of his army, but by conducting

fantastically dressed processions of penitents. These
processions had one good consequence. Cardinal
Charles of Lorraine unaccustomed to such barefoot
devotions, caught a chill which proved fatal. The
Protestants believed that he was carried off by the
devil; for "something more violent than the wind
tore down and whirled off into the air the lattices and
window bars of the house where he lodged."

While Henry III. was parading his puerile piety in
the papal city of Avignon, Damville held twenty
miles away, at Nîmes, a general assembly of the
Huguenots and "united Catholics." Discredited and
ridiculed, the King journeyed north to be crowned at
Rheims and the confederates were encouraged to
propose terms which implied not the humiliation
only but the ruin of the monarchy. Efforts were
made to continue the war with greater vigour, when
the Court was suddenly alarmed by the news of the
flight of the Duke of Alençon, who placed himself at
the head of the rebels (September, 1575).

Henry of Bourbon both disliked and despised
Alençon and chafed to see him occupying, as the
champion and leader of the Reformers, a position to
which he felt that he himself had a better claim.
Soon after the Duke's flight, Cecil's agent reports that
" Navarre was never so merry nor so much made of "
—but as time went on, his position at the French Court
became neither more secure nor more honourable.

It was humiliating to masquerade in Henry III.'s
penitential processions and still more degrading to be
the companion of debaucheries, which in themselves
were not attractive to an appetite for vice, which if

scarcely less keen than the King's, was less sophisti-
cated and jaded. And what if not even the sacrifice
of his self-respect, his dignity and his ambition could
secure his safety?

All his Huguenot servants had been removed, except Aubigné, the historian, who, like his master,
had hidden a serious purpose under a frivolous exterior, and one other : these two sitting by his bed,
heard him sigh and repeat the 88th psalm, " Thou
hast put away my acquaintance far from me and
made me to be abhorred of them. I am so fast in
prison that I cannot get forth." Upon this, Aubigné
drew the curtains and addressed to his master one of
those sententious speeches with which, if we may
believe his history, he would seem to have been
always provided. " Is it true, Sire, that the spirit
of God still dwells and works in you? You sigh to
Him for the absence of your faithful friends and servants, while they are met together grieving that you
are not with them, and labouring for your deliver-
ance. Are you not weary of trying to hide behind
yourself? you are guilty of your greatness and of the
wrongs you have endured. The murderers of St.
Bartholomew's Day have a good memory, and cannot
believe that of their victims to be so short.

" Nay, if what is dishonourable were but safe! But
no risk can be greater than to remain. As for us
two, we were speaking, when what you said led us to
draw the curtain, of escaping to-morrow. Consider,
Sire, that you will next be served by hands which
will not dare to refuse to employ poison or steel
against you."

It is probable that no eloquence was needed to induce Henry to attempt his escape as soon as occasion offered.   In the meantime he feigned to believe the King's protestations of good-will and to fear the hostility of Alençon, while he continued his apparently careless and trivial life.   In a letter to the Governor of Béarn, which he no doubt expected would be read by others, he describes the Court as being strangely distracted, " we are all ready to cut one another's throats, and wear daggers, chain vests and often corselets under our cloaks . . . the King loves me more than ever.   M. de Guise and M. de Mayenne [Guise's younger brother] never leave my side "; the partisans of Alençon, he goes on to say, hate him to the death, but in a Court where all others are his friends, he does not fear them.

He played the dupe so successfully, Henry III. was so convinced of his infatuation, that greater liberty began to be allowed him.   Toward the end of January (1576), some officers who bad been disappointed in their expectation of royal favour offered, if the King of Navarre would separate himself from the Court, to put him in possession of Chartres, le Mans and Cherbourg.   In order that they might have time for their preparations, and to enable his friends to collect a force near Paris, Henry postponed his attempt to escape till February 20th.

On February 4th as he came back towards night-fall from hunting near Senlis, he met Aubigné and two or three of his attendants galloping at full speed from Paris.   " Sire," cried Aubigné, "we are betrayed ; the King knows all.   The road to Paris

leads to dishonour and death, those to life and glory
are in the opposite direction." " There is no need,"
was the answer, " of so many words ; let us be off."
All night long they hurried through the  dark and
frozen woods, crossed the Seine as the day broke, at
Poissy, and without meeting any of the numerous
bodies of troops by whom the country was patrolled,
reached Alençon in safety the next day.   Here
Henry stood sponsor at the christening, according
to Calvinist ritual, of the child of his doctor.  As he
entered the meeting-house, the congregation were
singing the 21st psalm.  " The King shall rejoice in
thy strength, O Lord, exceeding glad shall he be of
thy salvation.   Thou hast given him his heart's
desire."

Hearing that the psalm had not been  specially
chosen, he said that he welcomed the omen.

During his long ride he had been thoughtful and
silent beyond his wont.   He now began to talk to
those about him with his usual cheery vivacity
and apparently careless good-fellowship.   He had,
he said, left in Paris only two things which he
regretted—the Mass and his wife.   The latter he
would have again ; the former he might make shift
to do without.

From Alençon Henry proceeded to Saumur on the
Loire, where he was joined by some of the numerous
Huguenot gentry of the neighbourhood.   Yet his
position was difficult.   Not only was Alençon recognised as the leader of the opponents of the Court,
but Condé had been acting as the chief of the Protestants, and it was doubtful whether his greater

services and more earnest devotion to the cause would not be held to outweigh the superior rank of the King of Navarre. The wisest course probably was to take no decided action, and to await the result of the negotiations which were being carried on between the Government and the rebels. This Henry determined to do, and in the meantime urged his friends to join him and thus strengthen his position whether for peace or war.

Catherine and her son in their terror at the alliance between Protestants and Politicians, and at a threatened invasion of German mercenaries due to the negotiations of Condé, released the Marshals Montmorency and Cossé. Montmorency bestirred himself to bring about an agreement which should end the war. Whole districts were being reduced to desolation. Both sides plundered the unhappy peasantry with impartial cruelty. But the German *Reiters* excelled in systematic rapacity and the atrocities perpetrated by their allies increased the popular hatred of the Huguenots in the North-eastern provinces.

The Court proposed terms which were generally acceptable (*Paix de Monsieur*, February, 1576). The conditions granted to the Protestants were more favourable than any they had hitherto obtained: complete freedom of worship throughout the kingdom except at Paris; the establishment of courts in all the Parliaments composed of an equal number of judges of both religions; the restoration of the Protestants and their allies, who were declared to be the good and loyal subjects of the King, to all their

honours and offices; the disavowal of the Massacre
of St. Bartholomew and the restitution of the property of the victims to their heirs; and the occupation
of eight fortresses as a security for the due observance of the treaty. In order that other grievances might be remedied, the States-General were
to be assembled within six months. Such were the
more general stipulations. Alençon further obtained
the addition to his appanage of the duchies of
Anjou, Touraine and Berry and of other lordships
which raised his revenue to 400,000 crowns. Condé
was confirmed in the government of Picardy.
Navarre in that of Guienne. A large sum was paid
to John Casimir, the brother of the Elector Palatine
for the wages of his *Reiters* and to compensate him
for the trouble and expense of his invasion of France.

# CHAPTER III.

## HENRY OF NAVARRE THE PROTECTOR OF THE CHURCHES.

### 1576–1586.

THE terms of the "Peace of Monsieur" were far too favourable to the Protestants not to excite the greatest irritation among the more zealous Catholics.

Henry III. had been determined to end the war, even, he said, should it cost him half his kingdom. He probably counted on the violent reaction which was certain to be provoked, and on the resistance which the Parliaments and clergy and other bodies would offer to the execution of the treaty, as an excuse for the non-performance of the concessions by which he bought peace. But if so, he ought to have seen how much his authority would be weakened by the double humiliation of yielding such terms to rebellious subjects and of subsequently excusing their violation by the plea that he was powerless to enforce them.

Humières, the Governor of Péronne, refused to surrender that strong fortress to Condé, who, according to the terms of the peace, ought to have been placed in possession of it as Governor of Picardy, and sought for support by forming an association between the partisans of the Guises and the most fanatical Catholics in the province. The Catholics as well as the Protestants had proved in the South the value of such confederations for political and military purposes.

The movement spread, and, although the better class of citizens and magistrates held aloof, was received with special favour in Paris, and soon grew into a general *Holy League*, or association of the extreme Catholic party throughout the kingdom.

A paper setting forth the objects of the association and the obligations which its members assumed was widely circulated. The preamble declared, that the Holy League of the Catholic princes, lords and gentlemen—it is significant that there is no mention of towns or burgesses—was formed to re-establish the authority of the law of God and of the Apostolic Roman Church; to restore to the provinces and estates of the kingdom their privileges and franchises, as they had existed in the time of King Clovis; to support the honour of the King and to obey him and after him all the posterity of the House of Valois, thus implicitly excluding the Bourbon Princes from the succession. The members bound themselves to obey loyally the head of the association, to punish with the utmost severity whosoever under any pretext whatever attempted to

withdraw himself from the League, and to regard as
enemies all who refused to join it, to defend each
other against any assailant, whoever he might be—
*i. e.*, even against the King—and to endeavour to
compass the objects of the association against *no
matter what opposition.*

The same articles of association were probably not
shown to all members, and those which were most
threatening to his authority were certainly concealed
from the King. Yet they could not long be kept
secret. From the first the League was regarded with
suspicion by all loyal Frenchmen, and Henry III.
endeavoured to obtain a promise from the Guises,
that they would form no associations which were
likely to lead to a breach of the recent peace.

But the reaction of popular feeling against the
Protestants was violent. They were attacked and
their worship disturbed by the populace; if they
appealed to the protection of the laws, they obtained no redress, and the obstinate ill-will of the
Parliaments prevented the establishment of the
mixed courts.

The King hoped by his statecraft and their mutual
rivalry to depress his opponents, whether Guises,
Bourbons or Montmorencys, and gradually to eradi-
cate heresy without having recourse to arms, and without subordinating French interests to those of Spain.
But to carry out such a plan required patient self-
control as well as extreme skill in perceiving and
utilising the force of opposing tendencies.

Henry III. studied his Commines and Machiavelli,
spun fine webs of policy and intrigue in his cabinet,

9

but either failed to carry them out, or carried them
out in such a manner that they only damaged his
position.

For instance, the idea of counterbalancing the
power of the great nobles by raising to an equality
with them, men who should owe their fortune to his
favour was not impolitic.  But Henry chose such
minions as Villequier, and the son-in-law of this
wife-murderer, the not less infamous D'O, recommended only by a common taste for debauchery.   His great favourites, Épernon and Joyeuse
were indeed men of a different stamp; the former
especially did him good service.  But that service
was more than counterbalanced by the discredit
and the reputation for weakness which the King
incurred by his foolish fondness and profusion.
Almost everything depended on the personal impression made by the King and on the practice of a
wise economy.   But Henry III. threw money away
with both hands, wasting it in frivolous, indecent,
but most costly feasts, squandering it on the ministers of his pleasures, buying curiosities and precious
stones at absurd prices.

He was in many ways very jealous of his royal
dignity, and endeavoured to introduce into his Court
the stately ceremonial of Spanish etiquette.   But
since this to some extent restricted the crowded
publicity in which the French kings had been accustomed to pass their lives, the innovations he made
were generally unpopular; and the worst interpreta-
tion was put upon the King's supposed desire to
avoid the observation of his subjects.   To a modern

reader the regulations which he published do not seem to indicate any morbid craving for solitude. The cup of beef-tea, on which the King broke his fast before leaving his bedroom, was to be borne in procession by the chief physician, accompanied by two chamberlains, one carrying bread, the other water, and by the cup-bearer, followed by the Cardinals and Princes, the great officers of state and the members of the council attending the *levée*.

On Mondays the King would hunt, on Wednesdays ride his managed horses, on Thursdays and Sundays play tennis or pall-mall in public. All day long he was followed about by a crowd of courtiers; at dinner a balustrade gave him the privacy of a beast in a menagerie. At night when he retired into his room, he found his " singing men discoursing music," and only after his boots were taken off, he went into his cabinet, into which none might follow but Épernon or Joyeuse bearing his bed candle.

But no elaboration of ceremonial could make his subjects respect the person or policy of a King, who —to mention his follies rather than his vices— dressed more like a woman than a man, who kept his council waiting for hours while he dressed his wife's hair or starched her ruffs, who at a serious crisis of his affairs found time to drive round Paris and steal the ladies' lapdogs; who gave solemn audience to ambassadors with a basketful of puppies slung from his neck by a broad silk ribbon ; who left the reports of his ministers unread, while he refreshed his memory of the Latin Grammar; who introduced the fashion of playing Cup and Ball in season and out ; and whose devotions were hardly more serious or more decent than his debaucheries.

He was soon so despised, that the dignity, the grace and the fascination which were his when he chose to assume them, lost all power. But indeed at the best his dignity was too much that of an actor on the stage, a hasty word or an aside would often betray that it was only assumed for the occasion ; his grace and fascination were those of a fawning, cat-like beast, whose treacherous claws may at any moment be darted into the flesh which it caresses.

The States-General had been summoned to meet at Blois in December (1576). The League exerted itself to the utmost to terrorise the elections, and it was assisted by the whole influence of the government. The Protestants and the Politicians, discontented at the non-fulfilment of the terms of the peace, and seeing that the Catholic associations and the Crown nowhere allowed even a semblance of freedom to the elections, held wholly aloof ; no deputies of any of the Three Estates came from the districts and towns which were in their power.

They expected that measures would be passed fatal to their interests, and wished to leave no pretence for describing the States-General of Blois as a free and full meeting of the representatives of the nation. Yet in so acting the Huguenots and their allies made a grave mistake, since, notwithstanding their abstention and the terrorism of the League, only a bare majority of the Third Estate voted in favour of restoring the unity of the faith by force ; and that vote was rendered nugatory by the refusal of the supplies without which war could not be successfully waged.

As the proceedings went on, the members of the lay Estates showed more and more aversion to the League, and one of their number published a pamphlet in which he accused the Guises and other leaders of the association of seeking only how they might establish themselves as independent princes in their respective provinces.

After obtaining all he wished by the treaty of 1576, Alençon had been at little pains to conceal his dislike of his Protestant allies. He told his intimates that to know the heretics was to hate them, that La Noue was the only honest man in the whole set. It was therefore easy for the friends of the King of Navarre to establish his superior claim to be recognised as the Protector of the Reformed Churches.

But although he had been publicly re-admitted into the Calvinist communion (at Thouars or Niort, in June, 1576), Henry did not without difficulty obtain admission into the walls of La Rochelle. The citizens could not forget that he had fought in the ranks of their assailants and that even now there were among his followers many who had taken an active part in the massacre of St. Bartholomew's Day. At length he was allowed to enter the Protestant stronghold accompanied only by his sister and a few Huguenot attendants, and when with tears and ready emotion he deplored his enforced apostasy before the assembled congregation, there seemed to be no further reason to question the sincerity of his religious convictions.

From La Rochelle Henry journeyed through Guienne to his hereditary dominions in the South. The news which he received from Court made it clear that the treaty so recently concluded was not even to be a truce. La Noue, he wrote to Damville, had been with him and had given him good and faithful advice. It was the intention of their common enemies to destroy them ; an intention only to be prevented by their union.

While preparing for the impending storm, Henry received at Agen (February, 1577) a deputation sent by the estates of Blois, to express their regret that he had not seen good to attend their session, and their hope that he would assist their endeavours to restore unity and peace to France. He was moved to tears by the eloquence with which their spokesman, the Archbishop of Vienne, dwelt on the calamities which resistance to the King's commands would entail on the country ; but replied, that the evil advisers who persuaded his Majesty to break the peace would be responsible for those sufferings. They had urged him to embrace the true Catholic faith ; as to that, his constant prayer to God was, that if, as he believed, he held the true faith, he might be confirmed in it, but if not, that He might be pleased to enlighten him, and give him will and power to drive all error not only from his own heart, but also from his kingdom, and if possible from the world ;—a declaration which showed no very stubborn dogmatism, and not out of keeping with a profession of faith made a few days earlier in a letter to a Catholic friend. " Those who honestly follow their conscience are of my religion, and mine is that of all brave and good men." Sentiments, laudable in themselves; yet such professed latitudinarianism was unpalatable to the Calvinists, even before it could be interpreted by the light of later events. Yet, though on this as on other occasions Henry did not forget to treat his enemies as if they might some day be his friends, he was active in preparing for the hostilities which ensued, and in carrying them on when once begun. The man, he said, who after he has put on his breastplate still loves his ease, had better not meddle with war.

He had now for the first time an opportunity of showing how far he possessed the qualities of a general and a statesman; that he was brave and clement he had already given some proof. Entering the small town of Eausse in his county of Armagnac, he had been suddenly attacked with cries of "Aim at the white plume," by two hundred or more fanatics, who by dropping the portcullis behind him separated him from his guards. Accompanied by only four gentlemen, the King charged his assailants with such vigour that he was able to reach the porch of a house, where with his companions he kept his enemies at bay till his followers had scaled the walls. When master of the town, he forbade all reprisals, and only allowed the punishment of two or three of the ringleaders.

Among the four who fought at Eausse by the side of Henry of Bourbon, were two young men whose names and renown are closely connected with that of their master: Philip de Mornay, Lord of Le

Plessis-Marly, and Maximilian de Béthune, Baron of Rosny.

Philip de Mornay was born in 1549. Destined by his Catholic father for the Church, he matriculated, when eight years old, at the College of Lisieux in the University of Paris. Two years later his father died, and his education devolved on his mother, a Calvinist. Her care and circumstances combined to give him the training best suited to fit him for the part he was destined to play. He visited Geneva, he studied at Heidelberg and Padua, he travelled in Germany and Italy and the Low Countries. He was equally versed in books and in the manners and cities of men, in the accomplishments of a scholar, and of a soldier and statesman.

In his twenty-third year he submitted to Coligny a memorandum on the state of the Low Countries, which determined the Admiral to send him as confidential envoy to the Prince of Orange. The massacre prevented this mission with the other plans of the Protestant leader.

Mornay escaped immediate death by the humanity of his Catholic host. Disdaining the proffered protection of the Guises, he made his way by prudence and good luck to the coast and crossed over into England, where the warm recommendations of Walsingham obtained for him a favourable reception at Court and the confidence of the Queen's advisers. Recalled to France by La Noue, Mornay had taken part in the negotiations between Condé, Alençon and the Germans, and in the following campaign. In the midst of the bustle of diplomacy and war he found time to woo and wed Charlotte Arbaleste, a young Protestant widow, well fitted by her talents and character to be the worthy partner of his life and thoughts.

After the conclusion of the Peace of Monsieur, Mornay joined the King of Navarre, and was at once admitted into his council, where his intimate acquaintance with foreign courts and countries was of the greatest service. A manifesto, in which Henry justified his conduct, his attitude to the Estates, and his warlike preparations was the first of that admirable series of state papers written by Mornay, remarkable alike for their lucidity, dignity and moderation, which did much to raise the reputation of the King of Navarre in Europe as well as in France.

At Eausse he proved that he was as ready with his sword as with his pen, and although his exploits as a soldier were obscured by his renown as a statesman, the King had little reason to boast in his offhand way, when on a later occasion Mornay had done some notable service, " that he knew in case of need how to turn even an inkhorn into a captain." Not men only of the moderate party, such as l'Estoile and De Thou, but Leaguers who continued Frenchmen, like Jeannin and Villeroy, sought the friendship of Du Plessis-Mornay, and the verdict of his contemporaries has been confirmed by posterity. " Even in the caricature of the *Henriade*, where the figures of the wars of religion are set up in gilt gingerbread in the taste of the *Grand Siècle*, the noble lineaments of the Calvinist gentleman stand out as if incapable of disfigurement." " If," says a clear-

sighted though fanciful French historian, " if virtue
had a home on earth, it was in the heart of Mornay."

Very different was the character and the ambiguous reputation of Maximilian de Béthune,
Baron of Rosny, better known to posterity as Duke
of Sully. Like Du Plessis-Mornay, he had narrowly
escaped the massacre of 1572, partly by good-for-
tune, partly by a presence of mind remarkable in a boy
barely thirteen years old. A student at the College
of Burgundy he had, warned of his danger by the
master of the house in which he lodged, put on his
academical dress, and breviary in hand passed unmolested through the scene of bloodshed till he found
shelter in the house of the rector of his college.

As soon as it was safe to do so he sought out and
attached himself by his father's orders to the King
of Navarre and followed his fortunes when he
escaped from Paris.

The number of portraits extant often only in-
creases the difficulty of forming a consistent conception of the features of the dead, and the fact that
the character of Rosny has been sketched from the
most various points of view, does not enable us to
pronounce judgment with greater confidence on the
minister of Henry IV.

He was disliked by the Catholics as a Protestant,
who nevertheless reached the highest position in the
state ; the Huguenots suspected the sincerity of a
believer who constantly preferred the interests of
the monarchy to those of his sect, who approved or
even urged his master's perversion, who was the

rival of Du Plessis-Mornay, the friend of Du Perron, the ex-Huguenot, court divine and sophist.

The whole tribe of courtiers, place-hunters and publicans hated the man who was so austere a guardian of the public purse, and who, while ruthlessly reforming the abuses and peculations by which they trusted to become rich, himself amassed a colossal fortune. The lawyers could not pardon the disregard which Sully showed more than once for the authority and the pretensions of the Parliaments. Just or unjust, the King's will, he said, was law. Men of letters were estranged by the economy which checked the not too generous flow of the King's bounty. All alike were offended by rude and overbearing manners. Not only was Sully obstinate in saying no, but he never cared to take the edge off a rebuff by any softness or flattery in word or manner.

Though honest, Rosny was not disinterested; unlike Du Plessis-Mornay, who " put no farthing in his purse and acquired no inch of land," he grew rich in the service of his master. Even the war, to carry on which many Protestant nobles mortgaged their estates and cut down their timber, was to him a source of profit. In the escalade of La Réole, one of his earliest exploits, he gained booty worth 1,000 crowns ; from the sack of Cahors he carried off a strong-box containing four times as much ; when the royalists stormed the Faubourg St. Germain, he laid his hands on some 3,000 crowns ; during the siege of Louviers, on as many more. As if guided by some unerring instinct, he found his way to treasure with-

out the help of any divining rod. It has been remarked, and with truth, that though an excellent
man of business, Sully was no financial genius. He
looked upon the King's far-seeing attempts to encourage arts and manufactures, much as an old
fashioned and parsimonious bailiff would regard his
master's costly experiments in scientific farming.
But the evils which he was called upon to remedy
were gross and patent. To deal with them in his
common-sense fashion, needed only plain honesty,
unwearying industry, power of comprehending
minute and intricate details, combined with great
capacity for organisation and a most determined
and relentless persistence. These qualities may not
amount to genius; but their combination in such
perfection is rarer than any genius; and the man
who possessed them was invaluable to a prince called
upon to rule a country perishing, not because it
needed a revolution or the reconstruction of its institutions, but because those which it possessed were
threatening ruin from neglect, or so choked and encumbered by abuses that they no longer performed
any useful functions. Nor are other reasons wanting which account for the favour shown to Sully by
Henry IV. He was his faithful and constant companion in arms. At Coutras, Arques, Ivry, Aumale,
Rouen, Amiens, in a hundred nameless skirmishes
he fought, " as headlong," said the King, " as a cock-
chafer," with a fiery valour surprising in a man of
cold and calculating character. Sully moreover
combined a courtier's pliability with great outward
frankness, and even roughness of bearing in council,

for Henry, who justly prided himself on the patience
with which he accepted rebuke, and listened to unpalatable advice, was often flattered rather than irritated by contradiction.  He did not refuse services
which the more austere integrity of Du Plessis-Mornay declined.  When, for instance, Henry desired
to obtain possession of a promise of marriage ex-
changed between his hardly used sister Catherine
and her cousin the Count of Soissons, Rosny spared
no artifice or lie till he had deceived the lovers into
entrusting the precious document to his keeping.
While, therefore, Sully, an exile from power, found
solace and dignity in the vast fortune of which the
foundation had been laid by horse-coping at the
Court of Pau, what other reward could virtue such
as Mornay's expect than to be praised and starve?

During the first part of the 17th century, Sully's
reputation was depressed by his personal unpopularity ; during the second half it was, like that of his
master, obscured by the rising sun of Lewis XIV.
But the eclipse and darkness in which that sun set,
led men to reflect on the different course of events
during the reign of his grandfather, when each year
saw some increase in the security, strength and prosperity of the country.  Moreover, the exaggerated
mercantilism of Colbert provoked a violent reaction,
and those economists who held the land to be the
true source of wealth, extolled the wisdom of the
minister who had proclaimed pastoral and arable
farming to be the breasts from which the whole sustenance of the country must be drawn.  Unlikely
as it may appear to the reader of that amazing and

mendacious compilation of pompous egotism, Sully's Memoirs have also exaggerated his posthumous fame; historians have largely used them as a valuable contemporary authority, and have in many cases, half unconsciously, adopted the view of his actions, the estimate of his importance, which he wished to prevail.

The Estates, though ready to vote resolutions urging the restoration of the unity of the faith, absolutely refused to sanction any further alienation of the Crown lands, or any other way of raising the resources necessary for a vigorous campaign. They were therefore dismissed by the King, who loudly expressed his disappointment, but probably was well pleased at the proved weakness of the party of the League. Meantime hostilities had begun and were carried on in a desultory fashion, though with some vigour and much ferocity, to the disadvantage on the whole, of the Huguenots, who were weakened by the defection of Damville, now by his brother's death Duke of Montmorency and head of his house. But his example was not generally followed by the Catholics of his party, nor even by his own family. His brother Thoré and his cousin Châtillon, the son of Coligny, were on the point of attacking him under the walls of Montpellier when news came that peace had again been concluded.

The King of Navarre, who was not on good terms with his cousin Condé, and whose little Court was distracted by the enmities between his Protestant and Catholic followers, listened readily to the proposals of the King and Queen-Mother for a general pacification.

The Peace of Bergerac (September 17, 1577) was based on a fair compromise. Protestant worship was allowed in the towns then held by the confederates, and in one town in each *bailliage* and to the nobles in their houses. The Protestants were to be fairly represented in the law courts. Eight cautionary fortresses garrisoned at the King's expense were to be left in their hands for six years. All leagues and secret associations were forbidden. This settlement was gladly received by moderate men of both parties; it was honestly meant by the King, and might have been lasting, but for the turbulent ambition of the House of Lorraine, the intrigues of Philip II. and the influence of events in other parts of Europe.

If he could not compel the Protestants to conform, Henry III. wished to keep on good terms with them; since he and they had the same enemies, Spain and the Guises. The subsequent infractions of the edict of which the Huguenots loudly and justly complained, were due, not so much to the bad faith of the King, as to the disobedience of governors who, like Montmorency in Languedoc, or Guise in Burgundy, acted as if independent sovereigns, and to the fanaticism of the populace encouraged by the stubborn ill-will of the law courts. When their own leader succeeded to the throne, the Protestants found that their position was not bettered, and looked back to the years which followed the Peace of Bergerac as to the time when on the whole their condition had been most tolerable " for good but ill, for ill yet passing good."

The King of Navarre as Protector of the Reformed Churches was zealous in calling the attention of the Government to their grievances; and not less importunate in demanding the payment of his wife's dower, and in protesting against the sequestration of the revenues of his wide domains in the north and centre of France.

To satisfy his claims and to settle the points still in dispute, Catherine de' Medici accompanied her daughter to the Court of Navarre, rejoicing in an opportunity of diplomatic intrigue and trickery. Margaret of Valois was not sorry to rejoin her husband; she hated her brother Henry III., and had chosen her lovers from among the favourites of the Duke of Anjou, between whom and the King's minions insults, broils and duels were of constant occurrence.

With the two Queens came a bevy of ladies, among them Madame de Sauves, a woman who had given Henry of Bourbon some early lessons in profligacy. It was not without reason, that when writing to ask the Huguenots to send representatives to assist him at the approaching conferences he also bade them "pray God to fortify him with sobriety and prudence, in order that he might withstand the wiles and artifices of those who are plotting the ruin of the churches."

Catherine remained eighteen months with her daughter and son-in-law. He fell in love with one of her girls, Condé with another, the Viscount of Turenne, the most powerful of the Protestant nobles, devoted himself to the Queen of Navarre. This was what the Queen-Mother had hoped, her main object being to sow dissension between the King of Navarre, the Prince and Turenne, and to prevent any close understanding between Margaret and her husband. The Florentine was so far successful that Henry and his young courtiers yielded at once to the allurements of her " flying squadron." Even an old and sober Calvinist captain, a pillar of the Church, was seduced by one of these girls to betray La Réole, an important Huguenot stronghold. The King of Navarre heard of this treachery when entertaining the Queen-Mother with a ball at Auch. He silently slipped from the room, summoned a few trusty companions and before morning escaladed Fleurance, a small town in the neighbourhood, held by a garrison of French troops. Catherine when she heard of the exploit, only laughed : " It is his revenge for La Réole ; cabbage for cabbage, but mine has the better heart."

The Queen-Mother was disappointed in her hope of profiting by the estrangement of her daughter and son-in-law. Margaret even encouraged her husband's gallantries and taught him to tolerate her own. Thoroughly acquainted with the objects and methods of her mother's policy, she gave him advice which though inspired by base motives was in itself useful.

Catherine's negotiations ended with a promise of further securities to the Huguenots and of the complete redress of their grievances. The non-fulfilment of this promise was one of the pretexts of a futile resumption of hostilities by the King of Navarre in 1580—the so-called Lover's Cour--of which La Noue and the most sober Protestants disapproved, and in which La Rochelle and other towns refused to take any part. The desultory campaign which followed only deserves mention for an opportunity it gave Henry of conspicuously displaying that valour, not less obstinate than fiery, which so greatly impressed the imagination of his countrymen and established his influence and popularity among the warlike gentry of both religions.

He had never been able to obtain possession of the district of Quercy which had been settled on Margaret of Valois as her dower. The inhabitants of Cahors, the capital of Quercy, had been notorious usurers during the Middle Ages, and the town was still prosperous and wealthy. Defended by strong walls, by a garrison of 1,500 men, under a brave and trustworthy governor and still more by its position, for the narrow and steep streets wind up to the summit of a bold rock surrounded on three sides by a bend of the river Lot, Cahors appeared to defy any sudden assault.

Henry, who was at Montauban, marched thirty miles under a scorching summer sun with a force not more numerous than the garrison; and at nightfall approached Cahors under cover of the thick groves of walnut trees which grew close to where the road from Montauban entered the town by a bridge defended by two gates and other outworks. A heavy storm favoured the surprise. Even the explosion of the petards by which the gates were blown in was mistaken by many for a peal of thunder. But it was after they had penetrated into the town that the assailants realised the full difficulty of their enterprise. The garrison was zealously assisted by the towns-people, fanatical Catholics, who feared the punishment of atrocities perpetrated on Huguenot fellow-citizens. Every house was a fortress, every steep and narrow street a barricaded and well defended pass. For five days and nights the conflict was continued, amid an indescribable scene of uproar and confusion—clash of swords, clanging of bells, volleys of firearms, roar of burning houses, shouts of fighting men and shrieks of women and children. Spent with blows, worn out with want of sleep, their armour battered, their feet sore and bleeding, almost all wounded or bruised by missiles thrown from the housetops, those around Henry urged him whilst there was yet time to retire from so unequal a contest; especially since they were not sufficiently numerous to occupy the gates and to prevent reinforcements reaching the garrison. But he obstinately refused, and at length his perseverence overcame the resolution of his opponents and the sack of the town rewarded the constancy of his followers.

The capture of Cahors spread dismay among the Catholic towns of the South. Toulouse already saw before her gates the avenger of the innocent blood so often shed in her streets.

Henceforward none were disposed to laugh at Henry of Bourbon; but the establishment beyond all cavil of his reputation as a fearless and adventurous soldier was all that he gained by his brilliant feat of arms. The Huguenots, even had they been more unanimous would have been no match for

three powerful armies sent against them by the
King. That Henry III. consented to treat, and that
the conferences held at Fleix in Périgord were followed by a treaty confirming all previous concessions
to the Reformers and to their leader, seems some
proof that the King was sincerely desirous of peace.
No doubt also the exhaustion of his finances, the
ravages of a virulent epidemic, which is said to have
carried off 30,000 victims in Paris alone, the renewed
intrigues of Spain and the importunity of his
brother and mother, again absorbed by ambitious
projects in the Low Countries, inclined him to moderation.

Henry III. succeeded in putting an end to the
civil strife which desolated his kingdom, but he
failed to use the respite which he obtained so as to
guard against future troubles. L'Estoile certainly
exaggerates when he complains that nothing could
have been more perverse and monstrous than the
government; that the care of the finances was entrusted to the greatest knaves, of the army to the
greatest cowards, of the provinces to the greatest
fools. But his testimony is valuable because it shows
how completely Henry III. failed to secure the confidence of that moderate party on whose support his
strength depended, and whose opinions are faithfully
reflected by the Parisian diarist.

An edict embodying many useful reforms was
published in 1580. The remark of the same writer
that this, like all others of the kind, might have
been endorsed, " Good only for three days," is
borne out by the preamble to another ordinance of

1583, which complains that licence, disorder and confusion have so grown, that hardly a trace of old-fashioned integrity remains.

While the reputation of the King of France was sinking, the King of Navarre was rising in public estimation. No doubt there were vices and follies, intrigues and factions enough and to spare at the little Court of Nerac or Pau, where, says Aubigné, "we were all lovers together," and where the pretentious solemnity of Sully owns that in the soft southern nights and under the pleasant shade of garden walks planted with bay and cypress by Margaret of Angoulême, the only converse among courtiers and ladies was of love and of the delights to which it leads.

"Our Court," Queen Margaret boasts in her memoirs, "was so fair and agreeable that we did not envy that of France. . . . I had around me many ladies and maids in waiting, and the King my husband was attended by a gallant following of lords and gentlemen . . . in whom there was no fault to be found except that they were Huguenots." If Margaret could find no fault in her husband's courtiers except their religion, we may be certain that religion sat but lightly on them.

The negotiation of the Peace of Fleix was the pretext of a visit of several months paid by the Duke of Anjou with his train of roués and bravos to his brother-in-law and sister. Anjou, who had a monkey-like aptitude for mischief annoying to others though profitless to himself, succeeded in destroying the good understanding based on mutual toleration

which had so far existed between the King and
Queen of Navarre. It must also be allowed that
Henry showed a cynical indelicacy in the demands
he made on his wife's complaisance.

In 1581 Margaret left her husband's Court, on the
pretext of a visit to her mother, whose tenderness
could no longer endure so protracted a separation.

Aubigné contrasts the virtue of the Court of Navarre with the licence of that of France. There the
greatest were proud to minister to the King's foulest
pleasures; at Pau, Henry's mistress, the Countess of
Grammont, was neglected. Yet some credit is due
to this lady, if, after his wife had left him, the King's
life became more decorous. She is popularly known
as the mistress to whom he sacrificed the fruits of the
victory of Coutras. Yet it is possible that without
her Coutras might neither have been fought nor won.
Diana, or, as she was commonly called, Corisande
d'Andouins, widow of Philibert de Guiche, Count of
Grammont, was a year or two older than her royal
lover. Of the three women who so influenced his life
that it is impossible to pass them by in silence, the
Countess of Grammont was the most respectable.
She stimulated the ambition of Henry, assisted him
with her fortune, and shared his councils, nor, though
a Catholic, disliked and suspected by the Protestants,
has her fidelity been seriously impugned. Her position, that of a widow who had formed a lasting connection with a prince separated from his wife, was
not one which in those days appeared other than
honourable, nor did the King scruple to entrust his
sister Catherine to her care.

Henry was always anxious to marry his mistress for the time being, a proof that the reiterated and passionate protestations of constancy in which his letters abound, were not wholly insincere. Tossed by fate, ever in the saddle, not less restless by choice in his amusements than by necessity in the business of life, he had a strong yearning for the quiet joys and repose of home.

Aubigné tells us that his master charged him on his allegiance to give him true advice; and then, after citing thirty instances of princes who had married subjects, said that he had promised his hand to the Countess of Grammont in case he should, as he hoped, obtain a divorce from Margaret. If we may believe the garrulous vanity of the Huguenot historian's old age, he replied that his master must remember that he had three parts to play, as King of Navarre, as heir to the Crown of France, as Protector of the Churches, that in each character he was served by a different set of followers, who expected a different payment. The servants of the King of Navarre and of the Dauphin of France looked for honours and temporal rewards, either in the present or the future; the wages of those who followed the Protector of the Churches were less easily paid by a prince, for if in some things they were his servants, in others they were his fellows and for sharing his dangers they asked to be repaid by his zeal, by his noble actions, his virtues. Aubigné did not suppose, so he continued, that hating books as he did, the King had himself collected the mischievous examples he alleged, but he must remember how very different the position of those princes had been from his own. He need not give up his love—this concession from a sincere Calvinist is notable—but let him serve and honour his mistress by living worthily.

During the long visit paid by Margaret after 1581 to the French Court, the emnity between her and Henry III. increased. Provoked by her intrigues and her malice, the King avenged himself by publishing and exaggerating the scandals of her life. He came up to her at a ball in the Louvre and with loud anger enumerated her lovers and dalliances, reproached her with the birth of a bastard child, and bade her rejoin her husband ; she might live more decently with him, than where her presence was both scandalous and mischievous. After so intolerable an affront the Queen of Navarre hurried from Paris, exclaiming that she and Mary of Scots were the most wretched among women, that she wished some one would end her miserable life ; but such fortune was too good for her, she had neither friends nor enemies. Her husband refused to receive her. If the charges made against her were true she was not fit to be his wife, if they were false his honour required that her brother should withdraw and apologise for calumnies so atrocious, for an insult so humiliating. Aubigné, and then, with further powers, Du Plessis-Mornay, were sent to remonstrate with Henry III. on the want of consideration he had shown for their master's honour. Apparently, Henry III. repented of his haste. He made a half apology, he begged his brother-in-law not to take the matter too much to heart. The most virtuous

princesses were subject to such calumnies; he reminded him of old scandals which had been current
even about his mother the pious Jane of Albret.
" His Majesty," laughed the Bearnese, " does me too
much honour; he tells me I am a ——, by way of
excuse for calling my wife a wh——."

But neither Prince wished to quarrel; Navarre
expressed some willingness to receive his wife back,
if only the royal garrisons were withdrawn from his
frontiers, so that he might not appear to be acting
under compulsion, and he claimed credit for rejecting
the large offers made by Philip II.—the hand of the
Infanta Isabella, after Spanish influence at the Vatican should have obtained for him a divorce from his
dishonoured wife, and powerful assistance in money
and men against all enemies if only he would abjure
his heresy.   Nor can it be doubted that Philip II.
was sincere in making these advances.   He was discontented with the conduct of the Guises and eager to
avenge himself for the interference of France in the
Low Countries.

Henry III. expressed his gratitude to his brother-
in-law, sanctioned the continued occupation by the
Protestants of their places of security; and when the
uncertainty of the succession in the event of Anjou's
death was mentioned, showed surprise that the matter should be discussed as if open to question.   The
King of Navarre, a prince of exalted birth and good
parts, whom he loved, was his natural heir.   " I
know," he said to the Provost of Paris, " that some
are trying to supplant him, but I shall take good
care to prevent them from succeeding"; as for the

Cardinal of Bourbon who hoped to step into his nephew's shoes, he was an old fool. When Anjou was dying (May, 1584), Épernon was sent with a sumptuous retinue to invite the King of Navarre to come to Court to take his place as heir-apparent—after first hearing a Mass. The Catholics about him had for some time been urging him to remove by his conversion the only obstacle to his universal recognition as heir to the French throne.

Henry reminded his cousin, the young Cardinal of Vendôme, that a man's religion, could not be put off and on like his shirt. However lightly he held by his creed he may well have thought that there was as much to be lost as gained by sacrificing it at this moment.

Épernon was therefore answered with protestations of gratitude and loyalty—of readiness to receive instruction or to submit to the decision of a free and universal council; but the King of Navarre showed no eagerness to accept the invitation to Court, and still less to go straightway to Mass.

Yet the fact that the legitimate heir to the throne was a heretic made the renewal of the civil war inevitable. Even if all the means which the gold of Spain, the intrigues of the Jesuits and the ambition of the Guises could set in motion or suggest to excite the alarm and stimulate the fanaticism of the populace had not been employed, it is not likely that the Catholic majority would quietly have submitted to the rule of a Calvinist king. In England and elsewhere they had seen the religion of the country follow the creed of the prince. The intimate connection of the State and of the orthodox Church was held to be a fundamental law of the monarchy. Even moderate men, who were willing that the Huguenots should be tolerated, were alarmed at the prospect of their domination.

These feelings were shared by Henry III. Though it had little influence on his life, he was more sincerely attached to his religion than Henry of Guise, or Henry of Bourbon; for the former was suspected by those who knew him best to be a Lutheran at heart, and the latter, like James I. of England, believed that faith in God is sufficient to save a man let him belong to what sect he may; although there is no reason to doubt, that, as he told the historian De Thou five years later, he held the one in which he had been bred to be the truest and the best.

A rapid glance at the condition of the general conflict between Protestantism and Catholicism will explain the impatience with which Philip II. and his clerical allies saw France gradually settling down into something like tranquillity. In England, the plots for assassinating the queen, although approved by the Pope and encouraged by the promise of Spanish gold and honours, had failed, as well as the schemes of domestic rebellion and foreign invasion organised by the Spanish ambassador against the sovereign to whom he was accredited; and the abrupt expulsion of Don Bernardino de Mendoza made it clear that open war between the two countries could not much longer be avoided.

In the Low Countries there seemed little hope that without foreign help the exhaustion of the

States would be able to resist the skill and energy of Alexander Farnese; even before the murder of Orange, an English envoy had reported "that the cause was panting and all but dead." Dendermonde and Ghent had opened their gates to the Spanish troops already closing round Antwerp. In Germany the conversion of the Archbishop of Cologne would, if he could maintain himself, give a majority in the Electoral College to the Reformers; but in the South the Catholic reaction was making rapid progress, supported by the Emperor Rudolf, who had been educated at the Court of Spain, and who resembled in nothing his wise and tolerant father Maximilian II.

An eminent English historian believes that after the death of Orange, Henry III., could he have trusted Elizabeth, was willing to defy Spain and the League, to place Henry of Navarre at the head of his army and in close alliance with England, to fall with all his forces on the Duke of Parma. He would thus have secured the active co-operation of the King of Denmark and of the Elector Palatine, the Archbishop of Cologne would have been maintained in his electorate, and at the next vacancy the Imperial crown might have passed from the House of Hapsburg.

We must doubt whether even if he had been willing to break so completely with his past, to overcome his own prejudices and predilections, Henry III. could have taken up and carried out on a bolder scale the policy of Coligny. Not the Guises only, but his mother, his favourites, the ambitious Épernon not less than the Catholic Joyeuse, would have resisted to the uttermost, strong in the support of populace and church, a course of action which would have thrown all power into the hands of the heretic heir and his followers. Yet there was much in the conduct of the King well calculated to excite the alarm of the Catholic and Spanish party. After the death of his brother he publicly recognised the King of Navarre as his successor, and announced his intention of bestowing upon him the duchy of Alençon, which had lapsed to the crown. An embassy bringing from Elizabeth the insignia of the Garter was received with the utmost cordiality and magnificence, and the King showed himself in public wearing the badge sent by an excommunicated heretic. The envoys who came to offer the sovereignty of the Low Countries obtained, it is true, little but gold chains and fair words, yet the Austrian Resident assured his master that the active intervention of France was daily expected.

Parma, who dreaded a diversion which might compel him to raise the siege of Antwerp, joined with Mendoza in urging the League and the Guises to action. On January 15, 1585, a formal treaty was signed at Joinville by the Dukes of Guise and Mayenne in their own name and that of their family, by a representative of the Cardinal of Bourbon and by the Spanish agents Tassis and Moreo. Since no heretic might ascend the French throne, it was agreed that in the event of the death of Henry III., the Cardinal of Bourbon should be proclaimed king. The contracting parties bound themselves to do their utmost to extirpate heresy, both in France and in the Low Countries.　The King of Spain promised a subvention of 1,000,000 crowns for the first year, in return for which the French princes undertook to place him in possession of Cambray, to prevent French privateers from preying on Spanish commerce, to hand over to him Don Antonio, the pretender to the Portuguese Crown, who had found a refuge in France, and to renounce all further alliance with the Turks.

The Guises had now secured the co-operation of Spain by a formal document ; the preparations of their party at home were also well advanced.　The weakness of the League at the time of the States-General of 1576–77 had been conspicuous and unexpected.　It was not till after the death of Alençon, when the thought that the heir-apparent of the crown was a heretic thrilled Catholic France with horror, that it again started into new and vigorous life, and received that form and organisation which identified it with popular passions and aspirations, as well as with feudal and dynastic ambition, and which enabled it in close alliance with Spain to bring France to the very verge of ruin.

Paris was the heart of this organisation.　The capital was divided into five districts under five leaders, who with eleven others formed the supreme council, the notorious Sixteen.　These men were for the most part lawyers and tradesmen of middling condition, but distinguished for fanatical zeal and party spirit, well suited to be the instruments of cooler and, if not more scrupulous, yet higher placed and more cautious ambition.　The parish clergy, the

friars and the Jesuits vied in the violence of their
sermons.  Terror and pity were alike employed to
excite the mob.  A hundred pulpits re-echoed with
the legend of the virtues and sufferings of the sainted
Queen of Scots, whose charms and innocence were
in the eyes of her votaries beyond the reach of
calumny and years.  Great pictures were exposed in
the cemeteries and public places, exhibiting the tortures inflicted on Catholic martyrs by the English
Jezebel, the close ally of the Most Christian King,
under whose heretic heir the faithful in France must
expect the like treatment.  Nay, they need not hope
for so long a respite ; ten thousand armed Huguenots, it was confidently reported, were already lurking in the Faubourg St. Germain, awaiting a signal
to massacre the Christian people of Paris.  To guard
against such dangers, the council of the League were
diligent in buying arms and in drilling the stoutest
of their adherents.

Encouraged by the approbation of the Pope, the
confederates published their manifesto (March 30,
1585).  They declared that they were prepared to
draw the sword to restore the dignity and unity of
the Church, to secure to the nobility their ancient
privileges, to relieve the people from all new taxes
imposed since the reign of Charles IX., to drive
unworthy favourites and advisers from Court, to
prevent future troubles by settling the succession,
and to provide for regular meetings of the States-
General.  Until they should have attained these
objects, they, princes of the blood, cardinals, and
other princes, peers, prelates, officers of the Crown,

governors of provinces, lords and gentlemen, together with sundry good towns and corporations, constituting the best and soundest part of the realm, swore to hold together and persevere " until they should be heaped one upon another in the tomb reserved for the last Frenchmen fallen in the service of their God and country." Then followed a list of the leaders, the Cardinal Charles of Bourbon, "first Prince of the Blood," the Dukes of Lorraine and Guise, "lieutenant generals of the League," and the names of the King of Spain and other Catholic sovereigns.

The King seemed at first disposed to resent this bold defiance of his authority. Épernon, never wanting in audacity, and who had devoted some of the money lavished upon him to secure the services of a considerable body of mercenaries, urged him to lose no moment in replying to so insolent a challenge. Montmorency the governor, or rather sovereign, of Languedoc, was to be surely counted upon in a struggle against Lorraine and Spain, and would be followed by the moderate party. For every man whom his enemies could hope to enlist among the Swiss, two would hasten to the standard of the King of France. Nor was it likely that the majority of the smaller nobles, the country gentry, who had little to gain by the substitution of the nearer, more invidious and oppressive authority of a feudal ruler for that of the Crown, would forget their hereditary loyalty any more than that the lawyers would aid to overthrow the monarchy on which their own importance depended. As for the Huguenot gentry and towns, the King of Navarre was urgent in pressing their services and that of his own small but excellent army on the King. But Henry III., ever undecided, averse to strenuous action and preferring middle courses and the chances of diplomacy to war, closed his ears to bolder councils and allowed himself to be influenced by Joyeuse's Catholic fervour and jealousy of Épernon and by the advice of his mother, who, undeterred by gout, rheums and unwieldy bulk, hurried from Paris to negotiate with the Guises. Catherine had not become less pusillanimous with age, and it had ever been her way to bend before those who were in the ascendant, yielding everything with the comfortable determination to break her word as soon as it should be safe to do so. But on this occasion, she was at heart a traitor to her favourite son.

Like the rest of the world, she appears to have made up her mind that the King must soon die, and she had already survived so many of her children, that it seemed to her a matter of course that she should survive him. But to lose her power was unendurable, worse to see it pass into the hands of Navarre. The old Cardinal of Bourbon was a nonentity, a wine tun rather than a man, as Beza said, and after his death Catherine hoped to secure the crown for her daughter Claude, the wife of the Duke of Lorraine, a prince of weak character, whom she would easily control. Thus the Florentine, as if immortal, spun her schemes with characteristic incapacity to distinguish between what was and was not possible. Easily alarmed by present difficulties, she allowed her hopes to blind her to those still future. Yet it was easy to foresee that the Guises would work for their own aggrandisement and not for that of the elder branch of their house; and that if the Salic law was to be violated, Philip II. would not allow the superior claims of the Infanta Isabella, the daughter of Claude's elder sister, to be passed over.

After negotiations which lasted two months the League presented an ultimatum. The King must enforce unity of religion by an edict, which all the princes, peers and parliaments, officers of the Crown, governors of provinces and towns and other officials should swear to observe.

Henry III. still hesitated. He had written to the King of Navarre, warning him to be on his guard, and adding that he was glad to hear that he was on good terms with the Duke of Montmorency. He had not himself been able to prevent the evil designs of the Duke of Guise, but at any rate he would not conclude any treaty with the League to the disadvantage of his lawful successor. The Queen of England wrote a letter to the King of France, the vigorous style of which so pleased Henry of Bourbon that he sent a copy of it to his Corisande. "If you could know, my dear brother, the pain and grief I feel at the danger to which you expose yourself, I am assured that you would believe that there is no creature in this world on whose help you can more surely rely than myself. Good God! is it possible that a great king can bend himself without reason and against his honour to sue for peace to rebels and traitors, and not at once cut off from them all oppor-

CATHERINE DE' MEDICI.

tunity of exalting themselves, compelling them by his
royal power to submit to the yoke of their deserts.
I marvel to see you thus betrayed in your council
and even by her, who of all the world is nearest to
you, and that you should be so blind as to tolerate
such villany . . . Alas! think you that that cloke of
religion in which they wrap themselves is so well
lined that their hope of ruling France in your name
but at their own discretion, cannot be seen through
it?. And I pray God that that may content them,
for Princes held in subjection by their subjects are
rarely long lived." Let him only, she goes on to say,
pluck up heart and if he will accept her help they
will soon put his enemies to greater shame than ever
rebels felt. If he manfully took his own part, his
loyal subjects would come to his assistance; she ended
by praying God to help him and to raise his courage.
Brave words and at the time perhaps honestly meant,
for Elizabeth could not but feel that the victory of
the League and Spain in France, now, when Parma
was triumphant in the Low Countries, would be
the certain prelude to her own overthrow. But
Henry III. knew, none better, how little the acts and
words of the Queen of England were apt to cor-
respond; how often the shortest performance would
follow her largest promises.

In any case, Elizabeth and Navarre were far away,
the Queen-Mother was at his ear and her creatures,
who formed the majority in the royal council, played
upon the fears of the King, exaggerating the strength
of the League, the dangerous discontent of the Parisians. The rebels already held many of the most

important towns and fortresses. " The penitential sackcloth of the King," writes a contemporary, " was not of proof like the cuirasses of the League, they had already mounted their horses and he was on foot." On July 5th (1586) their demands were granted in the King's name by Catherine de' Medici.

On July 18th the King summoned the Parliament of Paris and caused the revocation of the Edicts of Toleration to be read and entered upon the rolls in his presence. Turning to the Cardinal of Bourbon who accompanied him, he said : " Against my conscience, but very willingly, I came here on a previous occasion to seek the relief of my people by the proclamation of that Edict of Toleration which I have now come to revoke, in accordance, it is true, with my conscience, but most unwillingly, since from this act will follow the ruin of my realm and of my people."

# CHAPTER IV.

## THE THREE HENRYS.

### 1585–1589.

T was useless, now that the forces of the Government and of the League were united to bring about the extirpation of heresy and the triumph of Spain, for the King to attempt to disclaim responsibility and to wash his hands of the blood that was about to be shed.

We are told that when the King of Navarre heard of the treaty between Henry III. and the League, pondering long and deeply, his chin resting on his hand, the half of his beard on which he leant turned white, so great was his apprehension of the evil times which he foresaw. The prospects of the struggle were indeed unfavourable to the Huguenots. Their numbers which had decreased after the Massacre of St. Bartholomew, had again grown since the Peace of Bergerac; but they had lost much of their old unanimity, and the zeal of many Protestant nobles had grown cold. The Duke of Parma had compelled Antwerp, the last and in every respect the most important stronghold of the Cause in Flanders, to surrender (August, 1585); it seemed unlikely that Holland and Zealand, now that William the Silent was no more, would long detain the conqueror, who might next direct his victorious army against the French heretics.

Contrary to all expectations the war was carried on with so little vigour in 1585 and 1586 that the Huguenots were able to hold their own. The King sent whatever supplies and money he could raise to Épernon or Joyeuse and crippled by his ill-will the operations of the Leaguers. The nobility generally showed little interest in the cause, disliking equally the alliance of the Guises with the fanatical democracy of the great towns, their disloyalty to the Crown, and their subordination to Spain. The support of the Duke of Montmorency (Damville), an unscrupulous and dissolute man, indifferent to the religious question, but the determined enemy of the House of Lorraine, secured the predominance of the Protestants in Languedoc, while in Poitou they had been greatly strengthened by the conversion of the young Duke of Thouars, the head of the great House of La Trémoille, and grandfather of that Countess of Derby who defended Lathom House so gallantly in the English Civil Wars.

The Huguenots might perhaps have been even more successful had they not, like their opponents, been divided by faction. Condé was the rival rather than the lieutenant of his cousin; the Viscount of Turenne and other great nobles were difficult to manage and too ready to sacrifice the common good to their private aggrandisement, but still the party had a head, and that head was Henry of Navarre.

His activity was prodigious. Not only did he appear to see everything and to do everything himself, but if there was any quarter from which assistance might be hoped, any friend whose zeal needed encouragement, any opponent whose hostility might be disarmed, there never was wanting some weighty despatch from the pen of Mornay, some shorter but pregnant letter written by the King himself, or one of those spirited notes, which, says a great critic, seem written when his foot was already in the stirrup, which breathe the fresh vigour of the morning and recall in their stirring brevity the note of horn or trumpet rousing huntsman or soldier.

What Gascon squire, ever ready for war and adventure, but must have felt his heart beat quicker on receiving such a summons as this: " Put wings to your best horse. I have told Montespan to break the wind of his. Why? That I will tell you at Nerac. Hasten, speed, fly. This is the command of your master and the prayer of your friend "; or this: " You will doubtless not have failed to sell your woods and they will have produced some thousand pistoles. If so, be sure to bring me all you can, for I never in my life was in such need; and I do not know when, or whence, or if ever I shall be able to repay you. But I can promise you abundant honour and glory, and gentlemen like you and me do not live on money."

Even before the conclusion of the treaty between

the King and the League, Henry had appealed to
his countrymen in a manifesto published at Bergerac
(June, 1585). He was a good Christian and no heretic, since he was willing to receive instruction from a
free and general council while a heretic is one who
obstinately persists in error. Neither was he, as his
enemies pretended, a persecutor. He had never
interfered with Catholic worship in the towns he
occupied, but had protected the monks and priests
and had left them the use of the churches, while he
retired to pray with his fellow believers in some private house. His enemies in their solicitude to settle
the succession to the throne had chosen as heir to
the Crown of France, an old and childless man of
sixty-six, as if the King who was married and in the
vigour of his life had only a year or two to live.
He was anxious above all to spare his country the
evils of civil war; for this he would even surrender
the towns held by the Protestants, although necessary, as experience had shown to their safety, provided that the chiefs of the League would also place
the fortresses they occupied in the King's hands.
If they would do the like, he would also resign his
governments. Should these offers not be acceptable,
the quarrel might be fought out without injury and
ruin to the Commonwealth, if the Duke of Guise
would meet him in single combat or with ten or
twenty champions on each side.

Next followed (August 10, 1585) a declaration
published in the names of the King of Navarre, the
Prince of Condé, the Duke of Montmorency and
" the lords, gentlemen, towns and communities of

Je vous envoy mes cheres amours mes regrets
des pres de vrē peynture, que j'adores
seulement pource quelle est faicte
pour vous non quelle vous resamble
Jan prys estre Juge competant, vous
ayant peynte au tonté perfectyon
dans mon ame, dans mon ame dans
mon cœur, dans mes yens,

FAC-SIMILE OF THE WRITING OF HENRY IV.

both creeds associated for the defence of the realm," accusing the House of Lorraine of seeking to over-throw the Monarchy and of being the source of all the sufferings of the country. In attacking these traitors, the associates protested that they had no aim but the service and independence of the King. The German Princes, the Kings of Denmark and Scot-land, the Protestant cantons of Switzerland, the Eng-lish nobles and their Queen were warned, that the Holy League had devoted them all to the same destruction, that nothing appeared inaccessible to the ambition of Spain, which already stretched across so many seas and lands. Therefore they should support those who were fighting in France against the common enemy and his allies, the rebels who had compelled their king to break his edicts and to attack his most faithful subjects.

Nor was the papal bull left unanswered, which Sixtus V., more violent though less favourable to the League and Spain than Gregory XIII., had ful-minated against Henry of Bourbon. The astonished Romans awoke one morning to see the celebrated statues of Pasquin and Marforio and the doors of the principal churches decorated by a document which professed to be a proclamation of Henry, by the Grace of God, King of Navarre and Prince of Béarn, in which he gave the lie to "Monsieur Sixte," self-styled Pope of Rome, asserted that he was prepared to prove him a heretic in a free and œcumenical council, and declared that he would avenge on the Bishop of Rome and his successors the insult done to the royal House of France in his person.

Sixtus, bold himself, appreciated boldness in others and was disposed to admire rather than to be angry with the audacity of Henry and the faithful courage of his agents. The insulting document itself was written not by a Protestant, but by a Gallican lawyer and placeman, L'Estoile, whose diary is one of the most useful documents for the history of this period, as a record of the feelings and opinions of the most enlightened, the most honest and moderate of the middle class.

The Parliament of Paris showed its hostility to the League and its readiness to support the King should he venture on a bolder policy, not only by vigorous protests against the infraction of Gallican liberties by the unauthorised publication of a Bull, excommunicating the first Prince of the Blood, but also by declaring that it was monstrous to expose millions of men, women and children to death without apparent cause on an ill-established and vague charge of heresy, and that it would not honour as royal edicts, the articles of an unconstitutional league, in arms not only against God but against nature, which commanded fathers to be no longer fathers, friend to betray friend, and which promised to the assassin the spoils of his victim.

The Guises on the other hand, conscious that they were hated by the King, and that at any moment he might turn against them, did not cease to discredit and undermine his authority, and their fears when Catherine began once more to negotiate with the King of Navarre, were not allayed by the protestations of the Queen-Mother and her son, that their only object was to prevent or delay the invasion of France by a powerful army of German Protestants.

The German Princes declared that it was to Francis I. and Henry II. that Germany owed the toleration of Protestantism, and that gratitude for what those kings had done compelled them to endeavor to secure the like boon for France. The Protestant Swiss cantons allowed 10,000 men to enlist for the service of the King of Navarre. These mercenaries, when united with the Germans and with a body of French refugees, formed an army of some 30,000 men. They were to march from the Rhine to the Loire and there to join the forces of the King of Navarre.

Henry III. determined to send his favourite Joyeuse against the Huguenots, and himself to take the command of the army opposed to the Germans. Even the Duke of Guise, lieutenant-general of the League though he was, could not pretend to the supreme command when the King in person was present.

At Coutras on the borders of Saintonge and Perigord, a few miles north of Libourne on the Dordogne, Henry of Bourbon met Joyeuse and won the first victory which had been gained by the Protestants in twenty-five years of civil war (October 20, 1581).

The King's minions and courtiers had crowded to serve under Joyeuse and vied in the magnificence of their arms and equipments. As the autumn sun shone on the first ranks of the Catholic army, wholly composed of nobles resplendent with embroidery

and gold, Henry pointed out the glittering line to
the Protestant gentry, who had cut down their timber and mortgaged their estates to equip themselves
and their followers with the bare necessaries of war.
His words have been compared to that proclamation
in which Bonaparte inflamed the zeal of his ragged
and half starved battalions by the prospect of plunder and licence in the fertile plains and luxurious
cities of Italy. "Here, my friends, you have before
you a very different quarry from any we have hitherto followed. A bridegroom [Joyeuse had been
recently married] with his wife's dowry still in his
pocket and accompanied by the flower of the Court.
Courage! there is none among you of so little
account that he shall not henceforth ride a made
charger and be served on silver plate." But it was
not with thoughts of booty alone that the Huguenots entered the battle. They threw themselves on
their knees to implore God's help. The young
courtiers round Joyeuse shouted, "They are afraid!
they are confessing themselves," and were urgent to
be allowed to charge, and the more so because the
enemy's artillery well directed by Rosny, was plough-
ing long furrows through their ranks. As the
Catholic army advanced, the Protestants, led by the
King's chaplains sang the triumphant verses of
the 112th psalm. "They came about me like bees,
and are extinct even as the fire among the thorns,
for in the name of the Lord I will destroy them."
While Henry turned to the Prince of Condé and his
brother the Count of Soissons, "Cousins, I have
only to remind you that you belong to the family of

Bourbon, and, God's life! I will prove to you that I am its head."

The King of Navarre handled his army, which though about equal to the enemy in infantry, was greatly inferior in cavalry, with great judgment. He made up for the light equipment and inferior numbers of his horse by drawing them up in deep masses and placing his matchlock men between their columns. It was not till Joyeuse's men-at-arms were within a few yards, the heavy men and horses tired with attempting to trot up the rising ground, and galled with the fire of musketry, that Henry headed the decisive charge upon their extended line. The pistols of the Huguenots emptied many a saddle, before they closed, and fighting hand to hand their opponents could not use their lances. In an hour the royalist army was in headlong flight. Joyeuse himself, 400 gentlemen and 2,000 soldiers were killed; the booty gained by the Huguenots, who lost but forty men, was immense.

Although so complete, the victory of Coutras had no important results. Henry has been blamed for not pressing on to join the advancing Germans, after which he might have fallen with superior forces on the King, or have extorted peace by a bold march on Paris. He sacrificed his victory to love, says Aubigné —and some years later, his chaplain D'Amours reminded him how he had vainly urged him on the morning after the battle to use to the utmost the victory God had given him. Yet we can scarcely believe that his conduct at so important a crisis was determined by his desire to lay his laurels at the

feet of the Countess of Grammont. Devoted
though he was to his mistresses, Henry maintained
that he never had preferred them to the interests
of the State, and after reading his voluminous correspondence, it is difficult not to allow, that, at
any rate during the earlier part of his life, the boast
was not ill founded, nor was Corisande the woman
to expect or encourage such weakness in her lover.

It was in part the completeness of the defeat of
the Catholics, which was their salvation. Henry
could not keep his army together, so eager were the
soldiers to secure and carry home their booty.
Moreover, a large part of his forces consisted of the
levies of the districts in the immediate neighbourhood, Poitou, Saintonge, Angoumois, who had come
prepared to fight a battle, but not equipped for a
campaign. These and other reasons for inaction are
alleged in a despatch to Elizabeth of England.

It may perhaps be thought that the eagerness with
which Henry excuses his failure to meet his allies,
argues a consciousness of some want of energy on
his part, but it was necessary to keep the Queen
of England in good humour, and she was naturally incensed at the futile conclusion of an expedition
to further which she had done violence to her
habitual parsimony.

John Casimir, the brother of the Elector Palatine, from some strange scruple about attacking the
neighbouring House of Lorraine, had not placed
himself at the head of the motley army he had assembled. He entrusted the command to Fabian of
Dohna, a Prussian noble of considerable military ex-

perience and of great zeal for the Protestant cause, but of neither sufficient reputation nor rank to command the ready and cheerful obedience of his subordinates. The Swiss, when they found the King of France in person opposed to them, refused to fight, and gladly accepted Henry III's offer to pay them 400,000 ducats to go home. The confederates reached the Loire. Instead of being met by a Protestant army they found the towns and bridges occupied by the King. The Guises were advancing in their rear ; and at Auneau surprised the Germans in their quarters and inflicted on them a loss of 2,000 men. After this slaughter and the desertion of the Swiss, the whole Protestant army barely amounted to 12,000. They were without any definite plan of operations, the season was late and inclement, the soldiers were exhausted by fatigue and disease, the line of march was marked by abandoned waggons, by the corpses of men who had fallen out of the ranks from sickness or fatigue and had been pitilessly slaughtered by the peasantry in retaliation for their rapine and cruelty. One woman boasted that she had with her knife cut the throats of seventeen of these accursed heretics, who had crept into a barn for a little shelter before they died. The Germans followed the course of the Loire till they saw before them the high mountains in which it rises. On the other side of the hills was a friendly district and towns garrisoned by their allies. Châtillon, the eldest son of the Admiral, who accompanied the invaders with a body of French refugees, undertook to clear the passes and lead the army into Languedoc in four days. But the offer of the King, to assist them to return to their own country if they would swear never again to bear arms in France, was too tempting to be refused. Bolder counsels would have been safer. The Guises treated the royal safe conduct as valid only in France; as soon as the retreating Germans had crossed the frontiers of Franche-Comté, they fell upon them and cut the greater number to pieces.

The campaign of 1589 had decided nothing. The hopes of the Huguenots were not crushed by the misfortunes of their allies; since the victory of Coutras they felt confidence in their own unassisted strength.

The enmity of Henry III. and of Guise was embittered. The failure of the German invasion was really due to the negotiations of the former, but all the credit was ascribed by the populace to the latter. He was a glorious conqueror, the King had treacherously saved the Swiss from his avenging sword and had given them money into the bargain. Henry III. found that he had only bestirred himself to increase the power and popularity of the Duke. He bitterly declared to his courtiers that the King of Navarre was not his worst enemy. The morning after Coutras, Henry of Bourbon had written : " Sire, my lord and brother, return thanks to God, I have defeated your foes and your army. You will hear from the bearer, whether, though I stand sword in hand in the midst of your kingdom, it is I who am, as it is pretended, your enemy," and the King of France was disposed to believe that his brother-in-law spoke the truth; that Henry of Guise was his worst enemy he at any rate did not doubt. A remarkable despatch, written by the English ambassador, throws light upon the situation and upon the character of the French King. Sir E. Stafford tells how secretly and by night he was brought to a house where he met Henry III. alone. The King began by saying that in the confidence that his words would be communicated to no one but the Queen of England he would explain openly and fully the position in which he found himself, so that his sister might consult thereon with her most secret councillors, she had such, and wise; he had no one whom he could trust. By the advice of the Queen-Mother and his council he had refused a proposal made by Elizabeth to mediate between him and the Huguenots; but he besought her to do so with all his heart; and above all to persuade Navarre to have a care of his own interests and to accommodate himself to him in such sort (*i. e.* by his conversion) that the League might have no pretext to undo him and France. He himself was a good Catholic, and wished all France to be Catholic, but he was not such a bigot as to prefer to ruin himself and his kingdom rather than tolerate the Reformers. If the Germans had shown valour and discretion they might have brought the League on their knees. Why had they not attacked Lorraine, Champagne and Burgundy, instead of following him to the Loire? He had been obliged to act as he had, so as not to leave all honour to the Guises. Stafford remarked that it hardly seemed to be to the King's interest that Henry of

Bourbon should conform. All men would then turn to the rising sun. The King was silent for a while. He then said every one could rule a shrewd wife except he that had her, and such was his case; he hardly knew which way to turn, yet he would rather risk what might come from Navarre.

The feelings with which they were regarded by Henry III. were well known to the League. Seditious pamphlets were hawked about the streets of Paris and the pulpits rang with discourses not less outspoken. The King, it was repeated, sympathised with the Huguenots; he had saved their foreign allies from destruction, he had advised his dear friend the English Jezebel to murder the sainted Queen of Scots. He left the troops who were shedding their blood for God and country to starve, while he squandered vast sums on the atheist Épernon, and on indecent orgies and follies. The Sorbonne in secret session—thirty or forty dirty pedants and masters of arts, grumbles L'Estoile—decided that incompetent and faithless princes may rightly be deposed.

The " Sixteen " and their most violent supporters plotted to seize the King's person. The Duchess of Montpensier, the sister of the Guises, whose fervid fanaticism and feminine recklessness were the useful instruments of her brother Guise's calculating ambition, boasted that she wore at her girdle the scissors which should give Henry of Valois his third crown, the tonsure.

The leaders of the faction met at Nancy and agreed upon new articles to be presented as an ultimatum to the King. In these they demanded that he should assume a less ambiguous attitude, wage a war of extermination against the heretics, dismiss all suspected ministers and officers, accept the decrees of the Council of Trent, establish the Holy Inquisition, place more fortresses in the hands of the Princes of the League, and provide for the payment of their troops; the last might be done by selling the estates of the heretics and of their allies, the skin of the living bear. The King again began to negotiate—not daring to reject these insolent proposals.

In the spring of 1588 the Invincible Armada was preparing to sail, and Parma had received orders to collect his forces and to be prepared to embark as soon as the Spanish fleet had swept the narrow seas. But if this was to be done with any degree of safety, it was absolutely necessary that the action of France should be paralysed. Otherwise so favourable an opportunity of interfering in Flanders, and the vital importance of not allowing England to become a Spanish province, would not suffer even the most supine and irresolute of French kings to remain inactive.

The Spanish ambassador was accordingly ordered to insist that the League should either compel the King to give satisfactory pledges of his devotion to the Catholic cause, or deprive him of the power of becoming dangerous.

Henry III., aware of the plots against his liberty, if not against his life, was fortifying himself in the Louvre, and had garrisoned that palace, the Bastille, and the Arsenal with a strong force of Swiss. The

Sixteen and the Spanish envoys urged Guise to hasten to the Capital.

Not only did Henry of Guise, in defiance of the King's prohibition, enter Paris where he was received with delirious joy as a conqueror and saviour, he had even the incredible audacity to venture almost unaccompanied into the Louvre. The King grew white with anger when the approach of the Duke was announced. "He shall die!" he exclaimed with a vehement oath. An Italian priest who stood by quoted the text, "I will smite the shepherd and the sheep shall be scattered." "Stone dead," said the soldiers about the King, "hath no fellow"; but the courtiers who feared the vengeance of the people, urged caution, they described the excited crowds who thronged the streets and even the courtyard of the Palace. While Henry hesitated, Guise entered, accompanied by the Queen-Mother; he looked pale and discomposed; he had passed through ranks of armed men; Crillon the Captain of the Guard had defiantly neglected to return his salute. "I ordered you not to come," were the first words of the King. "Sire, I received no express command," replied Guise, "or I should not have ventured into your presence, though I have but come to beg for justice against the calumnies of my enemies." Catherine, alarmed at the evident rage of her son, led him aside and urged him to do nothing which might provoke the fury of the people. What protection could a few thousand Swiss afford against the armed multitude of Paris? Guise took advantage of the opportunity to escape from so dangerous a situation. When he next visited the Louvre he was accompanied by 400 gentlemen, who wore arms under their clothes.

It was evident that the King was raging under the yoke of the League, and that he would throw it off if occasion offered. Épernon had occupied Lagny on the Marne with his troops, and was about to secure Rouen and Orleans. Holding these towns he could threaten Paris on all sides and interrupt the supplies and trade of the great city. The ferment among the inhabitants increased. The King ordered the municipal militia, supported by 6,000 Swiss, to occupy the most important points of the city. The trainbands either refused to obey the summons of their captains, or deserted the posts they were ordered to hold. Barricades arose everywhere in the narrow streets. The Swiss were surrounded by an armed mob, and themselves without shelter were exposed to the fire of enemies covered by the barricades and by the houses which they had occupied and turned into fortresses.

When Guise showed himself it was to protect the King's troops from the fury of the people, and to release those who had laid down their arms on a promise that their life should be spared. Unarmed, in a white silken doublet and a switch in his hand, he walked through the enthusiastic crowd deprecating their rapturous applause—" Enough, enough, dear friends, cry Long live the King." Next morning a threatening mob, the dregs of the people, led by a sacred band of friars and students of the University, assembled with cries of "To the Louvre,"

"Let us fetch brother Henry," for the fanatics now talked of nothing less than of deposing the King and compelling him to end his days in some monastery. Fearing for his liberty and his life the King fled through the one gate he still held, the Porte Neuve, situated near the middle of the great gallery of the present Louvre, and took horse at the stables of the Tuileries, accompanied by his courtiers and the majority of his Council. So unpremeditated was this flight that many mounted their horses unbooted, in silken hose and robes of office. The guards at the Porte de Nesle fired across the river at the motley cavalcade as it passed along the bank, while the people shouted taunts and insults. On the hill of Chaillot, Henry turned to look once more on the Capital he was never again to enter. "Ungrateful city," he muttered, "I loved you more than my wife."

No pursuit was attempted; Henry III. a prisoner in the Duke's hands would have been a terrible source of embarrassment; it would have been difficult to find a cage for such a bird. It is not likely that the ambition of Henry of Guise extended to the throne. He wished for the sword of Constable, the position of Lieutenant-General of the kingdom, and these he felt certain that he would be able to obtain by the vote of the Estates and from the fears of the King. The prize for which he strove seemed already within his grasp; but the death or captivity of the King would have revived the loyal instincts of the nation, his follies and vices would have been forgotten, a civil war would have been kindled, which would have invited the ambitious intervention of Spain, have given an opportunity to the Huguenots and at the end of which Guise, even if successful, could scarcely hope to be more powerful than he was already. If more splendid hopes dazzled his ambition their realisation would be easier, when, after the natural death of the last Valois, a distant collateral and a heretic was the heir of the Capets. Then the Constable and Lieutenant-General of the kingdom, disposing of the army and of the administration, might assert the right of the orthodox Church and people of France to prefer a prince of the old Carolingian line.

It is difficult to say what was the policy of Henry III. during the six months which elapsed between the Day of the Barricades (May 12, 1588) and the assassination of Guise (December 23, 1588).

It is probable that as yet he had no fixed plan, but, living from hand to mouth, left the morrow to take thought for itself,—a policy consisting in the absence of all policy, commoner, Aubigné remarks, among princes than those would readily believe who have not enjoyed their confidence.

The sufferings of the people, the anarchy and dissolution of every principle of order, could not escape the notice of the most careless observer. Already, as at the time of the English wars, the peasantry, tired of sowing when they were not allowed to reap, were abandoning the plough to live as brigands on the highways, or to collect in large bands among the forests. "Gallia silvescit," wrote Du Plessis-Mornay in 1587. "One who had fallen asleep twenty-five years ago, would, if he now awoke, imagine himself transported to some barbarous island."

To avoid an open breach with the League and such an outbreak of civil war as must complete the ruin of the country, the King offered to yield everything to Guise short of the entire government of the state; and when the Estates met at Blois (October, 1588) made another attempt to gain the confidence of the Catholic party.

He offered the largest concessions, the fullest confession of his errors in the past and the most explicit promises of future amendment. "I know gentlemen, that I have sinned, I have offended God—but for the future I will do better—I will reduce my expenses to the lowest limit, where there were two capons on my table there shall henceforth be only one." He even most reluctantly recognised the Cardinal of Bourbon as first Prince of the Blood, and assented to a declaration that, as a relapsed heretic, the King of Navarre had forfeited his right to the succession.

But no concession would satisfy his opponents; they drove him from point to point, inflicted humiliation upon humiliation, until at length he turned savagely to bay.

He was warned, even, it is said, by members of the House of Lorraine, who were jealous of their kinsman, that the Duke of Guise intended to procure a confirmation of his authority and the dignity of Constable from the Estates and carrying the King back to Paris to govern the kingdom in his name.

As Henry III. had before shared with his mother the mistake of supposing that the whole future and strength of the Protestant party depended on the life of Coligny, so he now seems to have believed that the League was incarnate in Guise, that if he could be removed, the Catholic party would welcome the King as their leader. Some of his most intimate advisers encouraged him in this view, quoting an Italian proverb, " No fear of the dead viper's venom." The Duke was repeatedly warned that his life was in danger. A few days before his assassination he debated with his friends whether he should leave Blois—in other words begin a civil war against the King, or continue to coerce Henry by his presence and by the authority of the Estates. The former course would have compelled Henry III. to make common cause with the Protestants and the Politicians, and unless he was prepared to become the mere tool of Spain, Guise was not strong enough to struggle against such a combination. Many of the nobles, who had at first adhered to the League, had been disgusted by the court it had paid to the democracy of the towns and by the contumelious treatment of the King. The League, it was said, had gained the Huguenots more adherents in three months than they could by their own efforts have secured in thirty years. The personal followers on whose devotion Guise might count, his advisers and confidants, were men of tarnished reputation and broken fortunes. He determined therefore not to risk the failure of his plans by leaving Blois: if he saw death come in at the window he would not, he said, escape by the door. Besides he too thoroughly despised the King, who affected to be more than ever immersed in frivolity and devotion, to believe him capable of any energetic and determined resolution. There was, he said, no spark of manliness or courage left in him. He forgot that the vilest reptile will turn when trodden on, that the most timid beast will defend itself if no way of escape remains.

In those days political assassination was regarded as one of the ordinary resources of statecraft, and, when we remember that even two generations later the chivalrous Montrose advised Charles I. to get rid in this way of Hamilton and Argyle, we must allow that the murder of the Duke of Guise, an undoubted traitor, too stout to be dealt with in the ordinary course of law, can scarcely be accounted a crime. Yet it was accompanied by dramatic circumstances which have impressed the imagination of posterity. The shivering, frightened King, rising in the black winter night, to prepare the death of his accomplice in a far bloodier scene of midnight slaughter ; his long suspense after he had placed his guards in the narrow passage through which the Duke must pass when summoned from the Council Chamber to his presence ; the meeting of the Council in the gray rainy December twilight ; the murderous scuffle heard by the old Queen who lay on her death-bed below ; all this has been often described. Guise in his death struggle dragged himself and his assailants as far as the King's room. It was told that there, as Guise sixteen years before had spurned the murdered Admiral, so Henry now kicked the corpse of his enemy, saying, as was noted by those who were curious in omens and in other

**DUKE HENRY OF GUISE.**
From the painting by F. Clouet.

obscure suggestions of the future, " He seems even greater dead than alive."

The Duke's brother, the Cardinal of Guise, the Archbishop of Lyons, Espinac, author of the *Gaveston*, a scurrilous libel in which Épernon and his master were compared to Edward II. of England and his favourite, together with the old Cardinal of Bourbon, were arrested in the Council Chamber and other leaders of the League on the same day, but of these only the Cardinal of Guise was put to death.

The King's first visit was to the Queen-Mother. He told her triumphantly that at length he was King of France, for he had killed the King of Paris. She said: "You have cut boldly into the stuff, my son, but will you know how to sew it together?"

Henry III. was indeed much mistaken in supposing that the death of the Duke would make him King of France—he was soon in danger of being little more than King of Blois. Yet, had he acted vigorously, it is possible that his position might have been improved by the bold stroke he had ventured.

He should have justified himself by some solemn form of judicial inquiry. This he might easily have done, for the treason of Guise was patent. He should have appealed to the loyalty of his nobles, recalled Épernon and his soldiers and taken the field at the head of his army. Even had he done so, the grief and fury excited among the popular and fanatical section of the League by the death of their idol might have stirred them to a resistance which he could only have overcome by the help of the Protes-

tants: but he showed no vigour. He remained at
Blois trying to persuade the Estates to be reasonable, seeking to conciliate when conciliation was impossible, and by the release of Brissac and other
violent partisans gave leaders to his rebels.

In Paris the news of the assassination of Guise
produced an uncontrollable outburst of sorrow and
passion. The tidings reached the town on Christmas
Eve. At once all signs of rejoicing and festivity
disappeared. The churches were thronged with
mourning crowds, who listened to funeral chants
unaccompanied by music, which took the place of
the cheerful services appointed for the most joyful of
Christian festivals. The preachers did their best to
raise the contagious emotions of the people to the
highest pitch of fury. They denounced in unmeas-
ured terms the treacherous murderer, the Ahab, the
impure Herod, the Judas possessed not by one but
by 10,000 devils, to whom they would no longer
give the name of king. The Sorbonne (Jan. 17,
1589) solemnly declared that, owing to his manifold
crimes, the subjects of Henry III. were released
from their allegiance. The Parliament attempted
to resist, by continuing to administer justice in the
King's name, but the more obstinate magistrates
were thrown into the Bastille, and the more pliant
compelled to make common cause with the municipality and with the Council which had been appointed
to carry on the government in the name of the Holy
Catholic Union.

The Duke of Mayenne, the eldest surviving brother
of Guise, presided, with the style of Lieutenant-

General of the Realm and Crown of France, over this Council, which was composed of the most important Catholic nobles, of some of the most prominent preachers and doctors of the Sorbonne, of a few members of the High Court of Justice, of representatives of the city of Paris and of the other towns which adhered to the League.   For the example of Paris had been followed by many other great cities—Rouen, Amiens, Abbeville, Troyes and Rheims, Toulouse, Orleans, almost the whole of Burgundy, Brittany and Provence, besides numerous towns in other parts of the country, refused any longer to recognise the King's authority.   On all sides he saw his power crumbling away.   Mayenne contemptuously rejected all overtures.   He would not give Henry of Valois the title of King.   He was, he said, a miserable wretch, in whose promises it was impossible to place any further confidence.   As the fanatics were irreconcilably hostile and his own unsupported strength was unequal to the unavoidable conflict, the King could no longer hesitate to accept the help offered to him by Henry of Navarre.

The small advantage reaped from the victory of Coutras, the discouragement of his German allies by the destruction of the forces they had levied, the ill-temper of the Queen of England, who complained that her subsidies had been wasted, the dread, common to all Protestants, of some fatal blow to be dealt to the Cause by the mighty armament collecting in the Spanish ports, the jealousy of the Princes of his family, the disunion among his followers, and, lastly, the complete submission, as it

seemed, of the King to their common enemies, had
severely tried even the serene and persistent self-
confidence of Henry of Bourbon. " The devil is
loose," he wrote in March, 1588, to his Corisande.
" I am indeed to be pitied, and it is a wonder that
I do not sink under my load. If I were not Huguenot I should turn Turk. Oh, by what violent trials
my head is racked! This year will be my touch-
stone ; I must assuredly either become mad or turn
out a clever man." But such moods of doubt and
depression did not last long. Two years before he
had written that his own head was the best part of
his Council, and that his judgment was rarely at
fault ; and although we must allow some credit to
his advisers, and above all to Du Plessis-Mornay, the
skill with which he steered through the dangers of
this crisis justify the boast.

In the field he maintained his reputation as a
skilful captain and fearless soldier. When, in November, 1588, the representatives of the Huguenot
Churches met at La Rochelle, a tone of manlier
resolution may well have been given to their deliberations by the sight of the standards taken from the
enemy, which decorated the roof of the hall in which
they met.

The death of Condé, March 5, 1588, who perished
the victim of a domestic crime, in which his wife
Charlotte de la Trémoille was implicated, freed
Henry from a rival in the affections of his party and
from comparisons not always to his advantage.

The King of Navarre sincerely lamented his
cousin. " One of the greatest misfortunes possible

has befallen me," he wrote to his mistress, "the sudden death of the Prince. They have poisoned him, the miscreants . . . a wicked woman is a dangerous beast," yet, he added, he lamented rather what his cousin ought to have been to him, than what he had been. He had discovered a new plot to take his own life. These murderers were all Papists, and he hoped that Corisande would abandon a religion which brought forth such fruits. To his Chaplain he wrote: "What a miserable age this is, which produces monsters who, though assassins, think to be held men of honour and virtue."

Though the Assembly at La Rochelle passed some useful measures, it was by no means to the taste of the Protector of the Churches. He bore with characteristic patience the exhortations of the ministers that he should amend the irregularities of his private life ; but he warmly resented the criticism of his public policy, and the proposal of some to place the French Protestants under the protection of the Elector Palatine : and did not conceal his displeasure at the appointment of a permanent Council consisting of princes and nobles and of representatives of the general and provincial synods. "If there is to be another meeting," he complained, "I shall go stark mad. But, thank God, all is ended and well ended."

The Assembly had scarcely dispersed, and Henry was collecting his troops for a winter campaign, when the news came of the assassination of Guise. Although Aubigné professes that the Huguenot gentry loudly lamented the treachery of which he had

been the victim, extolling the virtues of the dead
and the courtesies which many had received from
him, yet the general feeling was one of relief and
exultation. "How many men," Du Plessis-Mornay
exclaimed, "have been overthrown in this one man!
How many battles won, and towns taken! How
many years compressed into one morning; how
many poor souls raised up and churches restored!"
To his master he wrote that it was a signal mercy,
that without staining his hands he should have been
avenged on his enemy. He had, however, better do
nothing rashly. It was well to sleep a night on so
great an event.

The King of Navarre exulted in less seemly
fashion. If, in addition to this good news, he might
only hear that his wife had been strangled and that
her mother was dead, then, he said, he would have
every reason to sing the song of Simeon.

Meantime, he followed the advice of Mornay and
carried on the war with vigour, till he was suddenly
attacked by a pleurisy so severe that his life was in
danger. The Huguenots were in despair, valuing
their leader more highly now that they feared he
might be taken from them, and touched by the consolation which he sought and found in the singing
of psalms and edifying conversation. But the inaction to which he was reduced was not inconvenient.
He was relieved from the necessity of taking any
decided step before he could well judge what was
likely to be the future course of events.

Du Plessis-Mornay urged his master to hasten to
the assistance of Henry III. Châtillon was equally

eager to bring about a satisfactory understanding
with the Royalists.  The sternest Huguenots could
scarcely murmur at being called upon to help a
prince so deeply stained with the blood of their
brethren, when they saw the heir of the murdered
Admiral sacrificing his resentment to the welfare of
his country.  The Protestants and the Royalists had
the same interests and the same enemies.  It was not,
therefore, difficult, when sentimental obstacles were
laid aside, for them to come to an understanding.
A truce was concluded for a year, during which the
King of Navarre engaged to employ his forces
"only by consent or command of His Majesty."
Saumur, a strong fortress, commanding the passage
of the Loire, and one town in each province were to
be placed in the hands of the Reformers for the free
exercise of their religion and as a pledge of the
King's sincerity.

Henry of Bourbon advanced to the banks of the
Loire with a small but veteran army—5,000 infantry,
500 horse, and 500 musketeers.  The good economy
of Mornay had enabled him to pay his troops, and
therefore to maintain a discipline which contrasted
most favourably with the savage licence of the
Leaguers.  The Champions of Catholicism were not
less terrible to the orthodox than to heretics.  The
churches were often the scene of their vilest excesses.  They derided the holiest mysteries of their
faith, and trod under foot the consecrated Host,
the Body, as they professed to believe, of their
Redeemer.

When the soldiers of Mayenne first saw the uni-

12

form of the Protestants among the ranks of their opponents, they shouted to them — " Back, white scarves; back, Châtillon; it is not you who are our enemies, but the murderer of your father, the traitor King, who has betrayed you once and will betray you again!" But Châtillon replied that they were rebels and traitors to their country, and that, when the service of his Prince and of the Commonwealth was concerned, he cast under foot all thought of private interest and wrong.

When this was told to Henry III. he praised him, and ever after treated him with the greatest favour, and would, it was thought, had he lived, have advanced him marvellously. So, at least, Châtillon himself believed, for he was grievously afflicted at the King's assassination, and said that he had lost his good master and all hope of prosperity in this world. His friends pointed out that after all Henry III. had compassed his father's death, and that he might reasonably hope for more favour from Henry IV., to which he replied: " What you say is true. Yet be assured that the late King would have acknowledged and rewarded my services, while this one will rather abase me for serving him."

The King of Navarre had once sworn that he would never again enter his brother-in-law's presence, except between the ranks of his army. Yet, although warned that the King might offer his head as a pledge of reconciliation to the Catholics, he accepted an invitation to an interview in the park of Plessis les Tours. In the midst of a great and joyful crowd which had assembled to see the meeting of the Kings, Henry of Bourbon threw himself on his knees before Henry of Valois, who hastened to prevent him with repeated embraces.

It was observed by the spectators that the King of France excelled in grace and dignity ; but the vivacity, the soldierly bearing and the genial frank- ness of the King of Navarre won the favour of the people. He was in appearance the perfect type of the well-born, hardy, adventurous and restless Gascon soldier of fortune ; but there was also something about him of a crafty Ulysses who had seen the cities and evil manners of many men. He was of small but active and wiry make, with strongly marked ex- pressive and mobile features, piercing eyes, equally ready to laugh, to frown or to weep, surrounded by careful and cunning wrinkles, and glancing from under highly arched ironical eyebrows ; the long sen- sual nose of Francis I., but less villainous and more aquiline, drooping over a pointed chin, his hair thick and curly though prematurely grey—bleached, he used to say, by the breath of adversity—his short beard hiding a closely shut mouth. His dress was a brown velvet doublet, worn on the shoulders by his breastplate ; he was only distinguished from his fol lowers by his scarlet cloak and by the white plume fastened to his grey felt hat by a costly brooch. What more complete contrast could be imagined to the effeminate graces of the last Valois?

"The ice has been broken," Henry wrote to Mor- nay, "in spite of many warnings that if I went I was a dead man. When I crossed the river I committed myself to God, who in His mercy has not only pre-

served me, but caused the King to show extreme
joy." "You have done, Sire," was the reply, "what
it was right for you to do, but what none should have
ventured to advise you to do."

The reconciliation of the King with the Protestants
was far from displeasing to the Politicians and moderate Catholics.  They gladly acquiesced in a policy
which implied toleration, enmity to the League and
a vigorous opposition to the patron and master of it,
the King of Spain.  The League in the meantime was
daily becoming more hateful to a majority of the
nation.  At Paris it rested on the support of the
lower classes, who were propitiated by an exemption
from the obligation to pay their rent,—a communis-
tic measure of confiscation odious to the middle class.
In Normandy the Catholic leader, Brissac, had made
common cause with an agrarian rising of the peasantry,—a sure method of alienating the sympathies of
the landowners.  While all who were less Romanists
and Guisards than Frenchmen were disgusted by the
ever growing subservience to Philip II.  The Spanish
envoy Mendoza, whose insolence and love of intrigue
had caused first Elizabeth and then Henry III. to
refuse to tolerate him at their Courts, enjoyed greater
authority in the Council of the Union than Mayenne
himself, who apologised humbly to the Escurial, on
the plea of haste and urgency, for accepting the
authority conferred upon him, without the previous
permission of the King of Spain.

The Royalists and the Protestants flocked to the
army of the two Kings; they were joined by a
powerful body of Swiss, enlisted by the Protestant

cantons, and were soon able to advance upon and threaten Paris. Nothing had been neglected which might arouse enthusiasm or coerce and crush any growing spirit of moderation among the citizens,— frantic and sanguinary sermons, processions of men, of women, of relics. Four thousand children were paraded through the streets with torches in their hands, singing the "Dies Irae." As they halted before the churches they turned the torches to the ground, stamped on them with their feet and cried, "Thus may God quench the House of Valois." Wonderful tales were told of the crimes and cruelty of the King, of his determination to glut his revenge on his rebellious Capital. All who were suspected of being Royalists were imprisoned or watched with malevolent suspicion. The slightest symptom of disaffection was punished by fine and imprisonment, frequently by death. A servant accused her mistress of having laughed on Ash Wednesday; the charge was sufficient to endanger the life, not of the lady only, but of her whole family. Yet without large and immediate assistance from the Spaniards, Paris could not be held against the overwhelming forces of the kings of France and Navarre. The day for the assault was already fixed. The respectable citizens, disgusted by the licence of the mob, the ruin of trade and the prospect of famine, desired at least as much as they feared the entrance of the King. The monks, students and paupers, whatever their zeal, would be no match for the Swiss and for the veterans of Épernon and Navarre.

But although the devotion of many to the Catholic cause had cooled, popular passion, as is often the case, became incarnate in an individual, entered into and took possession of him.

Jacques Clément was a Burgundian monk, ignorant, violent and fanatical; encouraged by his superiors he determined to strike down the murderer of the champion of the Church, the ally of heretics, the persecutor of God's people. No means were neglected which might raise his enthusiasm to the highest pitch. He was introduced to the Duchess of Montpensier, perhaps to other leaders of the League, who promised him all that could tempt the ambition of a friar in this world and the next.

He executed his purpose with the deliberate simplicity and success of a man too much in earnest, or too stupid, to be distracted by any apprehension of consequences to himself or others.

The assassination of Henry III. saved Paris. The Duchess of Montpensier fell on the neck of the messenger who brought her the tidings of the King's death; the townspeople gave way to transports of unreasoning joy. The assassin was honoured as a saint and as a martyr, his image and those of the two Guises were placed on the altars of the churches and received the adoration of the faithful.

# CHAPTER V.

## CAN A HERETIC BE KING OF FRANCE?

### 1589–1592.

HE death of the last Valois, worthless man and weak King though he was, appeared a most serious calamity to the few statesmen whose love for their country was not obscured by the spirit of faction or fanaticism.

Three parties in the state had a clear conception of their own aims and were prepared to bestir themselves to attain those aims.

These were first the Romanist and Spanish party, composed of men who, sooner than that France should cease to be orthodox, were prepared to sacrifice her national existence.

Secondly, there was the faction of Lorraine, the Guises and their adherents devoted, under the pretext of religion, to the aggrandisement of their House.

And thirdly, the Huguenots who wished to overthrow the religious system hitherto accepted by the nation, or, at the least, to destroy the connection between Church and State.

Besides these the many princes and nobles who sought only to advance their own personal fortunes, to become hereditary rulers in their governments, whether of province, town or castle, knew clearly what they wanted. Believing and even hoping, that the ship of the state was breaking up, each tried to possess himself of some fragment; but these selfish wreckers can hardly be said to have had a policy. The great majority of the nation were indeed conscious of the evils under which they were suffering, but stood hesitating and uncertain by what means they might be remedied.

Henry of Bourbon was the lineal descendant of St. Lewis, but for ten generations none of his ancestors in the male line had sat on the French throne. He was the champion and leader of a violent minority; if he, a heretic, was enabled by the swords of his Huguenots and by virtue of strict legitimist principles to establish his claim to the throne, this would be the triumph of one, and that the least popular, of the three existing constitutional theories.

It was only a minority, chiefly composed of lawyers, who asserted that indefeasible hereditary right must, under all circumstances, determine the descent of the Crown.

The principle of ultimate popular sovereignty, that the King derives his power, if not from election, at least from the consent of the people, historically true of the earlier Capetian monarchy, and never wholly forgotten, had been recently revived, mainly

by the Huguenot writers.   The greater part of the
Catholic clergy and many of the laity believed in the
indissoluble connection of Church and State.   In their
eyes the title of the "Very Christian King" depended on his coronation and unction with the
miraculous oil at Rheims.   It could hardly therefore
be expected that the conservative and personal
feeling which had attached the majority of the
nobility and of the magistracy to Henry III. would
be transferred to Henry IV.

On hearing of the attempt on the King's life,
Navarre had hurried from his quarters at Meudon
to the bedside of Henry III. at St. Cloud.   Holding
his successor's hand the dying man had said to the
nobles who were thronging the room, " I beg you
as my friends, and command you as your King, to
recognise my brother here after my death."   Upon
which all present had with many protestations
pledged their faith to Henry of Bourbon.

But all was changed when sixteen hours later he
again came to the royal quarters.   He was received
as their liege lord by the officers of the household,
but in the chamber of death he found the corpse
watched by two friars and many courtiers, who, after
a scanty salute, gathered in knots with scowling
faces and angry gestures, loudly protesting to each
other that they would rather die a hundred deaths
than serve a heretic master.

D'O, a man of the vilest reputation, who, by the
ignominy of a "mignon" and the arts of a swindler,
had earned the office of minister of finance, whose
shameless prodigality was supported by an insatiable

rapacity, had the effrontery to present himself before
Henry, as the spokesman of those whose tender conscience would not allow them to acknowledge an
unorthodox Prince.   If he would at once abjure
his heresy and engage not to confer office on any
Huguenot, then they were prepared to be his obedient subjects.

But Henry, who had found time to consult some
of his most trusted advisers, though paling with
anger, restrained his indignation and returned a
politic as well as spirited answer.   "Would they
take him by the throat in the first moment of his
accession, and forgetting the oath which they had
sworn but a few hours before to their murdered
master, seek to compel him to a compliance which
so many simple folk had been able to refuse, because
they knew how to die?   Who but a man entirely
without religion would change his faith in such
fashion?   Would they prefer an atheist for King?
or to be led on the day of battle by a man without
any fear of God?   He was ready—as he had always
been—to receive instruction from a council of the
Church, and meantime would refuse no reasonable
pledges to the Catholics ; although his past treatment of them was the best guarantee for the future."

He had scarcely spoken when Givry, one of the
most gallant of the late King's officers, who had
been sent to sound the disposition and to secure the
adhesion of the camp, came in and clasping the
King's knee, said "in his pleasant way," "I have
seen, Sire, the flower of your brave gentry.   They
are impatiently awaiting your commands.   You are

the King of all brave men—none but cowards will
desert you."

Almost at the same moment Sancy introduced the
forty captains of the Swiss companies who had come
to kiss the King's hand and to offer their services.
Sancy was renowned as a skilful diplomatist, but he
had never given a more striking proof of his ability,
nor one more useful to his country than by now persuading these mercenaries so far to abandon their
native prudence as to promise to serve the King of
France three months on credit. Henry embraced
him and grasped the hands of the Swiss leaders; to
them, he said, he should owe his throne.

The Marshal Biron, who of all the Royalist captains had the greatest military reputation and most
authority with the army, reproached Sancy for his
too great zeal. "I thought you," he said, "a wise
man, but you are doing your best to spoil a good
opportunity of making our fortunes." But the
promise of the county of Perigord and of other
bribes to his insatiable greed and vanity, induced
Biron not only to undertake to serve the King himself, but also to act as a mediator between him and
the malcontents.

The result of this negotiation was that, ten days
later (August 4th), Henry signed a declaration in
which he solemnly undertook to maintain free from
all innovations the Catholic, Apostolic and Roman
faith, to submit himself to the instruction of a
general or national council within six months if
possible, to deprive none of the dignities and offices
they had held under the late King, to appoint no

Protestants during the next six months to any vacant dignity or office and to grant to the Huguenots no privileges of worship or other advantages to which they were not already entitled by the treaties and edicts of Henry III. In return for these concessions, the majority of the Catholic nobles consented to recognise him as their King.

Yet the royal army began to melt away. Épernon left the camp with 7,000 men; he professed that he could do the King better service in his governments of Saintonge and Angoumois. His intention was to watch the turn of events, and if the opportunity offered, to establish himself as an independent ruler. Many other nobles followed his example.

It was perhaps the hope that he might succeed the King of Navarre in the protectorate of the Churches which made the Duke of Thouars (la Trémoille) hurry back to his fiefs in the Protestant districts of the South-west. The Gascon and Poitevin Huguenots who followed him might with more reason excuse their departure by the state of destitution in which they found themselves.

Soon the royal army was reduced to half its numbers, while that of the League was constantly strengthened by the arrival of Spanish or native reinforcements. To persist in remaining before Paris was to invite disaster, yet the retreat of the King appeared a confession of weakness and encouraged the impression that he would be no match for his opponents. The League not only held Paris but most of the great towns. They already outnumbered the King in the field, and would soon be

joined by the mercenaries who were being levied
with Spanish and Papal money in Germany, and if
thèse did not suffice, Philip II. promised the support of Parma's invincible veterans.  Henry IV., on
the other hand, was penniless, even his Huguenots
were beginning to desert him, and it was believed
that he must either retire south of the Loire, or be
driven to seek a refuge at the court of his ally the
Queen of England.

But in truth the strength of the League was more
apparent than real.  That it became more and more
subservient to Philip II., more and more dependent
on Spanish money and Spanish soldiers, was at once
a proof and a cause of its weakness.  Why, if it was
so strong and popular, was it compelled to rely on
foreign support?  Villeroy, an able statesman, though
timid to the verge of dishonesty, and who, dismissed
from office by Henry III., had joined Mayenne,
wrote, "We must render to the King of Spain the
credit and the gratitude due for our existence."
But it was the conviction that they could only maintain themselves by Spanish help which made him,
and all the less fanatical and reckless among his party,
anxious to come to terms with the legitimate heir
to the crown, and opponents of the extreme courses
which made a future reconciliation more difficult.
Nor was there any agreement on other points among
even those who were unanimous in inveterate hostility to Henry of Bourbon.  The spurious ultramontane democracy of the great towns was eager only
to secure the re-establishment of Catholic orthodoxy
and a large measure of local independence.  The

leaders of this party, who revered in Philip II. the champion and temporal head of Romanism and the dispenser of the treasures of the New World, would willingly have thrown the Salic law overboard, and at once have recognised the Infanta Clara Eugenia (Isabella), the granddaughter of Henry II., as their Queen. When we condemn this subservience to Spain, it is only fair to remember that Artois, Franche Comté and other French-speaking provinces among the dominions of the Spanish King, enjoyed a large measure of provincial independence and did not feel their nationality to be endangered. But the pretensions of Philip II. were odious to the Guises and to the few great nobles who had joined their faction. The personal government of the Escurial would not be compatible with the feudal independence which it was hoped to re-establish, nor was the House of Lorraine struggling to snatch the Crown from the Bourbons in order that they might place it on the head of the Hapsburgs.

The Guises themselves were not united. The Duke of Mayenne was jealous of the rising popularity of his nephew, the young Duke of Guise. He could scarcely venture to hope for the Crown himself, and apparently did not see how any settlement satisfactory to his ambition could as yet be brought about; he was therefore content that matters should drift on, his only policy was to prevent, so far as in him lay, every definite solution, in the hope of profiting by any, as yet, unforeseen chance.

The wholly selfish and unpatriotic aims of the leader of the League were not compensated by any exceptional ability, by any special aptitude for the part he was called upon to play. That Mayenne should have been praised, even by Protestant historians, for probity and humanity, that he should evidently have been regarded as a Prince of more than average virtue, is most damning testimony against the age in which he lived. He was suspected of more than one murder, not to mention the assassination with his own sword of a soldier of fortune who had dared to aspire to the hand of his step-daughter. He was cautious and prudent both in policy and in war, but these respectable qualities prevented him from venturing to seize the object of his ambition when it was perhaps not beyond the reach of audacity, and did not fit him to cope with the restless and daring energy of his opponent.

It was also fortunate for Henry IV. that being unable to agree in the settlement of the succession, his opponents sought to postpone the difficulty by proclaiming the old Cardinal of Bourbon King. By so doing they recognised the legitimacy of the claim of his family to the throne and set up as the rival of the undoubted head of the house an old man, nearly imbecile, of whom, even in his youth, Calvin had said that unless quickened with wine he was more lumpish than a log, and that he might well be mistaken for a wineskin or a cask, so little had he of the semblance of a human being ;—an old man, moreover, who, at this juncture, was a prisoner in the hands of his nephew.

Although the League held the Capital and many of the most important towns, it may be doubted whether it anywhere commanded the hearty allegiance of a majority. In Paris we are assured a violent minority terrorised the loyal and law-abiding citizens by means of foreign mercenaries and of the rabble, hired by the doles of the convents and the bribes of Spain.

But if his opponents were so weak, how came it that so long and doubtful a struggle had still to be waged before the authority of Henry IV. was universally acknowledged? The King's difficulties were, we shall find, due not so much to the strength or statecraft of his native opponents as to the intervention of Spain and to the want of loyalty and unanimity among his own partisans, and perhaps also to the misery and exhaustion of the nation, so reduced by suffering that it lacked the strength and spirit needed for the vigorous effort by which alone it could throw off the maladies under which it was perishing.

The body politic appeared to have reached the last stage of dissolution, and it profited but little that there should now be a vigorous will at the centre of the government, when all the departments of state, the nerves, so to speak, by which that will might have set the limbs in motion, were paralysed or disordered, and those limbs themselves wasted and powerless through misery and privation; when the supplies which are as necessary to the political, as food is to the physical organism, were either not to be obtained, or if obtained were diverted from their natural and wholesome uses, further to inflame the peccant humours.

"France," says a contemporary poem, "is like a

storm-tossed vessel surrounded by reefs and breakers, whose crew have deserted the care of sails and helm to turn their guns upon each other. Conquerors or conquered, the most they can hope is to be the last to perish in the universal wreck. Her cities are full of injustice and violence; the just judge is dragged before the judgment seat of the criminal. Yet those who in walled towns snatch, arms in hand, a precarious sleep are happy compared with the miserable country folk. All that the earth can do for those who taught the streams to water her green fields and enamel them with flowers, who decked her with golden harvest and purple vintage, is to offer them the shelter of her forests, the covert of the boar and the lair of the wolf. There perhaps they may escape the soldiers, who to compel them to disclose their poor hoards, their only resource against starvation, suspend them by their thumbs with cutting cords, or scorch their greased and naked bodies with burning brands, or hang by the feet their children, torn from the breast. . . . Man is no longer a man when he feeds on grass and roots, on raw flesh and carrion, when the starving children gnaw the bark of the forests, while the village streets are the abode of wolves and foxes, the houses, without furniture, doors or windows, bearing mute witness to the crimes that they have seen." This might perhaps be thought poetic rhetoric, but the sober lawyer, L'Estoile, is not less emphatic. " In this month the people almost throughout France were dying of famine and went in bands cutting and eating the unripe ears of corn." " In this month companies of robbers went through

13

the land robbing and plundering the houses of gentry and labourers of all they contained." Such are the constant entries in his diary. So also Villeroy complains that the towns which were rich before the Civil Wars had now become desolate and poor; that there was no longer any justice; the magistrates being no longer paid, lived in constant apprehension and misery. That all cities, and Paris more than any, were full of fear and discontent, confusion, faction and poverty; while if the towns were wretched no words could describe the misery of the open country, the villages deserted, the fields fallow, the face of the earth hideous and deformed.

No wonder that the peasantry were beginning to join together in armed bands, for those who had been robbed of all could still fashion some rude weapons formidable in the hands of despair, and that gentry and nobles dreaded a revival of the Jacqueries of the Hundred Years' War.

Such, however, was the state of things which many among the King's followers were anxious to perpetuate. So long as the war lasted and his authority was disputed, they believed that they could extort a high price for their services and immunity for their crimes and extortions.

So much was clear, that the rule of Henry of Bourbon would be a very different thing from that of the last Valois,—that it would at least be a reality. It was therefore dreaded by all those who had usurped or who still hoped to usurp an authority which did not belong to them, by all those who profited by abuses and irregularities which a strong government was certain to check, and there were many such among the nominal adherents of the King.

Nevertheless there can be little doubt that, without Spanish intervention, Henry IV. would before long have overcome the obstacles raised by the open hostility of the League, and by the treacherous jealousy and ill-will of his own followers.  Yet that intervention, although it protracted the struggle in France, is not to be regretted by Europe.  It diverted from the Low Countries the treasures and the men which might have enabled Parma to complete the subjugation of the Dutch.  The Spanish invasion of France in 1590 postponed for two years Henry IV's entry into his capital, but it gave Maurice of Orange an opportunity and a sorely needed breathing space.

Breaking up his camp before Paris the King sent the levies of Picardy under the command of the Duke of Longueville, and accompanied by 3,000 Swiss, back to their province, and the Marshal d'Aumont to Champagne with the same number of Swiss and the gentry of that district ; while he himself with the rest of his forces,—some 10,500 men— marched into Normandy.

He wished to prevent the Leaguers from drawing money and supplies from the wealthiest province of France, to confirm the loyalty of the well-disposed nobility and governors, to determine those who were wavering and by threatening Rouen to divert Mayenne from attacking the Royalist garrisons round Paris.  A third motive was the necessity of securing a port, conveniently situated, for keeping up communications with England.  Elizabeth had at first demanded a promise to cede Calais as the price of effective help, but Henry IV., at the time of his utmost necessity, and when his opponents were bribing the King of Spain and the Duke of Savoy by hopes of the partition of France, refused to cede an inch of French territory, and the English Queen, with more than usual generosity, had without further huckstering promised ample assistance of supplies and men.

Many of the Norman towns opened their gates at the King's approach, others he occupied by force. The governor of Dieppe had been among the first to recognise the King's authority.  (August 6, 1589.)

Dieppe was the wealthiest and most prosperous of the Norman ports.  The tidal harbour was safe and convenient for the largest ships which at that time navigated the Channel.  The population of the town, composed for the most part of wealthy traders, and of hardy fishermen and sailors, well trained in the use of arms, was more numerous than that which now brings home the cod of Newfoundland and the herrings of the North Sea, or ministers to the wants of a fashionable crowd of summer visitors.

Of the twenty-five or thirty thousand inhabitants a large proportion were Protestants : while the Catholics among the rich merchants and other leading men were like their governor determined enemies of the League.  The Spaniard was the natural enemy and prey of the seafaring population on both sides of the Channel.  The fortifications of Dieppe were strong and in good repair, well supplied with artillery and defended by a garrison—including the local militia,—6,000 strong, all well drilled and equipped by the care of the governor and the liberality of the townsmen.

Towards the end of August the King with a small escort rode from his camp at Darnetal, three miles from Rouen, to Dieppe. The inhabitants received him with enthusiastic loyalty, but he cut short the laboured discourses of the magistrates : " No ceremony, my children ; I only want your love, good wine, good bread and friendly faces."

Two days sufficed to confirm the zeal of the citizens, to inspect the fortifications and to learn the military capabilities of the neighbourhood. Scarcely was the King back at Darnetal when the news came that Mayenne was on the march from Paris. Eight hundred thousand gold crowns sent by Philip II., and the contributions, voluntary or forced, of the richer citizens had enabled him to collect a formidable army of 25,000 foot and 8,000 horse.

He boasted that he would soon bring back " M. de Béarn," " the Gascon heretic," or drive him into the sea, and the more fervent and credulous of his partisans already began to hire windows from which to view his triumphal entry into the Capital.

It would have been madness for the King with his small army to have awaited the attack of his opponent at Darnetal, with the great and hostile town of Rouen in his rear. He therefore fell back upon Dieppe, where he could face his enemies and await the English, Scotch and Dutch succours and the approach of the other divisions of his army under Longueville and D'Aumont. The position he had chosen, five miles from Dieppe, was defended by three little rivers, by woods and marshes and rested upon the village and castle of Arques. The zeal of the inhabitants of Dieppe, who turned out to work, men, women and children, enabled the King to strengthen his line by earthworks and by an entrenched camp, commanding the main road to Dieppe. The slow and cautious approach of Mayenne gave Henry full time to make every preparation that prudence could suggest. There was nothing to which he did not himself attend ; his indefatigable activity was a marvel to all—even to himself. " It is a wonder that I am alive," he wrote to Mme. de Grammont, " I am so hard worked ; but I manage to keep well, and my affairs prosper better than some folk expected. . . . I hope, with God's help, that if they attack me they will find that they have made a bad venture." This was written on September 7th ; on the 13th Mayenne was in front of the royal lines ; on the 16th he attacked the suburb of Le Pollet, which he hoped to carry without much difficulty and the possession of which would have given him the command of the harbour and prevented the English reinforcements from reaching the King. But meeting with an obstinate resistance, both there and at Arques, where he had attempted a diversion, he drew off his troops and, after the next day had been spent in sallies and skirmishes, determined to mass his men for a decisive attack on the entrenched camp and other works defending the direct approach to Dieppe.

Three days were spent in preparations. Early on

the morning of September 21st (about 5 or 6 A.M.),
the Leaguers silently advanced to the attack under
the cover of a thick autumnal fog, which not only
concealed their approach, but also, when the attack
had begun, prevented the King from using his artillery.   Yet the Catholics were unable to make any
impression on the Royalist position, till their German
mercenaries cried out that they too were Protestants
and wished to surrender, upon which their countrymen and the Swiss in the royal service held out their
hands and the butt end of their lances to help them
over ditch and rampart.   These lansquenets at first
obeyed the orders of the King's officers to draw up
apart, but when some of the Leaguers appeared to
be about to force the entrenchments, then, either
from premeditated treachery, or because they wished
to earn their pardon from those whom they now
believed to be the victors, they suddenly turned upon
the Royalists.   For a time it appeared as if Henry
IV. must fall back.   The treachery of the Germans
had driven him from his first line.   He had charged
ten times at the head of his division, and two horses
had been killed under him, but neither his own exertions nor those scarcely less determined of his followers would have been able to keep in check the
heavy masses of Mayenne's mail-clad horse and the
serried columns of his Swiss and German infantry,
had not the sun at the most critical moment scattered the fog, so that the guns of the Castle of
Arques began to play upon the advancing Leaguers,
while at the same moment Châtillon appeared leading the Huguenot garrison of Le Pollet.   " Here we

are, Sire," their commander shouted as they passed
the King, " ready to die with you," while his men
broke into that fierce chant, " Let God arise," which
on so many fields from the Danube to the Boyne has
struck dismay into the hearts of the enemies of Protestantism.   The Leaguers were driven from the positions they had won, and Mayenne fell sullenly back.

Long after Aubigné asked the Captain-General of
the League to what cause he should  ascribe his defeat at Arques.    After a moment's pause the Duke
replied : " Write that it was due to the valour of the
old Huguenot phalanx, composed of men, who, from
father to son, were hail fellow well met with death."

The army of the League had only lost from 600
to 400 men, and Mayenne was  able, five days afterwards, to march round the King's position and occupy a height from which he could  bombard the town
of Dieppe.   But  English vessels had already run
into the harbour, bringing ammunition and supplies.
On September 29th, 1,200 Scotch landed, and three
days later Elizabeth's fleet disembarked 4,000 men.
Henry IV. dined on the Admiral's ship, and the
besiegers might  hear the  salvos of ordnance, while
kettle-drum and trumpet brayed out the triumph of
the toasts he pledged.

The  armies of Longueville, D'Aumont and La
Noue  were  collecting in the rear of Mayenne, his
supplies were  intercepted by the  King's garrisons,
his army  was  melting away—the day after the engagement at  Arques 3,000 men, mostly Parisian
militia, left his camp.   The trainbands of the towns,
like the noble volunteers, only conceived themselves

bound to serve during their good pleasure. Since
the arrival of the English reinforcements, whatever
chance there might have been of reducing Dieppe
was gone. The General of the League, therefore,
broke up his camp and retreated, glad that the necessity of obtaining help from the Spaniards gave
him a pretext for hurrying to Amiens and spared
him the mortification of returning baffled and defeated to Paris.

Shortly before the attack on Arques the Count of
Belin, a Leaguist officer, had been taken prisoner
and was received by the King with the courtesy and
caresses by which he generally sought to disarm and
win his opponents ; he was a very spaniel, his old
followers grumbled, whom you must beat if you
would have him fawn upon you. Belin in return for
the King's civilities said that from what he saw of
the strength of his Majesty's forces he feared that
he would not be able to resist the great army about
to attack him. "You forget, M. de Belin," was the
reply, "that part of my strength which you do not
see—the help of God and my good cause." The re-
pulse of the army of the League opened the eyes of
many to what M. de Belin had been unable to see.
It appeared likely enough that Heaven would help
one so indefatigable and brave in helping himself.
And it was seen that on earth, too, he had allies ;—
the ships and soldiers of the Queen of England,
fresh from the defeat of the Invincible Armada, the
treasures of the Dutch who thought their money
not ill spent if it should aid in diverting Parma to
France. "Arques," said a young prince who fought

in the Royalist ranks, " was the gate through which
the King entered upon the path of his glory and
prosperity."

That Europe thought so too was shown by the
action of the Venetian Senate. That prudent oli-
garchy, in spite of the protests and threats of the
Spanish ambassador and of the papal legate, determined to recognise Henry IV. and to send an
embassy to his Court. That these wise statesmen, so
careful to trim the sails of their shattered bark to the
wind of success, should thus show that they believed
the future to be on his side, was an omen of sad im-
port to the French King's enemies and greatly raised
the hopes of his friends.

The first use made by Henry IV. of his victory
was to let it be understood that he was prepared to
grant the most liberal terms to Mayenne, not, he
said, that he feared him, but that his heart bled for
the sufferings of his people. The Lieutenant-General of the League, deaf to the arguments of Villeroy
and of the most honest among his advisers, rejected
all overtures.

After uniting his forces with those of his generals
the King advanced upon Paris with an army of
20,000 men. Slowly at first, hoping that Mayenne
would hurry to the defence of the Capital and give
him the opportunity of winning a pitched battle.
Then, finding that his opponent did not accept the
challenge and encouraged by messages from his partisans within the walls, by forced marches. Before
daybreak on November 1st, and in a thick fog, his
columns carried by assault in three places the sub-

urbs on the right bank of the Seine and all but succeeded in entering the city itself pell-mell with the fugitives they were driving before them. It was perhaps well for the Royalists that they did not succeed in penetrating into the town, where they might have been lost and overwhelmed in the labyrinth of narrow and barricaded streets.

The suburb of St.-Germain was sacked, and it is said that the slaughter of the Parisians by Châtillon's men to the cry of "Remember St. Bartholomew!" greatly impaired for a time the popularity of the King's cause in Paris. Yet the churches were respected, no violence was offered to women, nor were any victims slain in cold blood. Meantime the Duke, hearing that Paris was in danger, had left Amiens and was advancing with all possible speed. He entered the town two days after the attack on the suburbs. Henry, after drawing up his troops and offering battle in the plain of Mont-rouge retired slowly towards the Loire, reaching Tours on November 21st.

Through the province of Maine, which submitted after the surrender of the Capital, Le Mans and Brittany, where he was welcomed by the Parliament of Rennes and by a loyal minority among the nobles, the King marched into Normandy and in less than a month had reduced to obedience all the important towns and fortresses, with the exception of Rouen, Hâvre and Avranches.

His necessities compelled him to levy contributions, but all plunder and licence were severely punished ; he showed the most scrupulous respect for the churches, and received all who submitted with the most gracious courtesy.  A harmless sarcasm was the worst they needed to fear.  When the magistrates of a town which had only opened its gates after it had been played upon by the royal batteries assured him in a set harangue of that loyalty which was his by divine and civil law, he corrected them with a smile : "Cannon law you mean, gentlemen."

Meantime Mayenne was playing a difficult game with considerable skill in Paris.  Philip II's envoys, Tassis and Mendoza, urged that their master should be proclaimed "Protector of the Kingdom"; if he was, he would pay the cost of the war.  The taxes of France should be devoted to paying her debts, and Frenchmen should share the trade and wealth of the New World with the subjects of his Catholic Majesty. After the death of the Cardinal of Bourbon, the succession might be settled on some French prince with the hand of the Infanta Isabella ;—offers, tempting in themselves, but as little agreeing with Mayenne's ambition as with the patriotism of those of his advisers who had not forgotten that they were Frenchmen.  The authority of the Lieutenant-General of the Union would pale before that of the Protector of the Kingdom, and since the Duke was married he could not hope to be the Prince favoured with the hand of the Infanta ; while the sounder part of the Catholic party, men who, believing in the intimate connection of Gallican Church and State, felt unable to recognise an enemy of that Church as the Most Christian King, were far from wishing to see their country the tributary of Spain.

As a temporary compromise all were willing to recognise the Cardinal of Bourbon. It was known that he could not live long, and meanwhile the Span-lards trusted to be able, with the help of the Jesuits and their other allies in the confessional and the pulpit, by large bribes and still larger promises, to prepare public opinion for the succession of the Infanta. The more patriotic Leaguers, statesmen such as Ville-roy and Jeannin, hoped that time would be gained for the conversion of Henry of Navarre, or, if he proved obdurate, for securing the accession of some Catholic prince of the House of Bourbon; while Mayenne, too cautious to attempt to seize the Crown himself, could not hope to have more power than while carrying on the government in the name of an old man, a prisoner in the hands 'of his opponents. Charles of Bourbon was accordingly proclaimed King, and his supporters pledged themselves to labour for his release and coronation at Rheims.

After this, on the ground that the large powers which it claimed to exercise were inconsistent with the authority of a legitimate and orthodox monarch, Mayenne no longer summoned or consulted the "Council General of the Union," but appointed a Council of State attached to his person, composed in part of the more important members of the Council General, in part of Secretaries of State nominated by himself. This was a revolution in the constitution of the League. The Council General had been largely representative and democratic—the Council of State was the mere instrument of Mayenne's personal government.

But while the Spaniards, Guisards, Politicians and Fanatics were intriguing against each other at Paris, the King was extending his conquests. Meulan had been relieved, Poissy taken, and now he was threatening Dreux. The possession of the towns on the Seine enabled the Royalists to prevent the supplies of Normandy reaching the Capital. If Dreux fell, the rich crops of the fertile plain of the Beauce would also be lost. Already the pressure of want was felt. Mayenne, who had been joined by 2,000 Spanish and Walloon men-at-arms under the command of the Count of Egmont, and by some German foot in the pay of Spain marched to the relief of Dreux. The King, whose army was very inferior in numbers, was compelled to raise the siege, and Mayenne, having attained his object, would have fallen back without offering battle, had he not yielded to the representations of his officers. They pointed out to him the superiority of his army to that of the King; the Count of Egmont, zealous in the service of his father's murderers, protested that his mailed lancers would ride down the lightly armed cavalry of the King. More trusted advisers whispered to the Duke that the general of a victorious army might boldly demand the Crown from the representatives of the nation. If he could hope to meet them on anything like equal terms Henry IV. was not the man to baulk his opponents of their wish to fight a pitched battle. During the two days which intervened between March 12th, the day on which he broke up his leaguer before Dreux, and March 14th, that on which the battle of Ivry was fought, his army was considerably increased by reinforcements from Normandy and Picardy and even from Champagne and the banks of the Loire. Though impatient of a protracted campaign, the French gentry scented a battle from afar, and eager for the fray hastened to swell the King's ranks. But even so, he was greatly outnumbered, and could oppose only 2,200 cavalry and 8,000 infantry to Mayenne's 4,000 veteran horse and 12,000 foot.

Du Plessis-Mornay, always first where he could serve his master with pen or sword, reached the field in time to charge in the first line of the King's division, composed almost entirely of men of birth and quality, but after the day was won he exclaimed : " You have, Sire, committed the bravest folly that ever was, in staking the fate of a kingdom on one cast of the dice."

Yet Henry IV. had been careful to leave as little as possible to chance. Nothing was omitted which might enable his men to enter the battle with stout hearts and vigorous bodies. The March night was stormy and cold, but most of the royal troops were lodged in the villages on the fringe of the plain of Ivry, and large fires, tents and shelter were provided for those who were compelled to encamp in the open. A plentiful supply of wine and provisions was distributed to all. The King himself visited their quarters with such words to officers and men as were likely to raise their enthusiasm to the highest pitch. The Count of Schomberg, the Colonel of the German mercenaries, asking on the previous day for the arrears of pay due to his men, had received a curt reply: "Men of honour did not ask for money on the day before a battle." Now Henry sought him out: "M. de Schomberg, I insulted you. This may be the last day of my life and I would not wrong the honour of a gentleman. Pardon me, and embrace me." "Sir," replied the German, "yesterday, it is true, your Majesty wounded me—but to-day you kill me; for the honour you do me obliges me to lay down my life in your service." Schomberg kept his word; obtaining permission to leave his command and to charge with the King's division, he forced his way into the densest ranks of the enemy and fell fighting valorously.

The King protested to his followers that he fought not for personal aggrandisement, but in the hope of restoring peace and unity to his unhappy country, and that it was his earnest prayer his life might not be preserved, unless it was for his people's good; and since he passed much of the night in private devotions it would be unjust to question his sincerity. The edifying example of their leader was followed by the royal army. The village churches were full of Catholic Royalists hearing Mass and confessing; while the Protestants sang their psalms and listened to the exhortations of ministers not less valiant than pious.

The zeal of the Swiss was stimulated by means more congenial to the practical genius of their nation; 40,000 crowns which the economy of Mornay had provided were distributed among them.

The King threw himself down to rest for a couple of hours, but before daybreak, was again astir, visiting his men, explaining his simple plan of battle to the officers and raising the spirits of all by his cheerful confidence. In an army of barely 10,000 men, all could hear the words, could at least see the countenance and be brought under the personal influence of their commander.

Henry's tactics were much the same as at Coutras. He supported each division of cavalry by infantry on both flanks; and drew up his horse in deep masses, so that they might be able to force their way through the gaps made by the musketry in the enemies' hedge of lances. Mayenne also placed his regiments of infantry in the intervals of his cavalry, and drew up his forces in the same order as those of the King, except that as his army was much the more numerous his line was in the form of a crescent. The Duke himself, with his best men-at-arms, placed himself with Egmont and his Flemish horse in the centre opposite the King. After the rebels had formed their line of battle they halted, and the King took advantage of their hesitation to álter by a skilful manœuvre the position of his men, so that they should not advance with the sun and dust in their eyes.

The engagement began by nine volleys fired with great effect by the King's cannon—some six pieces, —a respectable field battery in those days. But although Marshal d'Aumont drove the light cavalry of the League headlong from the field, fortune did not at first appear disposed to favour the Royalists. The German Reiters and the Walloons broke the lighter French horse, who in vain attempted to protect the

14

artillery. The Duke of Montpensier on the King's left was driven back by the Duke of Nemours; and the advance of Biron's division, which had been stationed somewhat farther back tnan the rest of the line, barely saved D'Aumont's cavalry from being overwhelmed by their numerous assailants. France, said an eye-witness, appeared to be on the very verge of ruin.

Henry IV. saw that the decisive moment was come, and himself prepared to lead his choicest troops in the supreme and desperate struggle. As his helmet, conspicuous by a vast plume of white peacock feathers, was placed on his head, he cried: "Comrades, God is on our side. There are his enemies and ours, and here is your King. Should your standards fall, rally round my white plume; you will find it on the path of victory and honour!"

Mayenne's horsemen outnumbered those of the King by three to one, but fortunately at the moment of Henry's attack his opponents had been thrown into confusion by the German Reiters, who after their charge had fallen back, as their custom was, to re-form behind their own line. Sufficient space for this manœuvre ought to have been left between the corps supporting them. But the Leaguist officer, on whom the duty devolved of seeing that the different bodies of troops took up the positions assigned to them, was shortsighted, and had placed them too closely together; and this mistake was the more serious, because, arranged as they were in a crescent, they converged in advancing upon the enemy. The Reiters finding no space left,

tried to force their way through Mayenne's and Egmont's ranks, threw them into disorder and checked
their advance, so that the King was among them
before they could get into a charge or use their
lances with effect. Yet the contest was fierce and
for a time uncertain. Though Henry amply justified
by his intrepid valour what else had seemed a bom-
bastic vaunt, plunging into the enemies' ranks two
horse-lengths ahead of his followers, nor resting till
his sword was beaten out of shape, his arm spent
and swollen with changing blows, some of his men
had fallen back, thrown into confusion by a volley
poured into them at twenty-five yards by Mayenne's
musketeers. But the greater number pressed on,
fired by their King's example and emulating his
courage. The Count of Egmont fell and his Walloons took to flight. Mayenne and Nemours seeing
their horse give way hurried from the field. The
infantry of the League as yet stood their ground
and outnumbered the whole army of the King; if
his cavalry had scattered in pursuit, the issue of the
day might have remained ambiguous and incom-
plete. But Henry had given most express orders
that his horse if they broke the enemy were to keep
their order and return to their positions. The Catholic Swiss, when they saw that the King's guns were
about to be turned against their squares, did not
care to be shot down in the cause of a leader who
had proved an indifferent paymaster, and surrendered without a blow. The German foot would
gladly have done the same, but the memory of their
treachery at Arques was fresh; and they were cut

down without compunction. A large part also of
the French infantry either perished on the field, or
were drowned in trying to cross the flooded Eure.
Mayenne, careful only to secure his own escape,
caused the bridge at Ivry to be broken down as soon
as he had crossed, but the King passed the river at
another place, and hunted him as far as the gates of
Mantes.

The victory was complete. The army of the
League was annihilated; of 4,000 horse, 1,500 were
dead or prisoners. The infantry had disappeared,
the standard of Mayenne, black lilies on a white
field, and the red cornet of the Count of Egmont,
were among the King's trophies.

The unexpected and complete rout of their army
caused such alarm and confusion among the partisans
of the League at Paris that it was generally believed
that if the King had ridden straight on to the gates
of the Capital he would have met with no resistance.
He himself wished to make the attempt, but, with
the noteworthy exception of La Noue, the most
authoritative voices in his Council were loud against
such rashness. Continuous rains had made the
roads impassable. The treasury was empty and the
most necessary supplies not to be obtained. The
soldiers had exhausted their ammunition. Specious
reasons, but few of the King's advisers wished his
triumph to be speedy and complete. Least of all,
Marshal Biron, whose opinion had the greatest
weight in military matters. Even among the Protestants, some like the Dukes of Thouars and Bouillon thought they had more to hope from the

necessity than from the gratitude of Henry, while many honest Catholics, believing that by his conversion he might at any moment disarm all serious opposition, did not wish him to secure the throne without paying the price which he already, so to speak, held in his hand. He might be honest in protesting that he intended no change in the established religion of the State; but as a heretic he must remain under the papal ban, and in a prolonged contest with Rome to what lengths might he not be driven? How painful in any case the dilemma to his orthodox subjects! On the other hand, if, as the official phrase ran, he received instruction, Sixtus V., whose hostility to the League and Spain was no secret, would without delay welcome him into the bosom of the Church. The more moderate of the King's opponents were not less desirous of his conversion than his Catholic supporters. Villeroy, who had left Paris, visited his friend and neighbour Du Plessis-Mornay, and endeavoured to prove to him the necessity that Henry IV. should conform to the religion of the large majority of his subjects, in order that the perishing State might be relieved from the misery of civil war; while he pointed out to Mayenne with a frankness creditable to a man constitutionally timid, that he was now entirely dependent on Spain, and that Spain insisted upon being paid for every soldier and every ducat by some strip of territory, some sacrifice of French interests and independence. The Guises asked for and expected Spanish doubloons, but Philip would send them Spanish veterans. Besides, who could believe that the Duke was fighting for the Catholic faith and the relief of the people, who saw how those who followed him served God by blaspheming His Holy Name, pillaging churches, violating every law human and divine. "Our Union," he concluded, "from top to bottom is nothing but disunion; our towns are full of lawlessness, riot and poverty!"

The King had probably from the moment of his accession looked upon his conversion as a concession which might become unavoidable, and he had, as we have seen, even before 1589 prepared the way for such a step by professing on all occasions his willingness to "receive instruction" and to renounce any errors of which he might be convinced.

Henry IV. was not an unbeliever, not inaccessible to religious emotion; in trouble or sickness he found comfort in prayer and in the psalms which had soothed his infancy, but his emotions were superficial and transitory, his ambition deep and enduring. His creed he said was that of all honest men. Yet it cannot be doubted that in his heart he held Protestantism to be nearer the truth than Romanism. D'Amours preaching before the King, when it was known that he had made up his mind to be converted, warned him not to provoke God's judgment by wilfully sinning against light. The Catholic courtiers cried out that such insolence should be punished. "Why," said the King, "what would you have? he has only told me a home truth."

Perhaps Henry still hoped that he might be able to establish his authority while remaining a Protestant. Elizabeth of England had tried the policy

of comprehension; like him a latitudinarian, she had
endeavoured to establish a national Church on so
broad a basis that by degrees both Catholics and
Reformers might, it was hoped, be induced to attend
its services and be able to interpret its doctrine to
their own contentment. This attempt had failed.
The hostility of the Romanists was growing more
and more marked, and there were already signs that
the more logical Protestants would before long as
unequivocally reject the Anglican compromise. In
France, at any rate, it was clear that comprehension
was utterly impossible; and Henry was determined
to adopt the other alternative, toleration.

But then the old principle of the French Monarchy—" one king, one faith, one law "—must be
abandoned, the close connection between Church and
State must be severed or at least relaxed. A State
Church, an established Church, might continue to
exist, and that Church could be none other than the
Roman Church, the Church of the vast majority, but
it would have to be recognised that those who were
not within its pale might be good and loyal members
of the State.

This could perhaps be best brought about if the
King, the personification of the State, the symbol of
national unity, was himself a Protestant, sufficiently
liberal and honest to respect the position and privileges of the Establishment.

If the King was Catholic, the identification of
Church and State would again appear so complete
that heresy might lead to disloyalty, that a man
who rejected the King's creed would not un-

reasonably be suspected of wishing to impair his authority.

Besides it was evident that the Protestant minority must have an organisation—for the government of their Church, if not for self-protection; if the King was a Huguenot he would be the natural head of this body, if he was a Catholic the Protestant community might become a danger to national unity.

The army of the League was so entirely annihilated at Ivry that Mayenne was scarcely able to collect 6,000 men in the course of the next five months. Nor had his partisans been more lucky in other parts of the country. It was noticed by the Royalists as a remarkable and auspicious coincidence that on the very day of the great victory the Leaguers of Auvergne were routed and their leader slain, and an attempt to surprise the garrison of Le Mans defeated.

Henry IV., now that he was undisputed master of the open country, determined to starve the Capital into submission. Even had it appeared an easy thing to take by assault a town defended by a garrison of three or four thousand regular soldiers and ten times as many armed and trained citizens, the King was unwilling to expose his Capital to the horrors of a sack.

When the first panic caused by the news of Ivry was allayed, vigorous preparations were made for the defence of the city. The Spanish ambassador, Mendoza, was foremost in authority and counsel. To him and to his master the defeat of Mayenne was not wholly unwelcome; for the Duke was now com-

HENRY IV.

pelled to lay aside all affectation of independence
and to approach Philip as an humble suppliant, although secretly as determined as ever to play for his
own hand.

Careful inquiry showed that Paris which contained
220,000 inhabitants was provisioned for about a
fortnight.

The King's garrisons commanded the rivers and
roads, but the venality of their officers allowed many
convoys to pass. Eight thousand measures of corn,
10,000 barrels of wine were added to the public stores.
For a month no scarcity need be feared, and long
before then, so the preachers assured their congregations, Parma's matchless veterans would relieve
the Catholic King's "good city," or else God would
raise up a second Jacques Clement to save His
people in the hour of their need. And this perhaps
was the hope on which most reliance was justly
placed, for, as Henry wrote to his mistress, the number of assassins who were persuaded to attempt his
life was scarcely credible. The usual means, processions, placards representing atrocities inflicted by
heretics and Royalists, virulent broad-sheets and
more virulent sermons, were employed to rouse the
fanaticism of the mob. The Sorbonne declared
(May 7th) that even if Charles of Bourbon on his
death-bed were to recognise his nephew as his heir
(the King of the League died in prison two days
later), and Henry abjuring his heresy were absolved
by the Pope, even then he would be incapable of
succeeding to the Crown.

Scarcely had this decision of the Faculty of Theology been promulgated, when the citizens saw from the walls the Royal army, 12,000 foot and 3,000 horse, drawn up in order of battle before the suburbs of St. Antoine and St. Martin. Charenton and all the fortified places in the neighbourhood fell, and although an attack on St. Denis was repulsed, the city was soon closely invested.

Before the beginning of August, although some precarious supplies had found their way through the royal lines, and although the Jesuits and other religious houses had been compelled to produce their private stores, the Parisians had well-nigh exhausted the disgusting though common dietary of famine, rats and other vermin, boiled leather, offal and the like, and were compelled to have recourse to even stranger and more hateful viands. By the advice of the Spanish ambassador bones were collected from the cemeteries, ground down and baked into loaves. But those rarely survived who ate of this so-called "bread of Mme. de Montpensier." That lady herself refused, it was said, 2,000 crowns for her lap-dog, reserving it for her last meal; but on what, meantime, was the animal itself fed? A woman, and she one of the wealthier sort, salted down her infants who had died of starvation, but found in this Thyestean banquet no sustenance, only madness and death. The stomachs or fancy of the lansquenets was less nice, if, as was believed, they carried off and roasted any stray child they met.

On July 24th, the royal army, which had been considerably reinforced, assaulted and carried the suburbs. The walls of the city itself might no doubt

have been stormed, but the King knew the extrem-
ities to which Paris was reduced, and believed it
to be impossible that it should hold out for more
than a few days. The people were daily dying by
hundreds, their corpses lay unburied in the streets,
noisome reptiles, toads and adders, multiplied in the
empty houses. Processions, sermons thrice daily,
the Host permanently exposed on the altars, nay
even Spanish silver could not stay the pangs of starvation. Everywhere the cry, " Peace or Bread," began to be heard. Parma indeed had sent word that
he was preparing to march, and hoped to unite his
forces with those of Mayenne on or before August
15th; but these tidings only increased the popular
despair. Why could not this have been done a
month, two months earlier? In a fortnight more
Paris would no longer be a city of the living, but a
vast charnel house !

To satisfy the people, Nemours and his council
were compelled to send Gondi, the Bishop of Paris,
and Espinac, Archbishop of Lyons, to open negotiations with Henry. Although they styled him King
of Navarre, he received them with courtesy, only re-
marking that their feet would be well scorched in
the next world for so misleading their flocks in this.
But he flatly refused to allow questions concerning
the general settlement of the nation to be mixed up
with a treaty for the capitulation of Paris.

It seemed impossible that the patience of the
citizens could endure for another week ; yet the
siege continued more than twenty days longer.
Henry's humanity prevented his triumph. He al-

lowed many of the starving inhabitants to pass his lines, three or four thousand miserable wretches on one day ; thus exciting the indignation of his good ally, the Queen of England. "If God," she wrote, "shall, by His merciful grace, grant you victory, I swear to you it will be more than your carelessness deserves." He sent presents of food and of dainties to the Princesses, even to his most determined enemy, Mme. de Montpensier, and thus seemed to sanction similar attentions to their friends on the part of the nobles in his camp. The officers and even the private soldiers at the outposts thought it no great harm to sell small quantities of provisions at enormous prices to the starving citizens; an irregularity which it was difficult to check, since the King could not pay his troops and did not choose to bribe them by the prospect of the sack of the great city.

But though such chance supplies might enable the besieged to struggle on a few days longer, Henry IV. was confident that the final catastrophe was none the less inevitable and near. Mayenne, whom he had all but captured on his way to Laon, he did not fear, and he could not believe that Parma would leave the Netherlands and his all but accomplished task, to march to the relief of the League, letting the substance go, to grasp at the shadow, as the Prince himself complained to Philip II.

It was therefore a most unwelcome surprise to the King to hear that the Governor of the Netherlands with 13,000 men had joined the Lieutenant-General of the League at Meaux on August 23d, and that they were marching upon Paris.

La Noue, Bouillon, Henry himself, wished to leave a sufficient force to prevent any convoys of provisions entering the Capital,—the Parisians were so reduced, that it need not be numerous,—and with the rest of the army to take up a strong position at Claie, three leagues from Meaux, thus compelling Farnese either to make a long circuit or to give battle in a position advantageous to his adversaries. In the latter case, there was every hope that a decisive victory would end the war, in the former that before the Spaniards could reach Paris the Royalists would be within the walls.

The Leaguer Villeroy and the Huguenot Aubigné agree that this plan would have been successful. But the strenuous opposition and specious arguments of Marshal Biron induced the King to withdraw his forces from all the posts they occupied round Paris, and to offer battle to Parma in the plain of Bondy.

The forces of the Duke of Parma were about equal to those of the King of France. His Spanish veterans had proved their quality on many a battle-field amid Dutch dykes and swamps, in many a wearisome siege and fiery assault; their stubborn valour and discipline, their rapacious and devilish cruelty were the admiration and the dread of Europe; but to their general this expedition into France was but an episode, and an unwelcome interruption in the great contest to which he had devoted his genius and his life, seeing the resolute countenance and brave array of his opponents, he had no mind to risk in a pitched battle the army without which he could not hope to attain the object of his ambition. When he found himself confronted by the French army he took up a position which was soon made too strong for attack by the labour of his men, trained like the Roman legionaries to the use of pick and spade. Henry IV., following the usage of feudal warfare, sent a herald to offer battle. Parma replied, that he would fight when and where it was convenient to him and not before. Five days the armies remained opposite each other. Then by some skilful manœuvres Farnese threw part of his forces across the river, and taking Lagny, opened the navigation of the Marne. Convoys of provisions were now pouring into Paris, the King in vain attempted to lure or compel the Spaniards to fight. The royal army melted away. Henry did what, under the circumstances, was probably the best he could. He distributed his mercenaries as garrisons in the towns near Paris, and himself retired into the Beauvaisis with the most faithful of his friends and a small force composed mainly of cavalry.

On September 18th Mayenne entered Paris, but the past sufferings had been too severe, the future was too threatening for the sight of the Prince who called himself their deliverer to excite any enthusiasm among the inhabitants. Parma also visited the city he had relieved. But he pleased few. He humiliated Mayenne, making him feel that the Lieutenant-General of the Crown of France must not presume to think himself the equal of the Lieutenant of the King of Spain. Even those Leaguers who were not unwilling to be the servants of Philip were disgusted when

they found that the doubloons earned by their subservience were not forthcoming. The Parisians bitterly complained that the Spaniard did not clear all
the neighbourhood of the Royalist garrisons. Parma
did indeed take Provins and one or two small places
and next attacked Corbeil, but Corbeil resisted for
three weeks and the siege cost the lives of many of
his veterans. A few more such captures and his
army would be undone. Deaf therefore to the
entreaties of his allies and the outcries of the citizens
the Italian marched away, compelling Mayenne to
accompany him, pursued and harassed as far as the
Belgian frontier by the King and his horsemen.

No sooner had the Spaniards turned their backs
than Paris was once more surrounded on every side
by hostile garrisons. Yet two things had been
achieved by Farnese. He had proved to Mayenne
that he was powerless without Spanish help and he
had prevented Henry from entering his capital a conqueror and a Protestant. Yet it may well be doubted
whether he would have accomplished even so much,
but for the fatal advice of Biron. The Marshal was
determined to prolong the Civil War, that work-shop,
as La Noue terms it, of every iniquity detestable to
honest folk, but also, as Biron conceived, the work-
shop in which the edifice of his fortunes might be
completed. What to such as he was the ruin of their
country, the unutterable misery of thousands, compared with the satisfaction of their ambition?

Paris continued to be hemmed in by the royal garrisons. Provisions became ever scantier and dearer,
and strange diseases, the result of privation and un-

natural food, decimated the population.  Trade and
industry had ceased.  The colleges of the University
were deserted.  Desolate streets and empty houses
bore witness to the sufferings of a town which even
then owed much of its prosperity to the visitors who
were attracted by the fame of the gayest and most
pleasure-loving capital in Western Europe.  But an
unsuccessful attempt to surprise one of the gates was
made the pretext for introducing a Spanish garrison
sufficient to guard the city against the despair of its
inhabitants as well as against assault.

As Philip II. had previously embarked on the Invincible Armada the men and treasures which would
have completed the conquest of the Netherlands, so
he now left Parma to struggle with insufficient
resources against Prince Maurice, while he poured his
soldiers into France.  Four or five thousand Spaniards were sent into Brittany.  The wife of the Duke
of Mercœur, the Leaguist governor of that province,
was descended in the female line from the old ducal
House, and Mercœur had counted on Breton love of
independence for support in a struggle against a
prince in whose veins there ran no drop of the blood
of the Duchess Anne; but he was soon so hard pressed
by the Prince of Dombes, the chief of the Loyalists,
that he had been compelled to beg for help from
Philip II.  No sooner had the Spaniards landed than
Queen Elizabeth, who could not allow the Breton
ports to fall into the hands of Spain, sent 3,000 English to the assistance of the King's forces and Brittany
became the scene of a tedious war, little connected
with military operations in other parts of France, in

which English and Spaniards consulted rather their own interests than those of their native allies.

In Languedoc also the League had been unable to hold their own against the Duke of Montmorency without foreign help, and a small Spanish army of 4,000 men garrisoned Toulouse.

The Duke of Savoy, who had crossed the frontier as the champion of orthodoxy, was making rapid progress in Provence; he had been received with royal honours by the Parliament of Aix; had entered Marseilles and scarcely concealed the ambitious hope of reconstructing the Burgundian kingdom, a name applied at different times to states of very various extent, but embracing at least Provence, Dauphiné and the country between the Saone and Jura as well as Savoy and much of south-western Switzerland.

On all sides the neighbours of France were preparing to divide the spoils of the expiring monarchy, while the Spaniard was determined that the lion's share should be his.

The death of Sixtus V. (August 27, 1590), violent fanatic though he was, and the election of Gregory XIV. added to the difficulties of Henry IV. For Sixtus, though he hated heresy much, hated Spain more. Not long before his death he had been heard to say that Elizabeth of England and Henry of Navarre were the only sovereigns living to whom, had they not been heretics, he would have disclosed the great projects he meditated, and he had not concealed his displeasure that his legate Caëtano allowed himself to be the tool of the Spanish faction in Paris. One of the most ardent preachers of the League announcing from the pulpit the death of God's vicar, thanked Him for delivering Christendom from a "wicked and political Pope."

But the opposition of open enemies was perhaps not the greatest difficulty against which Henry had to contend. His Catholic supporters began to question the sincerity of the often repeated promise to receive instruction. If he was in earnest, why, it was asked, defer a step so advantageous to his interests? If a dozen bishops and divines could not supply sufficient learning to enlighten the royal conscience, would the more tumultuous theology of a council suffice?

The Huguenots, on the other hand, complained that it profited them nothing that a King of their own faith and supported by their arms had ascended the throne; their condition had been better during the last reign. Now, if three families met together to pray for the King's prosperity, if a citizen sang a psalm in his shop, or had among his wares a French bible or psalter, they were punished as criminals by the Royal Courts.

The Princes of the King's own family sought to profit by the general discontent. A letter was intercepted addressed to the Pope by the Cardinal of Bourbon, the brother of the late Prince of Condé, in which he excused himself for having hitherto adhered to the King of Navarre. He had done so in the confident hope of his conversion. But as he was now convinced that this hope was futile and that the head of his house was an obstinate heretic, incapable of reigning, he begged the Holy Father to assist him in establishing his right to the succession. His elder brother, the Prince of Conty, might indeed seem to have a prior claim, but he was deaf, as well as deficient in mental and bodily vigour. The Cardinal indeed was himself little better than imbecile; but his abler brother, the Count of Soissons, had joined in the intrigue to which many of those about the King were more or less privy, even his mistress, the Countess of Grammont.

Soissons, after fighting valiantly by his cousin's side at Coutras, had been encouraged to hope for the hand of the King's sister Catherine. The match was a brilliant one for a poorly endowed younger son, and the Princess herself was well worthy of a disinterested attachment. But Henry changed his mind and told Soissons that he must look elsewhere for a wife. The lovers thought that after he had himself brought them together the King had no right to insist upon their separation, and Mme. de Grammont, to whose care Henry had entrusted his sister, permitted or encouraged their correspondence, and listened to Soissons's schemes even when stretched beyond the bounds of loyalty. Perhaps she thus sought to avenge herself for the more frequent infidelities and the growing coldness of her lover.

Henry IV. had a pretty gift of writing love letters, in which Jove might have found matter for perennial laughter; and he was rarely wise enough to be off with the old love before he was on with the new, a want of prudence which was the source of much vexatious and undignified embarrassment.

Down to the end of 1590 he continued to write to Corisande with his usual protestations of eternal fidelity, kissing her fair eyes a million times and omitting none of the common forms of epistolary fervour, yet in the summer of the same year—not to mention more commonplace gallantries—he had been ardently courting a lady, who remained unmoved by an offer of marriage even though written in his blood, and by the well-known letter sent on the eve of an expected battle with Parma. " My mistress, I am writing this line to you the night before a battle. The issue is in God's hands, who has already ordained what it shall be, and what He knows to be for His glory and for the good of my people. If I lose it you will never again see me; for I am not the man to turn my back. Yet this I can assure you, that if I die, my last thought will be of God, to whose mercy I commit both you and myself; my last but one of you."

This Platonic infidelity to his Corisande was notorious; not less notorious the intrigues with the abbesses of Poissy and Montmartre which had relieved the tedium of the blockade of Paris. Mme. de Grammont, perhaps was conscious that she had become elderly, bloated, and red, and her coldly sceptical annotations on letters written two years earlier remain to show how little she was the dupe of her royal lover's professed constancy—a constancy he declared so great that it was a perpetual marvel to himself. She probably felt that her tenure of the official position of mistress was very precarious, and hoped by serving the ambition of the

younger Bourbons and the affections of Catherine
of Navarre to make herself friends who might receive her, if abandoned by the King.

Henry IV. on discovering the intrigue contented
himself with summoning his cousins to attend him,
trusting while they were under his eye to be able to
prevent any further treachery, and it is possible he
might have continued to throw himself at Corisande's feet and to kiss her hands—at least on paper
—had not a new passion led him to seize so decent
a pretext for ending a now irksome connection.

During the campaign of 1590 Bellegarde, a favourite officer, asked his master as they were passing by
Cœuvres, the seat of Antoine d'Estrées, to visit a
daughter of that gentleman whom he was courting.
The King went, and found that even a lover's tongue
had done scanty justice to the charms of Gabrielle.
No sooner had he left her presence, than he felt that
he must at all risks return; but Cœuvres was surrounded by parties of the enemy. Prudence and
dignity were laid aside; disguised as a wood-cutter, a
bundle of straw on his head, the King of France
found his way to the feet of his mistress. At first
she laughed at the swarthy, grizzled, hook nosed little
man who aspired to be the favoured rival of the brilliant Bellegarde, a model of manly beauty. But she
was dazzled by the splendid prospect of becoming
the acknowledged mistress of the King, and Henry
profuse in promise was scarcely less liberal in
performance.

To save appearances Gabrielle was married to a
M. de Liancourt, a widower with eleven children, so

ugly and elderly that he was not likely to provoke comparisons unfavourable to the King. To the young lady this was the least satisfactory part of the arrangement, and after the King had publicly acknowledged her first child, the superfluous husband was got rid of by an indecent divorce.

Mme. de Liancourt was successively created Marchioness of Monceaux and Duchess of Beaufort. The portraits of the fair Gabrielle scarcely justify the extravagant terms in which contemporaries celebrate her beauty; and some scepticism is perhaps justified when we reflect that during her lifetime there was every motive to flatter the all powerful favourite, and that when dead she became a legend.

When, in her twentieth year, Gabrielle first met the King, her figure, although already too mature, was exquisitely proportioned. Her complexion was fair and brilliant, her golden hair contrasted with dark, well pencilled eyebrows, and long lashes shadowing blue eyes, which though soft were bright and lively. Her regular and placid features—whose rare beauty, says Aubigné, was free from all wantonness—suggested a candid and virginal innocence strangely inconsistent with the scandals reported of her youthful depravity. These stories, too vile to bear repetition, were probably false, but the reputation of her family was thoroughly bad. Her mother, a woman of no character, was one of a house notorious for gallantry. She and her sisters had been known as the seven deadly sins.

It is not therefore surprising, that the virtue of Gabrielle was not of a kind to take alarm at the

bargain by which she passed into the King's possession, nor even sufficient to induce her to mitigate
the shame of it by observing from the first an inviolable fidelity to her royal lover. The King's
letters prove that Bellegarde at any rate continued
to be a not unfavoured rival.

" The influence your eyes have on me," he writes
on one occasion, " saved you from half my re.
proaches. But if I had known what I have since
learnt of my rival's visit, I should not have seen you,
but have broken with you for good. . . . What
more can you promise than you have already promised? What oath can you swear that you have not
twice broken ? " It is characteristic that Henry ends
his, no doubt just, complaints by protesting that he
would give four years of his life to reach his mistress
as soon as his letter, and that a few days later he
should thank her for the gift of her likeness in such
terms as these : " I am writing to you, my dear love,
at the foot of your picture, which I worship because
it is meant for you, not because it is like you. I am
a competent judge, since you are painted in all
perfection in my soul, in my heart, in my eyes."

Men who allow themselves the grossest licence
not unfrequently expect their women to attain to an
almost ideal standard of constancy and purity.
Henry was less exacting. His experience of married
life had taught him to give and take in such matters;
and Gabrielle, though not a woman of much ability
—her prayer-book was her whole library,—knew how
to flatter the King, " the bravest man in all the
world," as she called him ; she protested that the

least of his sufferings was mortal to her. " I am the Princess Constance," she writes, " full of feeling for what concerns you, insensible to all the world besides."

On the whole, and compared with the intrigues which caused much of the disquiet and sadly tarnished the glory of Henry's later years, his connection with Gabrielle d'Estrées was neither harmful to the State nor disgraceful to himself. Even austere Calvinists commended her modestly dignified behaviour, " that of a wife rather than of a concubine," and occupying a position most exposed to envy and malevolence she yet made few enemies.

Urged on the one hand by the Catholics to abjure his heresy, and on the other by the Protestants to make their condition under a king of their own faith more tolerable, the King determined upon one more effort to crush his enemies by force of arms, before attempting a final settlement of questions with which as a victor he would be able to deal more satisfactorily. To quiet the impatience of the Huguenots he meantime revoked such edicts as had been extorted from Henry III. by the League, and declared those of 1577 and 1580 to be still in force; while he endeavoured to allay the apprehensions of the Catholics by reiterating his promise to " receive instruction," and his firm determination to maintain the Catholic and Apostolic Church in all her dignity and privileges. He at the same time pointed out that religion was but the pretext under which his foreign and domestic enemies were pursuing the ruin and partition of the kingdom.

By assembling a strong army of regular troops, composed for the most part of foreign and Protestant mercenaries, the King trusted to avoid two of the difficulties which had hitherto prevented him from reaping the full advantage of his victories. The one was that of keeping the nobles and gentlemen who served as volunteers in the field during a protracted campaign or siege; the other was that which arose from the determination of many of his Catholic supporters that he should not be too easily successful and thus escape the necessity of abjuration.

Turenne, ably seconded by the arguments of an English embassy, was sent to the Protestant Courts of Germany, and when he returned at the head of 6,000 German Reiters and 10,000 lansquenets, he had fairly earned the reward of the staff of marshal and of the hand of the heiress of the La Marks, in her own right Duchess of Bouillon and sovereign Princess of Sedan.

Elizabeth also, urged by Walsingham and by Essex, forgot her wonted parsimony, and 6,000 men well supplied with artillery and with all the materials of war landed under the command of the favourite at Dieppe.

The English Queen once more asked for Calais as the price of her assistance; but to this demand Henry would not listen. It was as bad, he said, to be eaten by the lioness as by the lion; and whatever his enemies might do he would not buy the throne by partitioning the kingdom over which he aspired to rule. Like the true mother in Solomon's judgment, rather than receive part of a

mangled corpse, he would altogether forego the possession of his own.

He employed the spring and early summer of
1591 in reducing Chartres and other places in the
neighbourhood of Paris while his captains attacked
the towns held by the League in Normandy.  Before
the end of the summer, the double crosses of the
League floated only over the walls of Havre and
Rouen.

The Parisians were again sorely straitened for
food.  Mayenne was execrated for allowing Chartres,
the granary of Paris, to fall into the hands of the
enemy.  The preachers had promised their congregations that no such triumph should ever be granted
to the wicked.  Should this happen, exclaimed one
fanatic, might the devil have his soul—but no, never
would the Bearnese, that dog heretic and tyrant,
take Chartres.

Mayenne had summoned a meeting of the Estates-
General at Rheims, but on the day fixed so few representatives appeared that no attempt was made to
hold a sitting.  Yet clearly, unless the succession
was settled, a pretender to the throne selected and
recognised, the opposition to Henry IV. could not
be continued.

The King of Spain was urgent that the claim of
his daughter should be at once acknowledged.  He
was assured by the Sixteen and by the extreme party
that nothing could delight them more than that he
should reign over them; if that might not be, then
they and all good Catholics would be the loyal subjects of the Infanta and of any son-in-law it might

please his Majesty to choose.    The letters in which
the faction expressed their devotion to Philip II.
were intercepted by the Royalists and forwarded by
the King to Mayenne.    The Lieutenant-General of
the League was already sufficiently perplexed by
the escape from prison of his nephew, the young
Duke of Guise, whom he dreaded as his most
dangerous rival.    Guise, as the son of their martyred
hero, was highly popular with the Catholic mob,
and his marriage with the Infanta and election as
King by the Estates might have united the supporters of the House of Lorraine, the Spaniards and
the democratic party, and have reduced the Lieutenant-General of the League to insignificance.

Mayenne was therefore scarcely less anxious than
Henry IV. to prevent the marriage of his nephew
with the Spanish Princess.    His wisest and most
staunch adviser, Jeannin, began to urge what Villeroy
had seen from the beginning : that the League could
be maintained only by Spanish help.  "We cannot,"
he said, "do otherwise than ascribe to the King of
Spain the credit and gratitude due for our existence,
but the payment which he demands involves the
sacrifice of the independence and future of France."
He therefore maintained that Mayenne ought to
conclude an arrangement on the best terms possible
with Henry of Navarre.    The King's conversion indeed might be insisted upon, but, if this essential
point was secured, further resistance would be both
foolish and criminal.

The Duke affected to be convinced by the arguments of his followers, but was none the less de-

termined to let matters drift, careless, provided he could glut his selfish greed, whether France became Spanish or perished, the prey of more ignoble domestic enemies.

Meantime the sympathy of all decent citizens in Paris had been alienated by the violence of the fanatics, who, trusting to the support of the considerable Spanish garrison, had established a reign of terror, and appealed although in vain to popular passion. Privation, famine and pestilence had so broken the spirit of the mob, that not even the highly spiced invectives of the preachers and the prospect of licence and plunder could arouse it to acts of violence.

By the sale of Crown lands and of much of his private domain, the King had raised a considerable sum of money for the expenses of the campaign. He was joined in September by the English commanded by Essex, and on the last day of the month he met, in the valley of the Aisne, the Reiters and lansquenets of Turenne, led by the Prince of Anhalt. In November he undertook the siege of Rouen with an army composed of between 5,000 and 6,000 English, as many Swiss, 14,000 Germans and only 5,000 French—an army of Protestants and mercenaries. The capture of Rouen, the second town in the kingdom, would have made him absolute master of Normandy and of north-western France, would have dealt a fatal blow to the League, and have compelled the Parisians to acknowledge the authority of a heretic king. Unfortunately Henry was compelled to allow the Catholic nobles to occupy the most important posts in his army; had he not done so, it would have been said, that trusting none but heretics he obviously intended the ruin of the Church. As it was, the success of the King's plans was made to depend on the co-operation of men who were determined that they should not succeed : the baser, like old Biron, till their greed was gorged; the less self-seeking, till, by his conversion, he had pledged himself to maintain the established religion.

Now, when their services would have been of inestimable value, Henry must sorely have missed two men, so greatly trusted and respected both by Calvinists and Romanists that their employment would have given umbrage to none. La Noue, whose noble character and Christian resignation to the indignities and sufferings inflicted on him in his Flemish prison by the mean rancour of Philip II., had stirred the sympathy of the cold and pitiless Parma, whose integrity even Catherine de' Medici had not doubted, whose disinterestedness no temptation had ever shaken, who had been as unsparing of his fortune as of his blood in the service of his religion and of his country, who, keenly sensible of the pleasures of retirement, of study and family life, had spent his years hurrying from battle-field to battle-field—La Noue, the Protestant Bayard, without fear and without reproach, had fallen in August (1591) before Lamballe in Brittany. The day before his death, gathering a spray of laurel, and handing it to a kinsman he had said: " There, cousin, is all the reward that you and I may expect."

Scarely less lamented or less honoured by friends

and foes, Châtillon, Coligny's son, had died, consumed, so it was reported, by disappointment and melancholy, shortly after his skill as an engineer had compelled the surrender of Chartres. His house of Châtillon had been pillaged, his young brother D'Andelot had been taken prisoner, and, seduced by the caresses of the Guises, had forgotten his cause, his religion and his father's blood. His son, a mere child, had fallen fighting against the Spaniards in Holland. His services had been requited by neglect, although the King with ready tears lamented the worth he had slighted when living. "Alas! I loved him well; he should have opened his heart to me and it would have been my study to content him."

Biron, who had been sent to open the siege of Rouen in November, delayed the attack on the ill-fortified town and citadel until the Governor, Villars, a man prepared to sell himself to the highest bidder, but who, to enhance his price, was determined to give no ambiguous proofs of his valour and capacity, had had ample time to complete his preparations. Great stores had been accumulated. The old walls had been strengthened and new fortifications added on every side. All useless mouths and all who were suspected of royalism had been sent out of the city, and everything done to raise the spirits and confirm the resolution of those who remained.

Never would the citizens of Rouen acknowledge a heretic as King of France; such was the answer to the herald who bade them open their gates to their rightful sovereign; and this temper was sustained by constant processions, solemn oaths to resist to the death, fiery sermons and eloquent decrees of the Parliament, and lest these should not suffice, by gibbets prepared in all public places for the traitors who first spoke of treaty or surrender.

It was a perilous venture to begin the siege of a strongly garrisoned and well provisioned city in November. Yet it is possible that, had Biron not been wanting in loyalty or resolution, the city might have been carried by an immediate assault: in any case, the King was compelled to use an army which his finances could not maintain in idleness. Unfortunately the winter proved exceptionally severe. The trenches could scarcely be dug in the frozen ground; sickness and privations decimated the besiegers. Before the end of the year, Mornay had to be sent to beg for further help from Elizabeth.

The old Queen was in no pleasant mood. She complained that her men had been recklessly exposed, that they had borne more than their share of the hardships and privations of the siege; out of 5,000 barely 600 survived. Henceforth she would only assist the King of France with her prayers. She was highly indignant with Essex for not coming back when summoned and for exposing himself in the trenches. As for the King himself, his recklessness was incurable—apparently he wished to be killed, yet he must know that everything depended on his life. She even blamed the revocation of the edicts against the Protestants as impolitic.

The United Provinces were less easily discouraged —Parma might as well be fought in France as in the Netherlands. Early in January a Dutch squadron brought 3,000 men and large supplies up the Seine, and the losses of the besiegers were more than made up by the numerous French Royalists who hurried to the King's standard, when it was known that Farnese was assembling his forces for the relief of Rouen.

By the end of January, Parma and Mayenne had met and were advancing through Ponthieu. The King, who had been pushing the siege with indomitable energy, endeavouring by his personal exertions to remedy all that was done amiss or left undone by Biron, believed himself strong enough to hold the allies in check without breaking up his leaguer.

Leaving the Marshal with his infantry before Rouen, he advanced to meet the Spaniards with 3,000 Reiters, 2,000 French horsemen, and 2,000 dragoons, a name then first given to troops who were used as mounted infantry.

Near the little town of Aumâle he met the enemy 23,000 or 24,000 strong, and when himself leading a reconnaissance, was surrounded by a much larger force of cavalry. Speedy flight would have ensured his safety, but he persisted in charging to cover the retreat of his escort ; he was wounded by a ball which pierced the bow of his saddle, and was only saved from capture or death by the devotion of those around him and by the caution of Parma, who checked the pursuit, since he was convinced that the King of France would not have ventured so boldly unless supported by a considerable force. When he learnt what an opportunity he had lost, he exclaimed in his vexation that he had supposed himself to be fighting

against a general and not a guerilla chief.   In little
more than a week Henry was again in the saddle,
harassing the advance of the Leaguers, cutting off
their parties and beating up their quarters.   On
February 17th he attacked their camp by night, carrying off much booty and many prisoners.   Among
the latter the Count of Chaligny, a prince of the
House of Lorraine, was captured by Chicot, the
Court jester, a Gascon of sense and courage as well
as of merry wit.   " Here, Henriot," he said, bringing
his prize to the King, " is a present for you."   The
Count, enraged at the tone and quality of his captor,
struck him so violently on the head with the pommel
of his sword that Chicot never jested again.

The King's energy so delayed the advance of
Parma, that it was not till the end of February that
he found himself within striking distance of Rouen.
But Biron, instead of pressing the siege with energy,
had allowed himself to be surprised by Villars in
a furious sally on February 24th.   The Royalists lost 800 men, their ammunition and mines
were destroyed, their batteries overthrown, and
many of the guns triumphantly dragged into the
town.   The old Marshal himself was wounded
Parma might have now entered Rouen, but Villars
and Mayenne were so elated, that they trusted to
hold the town without the assistance of a Spanish
garrison.   More than one intercepted despatch of
Mendoza and Tassis had been forwarded to Mayenne
by Henry IV., and their contents had increased the
fear and suspicion with which he regarded his allies.
This jealousy of Parma perhaps counterbalanced

the injury done to the royal cause by the half-hearted
service of Biron.   But when Farnese fell back to the
Somme, the people of Rouen found that they had
been premature in thanking their patron Saint for
delivering them out of the hand of the Heretic, who,
after repairing and strengthening his works, was
again pressing the siege in person.   Elizabeth, less
bitter since the safe return of Essex, and moved
perhaps by her favourite's report of Henry's romantic admiration of the Virgin Queen, a topic on
which he never failed to dilate with Gascon emphasis
in her subject's presence, sent timely reinforcements,
while the Dutch fleet prevented any supplies reaching the town by water.

Urgent messages came from Villars to Mayenne
and Parma: unless relieved by April 20th he must
capitulate.

In four days the Spanish general marched from
the Somme to the Seine.   The King of France had
dismissed his cavalry; his infantry was scattered in
the towns round Rouen, where they had been
quartered to recover from the sufferings of the
winter.   Henry himself was at Dieppe when he
received the news that Parma was again marching
on Rouen (April 19th).   He at once flung himself on
his horse and rode without drawing rein till he
reached the camp.   It was midnight, but he found
his men already in full retreat.   Nor could he blame
the resolution of his captains.   It would have been
madness to attempt to hold their extended lines
against such an enemy as Parma, and when threatened both in rear and front by far superior forces.

The King determined that he would at any rate fall back no farther than was absolutely necessary. He took up a strong position three leagues from Rouen, and there awaited the feudal militia he had already summoned to his standard, and the troops dispersed in the neighbouring towns. On the next day 1,500 of the Norman gentry rode into camp, and before the week was out (April 26th) he was once more at the head of 18,000 infantry and 6,000 cavalry. Meanwhile Parma and Mayenne had destroyed the siege works, entered Rouen in triumph, reinforced the garrison and relieved the necessities of the inhabitants. Parma wished to attack the King at once before he had collected his forces; but Mayenne persisted that Rouen was only half relieved so long as the Royalists held Caudebec and commanded the navigation of the river. Caudebec accordingly was invested on the 24th of April and surrendered on the 26th. Parma, while directing the attack, had been wounded in the arm. Without changing countenance he continued to point out how his batteries should be placed. But his physical endurance was not equal to his courage; high fever set in, and he was obliged to leave the command to Mayenne, who, as soon as Caudebec had surrendered, took up his quarters at Ivetot, a few miles to the north.

When the King found himself at the head of an army superior in numbers to the enemy, he marched round their rear and threatened their communications with Hâvre and Lillebonne. Constant engagements were fought from April 28th to May 9th in which the Royalists had the upper hand. The supplies of the confederates were intercepted, and they were reduced to extreme want.

The King's hopes ran high—with a wide tidal river, commanded by the Dutch fleet, in their rear, either his enemies must starve or. they must attempt to force their way to Picardy or Rouen and give battle to an army superior in numbers, and which was daily growing. Surely, he said, they were delivered into his hands. But he forgot the ill-will of his own captains and the genius of his opponent. Parma, though his weak constitution was still suffering from the pain and fever of his wound, left his bed and during the night of May 10th led his army back towards Caudebec. Henry IV. fell on the retreating Spaniards, while Biron attacked Mayenne's French. The Leaguers were thrown into such confusion that the younger Biron engaged, if his father would give him 800 horse, to complete the rout. " What," shouted the Marshal with an oath, " would you send us back to plant cabbages at Biron ? " As he turned away the young man muttered that, were he the King, his father's head would not long remain on his shoulders. But even so, enclosed as he was by superior forces and by a river as broad as an arm of the sea, there was, Henry supposed, no escape for Parma.

But the Italian strategist while tossing in the fever of his wound had formed the plan which he now proceeded to carry into execution. For some days all available boats, rafts and pontoons had been collected by his orders at Rouen, and on the night of the 12th were sent down with the ebb tide to Caudebec. Before morning dawned the greater part of the

Catholic army had already crossed to the southern bank of the river.  Their cavalry and the guns of a hastily constructed fort kept the King's horse at a distance from the place of embarkment till the remaining infantry and artillery had been ferried across.  Then the Catholic horse retreated along the river bank to Rouen with such speed that the Royalists could not intercept them.

But although Farnese had accomplished a feat which raised to a still greater height his reputation as the first general of that century, he was far from having extricated himself from danger.  The King had, even yet, a chance of annihilating his opponents. They could not shut themselves up in Rouen, which was but scantily provisioned.  Henry IV. saw that it was possible for him to send his 8,000 cavalry across the Seine at Pont de l'Arche to break down the bridges across the Eure, and delay the advance of the Catholics until he should have time to throw himself with his infantry between his enemies and Paris.  But his generals protested that Parma had too great a start, that pursuit was useless.  The Swiss and some of the Germans refused to move till they had received their arrears of pay, conduct so much in accordance with the usual practice of these hirelings, that we need not suppose it to have been suggested to them by the traitors in the royal camp.

Farnese, suffering from his wound and from his constitutional ill-health, hurried on past Paris, leaving 1,500 Walloons to reinforce the Spanish garrison, and reached the Netherlands with an army reduced to half its numbers by sickness or the sword.

The subsidies of the Dutch had been well invested. Mayenne, who had gained little honour in the campaign, lay sick of an illness caused by debauchery at Rouen.

But the King was in no position to profit by the weakness of his enemies. His treasury was empty. He could not pay his Swiss and German mercenaries; and without pay they would serve no longer. The French nobles and gentlemen hurried to their homes, as their custom was after a campaign. It therefore only remained for him to dismiss with gracious words his English and Dutch allies, and to abandon the hope, so nearly realised, of crushing his opponents and of entering his capital, the master of his kingdom on his own terms.

In all parts of the country from Languedoc to Lorraine, and from Savoy to Brittany, the civil war dragged on during the summer, on the whole to the advantage of the Royalists. But the most marked result was the increased misery and devastation of the country, and that everywhere the Leaguers became more and more dependent on the money and men of Spain, and therefore more and more the obsequious clients of Philip II.

The death of Marshal Biron before Epernay, delivered the King from the exorbitant pretensions of a man whom he could not afford to offend, and whose insatiable vanity and selfish ambition made his great parts, improved though they were by study and knowledge of books, as well as by a wide experience of camps and courts, of little use to the cause he served, or to his country.

# CHAPTER VI.

## THE KING GOES TO MASS AND ENTERS PARIS.

### 1592–1595.

THE great hopes founded by Henry on the powerful army which had been so painfully collected, were baffled. Rouen and Paris had been snatched from his grasp. Yet it is not true that after a struggle of two years, after heroic exertions and brilliant victories, the King was in no better position than before Ivry.

Frenchmen had at least learnt to know what manner of man it was who claimed their allegiance as the legitimate heir of St. Lewis. His gay and chivalrous valour, his jovial wit, his genial affability, which, free from all condescension, rather raised those to whom it was shown than lowered him who showed it, his marvellous placability, his humanity, his ready sympathy, nay his very vices recommended him to his countrymen. Even the most credulous must have smiled when they heard Henry of Bourbon inveighed against from the pulpit, as a merciless and fanatical tyrant!

In Paris the Moderates at length began to stir. In the previous year (1590) Mayenne himself had broken the power of the fanatical faction. The Parliament, although composed of those members who had refused to follow their more loyal brethren when they seceded from the rebellious capital, had never entirely forgotten the conservative traditions of their profession; and, by acquitting a lawyer accused of royalist proclivities, aroused the anger of the " Sixteen." The people, they exclaimed, must seek by the dagger that justice which was denied in the law courts. Lists of the proscribed were prepared. Brisson, the first President of the Parliament, a jurist of European reputation, and two other magistrates of high position and character were seized, dragged before a tumultuary and illegal tribunal, and hurriedly executed. But the mob listened with apathy to the wild and inflammatory harangues of preachers and demagogues. So unusual was such moderation on the part of the excitable and violent populace of Paris, that in L'Estoile's opinion it could only be ascribed to an extraordinary and singular mercy of God.

Not only the Politicians, but all Leaguers who had any sense of humanity and justice, called upon the Lieutenant-General to put an end to the tyranny of a handful of murderers and fanatics.

Mayenne had no love for a faction which was devoted to Spain and which would gladly have assisted the young Duke of Guise to supplant him. He hurried to Paris, obtained possession of the Bastille, seized and executed four of the most active members of the Sixteen. Others not less guilty saved themselves by flight. An oath of obedience to the Lieutenant-General of the Union and to the Parliament, until the Estates should have elected an orthodox King, was imposed on all.

The vigour shown on this occasion by Mayenne, gave him for the moment an appearance of strength, yet it was but the appearance. He was hated by the fanatics, suspected by the Spaniards, neither liked nor trusted by the Moderates; he was supported only by a few personal followers, and by some ambitious nobles who hoped, by adhering to him, to sell themselves, when the time came, at a higher price to the King.

All this had happened while the royal forces were gathering round Rouen; and since then the desire for peace and weariness of clerical and Spanish domination had been growing. In the autumn of 1592 the Politicians and the more moderate Leaguers made the scarcity of provisions and the cessation of all trade a pretext for holding meetings to consider how the war might be ended and the sufferings of the people alleviated. A large majority were in favour of "summoning" the King of Navarre to abjure his heresy, and of endeavouring in the meantime to conclude some form of truce which would allow supplies to reach the capital.

Mayenne in alarm collected what troops he could, and came to Paris, where the Spaniards assisted him in preventing a step which would have amounted to an engagement to recognise Henry as soon as he should "receive instruction." Hitherto the accepted doctrine of the League had been, that as a relapsed heretic he had forfeited all claim to the throne, and that no simulated conversion, nor even the papal absolution itself, could relieve him from this disability.

Mayenne had promised to the Spaniards that the Estates should meet and settle the succession in the first months of the new year (1593). Philip II. had determined, if possible, to secure the Crown for the Infanta in her own right, or, if that might not be, as the wife of a prince, to be chosen by him and elected by the representatives of the nation. To obtain this end he intended that the Estates should meet in the presence of an irresistible Spanish army.

Parma was determined that if the thing must be done it should not be done by halves. If he must again abandon the war against the Dutch, to intervene in France, he would perform his task so thoroughly that it should need no repetition.

During the summer he had been recovering from his wound and nursing his constitutional infirmities at Spa. In the late autumn he ordered his Spanish and Italian veterans, his lansquenets and Walloon men-at-arms to assemble at Arras. He intended to enter Paris, where a palace was being prepared for him, at the head of an irresistible force, and to impose his master's will on Mayenne and the Estates, while he earned the gratitude of the citizens by driving the royal garrisons out of the neighbouring towns. This venture, at any rate, little as he approved of it, would not, like the invasion of England, be at the mercy of fickle winds and waves.

But fate can baffle men in many ways, and on December 3d, Alexander Farnese lay dead at Arras. His army dispersed: he had only been able to pay it by pledging his personal credit; for the master of Mexico and Peru was once more a bankrupt.

The Duke of Feria, with a few troops and a scanty supply of money, was left to attempt a task which the prestige and resources of Parma might hardly have accomplished.

The death of the great Italian was welcome news to Mayenne. Now he trusted to find Philip II. less stiff. Now he could look forward with less apprehension to the meeting of the Estates. Now he felt confident that, if the Spaniards did not close with the terms he offered, he would be able to hold matters in suspense till he compelled the King to purchase peace at a price which would entail the division of France into provinces ruled by hereditary governors, as independent of the Crown as the great feudatories of the 10th and 11th centuries.

The States-General were summoned to meet in January (1593). The partisans of Spain and the League were active in endeavouring to secure the return of their friends. "They say," the preachers exclaimed, "the Béarnese will go to Mass; so will a dog. Credulous blockheads! Don't you see the old wolf is only foxing, in the hope of eating the sheep? But go to! our good Politicians love this *Ventre St. Gris.* He is a spark to their taste, for they are swine whose bellies he has promised to fill. Good God! it is a fearful thing to imagine that there should be any peace possible with a bastard such

as he is, a heretic, a relapsed miscreant, a devil!"
But diatribes such as this excited only disgust, except
among the dregs of the mob, who lived on the doles
of the convents and the largess of the Spaniards.

On January 26 (1593), the representatives met in
the hall of the Louvre, to decide, so Mayenne assured them, the weightiest matter ever laid before
the Council of the nation.   At this first session there
were only 60 members present and among them
no representatives of the nobility.   When, afterwards, the deputies of the more distant towns and
provinces had arrived, the greatest number who
ever sat was only 128, among whom  there were but
24 nobles.   The lay Estates of the South-western
and Central  Provinces did not send a single representative.   According to Villeroy, those who came
were for the most part factious and needy men,
enemies of the public peace, elected for the express
purpose of supporting the designs of the Spaniards.
Such is the evidence of a Leaguer ; the Royalist De
Serre says that they were seditious and corrupt
fellows chosen from the very dregs of the people.
So contemptible in numbers and composition was
the Assembly which was summoned to subvert the
fundamental laws of the kingdom and to disinherit
the rightful heir of St. Lewis.   Yet a majority of
the representatives of Paris belonged to the moderate
party in the League, nor does the conduct of the
Estates generally appear to merit such uncompromising condemnation.   They showed some signs of
patriotism, some desire of peace, some wish to
escape the domination of Spain.

The Clerical and Spanish party suffered a defeat on the first question decided by the Estates. Mayenne had invited the Catholic nobles and Princes of the King's party to abandon an obstinate heretic, and to join the representatives of the people in bestowing the crown on a Catholic king. They had replied by proposing that the Estates should send envoys to a conference to be held at some place between Paris and the royal lines. These proposals, in spite of the opposition of the Hispaniolised fanatics, were accepted by the Estates. The chosen envoys left Paris amid loud rejoicings and cries of " Peace, peace — blessings on those who ask for and obtain it ; all others to hell and damnation."

But before the arrangements for the conferences at Suresne, between the royal commissioners and those of the Estates, had been completed, Feria, the plenipotentiary of Philip II., had entered Paris to make known the will of his master and what he was prepared to do for France and the cause.

Although the instructions given to Feria admitted the possibility of less favourable contingencies, Philip II., misled by the servile protestations of the extreme faction of the League, imagined that he could obtain France on his own terms. The Duke was first to demand from the Estates the recognition of the Infanta as the direct heir of Henry II. ; if the Salic superstition could not be overcome, he was next to suggest that they should elect as king the Archduke Ernest, who should receive the hand of his cousin with the throne. If, incredible as it seemed, the French should cling not less to the spirit than to the letter of the Salic law, and should refuse a foreign king, then let the Crown be bestowed on the Infanta and such French prince as her father should select as her husband within two months. Lastly, if the Estates should prove so unreasonable as not to be willing to leave the choice of a king to their benefactor, let them elect the Duke of Guise, and Philip would condescend to accept him as son-in-law.

The last was the only really possible alternative. If, from the first, Feria had said, " Elect Guise, and my master will marry him to his daughter and maintain the claim of the new King with his men and money," there is little doubt that the fervour of the Fanatics and Democrats, of the clergy and of the adherents of the House of Lorraine, would have overborne the open opposition of the more moderate, and the secret ill-will of Mayenne. The election of a pretender whose hereditary popularity and personal attractiveness would have excited some enthusiasm, and in whose assistance Philip would have strained to the utmost his still formidable resources, would certainly have revived the war, and postponed, even if it had not changed, the issue. But, fortunately for France and Europe, Feria was not the man to go beyond his instructions. Wrapped in the dense self-conceit of his Castilian pride, and mistaking an ill-timed dilatoriness for dignity, he did not even begin to negotiate with the States-General, until Henry IV. had communicated to their envoys at Suresne his determination to "receive instruction " within the next two months, without waiting till a council could be assembled, and until the retreat in miserable plight of the 4,000 or 5,000 men with whom the Spaniards assisted Mayenne to take Noyon, had proved how little was to be expected from their arms.

Two months elapsed in futile discussions before Feria had exhausted the previous alternatives and produced Philip's last offer—to honour Guise, if he were elected, with his daughter's hand. Abundant signs had not been wanting that it was mere waste of time to attempt to secure the Crown for the Infanta on other terms. When the Spaniards claimed the throne for her in her own right, Rose, Bishop of Senlis, one of the most rabid Leaguers, burst forth into a violent tirade. He saw that the Politicians were right when they said that Spanish zeal was all hypocrisy, a mere cloak for worldly ambition. Nay, he shouted, such pretensions would make him turn Politician himself. To break the Salic law was to ruin the kingdom.

As for the Parliament, they protested that it was treasonable even to debate proposals so subversive of the fundamental constitution of the realm, and proclaimed null and void any treaty for the election of a foreign prince or princess to the French throne.

Dreux meantime had fallen, and the last remaining road by which supplies could reach Paris was in the King's hands. It was certain that Henry IV. meant to conform; and, if he did so, by far the larger part of the League and the vast bulk of the Catholic population in Paris and in the other great towns would be anxious to end the war by submission to his authority.   Belin, the Governor of Paris, not unmindful perhaps of courtesies at Arques, said that if Henry went to Mass he and the other nobles would at once acknowledge him as their King.   It was idle for the papal legate to declare that only the Pope could absolve a relapsed and excommunicated heretic ; and when Mayenne with an air of compunction said, that Christ did not accept lip service and must be worshipped in heart, the audience laughed.

The King had invited various prelates and theologians to meet on July 15th, for his instruction. None could doubt that the League was at the last gasp, when in spite of spiritual and temporal threats, four of the parish clergy of Paris made their way to St. Denis, and among them one of the most furious of the preachers who, with such frantic and wearisome pertinacity, had beaten to arms on their drum ecclesiastic.

Henry, as it will be remembered, had promised at his accession to "receive instruction" within six months.   Four years had now elapsed and he was still listening with more or less profit to the sermons of his Calvinist ministers.   "The same," wrote Du Plessis-Mornay, "in religion, the same, alas, that I should say it, in his pleasures.   I rejoice when I see that he is not ashamed of Christ's gospel, I grieve when I see the shame his life does to the profession of that gospel."

The Catholics had looked upon the promise to be instructed, as equivalent to an engagement to conform to the Roman Catholic Church.   The Protestants had hoped that the King would preside over a

council in which both religions would be represented, and in which the superiority of the arguments of their divines would be so conspicuous
that Henry might fairly refuse to abandon a faith
the truth of which had been publicly and triumphantly vindicated. These hopes might perhaps
have been realised had the King been able to take
Rouen and to crush the League with his Protestant
army. He would then have been strong enough to
brave the discontent of his Catholic friends. But
now, although no enemy dared to meet him in the
field, he had more to fear from those in his own
camp than from his declared opponents. The majority of the latter openly protested that nothing
but his religion prevented them from acknowledging
him as King; while many of the former were already
plotting against him. The troubles of the country
would, they said, be ended if one of the Catholic
Bourbons were chosen King. An orthodox prince
would be readily accepted by the League, he might
satisfy Spain by marrying the Infanta; Mayenne
had his price, and such was the exhaustion and suffering of the country that no terms by which quiet
and peace were restored would be unwelcome to
the people. Even those who were more loyal were
discontented. They could, they complained, endure
this continual warfare no longer. They were weary
of serving a king who never rested day or night,
who was accustomed to live with his Huguenots on
the wretched plunder of peasants' hovels, to warm
himself by a blazing barn, to sleep among cattle and
horses in filthy stables.

17

D'O, weary of the care of an exchequer so empty that even his skill and experience could find nothing to steal, made himself the mouthpiece of the discontent of the old courtiers of Henry III. " Unless the King could make up his mind to go bravely to Mass he must expect the Catholics to mount their horses and leave him." Wherever he turned, writes a fervent Calvinist, the King saw cold looks and the hearts of his followers alienated from him. Every hour he was warned of attempts to corrupt the loyalty of the governors of his towns and castles. He was so uncertain whom he might trust that he surrounded himself with English troops.

On all sides he was plied with the same arguments: by his mistress, who imagined that the Pope might be induced to grant him a divorce, and who urged the tranquil delights they might enjoy if he were released from his perpetual anxieties and alarms; by the envoys of the Italian princes, who complained that they were in a false position, as the friends of an excommunicated heretic, but that all Italy, weary of the tyranny of Spain, would be the ally of a Catholic king of France; by his own most trusted advisers; and especially by the Huguenot Sully, who pointed out the many advantages the King might hope to gain by conforming to the church of the majority of his people: the submission of the moderate Leaguers and the satisfaction of his Catholic partisans, the rude awakening of his cousins from their ambitious dreams, his own safety and ease, the termination of the misery and sufferings of the country, nay, even the gain to the Protestants themselves, who might be better protected by a Catholic than by a Huguenot reigning on sufferance. He even went so far as to maintain that, in his opinion, the King need not be disturbed by any fear lest his spiritual welfare should suffer. Since surely " whoso believes the Apostles' Creed and dies obedient to the Decalogue, in charity with his neighbour, loving God with all his heart, and trusting in His mercy and the merits of Christ's death, cannot fail to be saved, whatever the sect may be to which he belongs." A fine sentiment no doubt, and true, but which does not meet the case of the perjured profession for worldly motives of a creed which is not believed.

The sophist Du Perron, Sully's friend, who had recently obtained the bishopric of Evreux and one or two latitudinarian ministers, who, it was suspected, had been not inaccessible to bribes, assisted in stifling the King's scruples.

Yet bolder and more honest advisers were not wanting. Aubigné, if we may believe his own testimony, assured his master, that matters were not so bad as they seemed: the majority of Frenchmen were so weary of the war that for the sake of peace they would gladly acknowledge him whether Catholic or Huguenot. If the Catholics chose a king, all the disappointed pretenders would turn against him. The insolent threats of the late King's courtiers, the plots of his cousins, were idle bugbears. But even if the worst were granted, God had raised him to victory and power from far lower depths. His chaplain D'Amours and the aged Beza, his

mother's friend and spiritual director, to whose outspoken admonitions he was in the habit of listening
with much good-natured respect and little profit,
begged him to beware of God's judgment if he became an apostate to what he knew to be the truth.
Surely it was unworthy of a brave and magnanimous
Prince to be driven to Mass by the fear of man.

But Henry had made up his mind, and that not
lightly or readily. His conversion would end the
struggle in which the country was perishing. It
would give him the repose, for which even his restless nature began to crave, in the midst of constant
campaigns and sieges, cabals, conspiracies and plots
against his life. It would really, so he persuaded
himself, be to the advantage of the Huguenots; the
most they could now hope for was toleration and
equal rights with their Catholic countrymen. As a
Protestant King, all that he attempted to do for his
fellow believers would be watched with the greatest
suspicion, opposed and rendered nugatory by law-
courts and officials. As a Catholic he would have a
far freer hand. He afterwards repeatedly said that
like St. Paul he had not refused to be anathema for
his brethren.

Du Plessis-Mornay, who some weeks before had
believed the King, when he assured the Huguenots
at Saumur that he did not mean to abandon the
faith in which he had been bred, was now convinced
that his purpose could not be shaken. Yet he
wrote, "I will trust in our tears, and that though
he forget God, God may not forget him . . .
only I fear that our life, which we ought to have

changed rather than our religion, may lead us even
to worse." Although Mornay had a taste for theological discussions he refused to be present at the
King's instruction. He was certain that Henry
would not be moved by his arguments, and with
pardonable self-complacency believed that after listening to them he would more than ever be sinning
against light. After the pervert had been received
into the Roman Church, Mornay at length obeyed
his reiterated prayers and commands to come to him ;
for the King feared that in their first dismay and
anger at his apostasy the Protestants might take
some rash step. He had kept the Dukes of Bouillon
and Thouars, whose ambition he most suspected,
near him, and he wished to consult Mornay, to convince him that he did not intend to neglect the interests of the Huguenots, and tò use his great
influence to pacify their discontent.

As soon as Mornay reached the Court, Henry
called him into his cabinet, and attempted to justify
his conversion in a private conversation which lasted
three hours. The arguments which he used were
probably those which had satisfied his own conscience. The position of his affairs had, he maintained, giving the reasons urged by Sully and others,
left him no choice. In his heart he was unchanged,
yet he trusted that God would be merciful to him,
since he acted for the good of his people. Also he
believed, that the differences between the two religions were not fundamental and had been exaggerated by the animosity of the preachers, and he
trusted to be able to compose them. Lastly, he

complained that the Protestants had not supported him as they might have done; Mornay himself had cared less for him than for the interests of the cause.

It was no doubt painful to Henry to abandon doctrines which he held to be true, and which he knew well how to defend. The Catholic theologians said they had rarely met a heretic better able to hold his own against them in argument, and he drily complained, that they had not satisfied him, as he had hoped, on the disputed points.

Before rising on the morning when he was admitted into the Catholic Church, he spoke long with his Calvinist chaplain La Faye, his hand resting on his neck, and kissed him two or three times. On the day before, when he bade his ministers farewell, he asked them with tears to pray fervently to God for him, ever to love him as he would love them; remember them and never permit any wrong to be done to them or violence to their religion. Long after, when he thought himself dangerously ill, he was tortured by the fear that, in abjuring a faith in which he believed, he had committed that sin against the Holy Spirit, of which there is no remission.

All this searching of the heart seems strangely at variance with the saying attributed to Henry—that "Paris was well worth a Mass." Yet he may have said that also. He passed rapidly from tears to laughter; from meeting-house or Mass to the chamber of his mistress. Since he had made up his mind to abjure his heresies, he carried out his resolution with the same light-hearted and cheerful assurance which he showed in battle, though he often shivered and turned pale while putting on his armour. "I begin this morning," he wrote to Gabrielle, "to confer with the Bishops in addition to those whom I mentioned to you yesterday. The hope I have of seeing you to-morrow prevents my writing at greater length. On Sunday I shall take the perilous leap. At this moment, while I am writing, I have a hundred troublesome bores on my hands, who will make me hate St. Denis as much as you do Mantes. Good-bye, sweetheart, come in good time to-morrow, for it seems to me a year since I saw you. A million kisses for the fair hands of my angel and the lips of my dear mistress."

On July 23d the King "received instruction" from the Archbishop of Bourges and four Bishops. They wished him to sign a detailed confession of faith in all the points of Romanist doctrine disputed by the Reformers. This he altogether refused. He was willing to live and die in the Roman Catholic Church, but he would not sign a confession containing puerilities *(badineries)* which he was certain they did not themselves believe.

The Bishops gave way, and a formula was prepared in which the King simply recognised the Catholic, Apostolic and Roman Church as the true Church of God, promised obedience to it and to the Pope, and renounced all heresies contrary to its doctrine.

On the next Sunday (July 25th), Henry, accompanied by his princes and nobles and by the great officers of the Crown, and escorted by his French, Swiss and Scotch Guards, passed through streets

thronged with a joyful crowd and strewn with
flowers to the old church of St. Denis, of which the
Kings of France were canons during their life, and
in which they rested when dead. It was noticed
that not a few of the thousands who rent the air
with their cries of " Vive le Roi " were Parisians
who had made their way through the fortifications
to witness an event which, it was hoped, would end
the war. The church doors were shut. The King
knocked ; they opened and disclosed the Archbishop
of Bourges surrounded by seven Bishops and a crowd
of clergy. " Who are you ? " asked the Archbishop.
" The King." " What do you seek ? " " To be received
into the fold of the Catholic, Apostolic and Roman
Church "; as he spoke, Henry knelt down and continued, " I protest and swear in the presence of God
Almighty, to live and die in the Catholic faith, to
protect and defend it against all at the peril of my
life and blood, and to renounce all heresies," handing at the same time his signed confession of faith
to the Archbishop, who thereupon gave him absolution and led him into the choir, the clergy following.
While the Te Deum pealed forth and the enthusiastic multitude shed tears of joy, the King was
heard in confession behind the High Altar, after
which High Mass was celebrated, Henry devoutly
casting himself on his knees at the elevation of the
Host.

The reiterated cheers of the populace, blare of
trumpets, salvos of artillery, and, as the night closed,
bonfires in all the neighbouring villages, announced
to Paris that the " most Christian King," the " eldest

son of the Church," had been welcomed back, a re-
pentant prodigal, into her communion. "It is a
perilous thing to do evil that good may come,"
wrote Elizabeth of England, lamenting the apostasy
of her ally. If this be true,—and who will care to
deny a truth which cuts away the root of that
casuistry which is fatal to public and private
morality?—then we cannot join those who praise
the conversion of Henry IV. as a sacrifice of private
feelings to public welfare. No doubt it facilitated
the work of pacification and shortened the material
sufferings of France, but at the price of setting up
before the nation an example of the sacrifice of
honour and principle, to expediency. The King
assured the friends, whose faith he formally abjured,
that he would never forget them ; that if need were
he was ready to die in their defence; and when in
his coronation oath he swore to drive all heresy
from his dominions he had fully determined to
secure toleration and equal rights to his heretical
subjects. This the Romanists knew, and therefore
his abjuration did not preserve him from their plots,
nor ultimately from the assassin's knife. If it was
necessary that the King of France should be a
Romanist ; if the connexion between Church and
State was so intimate that all heresy was politically
dangerous, then Richelieu who deprived the Huguenots of their political privileges, and Lewis XIV. who
refused toleration to their doctrines, were better
statesmen than Henry IV. The *dragonnades* of his
grandson were the logical consequences of the conversion of the first Bourbon King.

The establishment on the French throne of Henry IV. even as a Roman Catholic was no doubt of the greatest service to the Protestant cause in other parts of Europe. Personal enmity to Spain, ambition and patriotism combined to cause Henry IV. to pursue as a Romanist the same policy he would have followed as a Protestant. But when Spain was no longer formidable, Lewis XIV., the ruler and the idol of Catholic France, was but acting in accordance with his position, when he in turn became the champion of orthodoxy and of despotism, the scourge of liberty and of Protestantism.

The news of the King's conversion was received by all among the Leaguers who desired the preservation of the kingdom and of the Faith with as much joy, says Villeroy, as if they had been restored from death to life.

The fury of the Zealots, on the other hand, knew no bounds and became even more extravagant in expression. Not the Pope, not even God, said the preachers, could absolve a relapsed heretic. Where was the Balthasar Gerard, the Jacques Clément, who would rid the world of this monster? But with the exception of a few fanatics, the Leaguers listened with growing distaste and weariness to sermons sometimes three hours long, filled with abuse and scurrility. The more moderate among the clergy began to preach reconciliation and the Divine right of Kings.

The controversy was waged even more vigorously in the pamphlets and broadsheets which poured from the press, than in the pulpit, and here also the Royalists had the better of their opponents in wit as well as in moderation and good taste.

But the Spanish party had other weapons besides those of argument and of honourable warfare. In spite of many previous failures it was hoped that the assassin's dagger might eventually deliver the Church from her enemy. The Rector of the Jesuits and one of the parish priests of Paris encouraged a young man, not unwilling to lay down for the faithful, a life, which disappointed love had rendered worthless to himself, to join the royal camp, and to watch for an opportunity of assassinating the King. Fortunately an Italian Dominican, to whom the plot had become known, sent a warning. Barrière, so the youth was called, was arrested and broken on the wheel.

A week after the King's conversion, a truce had been concluded for three months with the Leaguers. Henry had consented to treat with Mayenne as with an equal, for he believed that when the country had once tasted peace it would not permit itself to be dragged back again into war; especially if, as he hoped, he in the meantime obtained absolution from the Pope. Clement VIII. had hitherto refused to receive his envoys, but he was now no longer a heretic. The Pope before his election had not been a partisan of Spain, and the Duke of Tuscany and other Italian princes promised to exert their influence at the Vatican to the utmost on behalf of the King of France. Mayenne also told Villeroy to assure Henry that he desired peace, that he was disgusted with the Spaniards and that he also would do his best to persuade the Pope to grant the absolution.

The Lieutenant-General of the Union had assented to the armistice because he had no choice. The mob threatened to throw the priests, whom they regarded as the main obstacles to peace, into the river; they turned their backs on the legate when he gave them his benediction and insulted Feria. The Spaniards indeed made large offers, to Mayenne, of little less than the partition of the kingdom. But to carry on the war, money and men were needed and not promises, which, moreover, the Duke did not believe to be sincere, for he knew that the Sorbonne had advised that everything should be promised to him and nothing given. Meantime, with characteristic double dealing he sent a secret envoy to Rome to urge the Pope on no account to absolve the King of Navarre, and his son-in-law to Madrid to persuade Philip II. to promise the hand of the Infanta to his eldest son.

The truce was prolonged till the end of the year. When it expired, all in arms against the King were to expect the punishment of rebels unless they submitted within a month.

The hope that the Pope would readily grant the absolution had not been realised. Clement VIII. scarcely deigned to receive the letter which Henry IV. wrote to announce his conversion. He would not listen to the Duke of Nevers who was sent as ambassador. "Don't tell me," he exclaimed, "that your King is Catholic. I could never believe him to be converted unless an angel from heaven came to whisper it in my ear.  As for the Catholics who have adhered to him, I do not say that they are rebels and renegades to their religion, but they are only the bastard children of the maidservant, while they of the League are the true lawful children— buttresses and pillars of the Catholic Church."   The Duke left Rome without having effected anything, or obtained any more comfortable assurance than a whisper from Cardinal Toleto, the chief adviser of the Pope, a moderate man, though a Spaniard and a Jesuit, that the Holy Father only wished to prove the King of Navarre's sincerity.

A pretext therefore still remained for those who, like Mayenne, wished to hold out on a scruple of conscience till they could obtain better terms.

In other respects the results of the truce were very much what the Royalists expected.  The Estates like a burnt-out candle had dwindled and gone out in such obscurity that it is impossible to determine the date of their final meeting.  The last ill-smelling flicker which attracted attention was the recognition by them of the decrees of the Coun- cil of Trent—a measure forced on their weariness and weakness by Mayenne, in order that reconcilia- tion might be made more difficult, since it was quite incompatible with the privileges of the Gallican Church, and with the principles of national indepen- dence stoutly upheld by the law-courts.

The impossibility of any tolerable arrangement with Spain, the duplicity and selfishness of May- enne were more than ever patent ; and many sepa- rate negotiations had been opened with the towns

and nobles of the League, the effect of which was
seen as soon as they had to choose between making
their peace with the King and the renewal of
hostilities.

Vitry, Governor of Meaux, one of the most able
and active of the Catholic captains, had been the
first of the officers of Henry III. to leave his successor, because he would not serve a heretic.  That
he had no personal animosity to the King he had
shown by consenting, while still in arms against
him, to hunt the royal hounds during an illness of
the huntsman.  He now told the citizens of Meaux
that as his Majesty was no longer a heretic he meant
to return to his service, and the townspeople determined to follow the example of their Governor.

Le Chastre, Governor of the Orleanais and Berry,
the uncle of Vitry, acted in like manner and the
municipalities of Orleans and Bourges united with
him in making their peace with the King.  The
citizens of Lyons had ended a long feud with their
Governor, the Duke of Nemours, by seizing and
imprisoning him in their citadel, and now in spite
of their Archbishop Espinac admitted a Royalist
garrison.  The submission of this great and turbulent town, the commercial centre of France, was a
great gain to the Royalists, and was likely to determine the hesitation of Villars, the Governor of
Rouen, with whom Sully was already negotiating.
The terms granted to the towns which submitted
were generally the same.  A complete amnesty for
the past ; the confirmation of all the municipal
privileges and franchises they already possessed ; an

engagement to build no citadel or to destroy those
which already existed; exemption from extraordinary taxation, together with large pensions and
gifts of money to their Governors. No doubt it
was better and even cheaper for the nation that the
gates of the hostile cities should be opened by
gold, that the King should buy back his kingdom,
than that the country should be devastated, agriculture, manufactures and trade, the sources of all
wealth, ruined by civil war. Yet, by purchasing
the submission of his rebels Henry IV. taught the
French nobility to believe that turbulence was profitable, a lesson not forgotten during the regencies
of Mary de' Medici and Anne of Austria. Nor did
it appear just that loyal subjects should bear a
heavier load of taxation in order that the rebel towns
and provinces might escape from the obligation of
contributing to the necessities of the State. The
King's most faithful servants had some reason to
complain when they saw not only their services un-
rewarded, but the sums lent to their master unpaid,
while wealth beyond the dreams of avarice was lavished on his enemies. " It is, I suppose, because I
am necessary, that the King keeps me necessitous,"
wrote Du Plessis-Mornay, who had never grudged
his money to the Cause; and the large sums which
La Noue had raised by mortgaging his estates were
never repaid to his heirs. It is true that the King
himself felt the pinch of want. He had not in the
winter of 1594 wherewithal to buy fodder for his
horses. " My plight," he complained to the treas-
urer D'O, " is indeed wretched; I shall soon have

to go on foot and naked." Turning to one of his attendants he asked how many shirts he had— "A dozen, Sire, and some of them torn."—"And how many handkerchiefs? Eight, is n't it?"—"No, Sire, only five." D'O, in excuse, said that to supply these wants he had ordered 6,000 crowns' worth of linen from Flanders. "Well," answered Henry, "it seems I am like those scholars who, when they are dying of cold, talk of the furred robes they have at home." Yet this destitution did not prevent him from giving to his mistress a service of plate and a diamond heart, "very appropriate for her if angels wear jewellery." It is seldom that a dissolute and ragged pauper whose children are starving is without a shilling for drink and tobacco.

Few could any longer affect to doubt that there was again a ruler in France, and two great events which took place during the first months of 1594 made it plain to all that there remained no colourable pretext for refusing to him the title of King. These events were his coronation and the submission of Paris.

The monarchy of the Franks had been elective like that of the other Teutonic nations. The Merovingian kings attempted to assert an unconditional hereditary right; but the Church which had assisted them to establish their authority, while she hedged round their Crown with a mystic and almost divine dignity, claimed the right of bestowing that dignity by a ceremony analogous to that which raised the priest above his fellow-men. Under the Carolingians the elective principle was reaffirmed, and the

nobles and prelates, who passing over the lineage of
Charles the Great chose Hugh Capet as their king
(987), doubtless intended to establish an elective
monarchy no longer confined to the members of one
family. For the next two hundred years the reigning monarch never omitted to procure during his
lifetime the election and coronation of his eldest
son. It was mainly owing to the fortunate chance,
that till the death of Lewis X. (1316) a direct male
heir never failed the house of Capet, that the descent of the Crown to the nearest male heir of the
deceased King came to be regarded as a matter of
course.

The presence of the peers of France at the King's
coronation became an antiquarian pageant, which
reminded only the most thoughtful spectators that
the royal power had once been based on a compact
between an elected ruler and his people.

On the other hand the religious and mystic importance attached to the coronation ceremony had,
if anything, increased. To lead her Prince to Rheims,
that he might receive the sacred unction, was the
final aim and crown of Joan of Arc's ambition; till
after that ceremony he was to her only the Dauphin,
nor does Froissart give him till then the style of
King.

One of the arguments used to determine the conversion of Henry IV. had been the question, how,
while he remained a heretic, could he be crowned?

This difficulty no longer existed. Rheims with
its cathedral and mystic oil was still in the power of
the League. But there were precedents for the per-

18

formance of the rite elsewhere. The coronation of Lewis VI. had taken place at Orleans and Henry determined to be crowned at Chartres, in the cathedral of which his ancestors had been patrons and benefactors. For once the tendency of relics to exist in duplicate was found useful. If the oil, brought to St. Remigius by an angel for the unction of Clovis, was not forthcoming, another scarcely less revered fluid of miraculous virtue was contained in a precious phial given by another angel to St. Martin, the apostle of Gaul. This was preserved in the convent of Marmoustier, near Tours, where it had by special mercy escaped a wholesale destruction of relics in 1562.

Everything was done to make the ceremony impressive. Henry of Bourbon claimed the throne as the representative of hereditary right, he had been opposed on the ground that sovereignty was conferred by the people, and that to exercise it was an office so sacred, so nearly a priesthood that it could not be held by a heretic excommunicated and unabsolved. Yet all the ancient forms were now carefully observed, forms from which, if all the annals of the French monarchy had perished, an historical student could have concluded with more certainty that it was originally elective and endowed with mystic sanctity by close connection with the Church, than the physiologist is able, from the presence of organs now useless and atrophied, to conjecture what were the conditions under which an animal has previously existed.

The greatest nobles present with the King, dressed

in magnificent and archaic robes, figured as the six
great vassals, the lay peers of the French Crown, the
Dukes of Normandy, Burgundy and Aquitaine, the
Counts of Flanders, Toulouse and Champagne.
Five Bishops represented the spiritual peers, the
Bishops of Laon, Langres, Beauvais, Châlons and
Noyon, who were either absent or dead. These
peers raised Henry from his seat under the High
Altar and presented him to the crowd, while the
Bishop of Nantes, acting for the Duke-Bishop of
Laon, asked whether they accepted him as their
king? Then having been acknowledged by all the
orders as their sovereign lord, he was clad in the royal
robes, emblematic, as it was supposed, of the sanctity of Holy Orders, the tunic of the subdiaconate,
the dalmatic of the diaconate, while the royal mantle
represented the chasuble of the priesthood, girt with
the sword, the rod of justice placed in his hands, and
anointed in seven places with the miraculous chrism.
After which he swore, his hand upon the Gospels
which he reverently kissed, to protect the peace of
the Church and of all Christian people ; to put down
iniquity and violence ; to deserve God's mercy by
enforcing justice, and lastly, to drive from his dominions (exterminate) all heretics. Then, and not
till then, did the officiating Bishop take the royal
Crown from the High Altar, and the peers each
touching it with their hands, place it on his head.
Next they led him to a throne raised aloft on a stage,
where they did homage to him in the sight of the
crowd who thronged the vast nave of the stately
Cathedral,—a crowd of nobles, magistrates and

soldiers scarcely less bright than those marvellous windows above them which the art of the middle ages has filled with translucent gems. The loud and reiterated shouts of joy spreading from the interior of the church to the populace collected outside drowned the blast of the trumpets and the proclamation of the heralds scattering largess.

The crowned and anointed King returned to the neighbourhood of Paris to conduct in person the negotiations which were to place him in possession of his Capital, while Sully continued to bargain with Villars, the Governor of Rouen ; and to endeavour to beat down terms, the extravagance of which was a vexation to his economic soul : perhaps also he compared the price demanded by Villars for ceasing to be a rebel, 1,200,000 livres, equivalent to nearly £500,-000, a pension of 60,000, equivalent to nearly £24,-000 and the revenues of six abbeys with the hardly earned rewards of many years of loyal service.

The higgling and hesitation of his agent excited the King's impatience. " It is folly," he wrote, (March, 1594) " to raise so many difficulties in a matter the conclusion of which is so important for the establishment of my authority and for the relief of my people. Do you not remember how often you have quoted the advice of a certain Duke of Milan (Francis Sforza) to Lewis XI. ? To separate by their private interests those who had leagued themselves against him under the pretext of the public weal. This is what I intend to attempt. I prefer, even though it should cost twice as much, to treat with each severally, rather than to attain the same end by

means of a general treaty with a single leader, who
would thus be able to keep together a faction in my
realm."

Thus urged, Rosny accepted Villars' terms, and
Henry IV. was undisputed master of Normandy. On
March 17th Sully received a letter from the King
bidding him join him before the 21st in order that
he might help to cry " Vive le Roi " in Paris.

Ever since the conversion of Henry, the Politicians and the more moderate and patriotic members
of the League would gladly have thrown open the
gates of Paris to a Catholic and national king.
Mayenne on the other hand had drawn closer to the
Spaniards, both because he felt their support to be
more necessary to him and because they encouraged
him to hope that Philip might marry the Infanta to
his son.

The Lieutenant-General of the Union felt the
ground trembling under his feet. He strengthened
the garrison, re-established the Council of Sixteen,
the committee of public safety of the League, perfected the organisation of the " minotiers,"—a militia
recruited by Spanish money from the lowest classes
to overawe the more respectable citizens, and banished some of the most prominent of the Moderate
party. Since Belin, the Governor of Paris, had not
scrupled to say that he was French and not Spanish
and that the time was come to end the Civil War, he
was dismissed and his place given to Brissac, the hero
of the Barricades, a favourite of the democratic faction. The study of antiquity had converted Brissac
to Republicanism in theory, but his actions were

solely determined by the intelligent pursuit of his
own interests.  He was not, therefore, likely to be
scrupulous in fidelity to a losing cause ; yet Mayenne,
who never allowed his own conduct to be hampered
by the most solemn engagements, trusted Brissac's
word, showing that strange infatuation which not
unfrequently exposes a swindler to be cheated more
easily than an honest man.  Feria was convinced
that a man could not be dangerous, who, instead of
listening to what passed in Council, amused himself
by catching the flies on the wall ; and the legate felt
that confidence was not misplaced in a Catholic so
scrupulous, that he cast himself on his knees to crave
absolution after an interview with his brother-in-
law, the Royalist St. Luc,—an interview which,
Brissac asserted, was rendered necessary by a law-
suit, in which his whole fortune was at stake, but
which really was to settle the price of his desertion.

During the next six weeks (January and February, 1594), each day brought the news of further
disaster to the cause of the League ; of fortresses
and towns returning to their allegiance.  At length
the Spaniards sent some troops to the frontier and
on March 6th, Mayenne left Paris with the avowed intention of attempting with their help to open a way
by which supplies might reach the Capital.  But since
he took his wife and children with him, his departure
appeared little less than a retreat from an untenable
position, and gave a great impulse to the negotiations carried on by the King's friends within and
without the walls.

Brissac was not more faithful to the League than

his predecessor, while his dissimulation and the trust reposed in him made him far more dangerous. The price he exacted from the King for his services was a high one, 20,000 crowns down, and a pension of 20,000, the confirmation of the dignity of Marshal bestowed on him by Mayenne, and the governorship of Corbeil and Mantes. The Parisian magistrates, who joined in the plot for opening the gates of the city to the King, deserve the praise of disinterestedness in comparison with the Catholic nobles. But few stipulated for private favours. The conditions upon which they insisted were such as they supposed to be for the public good. The maintenance of the privileges of Paris; the prohibition of Protestant worship within ten leagues of the walls; a general amnesty and permission to the foreigners in the town to depart uninjured. Since they had been invited and received as friends it would have been a treacherous breach of hospitality to have delivered the Spaniards into the hands of their enemies.

After the terms had been agreed upon, daybreak on the morning of March 22d was fixed upon as the time when the King and his troops should be admitted. A large force could not assemble near the gates without attracting the attention of the Spaniards and of the Sixteen whose suspicions were already aroused. Henry IV. was obliged to venture into the narrow and tortuous streets of the populous city with some 4,000 or 5,000 men. The Spaniards with their armed and disciplined adherents were at least three times as numerous. The safety and success of the King depended therefore, in the first

place, on the good faith and skilful arrangements of
his friends within the walls, and in the next, on the
sympathy, if not on the active co-operation, of the
citizens.

The plan of the Royalists was well conceived and
punctually executed. Never, perhaps, has a large
and unruly city, held by a powerful garrison, changed
hands with so little disorder or bloodshed.

Brissac on various pretexts got rid of two French
regiments whom he knew to be devoted to Mayenne, and persuaded the most energetic of the
Spanish commanders to leave the town, in the hopes
of intercepting an imaginary convoy. At the same
time he enrolled as new recruits a number of Royalist soldiers who slipped one by one into the city.

Feria and Ibarra were warned that the King would
enter Paris on the night of the 21st; but their in-
formant assured them that midnight was the appointed hour and appears only to have suggested
a possible complicity on the part of the Governor.
Feria accordingly, shortly before midnight, warned
Brissac to be on his guard, and sent his Spanish captains to visit the gates in his company. They were
ordered to stab him at the first sign of hesitation or
treachery. Brissac hurried them from post to post
till they were tired out, and brought them back to
Feria, well satisfied of his zeal and fidelity. Meanwhile all the trainbands, whom the Royalists could
trust, had been quietly got under arms. They were
told that peace had been concluded between Mayenne and the King, that it would be proclaimed on
the morrow, but that it was necessary to antici-

pate and prevent the resistance of the Spaniards and their adherents.

Brissac and the Provost of Paris, L'Huillier, accompanied by a strong body of citizens, seized the Porte Neuve—the gate on the bank of the river by the Louvre. The gates of St. Denis and St. Honoré were held by other magistrates privy to the plot, and the commandant of the Arsenal allowed the chain to be lowered which barred the river, so as to admit by water the garrisons of Corbeil and Melun. The Royalist troops entered the town from four sides, and then uniting with their friends, who had collected to hold and open the gates, occupied the great arteries which divided the labyrinth of narrow and crooked lanes,—the streets of St. Denis, St. Honoré and St. Martin. Then converging they marched upon the centre of the city where their friends were astir, and where they met with no resistance. When the Spaniards took the alarm they found themselves surrounded in their several quarters and deprived of any possibility of concerted action.

With the last of four bodies of troops which entered the Capital by the Porte Neuve came Henry himself. The Provost and Governor were waiting to welcome him at that same gate through which six years before the last Valois had fled, pursued by the execrations of his people.

The King received the keys of the town from the Provost, and embraced Brissac, saluting him by the title of Marshal, while he threw his own white scarf over his neck. The division which had entered immediately before the King, alone met with any resistance. As it moved along the quays a small detachment of lansquenets, stationed on the Quai de l'École, refused to surrender, but were promptly put to the sword or thrown into the river. Henry heard the noise of the skirmish, and, as he had entered the gate unarmed, called for his armour. For a moment, fearless soldier as he was, he hesitated to enter the gloomy streets which had so often been the scene of riot and bloodshed fatal to his friends and to the authority of his predecessors. But assured that his soldiers held the gates, that his adherents were in possession of the city, the Louvre and the two Châtelets, he proceeded along the street of St. Honoré towards the bridge of Notre Dame. The people crowded the street in silent curiosity and amazement at the unexpected sight, while the King advanced surrounded by his escort, trailing their pikes in sign of peace. Taking their clue from the shouts of the better class of citizens, first one and then another of the mob raised the cry of " Vive le Roi." Before the bridge was reached, the infection of enthusiasm had spread and the air rang with loyal acclamations. " I see," said Henry, " how these poor people have been tyrannised." Then, turning to a former Leaguer who was by his side, he asked, " What think you of seeing me here ? " " That what is Cæsar's, Sire, has been given to Cæsar."—" Given," said the King, looking at Brissac, who rode near him, " Given ! no, sold and for a good price."

When he approached Notre Dame and saw the clergy waiting under the great portal to receive him, he dismounted. The throng was so great that he

ENTRANCE OF HENRY IV. INTO PARIS.
(BY THE NEW GATE.)
From a contemporary engraving of a painting by N. Bollery.

was lifted off his feet. The guards would have made the people stand back, but Henry prevented them; the citizens, he said, had long missed the sight of a King, and should now look their fill. It was no small risk which he thus ran in exposing himself to the blow of any frenzied fanatic. When the Duchess of Montpensier was told that he had entered Paris, she exclaimed that surely some one would be found to plunge a dagger into his heart.

Meantime the bells pealed forth a joyous welcome, while the Te Deum re-echoed through the nave and aisles of the crowded cathedral.

Some futile attempt made by the Sixteen to rally their forces in the quarter of the university where they were strongest was repressed without bloodshed; and the King's heralds, accompanied by a shouting crowd of boys and children, rode through the town, proclaiming peace and amnesty.

The Duke of Feria and Don Diego Ibarra were glad to accept the terms offered by the King, and to evacuate the city with bag and baggage and the honors of war. At three o'clock, pelted by a pitiless March storm, 3,000 Spaniards, Italians and Walloons filed through the gate of St. Denis. The King, who had dined, was watching them from a window above the gate. Feria and Ibarra under circumstances which might have made other men feel and look sufficiently crestfallen, were sustained by their Castilian pride, and barely saluted him whom they still affected to call the Prince of Béarn. Henry returned a lower bow and shouted, "Commend me to your master, gentlemen, but don't come back." The other officers and the common soldiers, less proud, or more grateful for being allowed to depart with life and property, passed under the King's window bareheaded and with low obeisance.

Fifty or sixty of the most rabid Leaguers accompanied the Spaniards. The legate, who refused to see the King, was allowed to take with him the Rector of the Jesuits, and a priest who had instigated the would-be regicide, Barrière.

Henry IV. declared that he was determined to forget the past ; that it would be as unreasonable to hold the fanatics responsible for what they had done, as to blame a man who was beside himself for striking, or a madman for walking about naked,— a generous and politic sentiment, if not carried too far. But, as has already been remarked, a well founded confidence in his boundless placability, doubtless encouraged the intrigues and conspiracies which disturbed Henry IV's reign and confirmed the French princes and nobles in the belief that rebellion was a game in which there was much to win and little to lose.

The evening of his first day in Paris the King not only visited the mother of Mayenne, the old Duchess of Nemours, and the widowed Duchess of Guise, to assure them of his favour and protection, but even joined the card party of the Duchess of Montpensier, the termagant of the League, the patroness of Jacques Clément, and who a few hours before had been calling for some one to assassinate him.

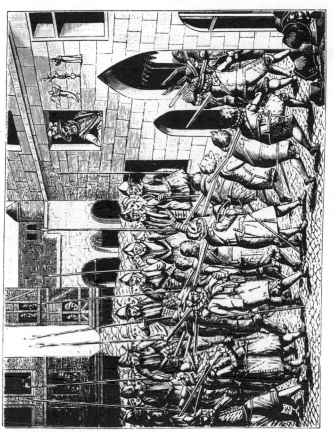

EXIT OF THE SPANIARDS FROM PARIS.
(BY THE ST. DENIS GATE.)
From a contemporary engraving.

Surely he had the right to forgive his own enemies, but, muttered the old servants of Henry III.,
was it thus he kept the oath he had sworn to avenge
the murder of his predecessor?

The possession of Paris, followed in a few days
by the news of the submission of Rouen, firmly
established the King's superiority over his enemies.
There was now little danger that the hope of obtaining the support of a dying faction would tempt
any prince to play the part of a pretender. The
Parliament, without awaiting the return of the
Royalist magistrates from Tours, eagerly annulled
all that had been done during the last six years "to
the prejudice of the authority of the Crown or of
the laws of the country," and summoned the Duke
of Mayenne and all others at once to recognise
Henry IV. as their lawful King, unless they chose
to incur the penalty of treason.

Even the University of Paris, so long the
stronghold of opinions which subordinated the
hereditary right of the Prince to the popular will,
and to the approval of the Church, yielded to the
pressure of circumstances and to the persuasion of
a new Rector, the King's physician. The Sorbonne
solemnly declared that, " notwithstanding the doubts
of certain men imbued with erroneous doctrine,"
Henry of Bourbon, the legitimate heir to the
throne, must be obeyed by all ; even though, owing
to the intrigues of the enemies of the country, he
had not as yet been recognised as the Eldest Son of
the Church by the Holy Father. " All power," as
St. Paul teaches, " is of God. The Powers that be

are ordained of God, and they that resist shall receive to themselves damnation."

But much remained to be done. The leaders of the League, who continued in arms, must be conciliated or subdued ; and if the King was to rule as an orthodox and Catholic monarch, if no pretext for disobedience was to be left to his subjects, he must be acknowledged by the Pope.

In the North, Laon, Soissons, Amiens and Beauvais were held by Mayenne and Aumâle, supported by the Spaniards at La Fère. The Duke of Guise was still master of Rheims and of the greater part of Champagne. Châlons, Dijon and most of the towns of Burgundy, though weary of the war, and anxious to return to their allegiance, were coerced by the garrisons of Mayenne. In the South, Toulouse and a considerable part of Languedoc were still unsubdued.

In Provence the Leaguers had acknowledged Henry's title, but were still in arms against the Duke of Épernon, the Governor. So universal was the discontent excited by the outrages of his Gascon mercenaries, and by Épernon's own avarice or cruelty, that the King was obliged to allow Lesdiguières to send assistance from Dauphiny to the men who were resisting his representative. The Duke, who protested that, rather than lose his government, he would sell himself to Spain or the Devil, began in revenge to negotiate with Philip II.

The exhaustion and misery of the country were greater than ever. Plains once rich with harvest were rapidly becoming barren moors or fever-stricken morasses. The wretched peasantry, driven by desperation and want, banded themselves together and became in their turn the robbers of those who still had something left. In the Limousin, Quercy and La Marche 50,000 men were in arms under the name of "Croquants." Partly by force, but more by policy, the royal governors dispersed these bands before the movement spread into Poitou.

When there were such troubles in the heart of the kingdom, and so many rebels and traitors in all the frontier provinces, the King of Spain might well hope that even if he could not seat the Infanta on the French throne, he might easily find sufficient employment for Henry IV. at home to prevent his becoming troublesome abroad.

The power of Spain was most dangerous on the northern frontier, and Mayenne was at Laon urgently pressing the Governor of the Netherlands, the Archduke Ernest, to send his troops into Picardy. Henry, therefore, marched in person against Laon, that hill fortress, which had been the capital of those Carolingians from whom the genealogists of the Guises derived their patron's claim to the throne.

Laon surrendered on August 2 (1594), but not without much loss to the besiegers. Givry, the gallant gentleman who had done Henry such good service on the day of his accession, was one of those who fell. A fortnight later, Amiens and the other Picard towns submitted.

The lieutenant of Guise in Champagne, a soldier of fortune, who, although the son of a gamekeeper, called himself St. Pol and Duke of Rethelois, treated

the Duke with insolent independence. In an alter-
cation between them he laid his hand on the hilt of
his sword, but before he could draw it, fell stabbed
to the heart by Guise. The dead man's mercenaries
at once opened the gates of the towns they garrisoned to the Royalists. The Duchess of Guise, won
by the King's courtesy, urged her son while it was
yet time to accept the generous terms offered :
400,000 crowns to pay his debts, pensions for himself and his brothers, and the government of Provence in exchange for that of Champagne.

The family of Lorraine imagined that their descent
from King René of Anjou gave them an hereditary
claim to Provence, which was not less a frontier province and exposed to Spanish aggression and intrigue
than Champagne. The majority, therefore, of the
Royal Council protested against the policy of entrusting it to the young man whom the King's
enemies had put forward as a pretender to the
Crown. But the event proved the wisdom of
Henry's decision. Guise, though young and fiery,
had a reserve of sober sense. In the days of his
popularity he had checked the foolish adulation of
the rabble, and had threatened to kill with his own
hand any one who addressed him as King. Épernon indeed, immediately on hearing that Guise had
been appointed governor, concluded his treaty with
Philip II., and persuaded the Leaguist magistrates
of Marseilles to follow his example. Marseilles, the
one great port between Barcelona and Genoa, had
long been the object of Spanish ambition. Carlo
Doria, with a Spanish fleet, was already in the

harbour, when a conspiracy and a rising concerted between Guise and the townspeople, who detested the yoke of Spain, drove the foreigners and their supporters from the town. It was no small triumph for Henry of Bourbon to have turned the son of the hero of the League into an instrument of his anti-Spanish policy. (Feb. 17, 1596.)

The Duke of Lorraine followed the example of his young kinsman, abandoned the League, disbanded his army and restored Toul and Verdun to France for 900,000 crowns.

After the submission of the Duke of Guise and the treaty with Lorraine, the only members of the Lotharingian family whose hostility was still formidable to Henry IV. were the Dukes of Mayenne and Mercœur. These nobles, although they could no longer hope to deprive him of the Crown, still trusted to be able to convert their Governments of Burgundy and Brittany into hereditary and independent principalities. The support of Spain gave them courage and strength to continue their rebellion; the fact that the King was still unabsolved by the Pope supplied a pretext.

In all the difficulties and dangers which he had encountered, Henry traced the persistent malevolence of his hereditary enemy, Philip II. To hurl defiance against the dreaded tyrant by an open declaration of war would not only satisfy his personal resentment, but might also be justified as politically expedient. Whether war was declared or not, it could not be doubted that Philip II. would do France all the injury possible. But the less Henry IV. appeared

19

to fear him, the less dangerous would he be. Much of his power to do harm depended on the dread inspired by the name of Spain, a dread based more on her old renown than on her present strength. Moreover, when once war had been declared, it would be impossible for Frenchmen any longer to pretend that in placing themselves under the protection of Philip II. they were not allying themselves with the enemy of their country. Henry's Protestant allies suspected him, since his abjuration, of a wish to come to terms with Spain at their expense. Open hostility would be the best reply to such suspicions. The English and Dutch promised that they would find Philip II. such occupation elsewhere, that it would be impossible for his armies to invade France. The Duke of Bouillon was certain that by means of his friends in Luxembourg, and other Spanish provinces, he would be able to do wonders for the King's service. Sancy boasted that he could induce the Swiss not only to connive at, but even actively to assist in, the conquest of Franche Comté, although they had guaranteed the neutrality of that province. Gabrielle d'Estrées, who had persuaded Henry to acknowledge and legitimise her recently born son, Cæsar, supported the war party. If Franche Comté was conquered, she hoped that it would be bestowed on him as an appanage.

Yielding to these arguments as well as to his own indignation, Henry determined on open war and closed his ears to Sully and other more cautious advisers, who urged him to wait till he had consolidated his power at home, before by an open defiance he roused the old King to exert to the utmost his still formidable resources. The Spanish monarchy was like some mighty beast of chase which, bleeding from many wounds and apparently exhausted, may yet, if the hunter approach too incautiously, gather its failing energies at the touch of his weapon and perish not unavenged.

# CHAPTER VII.

OPEN WAR WITH SPAIN—PEACE WITH FOREIGN AND
DOMESTIC ENEMIES—THE EDICT OF NANTES.

1595–1598.

EFORE the Spaniards were met in the field, it was necessary to deal with a domestic enemy scarcely less dangerous.

The Jesuits, alleging the traditional respect of their order for the Holy See, refused to offer up prayers in their churches for an excommunicated Prince.

It was not true that the Society of Jesus had been founded, as was pretended by their French opponents, to make the Church subservient to the ambition of the Spanish King. The primary object of Loyola and of his successors had been to maintain and to extend the authority of the Roman Church; to advance her frontiers over the realms of heathendom as well as to defend them against the encroachments of heresy. It was because, in the main, the policy of Philip II. had not been inconsistent with this object, because his enemies had also been the

enemies of Romanisn, and not because the founder
and the first generals of the Order had been the subjects of Spain, that the Jesuits had been the close
allies of the Spanish King.   They had been introduced into France by Henry II. at a time when
he had determined to join the crusade against heresy.
The rapid increase of their numbers, the crowds
who flocked to their churches, the popularity of their
schools, the noble and wealthy penitents who showed
by large gifts and bequests their gratitude for the
skill with which the fathers ministered to the
diseases of the soul, increased the jealousy and suspicion with which they were from the first regarded
by the constituted authorities in Church and State.

The Parliaments resented their assertion of papal
supremacy and their attacks upon the absolute
authority of the Crown.   The higher clergy, not less
anxious than the lawyers to maintain the liberties
of the Gallican church, were further incensed by the
immunity claimed by the Jesuits from episcopal
jurisdiction.   The older orders were irritated by their
popularity, their assumption of a name which seemed
to imply that they were the truer and more familiar
servants of the common Master.   The University of
Paris was jealous of their educational success, and
after affiliating on certain conditions their College
of Clermont, was even more indignant that the
popularity of their instruction should attract the
vast majority of students belonging to the higher
classes, than it was at the non-fulfilment of the
stipulated terms.   In 1565 the University, supported
by the Bishop and Clergy of Paris, as well as by the

municipality, ordered the Jesuits to close their lecture rooms. An appeal to the law-courts followed. Notwithstanding the ill-will of the lawyers, the support of powerful friends obtained for the Jesuits the permission of Parliament to continue their teaching, pending the final decision of their case and indefinitely postponed that decision. While the League flourished, the Jesuits had been all powerful in the University as well as elsewhere. But the old quarrel between the Order and the University remained in suspense, and appeared to the King's advisers to supply a convenient weapon against his most insidious enemies. The new Rector persuaded the Faculties to reopen the litigation. Not satisfied with demanding that the Jesuits should be forbidden to teach, he asked that they should be banished from the kingdom as the spies and tools of Spain. The case against the Society was argued at great length, with much eloquence and more learning by counsel representing the University and the parochial clergy of Paris. The advocate of the University was Antoine Arnauld, the father of a son of like name, destined to win undying fame in battle against the same antagonists.

Arnauld exaggerated the subservience of the Jesuits to Spain, but not the irreconcilable antagonism between the principles of the Order and Gallicanism. The Gallican Church had always maintained the supreme authority of œcumenical councils in things spiritual, and the independence in its own sphere of the temporal power. The Jesuits on the other hand taught that the Pope when he spoke as

Christ's vicar was the supreme and infallible head of the Church, and that an excommunicated Prince was a tyrant, to whom his subjects not only owed no allegiance, but whom any might lawfully slay.

To the charges of having violated every condition imposed upon them when admitted into the kingdom, of aiming at the subversion of the national laws in Church and State, of instigating rebellion and assassination, were added those other accusations to which, whether more or less founded, it has been the misfortune of the Order to be at all times exposed.

The counsel of the parochial clergy dwelt on the sinister characteristic which distinguished the Jesuits from other monastic bodies. The statutes and rules of the older Orders were fixed and immutable, while theirs could be changed or suspended by their superiors as season, place and circumstances might be thought to require. Yet so great was the influence of the Order, so numerous and powerful their friends, that they probably would have escaped condemnation but for an event which excited great popular feeling against them.

On November 27 (1594) after the King, on his return from a journey, had entered the house of Gabrielle d'Estrées, a young man slipped in, unperceived among the crowd of courtiers, rushed forward and struck at him with a knife. The blow might have been fatal if at the very moment Henry had not stooped forward to raise two gentlemen who had been presented to him and who were kneeling, according to custom, to clasp his knees. As it was, his upper lip was cut through and his mouth wounded. The would-be assassin proved to be a youth, Jean Chastel by name, a pupil of the Jesuits, whose weak intellect had been shaken by the discipline and the threats of damnation with which they had attempted to cure his moral depravity. He hoped by some deed of conspicuous merit to escape the punishment of his sins; nay, to exchange the pains of hell for the crown of martyrdom, should he perish in the endeavour to deliver his church and country from an excommunicated tyrant.

The attempt to assassinate the King was certain to produce consequences so inconvenient to the Jesuits, that they must be absolved from the charge of having directly incited the murderer. But they who excuse and glorify crime, cannot refuse responsibility for the fruits of their doctrine. The men who had exalted Jaques Clément as a saint and martyr were not less guilty than if they had placed the knife in Jean Chastel's hand. The Parliament no longer hesitated. On the same day that Jean Chastel was sentenced to suffer the barbarous punishment inflicted on regicides—his flesh to be lacerated with red-hot pincers, his right hand to be struck off, his limbs to be torn asunder by four horses—the Jesuits were banished from Paris and the kingdom. "It seems," jested the King, "that the reverend fathers could only be convicted by my mouth." There is no more convincing proof of the imperturbable serenity and healthy elasticity of Henry's temperament than the fact that it was not warped by the ever present danger of assassination, a strain under

which so many not ignoble natures have given
way. Soon after his accession he wrote to his mistress that the number of men suborned to attempt
his life was greater than could easily be believed.
But God, he added, would keep him. He could
scarcely be persuaded to take the commonest precautions. Yet it was with a sad and depressed countenance that he rode to Notre Dame to offer thanks
for his escape. When a courtier called his attention to the popular enthusiasm, he shook his head
and replied, " They are a mob [*C'est un peuple*]; if
my greatest enemy was where I am, and they saw
him pass, they would do as much for him as for me,
and shout even louder."

On January 17 (1595), war was declared against
Spain. The Duke of Bouillon (Turenne) had at his
own suggestion been sent to invade Luxembourg.
The Duke of Montmorency, on whom the King had
bestowed the sword of Constable, condescended to
show his gratitude by leaving his province of Languedoc to drive Nemours, and an army sent to his
assistance by the Duke of Savoy, from the neighbourhood of Lyons. But it was in Burgundy and
Franche-Comté that the King hoped to strike a
decisive blow. Burgundy was the province in which
Mayenne trusted, even if the rest of France slipped
from his grasp, to establish himself as an independent ruler. Franche-Comté was an outlying portion
of the Spanish dominions, inhabited by a French-
speaking population, which the King thought
might form an appanage for Gabrielle's little son,
recently created Duke of Vendôme. But money

was needed to carry on the war. The disorganisation of the administration, not less than the exhaustion and misery of the country, made it very difficult to obtain the necessary resources. However reluctant to impose new burdens on his people, the King could not begin the campaign with an empty treasury, and took the remonstrances of the Chambre des Comptes on the measures adopted in no good part. They raised objections, he told them, but suggested no other means whereby he could support his armies. If they had each offered him 2,000 or 3,000 crowns, or advised him to take their salaries, there would have been no need of these new edicts. He was not less outspoken to the Parliament, the fervour of whose new loyalty had not been strong enough to overcome their inveterate habit of seeking to exalt their own importance, by criticising and delaying the measures sent to them for registration. "You have," he said, "kept me waiting these three months, and I am now going to my army, as ill provided as ever Prince was. You will shortly see the injury you have done me. There are three hostile armies in my kingdom. I shall seek them out and I trust to bring them to account. I shall freely expose my life. God will not desert me. He has miraculously called me to the throne and assisted me till now. He will continue to help me. He does not leave His works imperfect. . . . Be as careful of what concerns the Commonwealth as you are of your own interests. Do your duty. Beware lest the venom of passion enter the heart. France is the man, Paris is the heart. I love you

as much as King can love. My words are not of
two colours. What I have in my mouth I have in
my heart. It is the nature of the French not to
love what they see. When you no longer see me
you will love me; and when you have lost me you
will regret me."

The King was eager to join his troops in Burgundy. Bouillon feebly supported by the Dutch
had effected nothing in Luxembourg; but the Duke
of Longueville, Governor of Picardy, had overrun
Artois, defeating the Spanish governor of that province, and, since the Archduke Ernest, Governor of the
Netherlands, had recently died (February 20th), it
was supposed that the Spaniards would not, during
that spring, attempt to do more than hold their own
on the Flemish frontier.

The younger Biron, who, since his father's death
had received the staff of Marshal and the government of Burgundy, had been sent to take possession
of his province. Assisted by the inhabitants, he had
driven Mayenne's garrisons from town after town,
and by the end of May had obtained possession of
the city of Dijon, although the citadel was still held
by Mayenne's soldiers.

Don Fernan de Velasco, Constable of Castile and
Governor of Milan, was ordered by his master to
collect forthwith all the forces he possibly could,
and to drive the French troops which had crossed
the frontiers out of Franche-Comté. Velasco with
10,000 men easily compelled the Lotharingian mercenaries, who, as yet, were the only French army in
the country, to retreat. He boasted that the Prince of

Béarn should rue his impertinent defiance of Spain, threatening to devastate France with fire and sword. Mayenne had joined him with an inconsiderable force, all that was left of the army of the League.

Biron urged the King to hasten to his assistance. Henry, who left Paris on May 30th reached Dijon on June 4th, the very day on which the Constable of Castile was preparing to cross the Saone, which divided the county from the duchy of Burgundy, the territory of the empire from that of France, at a little town called Gray, eight leagues from Dijon.

The King and Biron determined to take up a strong position at Lux, half way between Dijon and Gray, with their infantry, and to delay with their cavalry the advance of the enemy, till their position was entrenched and the siege works round the citadel of Dijon strengthened.   Henry, who was without any certain information of the Spaniard's movements, sent Biron forward with a small detachment of cavalry to discover whether some troops reported by his scouts to be advancing, were an isolated body of cavalry or the advanced guard of Velasco's army.

After passing Fontaine Française, a village not far from the frontier, Biron was met by an officer previously detached by the King, to discover the enemy's position, who assured the Marshal that their army was nowhere near; that the cavalry in front of them were only some two hundred men with whom he had been engaged.   Upon this, Biron at once sent word to Henry that he might safely advance, and himself hurried forward with his men, putting to flight some fifty or sixty skirmishers whom he met as he pressed on to the summit of a hill midway between Fontaine Française and Sainte Seine, another hamlet close to the frontier. From the top of the hill he commanded a wider view, and soon saw that he was on the point of being surrounded by a large force of cavalry supported by infantry. "Would I were dead," he exclaimed, "I have sent for the King and here is the whole Spanish army." He at once tried to fall back so as to warn the King, but was furiously charged by the enemy. Wounded in face and belly, covered with blood and dust, he maintained himself against ever increasing odds, till Henry came up. Even then but two or three hundred French horsemen were collected, while the enemy were four times as numerous. The King without stopping to put on his breastplate charged and drove back Biron's assailants, and then a few more of his men having come up, attacked in succession, and with such fury, three squadrons of the enemy's horse, each more numerous than his own, that he drove them back in confusion to seek the support of their infantry.

Four hundred Spanish men-at-arms had not been engaged. Mayenne urged Velasco to cut off the King's retreat with his infantry, and to allow him to lead the whole of the cavalry against the handful of French, who were exhausted by their repeated charges. If this were done, the defeat and probably the death or captivity of the King would be the result. But the Constable of Castile could not believe that the King would have been so foolhardy were not his army close at hand.

While the enemy's generals debated, new bodies of French horse were constantly gathering round their King, who soon found himself too strong to fear an attack. On the next day Velasco recrossed the Saone, deaf to Mayenne's entreaties that he would at least make some attempt to relieve the citadel of Dijon. Mayenne had no personal animosity to the King and had long cordially detested his Spanish allies. As they would do nothing to assist him he gladly acquiesced in a suggestion secretly made to him by Henry, that he should retire to Châlons, the only important town he still held in Burgundy, and remain there quiet and unmolested till they could come to terms.

The so-called battle of Fontaine Française, was only a brilliant cavalry skirmish, but by removing any inclination Velasco may have had to invade France, by securing Burgundy and determining the submission of Mayenne, it was as useful as the gain of a pitched battle. Henry, by his headlong bravery, no doubt imperilled a life of inestimable value to his country, but it was at the price of such risk that he maintained the reputation for chivalrous courage, which gave him his chief hold on the loyalty and affection of the French gentry.

During the next two months, the royal army wasted Franche-Comté without provoking the Spaniards to meet them in the field. The Swiss cantons, guarantors of the neutrality of the County, had been tempted to acquiesce in the French invasion by a promise that, if conquered, the province should be formed into a semi-independent state under their suzerainty. But reflecting how idle this suzerainty would be, they now alleged ancient treaties, and summoned Henry to withdraw his forces. He was anxious not to offend such useful allies, perhaps also, since his presence and his resources were urgently required in another quarter, glad of an honourable pretext for withdrawing from an arduous adventure too lightly undertaken.

Longueville, the Governor of Picardy, died soon after his success in Artois, and was succeeded by his brother-in-law, the Count of St. Pol. Philip II. strained every nerve to enable the Count of Fuentes, his commander in the Low Countries, to carry on offensive operations with a chance of success. Fuentes entered Picardy with 10,000 veteran troops and after taking Câtelet laid siege to Doullens. Admiral Villars, the brave and able defender of Rouen, and the Duke of Nevers were ordered to hasten with the forces they commanded into Normandy and Champagne to the assistance of the Count of St. Pol and of the Duke of Bouillon in Picardy. Bouillon, always impatient of an equal and insubordinate to a superior, quarrelled with Villars and was anxious to achieve something decisive before the arrival of Nevers, to whom the King had entrusted the chief command. Supported by St. Pol he insisted that the relief of Doullens should at once be attempted and would not listen to Villars who urged caution and the prudence of awaiting the hourly expected approach of Nevers and his army.

The result was a most crushing defeat (July 24,

1595), 3,000 Frenchmen, and among them 600 men of quality, were killed. Villars, after fighting bravely and with perhaps too much pertinacity, was taken prisoner and put to death in cold blood by the Spaniards as a " traitor." Doullens shortly after fell (July 31st). The atrocities which accompanied the sack of the town were marked by that cold-blooded devilry in which the Spanish troops surpassed all rivals.

Bouillon, far from learning modesty in defeat, lost no opportunity of thwarting Nevers, who had joined his colleagues a few hours after the rout. No attempt was made to prevent Fuentes from laying siege to Cambray with 18,000 soldiers besides 5,000 sappers and 72 cannon, a most formidable park of artillery for those days. Cambray, a free Imperial city, had been taken in 1581 by the Duke of Anjou, who had placed a certain Balagny, bastard of Monluc, Bishop of Valence, in command of the town and garrison.

On the 2d of October while the garrison was on the walls expecting an assault, the townspeople seized one of the gates and admitted Fuentes, who had promised to restore and respect the ancient privileges and liberties of the city. A week later the citadel in which Balagny and the French had taken refuge capitulated.

On hearing that Cambray was threatened, Henry hurried from Lyons towards the North-western frontier.

When Henry reached his army, he found the Spaniards in Cambray, and the French frontier-towns panic-stricken. Collecting all his resources and assisted by the Dutch with 2,000 men and the pay for 2,000 more, the King laid siege to La Fère, a Picard fortress surrendered by the League as the price of Spanish help, and in which great stores of warlike material and provisions had been accumulated by Fuentes.

The siege of La Fère continued throughout the winter. Meantime the leaders of the League found in the absolution of Henry by the Pope, a decent pretext for withdrawing from a hopeless contest.

Dislike of Spain, which he shared with the other Italian princes, the warm intercession of Venice and of the Duke of Florence, the advice of his confessor Baronius and of his minister Cardinal Toleto, led Clement VIII. to regret the harshness with which he had rejected the French King's overtures. It was an indication of his changed disposition that he authorised the monastic orders in France to mention the King in their prayers.

Notwithstanding the expulsion of their order from Paris and Northern France, the most influential Jesuits agreed with Toleto in approving of a conciliatory policy. Partly because they thus hoped to make their peace with the French Court and to obtain the revocation of the sentence of banishment, partly because the alliance of the order with Spain had broken down. Philip II. only tolerated the Jesuits with their secret and powerful organisation so long as they were thoroughly Spanish. In 1573, a Spanish Jew was about to be elected general. The party in the order opposed to Spain brought

20

about his rejection.    Henceforth Philip regarded
the order with dislike as a mere instrument of the
Papacy.    Their religious doctrine appeared questionable to the Dominicans of the Spanish Inquisition.    Their polemic against the Calvinists, their
desire to make things easy, so to speak, to put things
in a way acceptable to the common sense of the
average man, led them to express views not to be
reconciled with the theology of Aquinas, the canon
of Dominican orthodoxy.

The Jesuits, on the other hand, were too clear-
sighted not to see the growing impotence of Spain.
To make France subservient to their policy would
be a triumph not perhaps unattainable by patient
perseverance.

The adroit Du Perron, who had played a conspicuous part in his master's conversion, arrived at
Rome (July, 1595) to assist Cardinal d'Ossat in settling with the Curia the method and conditions of
the King's absolution.    Du Perron has been accused
of sacrificing his master's interests to the hope of a
Cardinal's hat ; a charge rendered credible by the
contemptible character of the time-server against
whom it was brought.    Yet he supported D'Ossat
in stoutly contesting every point, and those on which
they gave way were for the most part matters of
form and ceremonial; such as the blows which the
representatives of Henry knelt to receive, while they
kissed the Pope's foot, before he pronounced the
formula of absolution,— concessions which may be
justified as the price paid to the Holy See for the
surrender by it of the two most vital points at issue.

I. The French refused to admit that the heresy or excommunication of their King could affect his right to the throne or his claim to the allegiance of his subjects : and by allowing that he did not require " temporal rehabilitation " the Pope gave up that dogma of the supremacy of the spiritual over the temporal power, which, since the days of Hildebrand, it had been the aim of his predecessors to establish.

II. Clement VIII. had declared it to be impossible that he should absolve Henry of Bourbon, unless he would prove the sincerity of his orthodoxy by causing the decrees of the Council of Trent to be observed in his dominions. But by admitting a written stipulation that this should only be done so far as was consistent with public tranquillity, he gave back with the left hand what he took with the right, and sanctioned that toleration of heresy, which he pronounced to be inadmissible.

The final submission of Mayenne (January, 1596) was the outward and visible sign of the dissolution of the League. Yet the discredit of the Duke was so great, and his power had been brought so low, that the terms which he obtained might well appear extravagantly favourable. He received the government of the Isle of France, three fortresses as places of surety, Châlon-sur-Saône, Seurre and Soissons, together with the payment of all his debts. The Parliament remonstrated against such lenity ; but Mayenne had secured the intercession of Gabrielle d'Estrées, by promising, in the event of the King's death, to support the claim of her son, the infant

Duke of Vendôme, to the Crown. The debts of
the Duke grew like the hydra's heads. Directly
one was paid two more sprang up in its place, to
the profit of the debtor, if, as was suspected, this
was the source of his subsequent wealth. Yet it
must be allowed that Mayenne acted the part of a
defeated and pardoned rebel with some dignity and
honour. Unprincipled, and unscrupulous in his
ambition, and without those brilliant qualities which
dazzled the mob in his brother Guise, he was,
nevertheless, a man of considerable, though somewhat inarticulate ability. He had played the game
of conspiracy and treason and had lost, and was too
wise to return to it, when the chances of success were
infinitely less favourable. Henceforth, therefore, he
proved a loyal and useful subject.

His first interview with the King took place at
the country house of the royal mistress. Taking
him by the arm, Henry walked the Duke rapidly up
and down in the garden, till Mayenne, crippled with
the gout and of unwieldy bulk, was almost at his
last gasp. " One more turn," the King said in an
aside to Rosny, " and I shall have punished this fat
fellow for all the trouble he has given us,"—and
then aloud : " Confess, cousin, that I am going a
little too fast for you."—" Faith, Sire, it is true ; if
your Majesty had gone on, I think you would have
killed me."—" Shake hands, cousin," laughed the
King, " for, God's truth, this is all the ill you need
ever fear from me," and he sent him back to the
house to drink a couple of bottles of a favourite
vintage.

Not long after, Épernon, who had not published his treaty with Philip II., and who found the inhabitants of the towns and districts he held everywhere turning against him, thought good to make his peace on terms not less favourable than the other rebels. Henry's one aim was to conciliate his domestic enemies in order that he might direct the united strength of the country against Spain. He was so far successful that in the next year we find Mayenne, Épernon and Montmorency, representing the parties of the League, of the Royalists of the time of Henry III., and of the Politicians fighting together in the royal army under the walls of Amiens. Yet it was difficult for his faithful servants, many of whom could not obtain payment of the sums they had spent in his service, to see the traitors who had fought against him lavishly rewarded and caressed, without some feeling of discontent. These new courtiers had not been standing idly waiting to be hired in the market-place, but busily employed sowing tares, and trampling under foot the master's fields. And now, were they to receive a day's fair wage many times over, while the honest labourers who had borne the toil and heat of the day were sent empty away?

Although it was with the utmost difficulty that the King found the money to keep his troops together, the siege of La Fère continued. After the death of Francis D'O, he had placed his finances under the management of a board. Some of the members proved to be wanting in experience and vigour, others in honesty ; even Rosny, who was

among them, could effect nothing in the face of the
lethargy and ill-will of his colleagues. In the middle
of April (1596) the King wrote that it went to his
heart to see his people so ground down. That his
one wish was to relieve them from so many subsidies,
tallages and oppressions. But before anything could
be done, the Spaniards must be driven out of the
country. The 1,500,000 crowns of which his treasury
board had cheated him during the year, would have
sufficed for this. But, as it was, he was close to the
enemy without a horse that could carry him, without a whole suit of armour: his shirts torn, his
doublet out at elbow, his larder empty. For two
days he had been taking pot-luck here and there. It
is indeed probable, that but for a most timely loan
from the Grand Duke of Tuscany he would have
been compelled to raise the siege.

The master of the Indies, the ruler of Mexico and
Peru, was not less poverty-stricken than his antagonist; yet, early in 1596, he had been able by the most
desperate expedients to collect a considerable treasure. Part of this was devoted to preparing a great
armament for the invasion of England; but part
also was employed in supplying with a formidable
army, the new ruler of the Netherlands, the Cardinal-
Archduke Albert, who was about to exchange his
red hat for the hand of his cousin, the Infanta
Isabella. Twenty thousand men were collected at
Valenciennes, and it was generally thought that an
attempt would be made to relieve La Fère. Henry
hoped that the Archduke would fight a pitched
battle. But the movements of the Spaniards were

directed by a French renegade, De Rosne, a Marshal
of Mayenne's fashion, and a man of remarkable skill
and daring, to whom Fuentes had owed the successes
of the previous year.    Acting by this man's advice,
the Cardinal-Archduke sent detachments to make a
feint in the direction of La Fère, and marched the
bulk of his forces rapidly on Calais.

On April 14th the King was startled to hear that
the enemy had stormed the outworks of that town.
Within twenty-four hours he was on the march with
his cavalry and some light infantry.    Bad news met
him on the way.    The Governor of Picardy, the
Count of St. Pol, had been driven back by a furious
storm when near the mouth of the harbour with reinforcements.    No sooner were the walls of the town
breached, than the inhabitants, fearing the fate of
Doullens, compelled the Governor and garrison to
retire into the citadel.    But that also was defended
with little perseverance or courage.    The victors
acquired a vast booty, in addition to the possession
of a stronghold not less useful for their designs
against England than as a basis of operations in
Picardy.

Queen Elizabeth had once more overreached herself by trying to take advantage of her neighbours'
necessities.    The Spaniards had captured the port
which commanded the narrow seas almost in sight
of a powerful armament collected at Dover under
the command of Essex.    In a few hours 16,000
English might have been landed on the French
coast, a force sufficient to have compelled the hasty
retreat, or to have secured the defeat, of the Arch-

duke.　But the Queen asked for Calais as the price of her help.　Henry IV. replied that he would sooner see it in the hands of the Spaniards, from whom he trusted shortly to recover it, than of the English, who had so stubbornly held it for generations.　When Elizabeth relented, and the eagerly expected permission to sail reached Essex, it was too late, the Spanish flag already floated over the citadel.

Since he could not save Calais, the King strengthened the garrisons of the neighbouring towns and hastened back to La Fère, which surrendered on May 22d.　The Spaniards, meantime, had taken Ham, Guines and Ardres.　The gentry in the King's service hurried home, according to their custom, as soon as the siege was concluded, and the emptiness of the treasury made it difficult to keep even the mercenaries together ; yet Henry contrived to march towards the Archduke at the head of an army more formidable than the Austrian cared to meet.　The Spaniards recrossed the frontier and sat down before Hulst, which they took from the Dutch, at the cost of many men, much money and a loss far more irreparable, the life of Marshal de Rosne.

The recent successes of the Spaniards raised the hopes of those nobles who saw in the weakness of the monarchy a chance of enlarging their own privileges.　The Duke of Montpensier, a personage less ill-meaning than foolish, was put forward to suggest as an excellent plan for keeping an army on foot, that the King should grant the hereditary possession of their offices to all governors, whether of provinces

or towns, on condition that they should constantly
keep a certain number of men under arms for his
service.    Henry asked his cousin, whether he had
taken leave of his senses, but this brilliant suggestion
was a straw which showed clearly enough from what
quarter the wind was blowing.

On the other hand, Henry IV. probably owed to
the unfavourable aspect of his affairs, the signature
by the Queen of England and her clients, the
United Provinces, of an offensive and defensive
alliance with France against Spain (May 24th).
Elizabeth's friendship was ever warmest in his adversity.    Although the assistance promised by the
allies for the war in France was meagre, the moral
effect of the treaty was great.    It committed the
Queen to open war against Philip II.    She could
not, after so public an engagement, conclude without
indelible infamy a separate peace at the expense of
her allies, and exchange, as she had thought of doing, Flushing and Brill for Calais.

It was something to have secured the open alliance of England and of the United Provinces.    But
if the struggle was to be carried to a speedy and
successful issue, it was not only necessary for Henry
IV. to obtain further resources, but also to prove to
his enemies at home and abroad that he commanded
the support of a vast majority of the nation.

There were some who advised the King to con-
vene the Estates and thus to show that he possessed
the confidence of his people.    But the greater number of his councillors pointed out the opportunity
that would thus be given to intrigue and faction ;

the little good effected by recent meetings of the
States-General ; the weary debates that would ensue
accompanied by unprofitable complaints of evils,
which all must see and deplore, but which could
hardly be remedied while a hostile army was in the
land ; the certainty that the necessary supplies
would only be voted after long and perhaps ruinous
delay.    Henry, not more disposed to share his authority than other born rulers of men, listened readily to advice which fell in with his humour.    Nor
can it be denied that there was no general wish in
France that the Estates should meet.    The country
was inclined to acquiesce in personal government by
the same weariness of political strife, the same material exhaustion, the same desire of repose, the
same tendency to await reforms from above, which
led the national representatives, at the conclusion
of the hundred years' war, to surrender the power of
the purse by voting a permanent tallage, and which
at other periods have led the French to submit to
the usurpations of some " Saviour of society," a
Richelieu or a Napoleon.

The last meetings of the States-General had
merely been the preludes to civil war.    The traditions of constitutional government had been discredited by being used as the instruments of faction.
The reforming, the constitutional and progressive
party, so influential a generation earlier at the
States-General of Orleans and Pontoise, had been
composed of two kinds of men, the Huguenots
and the Moderates or Politicians.    The Huguenots
when the hope of seeing their creed adopted as the

national faith faded away, appear to have laid aside all wish to introduce constitutional reforms; the Politicians, weary of anarchy and of the insolence of Spain, were willing to support any government, strong enough to establish order at home and to make France respected abroad.   The King, therefore, met with general approval when he had recourse to a half measure, for which precedents were not wanting, and summoned a meeting of *Notables* for the Autumn (1596).

The Notables met at Rouen (Nov. 4, 1596), for an epidemic was raging in Paris.   One hundred and fifty nobles, prelates and magistrates had been summoned, but on the first day only eighty were present and these for the most part lawyers and officials. The King welcomed them in a characteristic harangue: "If I wished to gain the name of orator, I should have learnt some long and eloquent speech and have spoken it before you with suitable dignity; but, gentlemen, my wishes aspire to two more glorious titles, to be hailed the Saviour and Restorer of this State.   You know, to your cost, as I to mine, that when God called me to this Crown, I found France not only ruined but almost lost to the French. By the divine favour; by the prayers and good counsels of my servants who do not follow the profession of arms; by the sword of my brave and generous nobles—among whom I reckon the Princes, for the honour of a gentleman is our best possession; by my own toils and exertions, I have saved our country from annihilation.   Let me now save it from ruin.   Share this second glory with me, my dear subjects, as you shared in the former. I have not, like my predecessors, called you together merely to approve what I have determined. I have summoned you to take your advice, to believe and to follow it. In short because I desire to place myself under your guardianship, a desire seldom felt by a King, a grey beard and a conqueror."

The King's answer to some expression of surprise from his mistress that he should have spoken of putting himself under the tutelage of the Notables, has often been repeated, " Ventre St. Gris, so I said, but I meant with my sword by my side." It is not so well known that the draft of his frank and artless speech, written and elaborately corrected in his own hand, still exists in the French National library. Had they known that it was an after thought which made them " *Gentlemen* " and " his *dear* subjects," and that his love for his people was not at first *extreme*, the Notables might have distrusted their Prince's flattery. The King's impulsive frankness was indeed not wholly false : he often said what he really meant and said it simply, but this simplicity was the perfection of art. He boasts of everything, and even his frankness is the subject of his self-commendation. " I am grey without, golden within." " What is on my lips is in my heart . . . my words are not of two colours." If we examine his speeches we find in them little argument, but skilful flattery and sometimes scathing denunciation ; vague and often repeated promises of future benefits ; much praise of himself and energetic exhortation to others to go and do likewise.

The Notables protested their devotion ; suggested some reforms ; and, quite unconstitutionally, voted a duty of five per cent. *ad valorem* on all goods brought for sale into towns, villages and markets. This tax, called the Pancarte, proved eminently unpopular, and was withdrawn after no long time. The assembly was dismissed and the King returned to Paris, where, for the first time since his accession, he lived for a while the life of a pleasure-loving Prince, enjoying ballets and masques, hunting parties and sumptuous feasts. It was noted as a mark of sinful extravagance, likely in a time of general want and public poverty to provoke the wrath of Heaven, that *Bon Chrétien* pears at a crown a piece, and sturgeons which cost one hundred crowns, were served at the christening feast of the son of the Constable Montmorency.

Yet more serious matters were not neglected. Preparations were made to open the campaign of the next year by the siege of Arras, and stores and ammunition were collected at Amiens. As the citizens insisted that their privilege not to receive a garrison should be respected, they could guard their own walls with 10,000 armed men, the King ordered the Count of St. Pol, the Governor of Picardy, to take up his abode in the town and to watch over its safety.

But Hernantello de Portocarrero, the Governor of Doullens, an officer as fertile of resource as he was prompt and bold in action, heard that the train-bands of Amiens were not over-exact in performing their military duties. Accordingly a party of his men disguised as peasants on their way to market and driving a big waggon, appeared early one morning at the gates. As they passed under the arch of the portal the neck of a sack filled with nuts came undone, and while the guards were scrambling for the scattered contents, some of the pretended countrymen blew out their brains, or stabbed them with their concealed weapons, while others cut the traces of the cart horses, so that the waggon was left standing in the way and it was impossible either to close the gates or to drop the portcullis. Portocarrero and his men lurking in ambush hard by rushed up at the sound of the scuffle and were in possession of the town before the terrified citizens could collect or offer any effective resistance.

"On Wednesday, the 12th of this month" (March, 1597), writes the diarist L'Estoile, "in the midst of feasts and dances came the news of the surprise of Amiens, to the dismay of the revellers and of Paris. Even the King, whose constancy and magnanimity are not easily shaken, seemed stunned by the blow. Yet looking to God, as is his wont in adversity, rather than in prosperity, he said aloud : ' This blow is from Heaven. These poor people have lost themselves by refusing the small garrison I wished to give them.' Then, after a moment's thought, ' Enough of playing the King of France; it is time to be again the King of Navarre.' "

That same day, Henry determined on the measures to be taken for the recovery of the lost town, and suggested or approved of expedients for raising the money required for a long and difficult siege. Before nightfall he was on horseback, and on his way to the frontier. He sent Marshal Biron to invest Amiens on the north, to cut off the communications of Portocarrero with Doullens and to prevent reinforcements or supplies reaching Amiens from the Low Countries. He himself visited the towns on the Somme, reassured the panic-stricken inhabitants and strengthened their garrisons. Then he hurried back to Paris to obtain the necessary means for paying and supporting his army. The Parliament had refused to register the financial edicts. The creation of new judicial offices for the purpose of raising money by their sale, diminished both their emoluments and their dignity. Among other grounds for their opposition, they alleged that the King wasted money on his buildings. This Henry took much amiss; he ought not, he complained, to be grudged the little he spent in this way. Building was his only consolation and pleasure in the midst of his toils: hunting, gambling and women were apparently not worth mention. Yet in addressing the Parliament he restrained his anger and almost assumed the tone and attitude of a suppliant. He had come to beg alms from them on behalf of those who were spending their lives and toiling day and night to secure the tranquillity of their countrymen. " I have been," he continued, " on the frontier. I have done what I could to keep the people in good heart. I have encouraged the country folk. I have fortified their church towers. But I must tell you, gentlemen, that I felt their cries of ' Vive le Roi ' like so many stabs in my heart, knowing that I

shall be compelled to abandon them on the first
day" (of the enemy's invasion). The lawyers were
obdurate until the King held a "Bed of Justice"
and commanded instant registration. By this means
and by the zeal of Rosny, into whose hands the
control of the finances was gradually passing, some
2,700,000 crowns were raised and it became possible
to press the siege of Amiens with vigour and at the
same time to check the renewed aggressions of
Mercœur in Brittany, and of the Duke of Savoy on
the Eastern frontier, as well as to guard against the
intrigues and plots reported from various quarters,
last writhings of the scotched snake of the League.

During April and May the energy and care of
Biron prevented the Spaniards from throwing more
than one reinforcement of 600 men into Amiens and
drew a double line of entrenchments round the town
to the north of the Somme. Henry reached the
leaguer on June 7th and completed the investment
by extending his posts south of the river, but without protecting them by defensive works.

The King found an army of barely 15,000 men,
which after his arrival quickly grew to 25,000, the
gentry showing their usual zeal when there was an
opportunity of fighting under the immediate command of the King. Queen Elizabeth was with difficulty induced to fulfil her obligations under the
recent treaty and to send 2,000 men. The rebellion
in Ireland, the armament which, notwithstanding
the capture of Cadiz and of his fleet in the previous
year, Philip II. had again equipped for the invasion
of England, were more than mere pretexts. But in

addition to the Queen's contingent, English volunteers crossed the Channel, or came from Flanders to fight under so popular a Prince against the common enemy. Six thousand English and Dutch soldiers made up for the absence of the majority of the French Protestants, who, indignant that so little attention was paid to their complaints, and alarmed by the King's reconciliation with the Pope and by the concessions made to his opponents at their expense, listened to wild talk of rising in arms, seizing Tours and taking advantage of the King's difficulties to compel attention to their wrongs.

Although more than once Henry's resources were nearly exhausted, the care of Rosny never allowed the military chest to become quite empty ; and since the soldiers were paid, they could be kept under good discipline. The peasantry of the neighbourhood instead of being plundered and tortured were able to cultivate their fields and reap their harvest in safety, whilst they found in the royal camp a profitable market for their produce. It was perhaps the first time during these wars that the proximity of a large army was felt to be a blessing rather than a curse.

Sufficient accommodation, a well-supplied commissariat, excellent sanitary arrangements, good quarters and attendance for the sick and wounded bore witness to the King's humane and intelligent care for his men. It was usual in the sieges of this period for a quarter or even half of the assailants to perish from disease, privations and neglect, but before Amiens, notwithstanding much hard fighting, the French lost barely 600 men in four months. The Archduke Albert, though fully alive to the importance of holding Amiens—he would sooner, he said, see the enemy in possession of Ghent or Antwerp—could attempt nothing to raise the siege till he had money. But as the Spanish Government was entirely without credit, money was not procurable till the taxes were collected and the galleons had arrived from the Indies. Portocarrero, though unaided, showed the same enterprise and resource in defending as in taking Amiens, and his death on September 3d was an irreparable loss to the besieged.

It was not till the 12th of the same month, that the Cardinal Archduke succeeded in assembling his army, 18,000 foot and 3,000 horse at Douai ; on the 14th the sound of the guns he fired to announce his approach, was heard by the besieged. On the north of the Somme, the French lines were too strong to be attacked, but if the Spaniards could cross the river and approach the town from the south, they would either oblige the King to fight a pitched battle with only a part of his army, or to raise the siege.

On the 15th the Archduke attacked the village of Longpré, which lay outside the French lines and commanded the nearest bridge over the Somme. Marshal Biron, suspected of wishing, like his father, to protract the war, was accused of having left Longpré purposely unfortified and of having informed the enemy that this was the vulnerable point of the French position, but as the King had personally directed the siege for three months, he must share the blame of what was more probably a careless oversight.

In the absence of the King, who was visiting his posts south of the river, the Duke of Mayenne took the command of the French, sent the Swiss and all the artillery he could collect to Longpré and began hastily to throw up entrenchments. If the Spaniards had pressed resolutely forward, Mayenne with his inferior forces would scarcely have been able to prevent them from occupying the village and crossing the bridge. But they halted at the first salvo of artillery, then fell back and gave the Duke time to strengthen his position and to bring up more men. By the time that Henry returned to his army, the Archduke had lost his opportunity, and began to retreat after a futile attempt to throw a division of picked men across the river. He came on, Henry wrote to Elizabeth, like a soldier, but fell back like a priest. The King would have pursued and attacked the retreating enemy, but was restrained by the caution or jealousy of his officers; but the effect of a victory in the field could scarcely have been greater than that of the precipitate retreat of the relieving army and the consequent capitulation of Amiens (September 19th).

The recovery of Amiens after the futile attempt of the Regent of the Netherlands to raise the siege, the good order and discipline of the French army, the unshaken loyalty of the majority of the former leaders of the League, the unexpected resources obtained by the ingenuity and energy of Rosny, did more than any previous success to raise the reputation of the King and the opinion of his power at home and abroad.  He determined to make use of his superiority in arms and of the discouragement of his opponents to  ome to terms with his domestic and foreign enemies, and to satisfy, so far as was practicable, the demands of the Huguenots, before their despair or the ambition of some among their leaders led to new broils and complications.

The life of Philip II. was drawing to a close in the midst of sufferings so awful that his enemies could not but recognise in them the divine chastisement of a tyrant and a persecutor.  He had determined that the Netherlands should be the appanage of his daughter Isabella, and that she should rule there under the suzerainty of Spain, jointly with her cousin the Cardinal-Archduke Albert, whom she was to marry as soon as the Pope had released him from his priestly vows.  But the position of the new Governors of the Netherlands would be precarious if exposed to the enmity of France as well as of England and of the United Provinces ; nor did he wish to leave his young and incapable successor on the Spanish throne involved in the dangers of a great war.  He therefore gladly availed himself of the mediation of the Pope to open negotiations with the man to whom he had so long denied any title but that of Prince of Béarn.

Clement VIII. had for some time been endeavouring to bring about an understanding between the two great Catholic powers and to unite them in an attack upon England, the stronghold of heresy.

Early in 1597 he assured Cardinal d'Ossat, the French ambassador, that his master was not bound to keep faith with heretics, nor indeed, as a sovereign, to observe any engagements injurious to the interests of his country: " Salus reipublicæ summa lex." To these Machiavellian suggestions Henry IV. replied in a vein of impassioned honour: " I have pledged my faith to the Queen of England and the United Provinces to join my forces with theirs to resist the arms of the King of Spain. How could I then treat with him to their hurt, or even fail in a single one of those points I have promised to them, without betraying my duty, my honour and my own interests? No pretext, I think, could be sufficient to excuse such baseness and perfidy ; and if it could, sooner than avail myself of it I would lose my life. I have always found it better to trust in God than in the strength and works of men. Since His divine justice is infallible, I can never believe that He would favour an act of treachery so glaring as I should commit, if I were to desert my friends and allies for my own profit." Perhaps when the King sent this despatch, he protested over-much, perhaps he now argued, not without show of reason, that he had no intention of betraying his allies and turning his arms against them, and only contemplated opening negotiations and concluding a peace in which they might, if they pleased, be included.

No doubt he violated the express stipulations of the treaty concluded two years before, by which the contracting parties bound themselves to enter into no separate dealings or treaty with Spain, yet the severity with which some even among French historians condemn Henry's conduct, appears excessive.

When the French envoys signed the treaty with Elizabeth, they assured their master, " that no Prince can be bound by any treaty to do that which may endanger the safety of his people," and although he himself, as we have seen, appears to have repudiated this axiom of sixteenth-century statecraft, it was recognised by the English ministry when, after Henry's abjuration, they pointed out that the relations between France and England must henceforth be determined by considerations of self-interest. Elizabeth herself certainly never acted, nor intended to act, on any other principle. Again and again she had been prepared to betray her allies and clients, the Dutch, if only Philip II. had made it worth her while. At that very moment, so his agents assured the French King, she was secretly negotiating with the Archduke Albert, and would have concluded peace on the basis of an exchange of Flushing and Brill for Calais and Ardres. Henry at any rate contemplated no such baseness as this. He gave his plenipotentiaries the most stringent directions to conclude no peace to which his allies might not have the option of acceding. From the first he made no attempt to conceal his intentions from them. Soon after the recovery of Amiens he wrote to Elizabeth " that he knew it to be more than ever necessary for their common safety, that they should in all things be close friends. He himself would never weary of fighting for a cause so just as theirs; born and reared as he had been in the midst of the toils and

dangers of war, where glory, the best food of every
truly royal soul, is to be gathered like a rose amid
thorns.  But for all that, he might well be weary of
the evils and miseries inflicted by war on his people; since therefore the Spaniards were disposed to
negotiate, he could not do otherwise than enter into
treaty with them."

The French and Spanish plenipotentiaries met at
Vervins in February; the peace was signed on
May 2, 1598.

The terms between the two contracting powers
were settled without much difficulty.  Retaining
Cambray, the Spaniards evacuated Calais, the other
Picard towns and the port of Blavet in Brittany.
The French restored the county of Charolais.  The
negotiations were somewhat protracted by questions
concerning the allies on both sides.  The inclusion
of Mercœur in the treaty was absolutely refused by
the French.  On the other hand, Henry insisted that
the option of acceding to the peace within six
months should be offered to his confederates.

The Dutch refused to accept a truce which the
Spaniards were with difficulty persuaded to offer,
and Henry IV. promised to continue to assist them
indirectly by the most prompt repayment possible
of the large sums for which he was their debtor.

While his ministers began to negotiate the peace
with Spain, Henry left Paris for the west to receive the submission of Brittany.  The departure
of the English, recalled by their Queen on account
of the threatened Spanish invasion, and of serious
troubles in Ireland, together with the discontent of

the Huguenots, had given a respite to the Duke of Mercœur. But the Bretons, however much attached to their provincial independence, felt no hereditary loyalty to a Lotharingian Prince, and were weary of the civil war and of the presence of the Spaniards. As soon as the King's approach was known, town after town threw open its, gates. It seemed that Mercœur must either submit himself a suppliant to the King's discretion, or seek a refuge among his Spanish allies at Blavet. A little daughter of six years was the sole heiress of his vast riches and wide domains, and he offered her hand to the four-year-old Cæsar of Vendôme. After this he and his adherents were confirmed in all their possessions, offices and dignities, their zeal for the Catholic faith was commended in the public treaty, and by secret articles they were promised additional gratuities and pensions. The King probably persuaded himself that whatever Mercœur gained would be to the ultimate advantage of his son, and that the complete restoration of domestic peace could scarcely be bought at too high a price.

In forming our estimate of Henry IV's treatment of the Huguenots, we have to consider two questions: First, did he unduly delay the satisfaction of their just claims? Secondly, was the final settlement fair and equitable?

When Henry IV. succeeded to the throne, the Catholics feared that, if immediately victorious, he would disregard his promise to respect and protect the Roman Church, as the established religion of the State. The Protestants, when he abjured their creed, disbelieved his assurance that he would continue their friend and that if they were attacked he was prepared to die in their defence. Du Plessis-Mornay, generally just to the honesty of his master's intentions, expressed this feeling openly in writing to him. His conversion, he maintained, must either be sincere, or yielded to compulsion. If sincere, what have the Reformed Churches to hope from his affection? If compulsory, can he, who could not protect his own conscience, protect that of others? And if his conscience is enslaved, is his will likely to remain free? It is a shorter step from one wrong to a greater than from right to wrong, from idolatry to persecution than from pure religion to idolatry.

Both Romanists and Reformers were unjust to their King. He could not fail to see that while on the one hand the supremacy of Catholicism was too firmly established in France to be overthrown, on the other hand the disappointment and despair of the Protestant minority would be fatal to all possibility of a quiet reign. Had he felt no gratitude to the men "who had guarded his cradle and borne him to power on their shoulders," there were two sufficient motives to determine him to make the condition of the Huguenots as tolerable as possible. One of these motives was the wish to convince the Protestant powers that he was no enemy to their religion, and that they might trust him as their leader in that renewed struggle with the Austro-Spanish house, to which he looked forward; the other was the fear that the Huguenots might place themselves under the protection of England or of the Elector Palatine and so once more expose France to the danger of foreign intervention.

He who believed that no form of ecclesiastical polity was of divine institution, and who, while convinced that there was much error in the doctrine of Rome, suspected that his Calvinist friends had no monopoly of truth, was not likely to hold the balance unfairly, when the tranquillity of his kingdom and the success of his policy demanded that he should do equal justice to the jarring sects.

Nor do the complaints appear just which were constantly made by the Protestant assemblies, repeated by Aubigné and other Huguenot writers, and endorsed by their co-religionists down to the present time, that the King wilfully delayed the satisfaction of the demands of the Reformed Churches, that he granted their desire to all other factions and gorged his enemies with favours, before he gave a thought to his most faithful friends. After he was firmly established on the throne, he required all the authority, all the resources he had painfully accumulated to impose the acceptance and the observation of the Edict of Nantes on the courts of law, the magistrates and officials.

It was the constant and well-founded complaint of the Protestants that the moderate concessions made to them by the treaty of 1589 and by the edict of 1577, re-enacted in 1594, were rendered nugatory by the ill-will and disregard of the King's authority, shown by the Parliaments and by the Governors of towns and provinces. But if his authority was not sufficient to obtain for the Protestants a moderate instalment of what they might justly claim, how would it have been possible for Henry to enforce the complete satisfaction of their demands?

We may fairly ask those who accuse Henry IV. of neglecting the interests of the Protestants, to point out the time previous to 1598 when he could not only have promulgated an edict securing to them equal rights, toleration and liberty of worship, but also have enforced such a law.

Clearly he could not have done so at his accession. At that anxious time the utmost Du Plessis-Mornay ventured to advise, was, that toleration should be granted to what might be named the "so-called" Reformed Church, under colour of the old edicts set aside, but not legally repealed, by the League; while at the same time the Huguenots should be warned to behave with greater moderation.

Nor in 1591, after the victory of Ivry, does the same "Pope of the Huguenots" ask for more than the re-enactment of the edict of 1577 "under which, France had been prosperous, all the King's subjects satisfied, . . . the Catholic religion maintained in its dignity, the necessities of the Reformed religion provided for; by which in short it had seemed that the question had been so settled, that it ought not to have been re-opened."

After his conversion and the recovery of Paris (1594), Henry accomplished the desire of Du Plessis-Mornay, by re-enacting the edict of 1577 together with the clauses added to it by the treaties of Nerac and Fleix. Nay, more, since the Reformed Churches had lost their protector by his abjuration, and he neither would nor could allow a foreign prince or a powerful and ambitious noble to succeed him in that office, he not only permitted, but even suggested, that the Churches should organise themselves more efficiently for self-government and defence. The Huguenot community was divided into ten provinces, each province elected an assembly composed of an equal number of nobles, commoners and ministers, and these provincial assemblies nominated a general council composed of ten members—four nobles, four burgesses and two ministers. The ecclesiastical organisation, the consistories and synods, remained unaltered.

If then the position of the Reformed Churches was still unsatisfactory and precarious, this was not so much owing to the neglect of the King, or to the absence of legal guarantees as to the persistence of their enemies and the weakness of the central Government, which could not control the law-courts and officials, or punish the insubordination of the more powerful nobles. More ample concessions would have been valueless, since they would have remained a dead letter.

The Huguenots not only complained that the turbulence of their enemies and the ill-will of the judges rendered the protection of the law futile, but also that each treaty the King concluded with his rebels contained clauses impairing their right to that protection. The Catholic nobles and princes were allowed to proscribe dissent within their domains, the towns stipulated that it should not be tolerated within their walls. The sturdy importunity of the Protestant assemblies was not wholly displeasing to the King. He writes to a friend, that he wished that it might seem as if he granted whatever may be necessary for their welfare, rather because he cannot avoid doing so, than from his love towards them. Yet the Reformers not unreasonably suspected the sincerity of the royal intentions, when they saw the growing favour of their old enemies ; the presence of former Leaguers in the royal council ; the reconciliation of the King and the Pope ; the heir to the throne, the young Prince of Condé, taken away from his Protestant teachers and educated as a Catholic ; their own position becoming every day more precarious. Would Henry after he had come to terms with or subdued all his enemies, when his power was firmly established, care to provoke new discontent and to encounter fresh trouble in order that he might provide for their interests?

When Amiens was surprised the Protestant Parliament was in session at Saumur, that strong fortress overhanging the Loire, which under the government of Mornay was in some sort the metropolis of the Huguenot Church. The King desired them to postpone their debates and to hasten to his assistance. Mornay urged them to obey the summons. Although a few young nobles joined the royal army, the majority held aloof. Yet the violent counsels of some rash and unpatriotic men were rejected by the influence of the wiser and better part—perhaps also frustrated by other means. Henry IV. afterwards complained that the malcontents had nearly ruined

everything by their perversity and had only been
prevented doing so by the traitors among them who
accepted his bribes or sought his favour. "How
often," he concluded, "when I saw you so opposed
to my wishes, have I exclaimed to myself, O that
my people would have hearkened unto me! For if
Israel had walked in my ways, I should soon have
put down their enemies and turned my hand against
their adversaries."

To mitigate the impatience of the Protestants,
commissioners were appointed to treat with them
touching the satisfaction of their demands. These
commissioners were men of known impartiality and
moderation. The historian, De Thou, President of
the Parliament of Paris, and Gaspard de Schomberg,
Count of Nanteuil, a German by birth but no relation of the Schomberg whose death at Ivry has been
mentioned, or of that French marshal and English
duke of the same name who fell leading his men
to victory across the Boyne.

In addition to the liberty of conscience and toleration of their worship promised by previous edicts,
the Protestants demanded : (1) that they should
retain—at any rate for a considerable time—their
places of surety ; (2) that no one should be in-
capacitated by his religion for public office ; (3) that
all cases in which Protestants were concerned should
be tried by courts composed of judges of both
creeds (*Chambres mi-parties*). The negotiations
continued during the siege of Amiens and to the end
of the year (1597).

The King did not grant the demands of the

Protestants till he had not only settled the terms of the peace with Spain and stamped out the last embers of the civil war, but had also dispersed the Protestant levies which Mornay and De Thou had vainly urged the Dukes of Bouillon and Thouars to lead to his assistance before Amiens ; until, in short, he was sufficiently powerful to settle the question on his own terms. That he was able to give the Huguenots so much, is the best proof that he might have compelled them to accept infinitely less. If then the terms of the Edict of Nantes were fair and equitable ; if in it the principle of religious toleration was for the first time distinctly recognised and practically applied in the legislation of a great country, it is to Henry of Bourbon that the credit is due. An American historian of the Huguenots, no lenient critic of Henry's policy and character, allows that he from the first contemplated some such settlement, and that no one probably was better pleased than he when that settlement could finally be accomplished. We may then conclude that it was not the fault of the King, if the satisfaction of the claims of the Protestants was delayed ; neither can it reasonably be denied, that that satisfaction when made was as ample and complete as the circumstances permitted.

Henry IV., in the preamble to the Edict of Nantes (April 15, 1598), expresses his gratitude to God for having inspired him with courage and strength to struggle against the fearful disorders and troubles which he found at his accession. But all things could not be done at once. Therefore he had

chosen to remedy first those evils which could only
be dealt with by force of arms; postponing other
reforms till these civil broils should be ended.    For
the fury of arms scarce allowed the establishment
of laws.    " But now that it has pleased God to
grant us the enjoyment of some quiet, we think that
we cannot better use this tranquillity, than by enabling all our subjects to worship His Holy Name;
and, if it has not pleased him to permit, that this
should as yet be done in one form of religion, by
providing that it be at least done with one and the
same intention, and with such order that there
arise not hence any trouble or tumult."    He has,
therefore, determined to give to his subjects on this
matter a general, clear, definite and absolute law in
a *perpetual* and *irrevocable* edict, and he prays the
Divine Mercy to convince them that the chief
security for their union and peace, and for the re-
establishment of the State in its former lustre de-
pends on the faithful observance of this ordinance.

It was no doubt with the intention of disarming
opposition and allaying the alarm likely to be felt
by the Catholics, that the first provision of the
edict was in their favour.    The King had already
(December 6, 1597) engaged to leave the Protestants
in possession of the towns they occupied for eight
years and to pay their garrisons.    The edict ensured
to the Catholics the free celebration of their worship,
and the undisturbed possession of their churches in
these towns as well as in Béarn and in the domains
of the Huguenot nobles.

The members of the so-called Reformed Church

were to have full licence to settle wherever they pleased in the kingdom, without being called upon to do anything against their conscience. Protestant worship was to be permitted in all towns where it had been allowed by the edict of 1577, or in which it had been held in 1596 and 1597, and also in one town in each bailiwick, or *sénéchaussée*, as well as in the fiefs of the nobles of the religion.

The Protestants were to be freely received into, and to enjoy the benefits of, all colleges, schools and hospitals, to be allowed to found colleges and schools, and to print religious books in all towns where their public worship was sanctioned. They were to be capable of holding all offices in all places, notwithstanding any provisions to the contrary in treaties made by the King with Catholic towns and princes. In all places, portions of the churchyards, or cemeteries of their own, should be assigned to them. No minors should on any pretext of religion be removed from the guardianship of their parents, whose provisions by will for the religious instruction of their children must be respected and enforced by the courts.

The ministers of the Protestant Church were to be exempted from all obligation to military and other service inconsistent with their sacred functions, and the King undertook to contribute an annual sum towards their support. On the other hand, the dissidents were to pay tithe and to respect the holidays of the Church and not to contract marriages within the prohibited degrees.

A " Chamber of the Edict," consisting of magis-

trates of approved moderation, one at least of whom
was a Protestant, was to be established in the Parliament of Paris, and in those of Rouen and Rennes,
to take cognisance of cases in which Protestants
were concerned.   Three courts, at Castres, Bordeaux
and Gap, composed of an equal number of Romanist and Huguenot judges (*Chambres mi-parties*), were
to exercise a similar jurisdiction in southern France.
The political provincial councils of the Huguenots
were to be dissolved, and they were forbidden to
raise any common funds, or to form any confederation or league within or without the kingdom, unless
permitted by the King.

Such were the most important provisions of the
Edict of Nantes, which, if it only secured toleration
to the Calvinist Church, at least placed its members
on a footing of complete civil equality with their
orthodox countrymen.   But what especially distin-
guishes this from any previous edict favourable to
the new religion, is that the King, who granted it,
was determined that it should be no dead letter, but
as strictly observed as any other fundamental law of
the kingdom.

The Huguenots were not entirely satisfied, although the wiser part agreed with Mornay that the
King showed both wisdom and resolution and had
secured terms for them as favourable as they could
reasonably expect.   The clergy and the lawyers vied
in the loudness of their protests and in the virulence
of their opposition.   For nearly a year the Parliament of Paris resisted the repeated commands of the
King that they should register the edict.   For many

reasons he was unwilling to compel them to do so by the public exercise of his sovereign authority, and instead of holding a " Bed of Justice," he summoned the members to attend him at the Louvre. They found him in his private apartments and were welcomed by a speech, in which an inflexible determination to be obeyed was no way concealed by the tone of humour that tempered his reproofs.

" Before speaking to you about that for which I summoned you, I will tell you a story of which I was just reminding the Marshal de la Châtre. Soon after the day of St. Bartholomew, four of us playing at dice, saw drops of blood appear on the table ; and as they reappeared a third time after being twice wiped away, I refused to continue the game, and said it was an evil sign to those who had been guilty of so great bloodshed. M. de Guise was of the party." Then after reminding his audience that blood called for blood, the King continued : " You see me in my cabinet, where I have come to speak to you, not in royal robes, nor with sword and mantle like my predecessors, nor like a Prince giving audience to ambassadors, but in the guise of a father about to talk familiarly with his children ; what I want to say is this, that I pray you to verify the edict which I have granted to those of the Religion. What I have done is for the sake of peace. I have made peace abroad ; I wish to establish it within my kingdom. You should obey me, since I am your King, because of the obligations under which my subjects and especially you of my Parliament are to me. I restored some of you to your houses from which you were exiles; to others I restored the religion you had lost. . . . I know well that there are intrigues among you; that seditious preachers have been put forward. This was the way taken to the barricades and which led by degrees to the assassination of the late King. I shall be on my guard against all that. I shall cut off the roots of all faction and of all seditious preaching, by causing those to be cut short by the head who incite to them. I have overlept the walls of towns. I shall easily leap over a barricade. Do not make the Catholic religion your pretext. I love it more than you do. I am a better Catholic than you; I am the eldest son of the Church, which none of you are or can be. You deceive yourselves if you think that you are the Pope's friends. I am more his friend than you. When I choose I will have you all declared heretics for not obeying me. . . . Do what you will I shall know what each of you says. I know everything that happens in your houses, all you do, all you say. I keep a little familiar who reveals these things to me. . . . Those who desire to obstruct my edict wish for war. Very well. I will declare it to-morrow against those of the Religion, but I will not fight—no, you shall all go to the war in your robes and you will be like the processions of Friars with their muskets and frocks at the time of the League. I am now King and speak as your King. I will be obeyed. It is true that the Judges are my right arm, but if the right arm is gangrened and corrupt, the left must hew it off. . . The last word I shall say to you is just this: Follow

the example of M. de Mayenne. An attempt was
made to induce him to join in some intrigue against
me. He replied that he, like my other subjects, had
too much cause to be grateful to me ; and that he
for one would always risk his life to do me a service,
because, he added, I had saved France in spite of
those who sought to trouble her, while he himself
in the past had done what in him lay to ruin the
Commonwealth. . . . This is what the Head of
the League said. . . . Grant to my prayers what
you might have refused to my threats. . . . Do
quickly, I pray you, what I ask, and not for my sake
only, but also for your own and for that of peace."
The deputations sent by the Parliaments of Bordeaux and Toulouse to protest against the too favourable terms granted to the heretics, were given not
less plainly to understand that the King meant to be
obeyed. The magistrates of Toulouse had excelled
in fanaticism and faction and in addressing them
Henry assumed a tone of angry expostulation. "It
was strange that they could not cast off their perversity. It was plain the Spaniard still stuck in their
belly. Who could believe that those who have
risked life, goods, rank and position for the defence
and preservation of the kingdom are to be held unworthy of honour and public office, are to be hunted
and driven out of the country as traitors, while those
who have striven with all their might and main to
destroy this State are to be reputed good Frenchmen
capable and worthy of office ? I am not blind, I can
see clearly ; I choose that those of the Religion shall
live in peace and be capable of holding office, not

because they are of the Religion, but because they have served me and the Crown of France faithfully. I must insist upon being obeyed. It is time that we all, having had our fill of war, should learn wisdom by what we have suffered."

Henry IV. proved his sincerity by continuing up to the end of his life to watch over the interests of his former co-religionists.

Nothing had been more strenuously insisted upon by the Catholics or more carefully provided, not only by the terms of the treaty between the King and his Capital, but also by a provision in the edict itself, than that Protestant worship should not be publicly held in Paris or within a distance of five leagues from the walls. Yet in 1606 the King, moved by the hardships endured in winter by the Huguenots, and especially by the sickness and mortality which exposure, during a journey of thirty miles, caused among the children, authorised them to build a " temple " at Charenton, barely five miles from Paris. A vast building capable of holding 14,000 worshippers soon arose, although the Catholics protested against the King's arbitrary violation of his own edicts and engagements.

The rays of the royal favour fell perhaps most warmly on those who did not shame their master's compliance by constancy to their creed ; yet during the twelve years which separated the promulgation of the Edict of Nantes from the King's death, the Reformers enjoyed greater peace and prosperity than at any other time before 1789. "Our churches," wrote Du Plessis-Mornay, " enjoy, by the grace of

God and under the blessing of the King's edicts, a condition they are not disposed to change. The Gospel is freely preached, and not without making some way. Justice is dispensed to us, we have towns in which we can take shelter from the storm. If any infraction of the law occurs, our complaints are listened to and reparation is usually made. We might wish that in many localities our places of worship were nearer and more convenient, that we had a greater share in the distribution of honours and offices. . . . But these are things to be desired, not to be exacted."

So long as Henry lived, the law was observed, and the Protestants had little reason for complaint ; nor is it easy to see how he could have secured them against the evils to which they were afterwards exposed. After the promulgation of his edict, the King wished the national synod, the supreme authority of the Calvinist Church in spiritual matters, to elect the two deputies who were to attend the court as agents of the churches and defenders of their interests, but he eventually permitted the meeting for this and other purposes of the political assemblies, so that at his death both the ecclesiastical and temporal organisation of the Huguenots remained unimpaired, and knitted them into a compact and formidable body. They held seventy-five fortresses, some, such as Saumur, St. Jean d'Angely, Embrun, La Rochelle, Nimes, Montauban, of great importance, and among these seventy-five were not reckoned the towns and castles belonging to the domains of the great Protestant nobles.

Yet the Huguenots were but a small minority of
the nation. At the end of the sixteenth century
there would seem to have been about 800 Protestant
congregations ; these for the most part were confined
to Languedoc, Poitou, Guienne, Provence and Dauphiné. In Normandy there were about sixty
churches ; very few in the remaining provinces.
The Protestants were at the very outside some
1,250,000 souls—men, women and children, not
more than a twelfth, and probably less than a
fifteenth part of the population of France. It is
indeed true that these were the very flower of the
people ; the most intelligent and industrious artisans,
the most enterprising as well as the most thrifty and
diligent tradespeople, the most educated and public-
spirited of the gentry and the most enlightened
among the members of the learned profession. It is
true also that the democratic organisation of their
community, the temporal and spiritual affairs of
which were administered by popular and representative bodies, taught them those manly and self-
reliant virtues which are believed to be the best
fruits of popular institutions, and gave them interests extending beyond the narrow sphere of private
selfishness.

On the other hand not only were they a minority,
they were also an unpopular minority. The odium
of the excesses committed by both sides during the
civil wars fell upon them, just as the French people
hated the English, after the Hundred Years' War,
for all they had suffered at the hands of ruffians and
brigands of every nationality. Even the purity of

their morals made them hateful at a time of gross and general licentiousness; who were they that they should affect to be better than other people? Their success in trade, due, like that of the Quakers, as much to the help, which members of their community were ready to give to each other, as to their industry and probity, excited the rancorous envy of their competitors among the Catholic middle classes. The lawyers disliked their independence. Even those magistrates who, in other matters, opposed the Jesuits and Rome, sought to prove their orthodoxy by denying justice whenever it was possible to the Huguenots. These dissenters with their privileges were an anomaly which marred the uniformity of the fair edifice of centralised government and law. The prejudices and fanaticism of the populace were artfully aggravated by the professed enemies of the Reformers, Jesuits and others. Hence riots, which were made a pretext for inveighing against those, who suffered by them, as a danger to the public peace. Their funerals were so constantly disturbed by the mob, that they were obliged to bury their dead by night. Therefore they were called *Parpaillots*, night moths, creatures who shunned the wholesome daylight.

When, therefore, the loss of their King and protector left the Protestants exposed on all sides to the attacks of their enemies, the necessity of self-preservation compelled them to draw even more closely together, to become to some extent what their enemies reproached them with being, *imperium in imperio*, a separate community in the State. If the Government was hostile to them, even if it was neutral, and did not protect them against their adversaries, then they must either make shift to protect themselves or seek protection elsewhere. If they attempted the first, they were accused of arming against their country, if the second, they incurred the charge of allowing themselves to be made the tools of the enemies of France. Yet during the troubled regency of Mary de' Medici, amid the conflict of selfish factions and contemptible ambitions, although many Protestant nobles, Bouillons, Lesdiguières, and even Châtillons, were as false to their country as to their cause, the conduct of the Huguenots as a whole was marked by a loyalty, patriotism and forbearance, which, had they existed to the same extent among other classes, might have spared France long years of suffering and civil strife.

# CHAPTER VIII.

## THE REORGANISATION OF THE MONARCHY.

### 1598–1610.

FTER peace had been restored and the religious difficulty compromised, the most pressing need of the Government was to find some escape from the terrible financial embarrassment, due as much to extravagance, malad-ministration and dishonesty as to thirty-five years of civil and foreign war. Henry IV. was fortunate in having by his side the right man for the task, and he showed himself worthy of such good fortune by giving to that man full confidence and constant support.

The merit of Rosny lay, not in the possession of creative genius, but in an exceptional talent for administration and organisation ; in an inborn hatred of extravagance and disorder. His reforms were in no sense revolutionary ; and consisted for the most part in introducing a careful and orderly collection of the revenue ; in abolishing abuses not a necessary part of the existing system ; in establishing, wherever he was able, a rigid economy ; in restoring and fostering those sources of national wealth which had been choked or neglected during a generation of misgovernment and anarchy.   He was laborious, clearheaded, endowed with indomitable energy.   When conscious of the King's approval and support, his unbounded self-esteem and self-confidence made him as careless of giving offence to the most powerful noble as to the humblest officer of the revenue. " He treats all alike, worthy or unworthy, good and bad, deserving or undeserving, great and small ; receives, or rather scorns, all with the same scowling face," wrote Casaubon to Scaliger.   But this churlish and disobliging temper was of real service to the State, when it was necessary to disregard so many vested interests in fraud and robbery.

Rosny was one of the committee of the council to whom the King entrusted the management of the finances, after the death of Francis D'O.  His zeal, his determination to inquire into everything, above all his honesty, were insupportable to his colleagues. Finding himself thwarted at every turn by their ill-will, he withdrew from the board to be sent back with enlarged powers and promises of support.  For the King was convinced of the dishonesty of his opponents and influenced in his favour by Gabrielle d'Estrées, who had been courted by Rosny and who was eager to avenge on his rival Sancy the ridicule he had thrown on her ambitious hope of sharing her lover's throne.   Rosny's energy supplied the money which made it possible to retake Amiens and relieved the King's most pressing needs, by compelling the farmers of the taxes and other harpies to disgorge some part of their ill-gotten gains. His colleagues on the treasury board either yielded to his ascendancy or withdrew.

Each year he received increased marks of royal confidence and favour. He was appointed Controller of the Canals and Rivers of France (1597), of the Highways and Ports—*grand voyer,*—and Grand Master of the Ordnance (1599), Superintendent of the King's Fortifications and Buildings (1602), Grand Master of the Ports and Harbours, Duke of Sully and Peer of France (1606). Although *de facto* Minister of Finance from 1597, he only received in 1601 the official title and rank—*Surintendant des Finances.* He was also Governor of the Bastille, of Mantes, of Poitou. He managed his own exchequer not less skilfully than that of the State, and, although he kept the promise made to his master not to seek to enrich himself by underhand means, his income, 200,000 livres, equalled that of the wealthiest princes, and he had amassed valuables worth 2,000,000 livres.

The state of the French exchequer, when it was taken in hand by Rosny, might well have daunted the most intrepid financier. The public liabilities amounted to some 350,000,000 livres, of which one third was floating debt.* The causes of the financial confusion and distress were many and deep-seated. The right of levying some taxes had been assigned as security to the native and foreign creditors of the Crown. These taxes had generally been alienated at a valuation far below their real worth. The pro-

---

* The intrinsic value of the " livre " was at this time about 2 fr. 50c., the relative value perhaps three or four times as great.

ceeds, for instance, of a tax which produced 150,000 livres were assigned to the Duke of Montmorency as the equivalent of a pension of 27,000 livres; the difference represents the profit of the publican who farmed the tax.

As the creditors of the Government had often to wait long for their money, priority of payment depending on favour and bribery, those who had dealings with the State insured themselves by exorbitant charges against the risk of delay or default, and often sold their claims at a heavy discount to courtiers or placemen, who used their influence or official authority to obtain for themselves prompt and full payment.

The public accounts were so ill kept and carelessly audited that the Controller of the Exchequer could appropriate twenty per cent. of the sums which passed through his hands without fear of detection. At the time of the siege of Amiens, Rosny knew that of 500,000 crowns which he had paid into the treasury 200,000 must be remaining, since he had kept a careful account of the expenditure to which the money had been appropriated and could produce the receipts given him for his payments. Ignorant of this the Controller boldly asserted that the balance in his hands only amounted to 90,000 crowns. Rosny produced documentary proof that it must be 110,000 more. The Controller was compelled to disgorge, but neither punished nor even dismissed for his attempted fraud.

The taxes were farmed, not to the highest bidder, but as a matter of favour; the members of the

council, the King's favourites, or even the Minister
of Finance himself stipulating for a share in the
profits of the publican or becoming his partner.
The *Surintendant* D'O had a share in the farm of the
salt tax. The Government paid exorbitantly for
everything, not only because of the uncertainty of
payment, but also owing to the dishonesty of its
agents, who imitated the unjust steward in the para-
ble, " take thy pen and write so much *more*," but
unlike him did not wait for a consideration till dismissed. Another evil was the inordinate number of
officials of every kind.

Nor among the causes of public distress must we
forget the ruinous and oppressive nature of many of
the taxes, which became the more economically disastrous as the capacity of the country to bear the
load of taxation diminished. Commerce and manufactures totally ceased in many districts. Not only
were all ways of communication insecure, but the
very roads themselves had ceased to exist. It was
no uncommon thing for the inhabitants of a town
to be suffering the extremity of famine, while a few
leagues away the crops were rotting in the fields for
want of a market. The population was decreasing;
the land was going out of cultivation, partly owing
to the devastation of the country and the destruction of villages and towns by hostile armies, or by
bands of brigands and of desperate peasants, who,
robbed of all else, still found arms wherewith to rob
their neighbours; partly because of the excessive
tallage, just as in Egypt, before the English occupation, and in other Eastern countries, the peasantry

have not unfrequently abandoned their fields because the land tax has not left them a share of the produce sufficient to support life.

While taxation pressed more and more heavily on the poor, those who were best able to pay eluded their part of the public burdens. This they effected sometimes by claiming exemption, either as " noble " because they had borne arms in the King's service, or because they had acquired some small office, sometimes by bribery and corruption. The *élus*, who determined the quota of tallage to be paid by each parish, were no longer elected as their name implied, but petty officials, for the most part venal like their betters. The *asséurs* or assessors, who fixed the share of each individual, were not more incorruptible.

To reform, root and branch, the evils and abuses under which the country was perishing would have required a treatment perhaps more drastic than the condition of the commonwealth permitted, fevered and exhausted as it was by civil war and with wounds still too raw to be firmly handled. Moreover, as we have said, the temperament and talents of Rosny were those rather of an administrator than of a reformer. The services which he rendered to his country were so opportune as to be of inestimable value, yet what he effected was very simple. He introduced an orderly and business-like method of keeping the public accounts; prevented peculation; and caused the taxes to be levied in a manner as economical to the Government, as little oppressive to the public, as was possible without a complete change in the existing system. At the same time, supported, or rather urged on, by the King, he did much by the wise encouragement of productive enterprise to assist the wonderful recuperative power which France has always shown during her short periods of respite from foreign war or domestic disorder.

Rosny, *grand voyer de France*, was zealous in repairing and improving old means of communication and in creating new ones. The roads were soon in better condition than at any previous period since the time when they had echoed to the tramp of Roman legions. Long avenues of trees were planted to give shade and coolness to the wayfarers. The navigation of the rivers was improved. A comprehensive plan for uniting the Seine, Loire, Saone and Meuse, by canals, so as to establish a waterway connecting the Mediterranean, the Bay of Biscay, the Channel and the North Sea, was approved by the King. A canal was begun in 1604 from the Loire to the Loing, a tributary of the Seine, as a first step towards the realisation of this scheme.

Internal trade was restored by security and improved means of communication. The abolition of export duties on corn and wine threw foreign markets open to the agriculturist.

Sully well deserved the commendation of orthodox economists by his clear perception of the truth which is the foundation of the doctrine of free trade. "As there are divers climates, regions and countries, so it has pleased God to make them suited to, and fertile in, divers products, materials, industries and arts which are not common to other places, or there at any rate not equally profitable. So that by traffic and commerce in those things in which some countries abound, while others are wanting in them, intercourse to their mutual profit may be kept up between nations however distant."

He saw that as both parties to an act of barter must obtain something more useful to them than that with which they part, so no trade can be carried on between two countries which is not more or less to the advantage of both. He believed that nature had meant France to be a pastoral and agricultural country ; that this was the most profitable employment of her labour and capital ; and he objected to the attempt to foster arts and manufactures artificially, both because it might divert the productive energies of the country to less profitable uses, and because he believed that the sedentary and indoors life of large classes would be physically injurious to the nation.

Such considerations led Sully to regard with little favour his master's desire to encourage the introduction of new manufactures and to naturalise the production of strange commodities. Henry, on the other hand, believed that the ever increasing number of the unemployed in the large towns was a constant danger to public peace. In one single quarter of Paris there were, in 1596, 7,769 paupers. He was convinced "that the development of manufactures and industries offered the best security against civil broils and disorders." The protectionist may perhaps find some comfort in the success of that part of the King's commercial policy which offended the precocious economic orthodoxy of his minister.

Although the silkworm had been long introduced into France, by far the greater part of the silk stuffs, then so largely used, was imported from Italy.   So also were the brocades and the cloth of gold and silver, to the purchase of which a considerable part of the revenue of the upper classes was devoted at a time when a man of fashion often wore the value of his estate upon his back.   No doubt it would have been better had the wealth thus wasted been used in improving the land of the gentry, and in the employment of productive labourers ; thus increasing their wages and enabling them to create a new market for native produce, by the purchase of those necessaries which they were now unable to procure.   And this Sully would have attempted to effect by sumptuary enactments.   Indeed the insolent luxury and tasteless profusion of the publicans and usurers, parasites, who had taken advantage of the weakness of the body politic to settle upon it and to suck its blood, their tarts flavoured with ambergris, their hangings of cloth of gold and fountains of costly perfumes, their studs and harems, might well seem to deserve the lash of the law.   But sumptuary restrictions have rarely produced the intended result, and the protective legislation by which Henry IV. fostered the growth of manufactures to satisfy the wants of luxury and ostentation was so far successful that, in foreign markets as well as at home, the silks of Lyons and Tours, the cloth of gold of Paris, the tapestry of Gobelins, soon successfully competed with the produce of the towns of Italy and Flanders.   Thus, not only was domestic luxury made the means of finding employment for the urban population, but France obtained in exchange for the produce of labour, which would not otherwise have been employed, foreign commodities of more general utility.

More useful manufactures were not neglected. Although fine cloth was still woven at Rouen, the supply of coarser stuffs was practically a monopoly in the hands of the English, who sold it on their own terms to the French consumers.

Henry IV. encouraged the clothiers of Provins and Paris by advances of money, by concessions and privileges, to betake themselves again to their looms. Stringent regulations against fraud and careless workmanship protected the consumer and restored the reputation of native fabrics.

Sully was not more anxious to encourage maritime than manufacturing enterprise. He even opposed a measure imposing on foreign vessels when they entered French ports the same dues which were paid by French ships in the harbours of the country to which they belonged. He discouraged his master's desire to compete with Spain and England in the colonisation of the New World,—false, in this as in other things, to the tradition of his faith,—for, like the Puritans, the Huguenots had more than once instinctively turned to the great continent beyond the Western Ocean. Fortunately the King was in these matters both wiser than his minister and determined to have his own way. Commercial treaties which placed the countries on a footing of equality were concluded with Spain (1604) and with England (1606).

The Spaniards were compelled to withdraw a

differential duty of 30 per cent. levied on all goods
coming from France, which, by provoking a like
taxation of Spanish imports into France, had caused
all trade between the two countries to pass into the
hands of foreigners. The good effects of the King's
policy were soon felt. The export trade of raw
produce—corn, cattle and wine—as well as of manufactured goods vastly increased. Nowhere more so
than in the Mediterranean. The traditional friendship between the Most Christian King and the
Sublime Porte gave the French merchants great
advantages in the Levant.

The Venetian ambassador describes Marseilles as
the emporium of Europe, and the successful rival of
his own town. Three hundred ships of large ton-
nage lay in her land-locked harbour. The annual
profits of her merchants were believed to amount to
a sum equivalent to over £7,000,000—no doubt a
gross exaggeration.

No sooner was Henry IV. in peaceable possession
of the throne, than he sent a Breton gentleman as
his Lieutenant-Governor to " New France," as all
America between latitude 40° and 52° was then
called. The Lieutenant-General and his intending
colonists were wrecked, and it was not till 1604 that
a serious and successful attempt to found a colony
in the New World was made by a company of
merchants and gentlemen, to whom the King granted
a monopoly of the fur trade. De Monts, the chair-
man of the company, Vice-Admiral and Lieutenant-
General of the King, left Havre accompanied by
Champlain, a gentleman of Saintonge, and in 1605

occupied the peninsula of Acadia. In 1608 Champlain sailed up the St. Lawrence. It was not till after the King's death that he discovered the vast inland seas, the sources of that mighty river which bears the largest ships to the foot of the precipitous rock on which, four hundred miles from the ocean, he founded Quebec, the future capital of Canada ; yet the credit of having initiated the most successful attempt hitherto made, to find a home for the French race beyond the limits of old Gaul, belongs to Henry IV.

Sully and his master were heartily at one in promoting all plans for encouraging and improving agriculture. The King, says Scaliger, was capable of everything except keeping his gravity, or reading a book ; yet he at least turned over the leaves of the treatise on husbandry, written by Olivier de Serres, whom Arthur Young styles the Father of French Agriculture. Every day for the greater part of a year the book was brought to him after dinner, and he studied it for half an hour with apparent interest. Engineers were brought from the Low Countries to drain the marshes. The reckless destruction and waste of the forests was checked and new timber planted.

In 1598 Rosny travelled through the country, inquiring into the condition of the people, their sufferings and most pressing wants. The result was that in 1600 an important ordinance was published. By this all arrears of tallage due for years prior to 1597 were remitted, and the amount annually payable reduced by about 1,800,000 livres. Any fraud

or partiality in the assessment of the tallage was to
be henceforth severely punished, and *any* taxpayer
was enabled to bring corrupt or unfair assessors to
justice by a summary and inexpensive procedure.
An earlier edict had annulled all exemptions from
taxation granted during the last twenty years.   It
was now enacted that the mere fact of serving in the
King's army did not constitute a claim to exemption ; that none not born of noble parents in legitimate wedlock should presume to style themselves
esquire or noble.

The salt tax or *gabelle* was even more vexatious
and oppressive than the tallage.   It combined every
one of those characteristics which, according to
Adam Smith, are the mark of a bad tax.   It was
arbitrary, inconvenient, unequal, costly to levy and
more profitable to those who farmed it than to the
royal exchequer.

Sully would have liked to make the sale of salt a
Government monopoly throughout the kingdom—
leaving every individual free to buy as much or as
little as he chose.   But this would have injured too
many interests—and every " interest " can bring
pressure to bear on an administration except the
general interest of the community.   He was therefore obliged to content himself with remedying the
abuses of the existing system.   Above all he warned
the royal officers not to punish the poor too severely
if they evaded taking their full quota, or even for
having smuggled salt in their possession.   To sell
and to buy contraband goods were, he pointed out,
offences of very different gravity.   He reminded the

magistrates that in judging between the publicans, who farmed the revenue, and the taxpayers, they must not imagine that the interests of the former were the same as those of the State. They should recollect that it was the King whom they injured when they ruined his poor subjects by grievous fines and penalties.

Much was gained by checking the extortions of the tax-gatherers and by compelling all who were liable to contribute their fair share of taxation, while a few years of peace, order and decent government so restored the vigour of the commonwealth that it could have borne with comparative ease a burden as heavy as that which before had crushed it to the ground. But thanks to the skilful management of Rosny the load to be endured was actually lighter.

He began his reforms by introducing some order into the system of accounts. He assigned certain sources of revenue to defray the necessary expenditure, and devoted whatever remained over to meet the charges of the public debt. Undeterred by respect for persons he vigorously attacked the dishonest practices of the financiers, publicans and tax-gatherers, who cheated the exchequer and oppressed the people.

A " *Chambre Royale* " composed of magistrates of high position and character was appointed. Sully hoped that this court would punish these harpies and confiscate the ill-gotten wealth which enabled them to set the fashion and ruin the nobility who attempted to vie with them in ostentatious profusion. But, so the minister laments in his memoirs, the bolder brigands escaped by bribery and intrigues, the lesser fry, " petty pickers and pilferers," paid for their own misdeeds and for those of the stouter thieves. The King himself was loath to deal hardly with men in whose houses he could throw aside restraint and ceremonial and find the most costly instruments of luxurious and too often vicious indulgence eagerly offered by hosts who were proud to be the submissive ministers of his pleasures.

Yet if the past could not be amended, the future might be improved. Henceforth the farm of the various taxes was put up to public auction and allotted to the highest bidder, instead of being sold as a matter of favour at a low price. In this way and by redeeming those taxes which had been assigned as security for their interest to public creditors 1,800,000 livres were annually saved.

The abolition of numerous useless offices and sinecures, although a breach of public faith, since these had, for the most part, been bought with ready money, was a measure which both benefited the revenue and relieved the public from the vexatious interference of men who sought to obtain an equivalent for what they had paid by extortion, or by the pleasure of indulging in the insolence of office.

The custom of entrusting important public functions to those who could pay for the privilege of exercising them had long prevailed in France. The sale of judicial offices had survived the protests of generations of reformers and the promises of successive kings. The judges had acquired a prescriptive right to sell that which they had bought, and to resign their office in favour of a son or other competent person, provided that they survived the transaction for forty days. If they died before this period elapsed or before resignation, the patronage lapsed to the Crown.

Sully proposed that the hereditary tenure of their offices should be granted to' all functionaries of the courts of law and exchequer, on condition of the annual payment of a sixtieth part of their estimated revenue. The treasury by this gained each year a large sum, and any system, even a bad one, was better than the previous confusion. The judges themselves were at first highly averse to an arrangement which touched their pockets and appeared to impair their dignity, for this yearly payment was likened to a tallage.

The measure had wider consequences than were foreseen, either by those who promoted or opposed it. Not only were the magistrates relieved from the necessity of courting the favour of princes and no-bles, they were also made less dependent on the Crown itself. The dignified integrity and impar-tiality of the French judges during the following century contrasts very favourably with the servility of the English Bench to the Stuart kings. In theory nothing could be more difficult to justify than that functions which require high intellectual and moral qualifications should first be sold to the highest bid-der and then be transmitted by the accident of birth. But, as is often the case, what is indefensible in theory worked well enough in practice. There seems to exist in certain offices a traditional spirit

which shapes the character and conduct of those
who hold them, and such an influence is naturally
intensified if those offices are hereditary.   The highest places in the French magistracy were already to
a great extent held by the members of a few families, closely connected by descent and marriage ; and
these families were for the most part raised by refinement of life and culture, by decency and gravity
of manners above the roystering swashbucklers and
frivolous nobles who affected to despise them.   The
keen sense of professional honour, the learning, the
integrity which became hereditary in such families
as those of De Thou and Arnauld, of Seguier and
Harlay and Molé, not only supplied the Bench with
independent and capable magistrates but gave to
the *noblesse de robe* a consideration and an influence
which made it an equipoise to the feudal nobility.

It is impossible within the limits of this book to
attempt more than briefly to indicate some of the
most salient points of Sully's administration.   A few
figures may best enable us to appreciate his success.

In 1598 the public debt amounted to about
348,500,000 livres—the revenue to about 30,000,000.
Before 1609 he had liquidated over 100,000,000
livres of debt ; reduced the yearly interest on what
remained by some 5,000,000 ; redeemed no small
part of the alienated royal domain ; collected a treasure of 20,000,000 livres ; and raised the revenue to
39,000,000, while reducing the tallage by about
2,000,000.   And he obtained this result while amply
providing for the requirements of the public services
and for the personal expenditure of the King.

Not only, as we have already seen, were roads and canals constructed, harbours and bridges restored, the navigation of rivers improved, marshes drained and all useful enterprises encouraged by subsidies and bounties, but the army also was reorganised, the arsenals filled with military supplies and with an artillery more powerful and better equipped than any which had as yet been seen.   In the short war of 1600 against the Duke of Savoy, the army was accompanied by a field train of 40 guns, each requiring 47 horses : a battery which excited the marvel of contemporaries.

The fortresses were put into thorough repair and strengthened under the direction of a Lotharingian engineer, Errard, as great a master in his art as the better known Vauban.   He introduced the use of the glacis and perfected the system of angular fortifications, with a double line of defence.   First the ramparts with their cavaliers and bastions protected by a wide ditch, the soil excavated from which was used for the glacis, then an outer ring of redoubts, ravelins and trenches.

The strength of the French armies had hitherto consisted in a numerous and valiant but ill-disciplined cavalry, composed almost entirely of the feudal levies, whom it was not easy to collect, still more difficult to prevent from disbanding if the campaign was protracted or unsuccessful, and impossible to keep together after victory.   The infantry consisted mainly of foreign mercenaries, well armed indeed and well drilled, but not over trustworthy, addicted to plunder, costly to maintain and mutinous when their pay was in arrear.  In short the French army was partly feudal, partly foreign, a grievous burden to the country, yet wanting the cohesion and discipline necessary to make it an efficient instrument of scientific strategy.  Men fought, it was said, in France, but war was only waged in the Low Countries.  To lead his nobles in a dashing cavalry charge had been Henry's glory ; yet his first care was the reorganisation of the French infantry. By treating this as the most important part of his army, he changed the character of that army.  It had been feudal and mercenary, it became popular and national.  This policy accorded with the traditions of the party he had once led.  Coligny and his brother Andelot, successively Colonels-General of the French foot, had attempted to improve the organisation and to raise the importance of that arm.

Large sums were spent on buildings of public utility and on the improvement of the towns, especially of Paris.  Under the Valois, Paris appeared a mean and dirty town to travellers acquainted with the cheerful magnificence of Italian cities, although it contained some fine buildings, such as the religious houses in their vast enclosures, and the " hotels " built in the style of the French Renaissance, by great nobles or wealthy financiers.  Four hundred thousand inhabitants lived in narrow, crooked and filthy lanes, ill paved, and of course undrained.  The stories of the lofty houses, built of lath and plaster, projected on each side till they almost met and excluded light and air from above, while booths and sheds encroached on the narrow

space below.  In the summer, carpenters, cart-
wrights, workers in brass, dealers in every kind of
commodity plied their trades in the streets, while
the wares of tanners, dyers and cleaners flapped in
the fetid air, frightening the horses and threatening
ruin to the finery of the courtier or country
gentleman threading his way from his lodgings to
attend the King's levee at the Louvre.  As
in the East, a crowd of half-starved dogs disputed
the possession of the offal in the gutters with kites
and crows.  At night, bravos and cut-purses plied
their trades, parties of young courtiers and nobles
rose from a debauch to charge each other or the
watch, to insult the women and beat the unoffending
citizens.  It was in vain that directly an alarm was
raised all citizens were commanded to ring a bell and
to rush out into the street lantern in hand to join in
the hue and cry ; and that, to make the escape more
difficult, houses were not allowed to have a back
door.  It was a rare exception for offenders against
the public peace to be brought to justice.

The bridges across the Seine were either of wood
or encumbered by houses like old London Bridge or
the Florentine Ponte Vecchio.  The river was only
partially confined by quays, which made it the more
apt to overflow in other places, and frequent floods
added to the squalid discomfort of the lower parts
of the town.

Had he lived longer Henry IV. would have created
a new Paris ; as it was he did more than any previous
king to improve and change the aspect of his Capital.
The citizens were forbidden to encroach upon or

obstruct the streets, many of which were widened
and made more regular. Henceforth no houses
were to be built with overhanging stories. The
pavement was improved, and although the habit of
emptying noisome water from the windows of the
upper stories into the streets continued till this century to expose those who passed by to the danger
of a foul shower-bath, attempts were made to prevent accumulations of filth and refuse in streets and
public places. Numerous fountains supplied abundant and tolerably pure water. For the mis-called
sanitary arrangements of modern times did not as
yet pollute springs and river.

Since the death of Henry II. the old Palace of
the Tournelles surrounded by spacious gardens had
been abandoned to decay. On this site Henry laid
out the Place Royal surrounded by excellent stone
houses, built partly by himself, partly by individuals
to whom the land was sold at a nominal price on
condition of their following the plans of the royal
architects. His letters-patent declare that he intended the wide open space not only to be used for
tournaments and other martial exercises but more
especially to be a recreation ground for the inhabitants of the crowded suburb of St. Antoine.

Quays were erected to raise the banks of the river
and to prevent floods. The Pont Neuf was completed
and connected the Place Dauphine, the centre of
the trade of Paris, with the Rue Dauphine, which
extended in a straight line, and with a breadth of
thirty-six feet from the riverside to the Porte de
Bussy.

Although Henry did all this and a great deal more for the benefit of the public, the greater part of 8,000,000 livres spent on building was devoted to increasing the magnificence and convenience of his own palaces.    In the Capital he built the long gallery of the Louvre and began the other constructions which were intended to unite that palace to the Tuileries, and which were finally completed by Napoleon III.    He doubled by his additions the size of the palace built by Francis I. at Fontainebleau, his favourite residence owing to the good sport afforded by the neighbouring forest.

At St. Germains a magnificent pile was erected on the site of the present terrace; from the windows of which the King could look over terraced gardens sloping to the river, and ornamented in the Italian style with grottoes and statues, upon the fairest prospect in the valley of the Seine.

Henry IV. was more successful in improving the material aspect of his Capital than in establishing an efficient police or in checking the general violence of manners.    The diarist L'Estoile records that in one month of the year 1606 nineteen murders were committed with perfect immunity in the streets of Paris. He and other contemporary writers frequently complain that life and property were safer in a forest glade than in the Capital.    Thieves found their way into the houses of citizens, and, holding a dagger at their throats, compelled them to surrender their money and valuables.    A President of the Parliament, a steward of the Duke of Mayenne and other men of position were thus robbed.    The vulgar bul-

lies who elbowed peaceable wayfarers into the kennel
and broiled with each other at every corner, did but
imitate the manners of their betters.

The practice of duelling, so fashionable under the
later Valois, became a deadly epidemic when the
cessation of the war deprived the gentry of the
opportunity of vying in valour and of indulging
their taste for violence in legitimate warfare. In
twenty years of Henry's reign (1589–1609) over
7,000 pardons were granted to gentlemen who had
killed their adversaries in " affairs of honour." In
1602 a royal edict threatened all who sent or accepted a challenge, or acted as seconds in a duel,
with the penalty of death. But this attempt to
check the evil proved utterly futile. Death was too
severe a punishment to be inflicted for an offence
which the public generally and the King himself regarded as venial.

J. A. De Thou tells how at the table of the Prince
of Condé, the conversation once turned upon duelling. Some of those present defended the practice,
whereupon the Prince " with an air of authority
becoming his rank " condemned it as absolutely
repugnant to God's law. It was, he added, a sin to
draw the sword except by order of the sovereign,
and for the defence of life and country. Yet he had
himself challenged and fought with the Duke of
Bouillon, a fact recorded by the latter in his memoirs
with much complacency, although in the same
breath he warns his sons to be meek and gentle, and
careful of giving offence. The King could not perhaps seriously condemn a custom all but unanimously

approved by those with whom he lived and which was so consonant to his own character. Yet he might deplore an indulgence in this privilege of gentle birth—for so it was esteemed—so excessive, that France lost every year many hundred brave men. The judges and those who by birth and education were led to regard the laws of God and man as of not less obligation than a conventional code of honour, were urgent that the King's solemn edict should not be allowed to remain a dead letter. Accordingly, in 1609, a new ordinance was promulgated, which, as it was less severe than that of 1602, might have proved more efficacious, had not the murder of the King in the following year paralysed all authority.

It would be absurd to blame Henry IV. for not having created a new heaven and a new earth during twelve years of peace indeed, but of peace disturbed by intrigues and cabals, by the plots of foreign and domestic enemies. Yet it is noticeable that historians have generally exaggerated the well-being of the people during the last years of his reign. So far was the proverbial fowl from being in every pot, that there were still many parts of France where the lower classes scarcely knew what it was to have a full meal, and yet more where the standard of living was so low that a short harvest was followed by famine. But none the less the greatness, the astounding greatness, of the results achieved during so short a period by the King's efforts to restore material order and prosperity to his kingdom cannot be disputed.

Henry IV. had an unfeigned desire to improve the condition of his subjects. He believed their interest and his own to be the same. " He who injures my people," he said, " injures me." He had also a true sympathy with the sufferings of the poor and humble, and he took some pains to discover what they were and how they might be relieved.

When travelling through the country he would constantly stop to speak with those whom he met on the road, asking them whence they came and whither, the nature and price of the wares they carried, the profits of their trade and other details of their daily life. Other princes, he said, think scorn to know the value of a ducat; I would know the exact worth of a farthing, what it buys, by what labour it is earned. When separated from his attendants in hunting or by any other chance, he would ask the hospitality of the nearest peasant or sit down with the drinking boors in some country inn, freely bandying talk and jest with those he met. He constantly vexed Sully by the demands he made on the treasury to satisfy his mistresses and to pay his gambling debts, yet it pricked his conscience that this self-indulgence should add to the load of taxation which made life harder to the poor. He tried to cheat his remorse by insisting that the 1,200,000 crowns he annually spent should be drawn from that part of the revenue which was not derived from the tallage.

The popular conception of the Bearnese, that he was untiring in love and war and that he wished every peasant to have a fowl in his Sunday pot, is, so far as it goes, not untrue.

M. Poirson, the last and most laborious French historian of the reign of Henry IV., has been at pains to show that his hero was not less industrious and successful in promoting the intellectual and moral than the material well-being of his people. But an impartial student can scarcely avoid the conclusion that his efforts in these directions both obtained and deserved far less success.

The studies of the University of Paris were re-formed. The task was entrusted to a commission of which such men as De Thou and Harlay were members and was therefore not ill performed. The study of the best classical authorities replaced that of the hand-books and compendiums of the Middle Ages. Perhaps in part, the obscurantists owed their defeat to the fact that they had been the inveterate political enemies of the King. The prince of six-teenth century scholarship, the " phœnix of learning," Joseph Scaliger, had been permitted or rather en-couraged by Henry IV. to leave France and settle at Leyden, but the scarcely less erudite Casaubon was summoned from Montpellier to Paris. Casau-bon's gentle disposition, his moderation and the pressure of a rapidly growing family encouraged Du Perron and others about the King to hope that he might be persuaded to conform. The proud in-dependence of the descendant of the lords of Ve-rona—or as his enemies called it his extravagant self-conceit—was known to be intractable.

The care of the public library, formed by uniting the books of Francis I. and Catherine de' Medici, was entrusted to Casaubon and attempts were made

to induce Hugo Grotius and Justus Lipsius to restore by the lustre of their names the supremacy of
European learning to the University of Paris.   New
endowments encouraged the study of anatomy and
other kindred subjects, which were recommended by
their practical utility to the King's philistine common-sense.   The Huguenots in the midst of a struggle for life or death found means and leisure to
establish schools and colleges.   The children of even
the poorest of the Religion had the opportunity of
a decent education.   But although Queen Jane of
Navarre had specially distinguished herself by her
zeal in providing for the instruction of youth in her
hereditary dominions, her son made no attempt to
raise the intellectual condition of the mass of his
subjects.   Even the reform of the University of
Paris may have been due rather to a wish to introduce into that body a more loyal and less fanatical
spirit, than to any true sympathy with erudition and
culture.

Henry's former tutor, Florent Chrestien, wrote to
Scaliger that though the Princes of France excel all
others in war and deeds of arms, learning must look
elsewhere for patronage and encouragement.

The last Valois kings had shown a real interest
in learning and culture ; Henry IV. was a soldier, a
sportsman, a practical statesman—but incapable of
any sedentary occupation.   Even his business was
generally transacted walking up and down in his
gardens or in the galleries of his palaces, or between
the burnished rows of cannon in the Arsenal.   The
grandson of Margaret of Angoulême had literary

instincts, for in their way his letters are models of
style, but he had none of the tastes of a scholar and
no sympathy with scholarship.　Classical studies
were therefore not fashionable at his Court.　During
the previous reigns it was not only grave ambassadors like Paul de Foix, who carried with them a
travelling library which was unpacked for their use
and that of their attendants at each resting-place,
men of pleasure like Bussy d'Amboise affected even
if they did not possess a taste for reading, and professional soldiers like the gallant Givry and St. Luc,
who was killed while commanding the artillery during the siege of Amiens, were serious students of
antiquity.　Among the Huguenots the best learning of the age was even more widely diffused; Du
Plessis-Mornay and La Noue were but perfected
types of the accomplished Protestant gentlemen.
Great nobles like La Rochefoucauld, Count of
Roucy, were proud of their skill in writing Latin
verses.　After the accession of Henry IV. there is a
great change in the attitude of the fashionable world
to letters.　The younger Biron, when some discussion arose on an antiquarian question, showed by
his remarks that he possessed considerable classical
knowledge, but he did so as if ashamed, and fearful
lest he should seem to know more than was consistent with the character of a soldier and a man of
fashion; a generation earlier he would have ostenta-
tiously paraded his knowledge.　Lesdiguières, perhaps the most able of Henry's generals, had been
trained to the law and was a fair scholar, but he was
sneered at by some, as if learning and valour were

incompatible. A scarcely less significant symptom
of the change in feeling was the King's boast, that
he could transact the most difficult business with
the help of his Chancellor who knew no Latin and
of his Constable who could barely read or write.

The King, who wished to decorate his new palaces
with statues and frescoes, was a more liberal patron
of sculptors and painters than of scholars. He paid
pensions to promising students whom he sent to
pursue their studies at Rome, directing his ambassador to watch over them with the care of a father.
Some came back imitators at second or third hand
of the Caracci; others learnt to combine the exaggerated action and defective composition of John of
Bologna with the affectation and want of dignity
which had begun to be the besetting faults of French
sculpture.

France was exhausted by half a century of civil
discord in which both parties had seen their hopes
cheated and had come to suspect that the ideals they
had cherished were unattainable. The nation was
absorbed in the effort to repair the ruins of the
material fabric of society, and had little energy to
spare for artistic and literary creation. The poet,
says the Roman Satirist, who is to sing of the loftiest
themes must be free from the sordid cares of daily
life. Disappointed aspirations, weariness of past
struggles, fear of future disorders, inspired even the
better citizens with a preference for all that appeared
practical, approved of by sound common-sense,
orderly and well established, with a distrust of everything that was vague, unsubstantial and utopian.

In the many this temper produced an eagerness to enjoy common and material pleasures.

When the Duke of Bouillon, writing for the edification of his children, contrasts the corruption around him with that virtuous Court of Catherine de' Medici, in which his boyhood had been trained, we smile to see the former lover of Margaret of Valois praising past times and affecting in his old age to inculcate austerity of morals. Yet there is abundant evidence that under Henry IV. the French Court was no school of virtue; and that preachers and moralists complained not without reason that the sensuality of the upper and middle classes had never been so gross and unrestrained. The Court of the Valois had excelled in perverse and morbid depravity, but the restoration of public tranquillity under Henry IV. appears to have been followed by a widespread indulgence in coarse vice, and selfish profusion which can scarcely be paralleled, except possibly by what was afterwards seen at Paris under somewhat similar conditions during the Directory. The disappointed renunciation of ideal aims, absorption in material cares, eager pursuit of animal pleasures, whether they be sought in the innocent gratifications of a respectable citizen, meat and drink, a warm roof and a comfortable bed, or in the more guilty satisfaction of sensual lusts, are scarcely compatible with literary or artistic excellence. Yet, although the reign of Henry IV. produced no writer of the first rank, it was a most important period, a period of transition in the history of French literature. During the Civil Wars and the years of apathy which followed, the old school, the school in poetry of Marot, of Ronsard and the Pleiad, in prose of Rabelais and Amyot, of Montaigne and Aubigné passed gradually away.  Men of such second-rate ability as Malherbe and Balzac would not have been able to decide the form assumed by the master-pieces of the next generation, had not circumstances inclined the taste of the times to prefer smoothness to vigour, a carefully chosen to a copious vocabulary, logical lucidity and correctness to variety of con-struction, to a picturesque and pregnant sententious-ness varied by carefully constructed sentences of classical prolixity, which arrest the attention of the reader, even though they may sometimes strain his patience.

But our space forbids the attempt to sketch even in outline the history of French literature during the reign of Henry IV.  Nor would it be a profitable task to enumerate names, even with the addition of a jejune criticism, unsupported by copious quota-tions.

# CHAPTER IX.

## THE DIVORCE AND SECOND MARRIAGE OF
## THE KING.

### 1598—1601.

HE country was at peace and her wounds were slowly healing. But the continuance of tranquillity, the enjoyment of what had already been secured, the realisation of future hopes, everything depended on the King's life. What if the King had succumbed to an illness, which was believed to have endangered his life in 1598, or if one of the numerous plots to assassinate him in that and the following years had been successful? The heir to the throne, the Prince of Condé, was a boy of feeble constitution and character, his birth discredited by rumours based, it would seem, on better evidence than is usually the case with such scandals. Even if his claim to the throne were not challenged, to whom would the Regency be entrusted? His mother was a woman of private birth, defamed as an adulteress and who would have been publicly tried as an accomplice in the murder of her

husband, had she not purchased impunity by abandoning her religion. All therefore who cared anything for the welfare of France were anxious to see Henry the father of legitimate children.

To this there were two obstacles. In the first place, he already had a wife, but one who could never be the mother of his children, and secondly, as years went by, Gabrielle d'Estrées' influence over him was confirmed by long habit, and his passion for her became more fervent. She had reformed that levity of conduct, which during the earlier part of their connection excited the reproaches of the King and gave a handle to her enemies. Her lover treated her with the consideration due to a lawful wife, and expected others to show her the like respect. He created her Duchess of Beaufort. He legitimised her children. Their baptism was celebrated with all the ceremonies and pomp reserved for the " Children of France." When absent, he wrote to her daily, and if he was not always faithful he at least paid her the compliment of simulating constancy ; decent hypocrisy contrasting favourably with the cynical effrontery which afterwards imposed an odious promiscuity on his lawful wife.

Meantime Queen Margaret had been living since 1587 in the castle of Usson in Auvergne. When, after her quarrel with Henry III., her position had become not less unpleasant at Nerac or Pau than at Paris, she took refuge at Agen, a town which formed part of her dower. The people of Agen rose against her, and, trying to make her way to Ivoy, a castle belonging to her mother Catherine, she was seized by Canaillac, Governor of Usson, who had been ordered by Henry III. to confine her in that castle, fortified as a State prison by Lewis XI. But although Canaillac had passed the middle stage of life, was heavy in bulk and sedate in disposition, he could not resist the fascinations of his captive, and the prisoner became the mistress of the fortress as well as of its Governor. Yet, whatever her position, so long as she remained in a remote valley among the mountains of Auvergne, Margaret could do little harm, and the contemptuous toleration of her husband allowed her to live on unmolested at Usson ; " a hermitage," so she said, " miraculously provided to serve her as an ark of safety." There she found solace for her isolation in books and music, as well as in the pleasures of the table and vulgar gallantry : for Margaret combined in a remarkable degree the coarse sensuality and intellectual refinement characteristic of the House of Valois, and to some extent also of her Florentine ancestors.

Du Plessis-Mornay appears to have been the first of Henry's advisers earnestly to press upon him the duty of providing for an undisputed succession (1591), urging him to marry again and to cease imperilling body, soul and honour in licentious intrigues. " Why then," said the King, " don't you find me a wife ? " " There is a double difficulty," replied Mornay, " you have to be first unmarried ; but I will see what can be done." Whereupon he went to the legal adviser employed by Queen Margaret to defend her interests at Court, and assured him that the King had made up his mind. He had many and

MARGARET OF VALOIS.

grave reasons which would justify him in treating his wife with severity. It would, therefore, be to the Queen's interest and honour that she should herself ask for a divorce, to relieve her conscience and for the good of the kingdom, on the ground that she had been married without her consent, within the prohibited degrees and without the papal dispensation. Margaret, weary of Usson and of a retirement which did not protect her from the importunity of her creditors, consented, and wrote a graceful and grateful letter to Mornay, thanking him for his good service and advice. But for several years matters made little progress. The Queen was very willing to agree to a divorce on the liberal terms proposed by her husband, the payment of her debts, an abundant revenue, permission to live in Paris with the title and precedence of Queen of Navarre and Duchess of Valois. She wrote again and again to Mornay, urging him to press on the business, and sought to stimulate his zeal by a present of 14,000 livres. But to establish the validity of a subsequent marriage beyond dispute it was necessary that the divorce should be pronounced by a competent and generally recognised tribunal, and as yet the Roman Curia was hostile and not likely to strain a point to oblige the King of France.

Henry himself, up to 1594, was anxious for a divorce and to find another wife. Then his interest flagged, till he again took the matter up warmly in 1598, urging his agents at the Roman Court to press for the Papal sentence annulling his marriage. We may conjecture that his affection for Gabrielle d'Estrées was sufficiently strong after the first two or three years of their union to render the idea of marrying any one else distasteful, but that it was not till 1598 that it could outweigh the obvious objections to making her his wife and Queen of France. Unseemly in itself, such a match would have failed to secure that undisputed succession, which was the chief advantage desired by those who begged the King to take to himself another bride. The jarring claims of those children of Henry and Gabrielle, who were born out of wedlock, and of the legitimate offspring of a subsequent marriage would only have added another element of discord to those already existing.

The Duchess of Beaufort had endeavoured to secure future support by using her influence to obtain favourable terms for the Dukes of Mayenne and Guise, and by betrothing her eldest son to the heiress of the Mercœurs. She also courted the favour of the Huguenots. Aubigné tells how on one occasion, when the King had good reason to complain of the factious conduct of some among the Protestant leaders, he came unexpectedly to Court and was well received by Henry, who bade him kiss his mistress, and sending for their little son Cæsar from his bed, placed him naked as he was in his old servant's arms, saying that he meant in another year to commit him to his care, in order that he might be educated among those of the Religion and win their affection.

After the conclusion of peace and when her lover was securely established on the throne Gabrielle persuaded him to entertain more seriously the thought

of their marriage.  Whenever Sully's name is mentioned in his memoirs we must be on our guard
against his mendacious self-esteem, and everything
he tells us about Gabrielle d'Estrées is to be received
with caution.  He hated her, because he believed
that but for her he might be the all powerful favourite and adviser of his Prince, and his hatred was
inflamed by all the rancour which a man morbidly
vain and wanting in generosity naturally felt towards
one whose favours he had repaid by ingratitude.
He also wishes to pose as the author of all good, the
opponent of everything injurious to king or kingdom.
Therefore he would have us believe, that it was he
who brought about the King's divorce, he who dissuaded his master from marrying Gabrielle.  Nay,
he apparently wishes to insinuate that he did not
shrink from complicity in a plot to murder a woman
whose influence might be so fatal to the country.
Throughout that prodigious monument of senile
garrulity the *Économies Royales*, the ex-minister,
to exaggerate his own importance and familiarity
with the King, forges and falsifies letters and other
documents ; and he is scarcely less anxious to depreciate the merits and influence of others than he is
to exalt his own.  The services of Sancy, Villeroy,
Jeannin, De Thou, of all the most trusted of the
King's advisers are ignored, their errors or failings
exaggerated.  But the great reputation of Du Plessis-
Mornay, his lofty character, his credit with the King,
made him the special mark of Sully's envious malignity.  The most artful malevolence sought in vain to
detect a flaw in Mornay's integrity, but the tempta-

tion to attribute to himself the credit of what Mornay
had done was irresistible to Sully. Accordingly we
find in the *Économies Royales* a fictitious correspondence between Margaret of Valois and M. de
Rosny, and an account of the events preceding the
death of the Duchess of Beaufort which recent in-
vestigations have shown to be little else than a
romance. We cannot therefore give full credit to
Sully's account of a conversation with the King,
towards the end of 1598. Yet we may well believe
that some such discussion as that recorded took place,
even if Sully exaggerates the freedom with which he
spoke to his master.

The King, he would have us believe, began by
saying that his ambassador at Rome and others about
the Papal Court assured him that the Pope was anxious to serve him in the matter of his divorce, and
that therefore he had decided to look about him for
a wife, who might bear him an heir and prevent the
evils of a disputed succession. He would like " that
not impossible she," his future wife, to be beautiful,
chaste, amiable, and accommodating in humour,
clever, of illustrious birth and great estate ; but he
feared such a one was either dead or not yet born.
He then enumerated all the marriageable foreign
princesses and French girls of high rank, beginning
with the Infanta Isabella, whom he said he would
take could he obtain the Low Countries with her, but
to that her father would never consent ; to all the
others he discovered some objection. " A pity," said
Sully " that the Queen of England cannot be made
young, or Mary of Burgundy or some other great heir-

ess of past time resuscitated for you, but since this may hardly be, what if you were to collect all the marriageable maidens of your kingdom, select the most pleasing from among them and then try to discover your paragon among the chosen few?" Henry laughed and allowed that it was absurd to expect perfection, but his bride must possess three essential qualifications: She must have good looks, good temper and be capable of bearing him a son. Sully replied that he did not think that it could be known beforehand of any woman that she would satisfy the King in these particulars, especially in the last. "At any rate," said the king, "I know that my mistress would."

By the end of 1598 it was generally known that the King intended to marry Madame de Beaufort. Queen Margaret wrote to her: "My desires are in all respects the same as yours and the King's. I speak my mind freely to you, as to one whom I consider my sister, and honour and esteem next to the King." As a substantial proof of her good-will she executed a deed conveying her Duchy of Étampes to Gabrielle.

The approaching elevation of the King's concubine to the throne excited general alarm. Not that the Duchess was herself unpopular. Her gentleness, the moderation with which she used her influence, employing it never to injure, and generally only to benefit others, won the affection of those with whom she came in contact; she had no enemies, says Aubigné, except the necessities of the State. But neither her birth nor her previous life fitted her to be the Queen of France; she had greedy relations, and the dread of a disputed succession haunted all who had a thought for the future of their country. The prospect of so splendid a station disturbed her own cheerful serenity; she became nervous and full of vague but distressing apprehensions. She may have felt that all had so far gone too smoothly; that fortune under so smiling a face must hide some treacherous intent. It was with tears and dismal forebodings that she left the King at Fontainebleau to spend the Easter of 1599 at Paris. She lodged at the Deanery, but on the evening of April 6th supped at the house of Zamet a rich Italian. This man, the son of a shoemaker of Lucca, and a former valet of Henry III., had enriched himself by usury and speculation. From being the servant he had become the boon companion of princes, who found him a merry and generous host, untroubled by scruples or pretensions. Gabrielle accepted an invitation to spend the evening of the 7th at the same house, but was then too unwell to leave her room. On the next day she was much worse and fell into violent convulsions; on the 9th she was artificially delivered of a dead child; towards the evening she became unconscious and died the morning after (April 10th). There is as little reason to suppose that she was poisoned as that her neck was wrung and her soul carried off by the devil. Both reports were current, but the latter was more generally believed by the populace, to whom it seemed that her great power over the King must be due to some supernatural cause. No contemporary writer acquainted with the

Court, except Sully, hints that there was any plot against her life.

The despair and grief of the King were extreme. Violet, the colour in which the sovereigns of France mourned, was not sombre enough to express his sorrow. He clad himself in black. He received in gloomy state the condolences of his Parliaments and of the ambassadors of foreign powers. No ceremonial was omitted, which would have been due to Gabrielle d'Estrées had she been the crowned consort of the King of France. But no courtly observance could do her such honour as the unfeigned tears of the Princess of Orange* and of Catherine of Navarre. The latter, whom her brother, with little regard for her feelings and for her long attachment to the Count of Soissons, had lately married to the Duke of Bar, forgot all unkindness and wrote in words of which we should be sorry to doubt the sincerity. " My dear King, I am well aware no words can heal your great grief. I only write these to assure you that I share in it as completely as I needs must, owing to my extreme love for you and to my own loss of so perfect a friend. I much wish I had been with you, to offer you in your affliction all the humble service I owe you. Believe me, my dear King, I shall always act a mother's part by my nephews and nieces. I humbly beg that you will remember that you have promised me my niece. If you will let me have her I will treat her with as much love and care as if she were my own daughter. . . . If it pleased God, my King, that I could lighten

---

* The daughter of Coligny and widow of William the Silent.

your grief by the sacrifice of some years of my life, I would pray with all my heart that it might be so, and upon this truth I kiss you a thousand times, my dear and brave King." Her brother assured her in his reply that her sympathy was a consolation to him in his grievous sorrow, a sorrow as incomparable as the object for whom he mourned. That henceforth regrets and lamentations must accompany him to the tomb. Since God had caused him to be born not for himself, but for his people, all his thoughts and cares should henceforth be devoted to the welfare and preservation of his kingdom. "The root," he concluded, "of my love is dead, and will never put forth another branch."

If the King expected no more pleasure in life, if henceforth he was determined to live for his country alone, then, as soon as he was released by the Papal sentence from the ties which bound him to Margaret of Valois, there could no longer be any reason to delay his union with a Princess who might bear the longed-for Dauphin.

The reigning Grand Duke of Tuscany had a niece, the daughter of his brother and predecessor, Francis, and of Jane of Austria daughter of the Emperor Ferdinand. The King's advisers, undeterred by the many ills of which a Florentine marriage had before been the cause, selected this young lady, Mary de' Medici, as, on the whole, the most eligible partner of his throne. The Grand Duke was wealthy and could give his niece a dowry which might extinguish a debt due to him, and leave a useful balance. No sooner was Gabrielle d'Estrées dead than the Florentine envoy and Villeroy began busily to negotiate the marriage treaty.

But while his ministers were higgling about the terms on which he should sell his hand, Henry had given away his heart, or what remained of it; some portion, we should like to believe, and that the better part, rested in Gabrielle's grave.  For it was to the fascination she exercised over the baser parts of his nature, his senses and his fancy, that his next mistress owed her fatal power.

After spending two months at Fontainebleau, where everything reminded him of his loss, he determined to seek distraction in a visit to the cheerful banks of the Loire.  On the road to Blois lay Male sherbes, a castle of Francis de Balzac, lord of Entragues and Governor of Orleans, a man of tarnished reputation, but of good family and the husband of Marie Touchet, formerly mistress of Charles IX., and the mother of a royal bastard, Charles of Valois, Count of Angoulême, to whom the old Queen Catherine, passing over her daughter Margaret, had left her county of Auvergne.  Among three children born by Marie Touchet to her husband, was a daughter Henriette, not surpassingly beautiful, for her nose was not above reproach, her lips were thin and when in repose ill-tempered, and there was more intelligence than charm in her high and well-formed forehead, yet marvellously fascinating by her grace, her vivacity, and her ready wit.

Few who were dazzled by her bright eyes and mobile smile could pause to note and criticise the defects of so brilliant a creature.  Henry, when in

the first week of June he came to Malesherbes, only
intended a stay of a few days to be spent hunting
in the woods which fringe the narrow valley of the
Essonne.   Before twenty-four hours were over the
disconsolate and elderly mourner was himself in the
toils of this Delilah of eighteen ; the end of July
found him still lingering at. her feet, and when he
left it was to follow his new flame and her mother to
Paris.

The room which Henry occupied during his long
and frequent visits to Malesherbes still exists, hung
with the same old tapestry, on which the eyes of the
King must often have rested, the vision of Ezekiel,
and below a quaint legend :

> *Mort, femme et temps, tout soit viel et antique*
> *Mondaine amour et chasteté pudique*
> *Tout prendra fin.*

It may happen that a mourner is attracted by a
resemblance in character or outward presentment to
what is no more, so striking and close that the new
passion is in some sort to be excused as but the con-
tinuation of the old.   But it must have been because
nothing in Henriette d' Entragues could remind him
of what he had lost in Gabrielle, that the King was
so easily fascinated by her.   No comparison was
challenged, in which his judgment might have been
biassed by tender regret.   Gabrielle's regular features,
her soft and alluring beauty were in keeping with a
gentle and placid disposition.   She had played the
part of a mistress with the modest dignity of an
honourable woman.   Henriette had been carefully

brought up by her mother, who, it was told, had stabbed with her own hand a page presumptuous enough to make love to her daughter; yet, though an inexperienced girl of barely eighteen, she had all the arts and tricks and depraved instincts of a courtesan, eager to profit by the passions she inspired without sharing. Her somewhat swarthy and vivacious features, her expressive eyes sometimes melting, oftener cold and imperious, her nervous mouth, her slim and active shape, were well in keeping with her restless and unscrupulous ambition, her malicious and cynical wit.

Since the King had been willing to marry the Duchess of Beaufort, there appeared to Henriette and her family to be no reason why, if they played their cards well, she should not be Queen. On public grounds there would be less to urge against such a match; no question could be raised as to the legitimacy of her children. Mademoiselle d'Entragues therefore did her best to inflame the King's passion. She herself would not bargain with her sovereign. She was his to command, and she gratefully received his gifts; rich jewels and a princely fortune. But her father's sense of honour was so nice that he could bear no blot on his scutcheon, and she was carefully watched by her mother. At length early in October, the King placed in her hands the following amazing document: " We, Henry by the Grace of God, King of France and Navarre, promise and swear before God and by our faith and kingly word to Monsieur François de Balzac, Sieur d'Entragues, etc., etc., that he, giving us to be our consort (*pour compagne*) demoiselle Henriette Catharine de Balzac, his daughter, provided that within six months from the present day she become pregnant and bear a son, then and forthwith we will take her to wife and publicly marry her in face of our Holy Church," etc. After this D'Entragues no longer refused to close his eyes to his daughter's dishonour. The negotiations with the Grand Duke of Tuscany were proceeding apace; it was also known that the King had been able to find consolation in other quarters. The young lady and her friends shrank from the risk of further delay. They no doubt hoped that her more intimate relations with the King would give Henriette not less influence over him than had been exercised by her predecessor. In November (1599), Henriette d'Entragues was publicly installed as reigning favourite in a house sumptuously furnished for her; such a bird, said Henry, deserved a fine cage.

In the early summer of 1600 the room of the Marchioness of Verneuil—so she was now styled—was struck by lightning, and the premature birth of a dead child relieved the King from his conditional promise. Had Henriette borne him a living son the situation would have been awkward, for already in the previous March the French plenipotentiaries had signed their master's marriage contract with Mary of Medici. The marriage itself was celebrated by proxy at Florence on the 3d of October. On the 17th, escorted by a Tuscan and Papal fleet, the new Queen of France sailed from Leghorn. Neptune, says Malherbe, anxious to contemplate her charms

as long as possible, showed his gallantry by so buf-
feting her splendid galley, inlaid without with ivory,
mother of pearl and lapis lazuli, and hung within
with cloth of gold and silk brocade, that it was
obliged to seek shelter in Porto Finale on the Ligu-
rian coast. It was not till November 3d that she
reached Marseilles, whence she proceeded by easy
stages to Lyons. There she was received with much
joy by the citizens, among whom were many of her
own countrymen. In that town, the emporium of
all trade between France and Italy, the natives of
Florence, Genoa and Lucca had churches and even
streets of their own. In the church of the Celes-
tines was the magnificent tomb of the Pazzi, the
exiled enemies of the house of Medici. This the
paltry spite of the new Queen of France condescended
to mutilate. Such a proof of a rancorous and ungenerous disposition was well calculated to alarm and
disgust her husband, so magnanimous in his treatment of opponents whether alive or dead, and who
used to say that of all faults vindictiveness appeared
to him the most unpardonable.

Henry had been actively engaged in a little war
against Savoy, and this had been his excuse for not
receiving his bride when she landed in France. He
had soothed her disappointment by letters couched
in his most amorous vein. Such descriptions of her
had reached him that he loved her, he said, not as a
husband ought to love his wife, but as a passionate
lover adores his mistress. He was suffering from a
fever, but the sight of her would cure him. All this
time, when he was not with Henriette, and he had

sent for her to Dauphiny, he was writing to her " his
sweetheart, his very own " in terms of more heartfelt
tenderness.   The King joined his wife a day or two
after her arrival at Lyons, where the Cardinal Legate
gave the nuptial benediction in great pomp to the
newly wedded pair.

Henry professed to be much pleased with the person and the gentle and submissive manners of his
wife.  Mary of Medici, though twenty years younger
than her husband, was no longer a girl, and a full and
rather heavy figure made her look older than her
age, twenty-six.   She had pretty hair, a good complexion, fine arms and a white skin, which she displayed liberally, but her forehead was heavy, her
nose coarse, her mouth sensual, her flat bold eyes
wanting in expression.   Even when compared with
the crowd of full-blown Flemish nymphs who sur-
round her in the allegorical compositions of Rubens,
she appears wanting in grace and distinction.   The
Queen looked good-natured, and was not unwilling
to please her husband, but from the first he was
plagued by the pretensions and quarrels of her Italian
followers.   Two of these were destined to exercise
a fatal influence on the fortunes of their mistress
and of France.   Leonora Dosi or Galigai had been
brought up with Mary of Medici as a humble play-
fellow and companion, a black-eyed swarthy little
creature like a gipsy changeling, full of malice and
ambition, whose restless energy had won a complete
ascendancy over her phlegmatic mistress.   The
knowledge of her power over the Queen induced a
certain Concini, a younger son of good family—his

**MARY DE' MEDICI.**
From the painting by F. Porbus in Prado Museum in Madrid.

father had been the Grand Duke's minister,—who hoped to find his fortune in France, to pay Leonora some court. He was only too successful. Her ardent passion scorned all disguise. Their amorous dalliance in the Queen's room and presence provoked malicious comment, and Mary of Medici, not ill-disposed to the handsome gallant on her own account, was induced by her confidante to treat him with an indulgence compromising to both mistress and maid. The Galigai was not loved and Concini was detested by the Italians about the Queen. Henry therefore had abundant warning that they were ambitious and dangerous intriguers. He refused to listen to his wife's entreaties that Leonora should be appointed her Bedchamber woman. The proposal was, he said, preposterous; the place was one which had always been held by a lady of quality. If Leonora and Concini would marry he would gladly find a dowry, but on condition that they returned to Florence,—a suggestion received by Mary of Medici with sullen obstinacy. The thought of parting with Leonora was unendurable, and Concini grew daily in favour. Eventually Leonora obtained the desired appointment, but through the intervention of Henriette d'Entragues with whom she formed a temporary alliance—a result well calculated to increase the resentment of the Queen, who saw her husband grant to the suggestion of his mistress what he had refused to the prayers of his wife.

On the 20th of January, 1600, peace was concluded with Savoy. The King declared that his presence was needed in the North, but that the

health of the Queen must not be endangered by a
hurried journey in an exceptionally cold winter.
Leaving her therefore to follow by slow stages, he
rode post to Fontainebleau, to throw himself into
the arms of Madame de Verneuil.

Two or three weeks later the Queen reached Paris.
On the very evening of her arrival Henry persuaded the Duchess of Nemours to introduce
Henriette to his wife. As she came forward he
explained who she was, "This young lady is my
mistress, she will be your very obedient and humble
servant." As a scanty courtesy appeared to hold
out little prospect of the fulfilment of this promise,
he placed his hand on Henriette's head and bent it
down till she had kissed the hem of the Queen's
dress.

He must be allowed to have so contrived the introduction of the rivals as to exasperate to the utmost
the tempers of both women. The ideal of married
life which he appears to have formed was such as
might have occurred to an amiable Turk emanci-
pated from the jealous prejudices of the East. A
Sultana to be the mother of his heir, and a reigning
favourite chosen from among a bevy of women,—to
one or another of whom the royal handkerchief
might from time to time be thrown,—were to show
their gratitude for the good-humoured indulgence
with which he was prepared to treat them, by living
amiably and cheerfully together. To realise such a
dream of domestic felicity would nowhere be easy,
but the attempt could hardly have been made under
conditions more adverse than those against which

Henry IV. had to struggle : his wife, disposed to jealousy, ruled by unscrupulous favourites, alternately passionate and sullenly obstinate ; his mistress a very demon of malice, with a cold heart and a hot head ; both eagerly watched by those who sought to use their ambition and their mutual hatred to annoy the King and perplex his policy.

A letter of the Duchess of Thouars has preserved a vivid picture of the royal household. She found, she says, the King and Queen walking up and down together, while Mademoiselle de Guise—who, it was whispered, since she could not be Queen, would have been satisfied to be reigning mistress—sat embroidering strips of canvas. Madame de Verneuil came into the room at her pleasure and though the Queen flushed with anger, began to talk to her, or flouted and jeered at the King. The Court was full of jealousies and quarrels and not much frequented by people of quality. The Queen was on bad terms with Madame de Guercheville (a lady of character and the first in position of her French attendants) and the King with Signora Leonora.

Matters were scarcely improved by the birth of the longed-for heir—Sept. 27, 1601. Henry indeed was delighted and characteristically wrote to Madame de Verneuil, expatiating on the beauty of her rival's baby. There is a touching simplicity in his apparent confidence that she would sympathise with his pride and delight in the child.

Henriette herself gave birth to a boy a month later, and in the pride of her motherhood scoffed at the banker's fat daughter, who had indeed got a son, but not the Dauphin, for the King was her husband, she had his written promise, and it was she who held the Dauphin in her arms; he at any rate, she added, should not go to St. Germains to be brought up with the royal bastards.

# CHAPTER X.

WAR WITH SAVOY — SPANISH INTRIGUES — CON-
SPIRACIES OF BIRON AND OF THE ENTRAGUES.

## 1599–1609.

THE Peace of Vervins had not decided
whether or how the Marquisate of
Saluzzo, occupied by the Duke of Savoy during the civil troubles in France,
should be restored. In the winter
of 1599, Charles Emmanuel came
himself to the French Court, trusting by means of
400,000 crowns, which he brought with him, to secure
such support among the King's advisers, that he
would be allowed to keep his acquisition on easy
terms. He was indignant that his father-in-law,
Philip II., passing over the Duchess of Savoy, should
have bestowed the Netherlands on her younger sister
Isabella, and offered, if well treated by Henry IV.,
to help him, when the time came, to attack the
House of Austria in Italy and Germany. But the
French Government persisted in demanding the immediate cession of the Marquisate or of an equivalent.

Since the Duke, on futile pretexts, delayed to
accept either the one or the other alternative

war was declared against Savoy (August, 1600).
When operations commenced the season was late
and the snow already deep on the mountains. The
Duke was assisted by 4,000 Swiss sent by the Spanish
Governor of Milan and by the ill-will of Biron the
principal French general, yet such was the energy of
Lesdiguières and of the King, so effective the new
organisation of the army, that before the end of the
year Charles Emmanuel was suing for peace and had
reason to esteem himself fortunate that he was able
to persuade the King to accept an indemnity of
800,000 crowns with the county of Bresse and other
lordships on the western side of the Alps, forming
the modern department of the Ain. Fort St. Catherine, built by the Dukes of Savoy to be a constant
threat to the Genevese, had been taken by the King
during the campaign. It was now razed, never again
to be rebuilt (Jan., 1560).

The Duke of Savoy, after his fruitless visit to the
Court of France, hearing the taunt that he had carried
away with him nothing but the mud of his winter
journey, replied: " The mud can be brushed off, but I
have left behind me traces, which the sword alone
can obliterate." An adept in intrigue, he had noticed
the restless discontent of many of those nobles who
had fought on the King's side against the League.
They contrasted their rewards with the favours obtained by their former adversaries and complained
of their master's ingratitude. Their importance had,
they felt, depended on the war, and was likely further to diminish as the country became more settled,
and the authority of the Crown better established.

Foremost among these malcontents was the Marshal Duke of Biron, the inheritor of his father's ambition, vanity and martial reputation. If miserliness and ingratitude were defects in Henry's character, he had not shown them in his treatment of the companion-in-arms whose life he had twice saved in battle at the risk of his own. He had made him Marshal, Duke, and Peer of France, Governor of the wealthy and important frontier province of Burgundy. But no rewards appeared adequate to Biron's extravagant estimate of his deserts, no wealth could fill the bottomless purse of an inveterate gambler and spendthrift. Biron liked to boast that his own and his father's services had given the King his crown, and made no secret of his disgust that he was not all powerful at Court. His need of money was as well known as his extravagant ambition, and he became the dupe of alchemists and of adepts in occult sciences, who fooled him with the prospect of boundless wealth and high fortune.

The Duke of Savoy found such a man a willing recipient of a part of the treasure he had brought for the corruption of the French Court, and ready to incline his ear to any scheme which implied his own aggrandisement. One La Fin, an adventurer and charlatan, who, after wasting his own substance in the pursuit of the philosopher's stone, had acquired the confidence of the Marshal by his skill in alchemy, astrology and magic, conducted the negotiations between him and Charles Emmanuel. Nothing definite was settled before the war of 1600. The support of Spain was indispensable to the confederates, but

Philip III. was phlegmatic and timid : his minister, the Duke of Lerma, as incompetent as he was greedy and aspiring, distrusted his own ability to cope with such an adversary as Henry IV. Accordingly the Spanish Court declared that during the King's life nothing could be done, suggesting at the same time that this obstacle might be removed. Various plans for the assassination of Henry were discussed, as well as the terms on which the Duke of Savoy would bestow his daughter's hand on the Marshal.

Henry knew something of what was going on, and took such precautions that Biron was compelled to assist in the defeat of his confederate. On the conclusion of the war, thinking that nothing could be done for the present, and wishing to guard against the danger of detection, Biron made a merit of confessing to the King that he had had some dealings with Savoy and in a moment of pique had asked the hand of the Duke's daughter ; and for whatever he had done amiss he implored a pardon which was readily granted.

Scarcely however had the peace been signed before Biron was again listening to the offers of the Duke of Savoy and of the Spaniards. The hand of a princess, a dowry of 300,000 crowns and the independent sovereignty of Burgundy were irresistible baits to his ambition and poverty. He preferred, he said, death on the scaffold to an almshouse, and became the centre of all who plotted against King or country in France. He affected to be a zealous Catholic and deplored the sinful tolerance of the King, while at the same time he and Bouillon endeavoured to persuade the Huguenots that their extermination had been promised to the Pope.

The towns were excited by an artfully disseminated report that the hated *pancarte*, or tax on sales, was but the beginning of a new system of fiscal oppression. The inhabitants of those provinces which were exempt from or had compounded for the *gabelle*, were informed that Sully intended to impose a uniform salt tax on the whole kingdom.

It is not likely that any definite treaty was drawn up between the Marshal and his foreign allies ; but the understanding appears to have been, that, after the King and his family—" the lion and his whelps " —had been cleared out of the way, the Crown of France should be declared elective and the great vassals, like the Princes of the Empire, be practically sovereign in their respective territories. An independence as great as that of the free imperial cities would, it was hoped, induce the larger towns to acquiesce in the disruption of the kingdom. Such a scheme was well calculated to tempt the selfish ambition of the more powerful nobles. The Constable Montmorency, Épernon and many others appear to have been privy—at least in part—to the conspiracy. The half-brother of Henriette d'Entragues, the Count of Auvergne, took a more active part in the plot, and his sister certainly knew something of what was going on. The restless ambition of Bouillon could not resist the temptation of the sovereignty of an independent Protestant State to be formed beyond the Loire, but he attempted in vain to draw the other Huguenot leaders into the design.

In September, 1601, Henry was at Calais, and
Queen Elizabeth came to Dover, partly in the hope
that her old ally would visit her to discuss how best
they might humble Spain.   Henry IV. would gladly
have done so, but he feared to alarm the Catholics,
and was unwilling to do anything which might lead
to an immediate renewal of the war.   He sent Biron
to offer his excuses and regrets, and Elizabeth invited the Duke to accompany her to London.
Taking him by the hand, as he was talking to her in
a room of the Tower, she led him to a window, and
pointed to where the once loved head of Essex was
rotting in wind and rain.   " Had he but confessed
that he deserved death I would have pardoned him.
He bowed before the headsman, because his pride
would not endure to stoop to me.   If I grieved for
the death of that poor wretch, it was for his ingratitude."   Then looking fixedly into the Marshal's
restless and sinister eyes, deep set in his swarthy
face, she continued: " If the King would believe
me, there are as many heads which need to be cut
off in Paris as in London."

That same month the Dauphin Lewis was born ;
perhaps Biron's heart misgave him, more probably
he distrusted his confidant, with whom he was no
longer on the best of terms, for he wrote to La Fin,
" God has given the King a son, let us forget our
dreams."   Yet shortly after he renewed, through
another agent, his negotiations with Spain and
Savoy.   La Fin, on the offer of a free pardon and
great rewards, came to Fontainebleau, told all he
knew, and placed in the King's hands letters

written by Biron and containing ample proof of his treason.

Henry, alarmed at the extent of the conspiracy, wrote to Biron, that what he had heard from La Fin had entirely satisfied him, and begged him to come to court; while he himself hurried into the western provinces, where he feared the discontent of the towns and peasantry and the influence among the Huguenots of the Dukes of Thouars and Bouillon. He reassured the Protestants, contradicted the malicious reports about new imposts and the extension of the salt tax and received protestations of loyalty, which it was politic to believe, from Montmorency and Épernon. The latter he brought back with him to Fontainebleau, and he once more summoned Biron. If he obeyed and came, he would not believe a word of the charges against him. Conscious of guilt the Marshal would gladly have stayed away; but Sully had stripped the fortresses of Burgundy of their guns, on the pretext of replacing them with better artillery; 6,000 Swiss and French troops commanded by loyal officers were quartered in the province and in the neighbouring districts; as many more were on the march. Montmorency and Épernon had drawn back. The Huguenots would not listen to Bouillon; Spain, averse to active interference in France, would certainly not come to his assistance. The short campaign of 1600 had inspired the Duke of Savoy with a prudent dread of French arms. Biron had no choice but to obey or to fly the country, a powerless and dishonoured exile. He therefore determined to go to Fontainebleau, to appeal to the King's old friendship, and to oppose a brazen denial to any charges brought against him, which would be, as he supposed, little more than vague surmises resting on no certain evidence.

No one was less vindictive and more humane than Henry IV., and we may well believe his assurance that if his own safety alone and not that of his family and country had been at stake, he would still have pardoned his old friend and companion in arms. As it was, he assured Sully that if Biron would make a clean breast, confess everything and sue for pardon, all should be forgiven and forgotten. He probably justified such clemency by the reflection that the Duke after such abasement would no longer be dangerous. He bade the minister go to him and advise him to conceal nothing, and to hope everything from his master's affection. But Biron was obdurate. He protested both to Sully and to the King, with whom he had two interviews, that he had been foully calumniated, that he had done nothing, knew nothing except what he had already confessed at Lyons.

The evening of the second day after his arrival he played cards till after midnight at the Queen's table; as he rose to leave, the King called him aside: "Biron, you know that I have loved you. Confess the truth to me and I will pardon you." Again Biron said he had nothing to confess. "I see," replied Henry, "that I shall learn nothing from you. Perhaps the Count of Auvergne will tell me more. Good-bye, *Baron* de Biron." As soon as he passed the door he was arrested by the Captain of the Guard, who asked for his sword. The Marshal broke out into laments and protestations. What! his sword that had done such service! Was this the reward of his campaigns, his thirty-two wounds, his father's merits? He must and would speak to the King; at length he surrendered his sword and was led to the Bastille, where his captivity was shared by the Count of Auvergne.

Biron was forthwith arraigned of high treason before the Parliament. The peers of the realm were summoned to take their place among the judges, as was customary when one of their number was on his trial. But none appeared. They were unwilling to condemn yet dared not acquit. The evidence of the guilt of the accused was overwhelming and the court unanimously sentenced him to a traitor's death (July 29, 1602).

The Chancellor and other officials went to the Bastille to communicate the judgment to the prisoner. He was occupied in astrological calculations, seeking to discover his fate from the stars. When he learnt on more certain authority what it was to be, he burst forth in a passion of violent invective. Was this the King's gratitude? Why did he refuse to pardon him and let greater culprits go scot free? How many times had Épernon betrayed him, and Mayenne? Queen Elizabeth was ready to forgive Essex, had he asked for mercy. Well, if he must die, he must, but the King had not learnt all his secret, and never should from him. Even yet he could not believe that he would be executed. So

contrary to all precedent did it seem that a great
noble and officer of the Crown should be capitally
punished for conspiracy against the King's life and
the peace of the country. He showed no vestige of
religious feeling; he would not even pray, fearing,
says a contemporary, the devil more than God. But
he bade those about him tell the people that he died
a good Catholic; he would send no message to his
mother because she was a heretic. He wished it to
be believed that he died a martyr, and thus to stimulate the zeal of the fanatics, who daily plotted
against the King's life.

When he was brought out to the scaffold in the
courtyard of the Bastille, for he was spared the ignominy of the Place de Grève, the spectators marvelled
that a man famous for the most undaunted valour,
should on that last scene display so little self-
possession or dignity. But it was rage not fear, the
hope that at the last he would be pardoned and bitter
disappointment that this hope was not realised,
which made him three times snatch the bandage from
his eyes, threaten the executioner that he would
strangle him if he but laid a finger on him, and alarm
those who stood around by his fierce words and angry
gestures. At length the headsman took him una-
wares and with marvellous dexterity struck off at a
blow his bull-necked head; three times it is said to
have bounded from the ground, "impelled by the
fury which possessed it."

Henry IV. was probably glad that Biron had died
without making any full and public confession. He
had learnt all that it concerned him to know from

La Fin and from the base terror of the Count of
Auvergne, who, to save his life, offered, King's son
though he was, to play the part of a spy and to continue to communicate with his confederates in order
that he might disclose their plans to the Government.
The King neither desired a war with Spain and
Savoy, whose ambassadors expressed to him their
masters' satisfaction that he had crushed so dangerous a conspiracy, nor to disturb the peace of the
country by punishing the great nobles who had been
to a greater or less extent the accomplices of the
Duke of Biron.

Bouillon after disobeying repeated commands to
come to Court, and conscious that he had carried his
ingratitude and treason further than others, fled the
country and sought a refuge with his brother-in-law
the Elector Palatine.    He tried to excite sympathy
as a sufferer for the Protestant cause, and did what
he could to persuade the Germans that the King of
France had become a persecutor, at the very moment
when Henry was negotiating for the formation of a
league of the German Protestants, the main object
of which was to be the election of a non-Austrian
prince as King of the Romans. Failing in this
Bouillon retired to Sedan, the impregnable capital
of his wife's dominions.   The execution of Biron was
an impressive warning that the game of treason could
not henceforth be played with a light heart and the
certainty of impunity ; but a fanatic does not pause
to weigh consequences, and an assassin may hope
to escape in the confusion and consternation of
his success.   The notorious book of Mariana, *De*

*Rege et Regis Institutione* (Toledo, 1599—Mayence, 1605) had justified tyrannicide, and glorified Jean Chastel, and the King, says Aubigné, who feared nothing else, dreaded the Jesuit's knife. The Jesuits indeed pointed out that Mariana was a rebel to authority, the leader of the Spanish faction and the chief opponent of their General Aquaviva; that his book was no exposition of their true doctrine, that they did not teach regicide, nor even the supremacy of the Pope in temporal matters—at least he had but an *extraordinary* supremacy, one only to be used when absolutely necessary for the salvation of the souls of the faithful. It was a vile calumny to call them the tools of Spain at the very moment when they were being persecuted by the King of Spain and his Dominican Inquisition. All this and much more was urged by Father Cotton, afterwards the King's complaisant confessor, who had been allowed to come to Court to plead the cause of his Order.

Cotton was the very man for the task, supple, unscrupulous, the typical Jesuit of Protestant controversy, disarming suspicion by an apparent simplicity which bordered on folly. Everything that persuasion, everything that intrigue could effect was done to induce the King to permit the Order to return to Paris. They only wished to be allowed to reopen their schools. They would not preach. They would obey the ordinary. There were no bounds to their submissive humility. His mistress Henriette, La Varenne his confidant and pandar, the majority of his Catholic ministers, urged the King to gratify the

Pope and to prove his love of toleration by allowing the poor fathers to return. Sully vainly pointed out that the Jesuits, who were the soul of the counter Reformation, who were supreme at the Courts of Vienna and Brussels, must necessarily be the inveterate opponents of a policy based on toleration, and which aimed at overthrowing the power of the Hapsburgs by consolidating German Protestantism. "No doubt," replied his master, " but I must do one of two things : Receive them and learn by experience the value of their protestations and promises, or by a decided refusal reduce them to such despair, that they will certainly attempt my life, which will be made so wretched by the constant fear of dagger or poison that I would far rather be dead." The Parliament protested in vain. The decree authorising the return of the Order was registered (September, 1603). The King showed the Jesuits much favour, liberally endowed their college at La Flèche and other institutions. But he at the same time allowed the Huguenots to open their place of worship at Charenton, and endeavoured to persuade them by word and deed that they might trust to his affection and policy for protection against their enemies. The Jesuits had hoped with the aid of their friends among his advisers to make Henry their confederate in the struggle against heresy. When they found that he was still the ally of their opponents and the strength of the resistance to the further progress of Romanism, were they not likely in their disappointment to become even more bitter and dangerous enemies, and that too, as Sully said, after they had been admitted into the very heart of the place ?

Modern historians have shown that the " Grand Design," attributed to Henry IV., of a Christian Commonwealth composed of fifteen Confederate States, Protestant and Catholic, republican and monarchical, elective and hereditary, was an invention of Sully's vanity and leisure. Such a visionary scheme would not have recommended itself to the essentially practical mind of the King, the aim of whose policy if less ideal and disinterested was at least more attainable.

The Peace of Vervins ended the hostilities in the field between the two countries ; but indirectly, and with the weapons of diplomacy and intrigue, the struggle between France and the heirs of Charles V. was carried on with unabated animosity. Henry IV. complained with good ground, that the insubordination of his nobles, the disappointed ambition of his captains, the humours of his wife, the far-reaching hopes and rancour of his mistress, the troublesome fanaticism and ignorant prejudices of a part of his people and clergy were encouraged and inflamed by Spanish intrigue : that all who plotted or attempted anything against him or his Government, did so with the full assurance of Spanish help, or of finding, at the worst, a refuge on Spanish territory.

But he was himself not less assiduous in his efforts to injure the House of Hapsburg, not less careful to encourage its enemies and to prepare by his diplomacy allies for himself in the war, upon which he

was determined as soon as he had re-established
order, restored the finances of France, reorganised
his army and collected sufficient resources for a
struggle destined to change the face of Europe.
For it was no doubt his hope to separate the
Netherlands from Spain, to unite the Protestant
princes of Germany in a firm alliance, and with their
help to deprive the Austrian House of the Imperial
crown, while he at the same time assisted the Italian
princes to drive the Spaniards out of the peninsula.
Had he been able to effect this, even without any
extension of territory, France would have become
the arbitress of Europe. But he contemplated no
such disinterested policy. He would have been glad
to annex the whole of the Netherlands, and, if Dutch
love of independence and English jealousy made
this impossible, he at least hoped to obtain Artois,
Hainault and Franche-Comté, with Roussillon, as
the reward of his efforts for the common cause. It
was thought also that he had not quite forgotten the
traditional French claims to the two Sicilies and
Milan, yet as it was not likely that the Italian powers
would help to overthrow the domination of Spain
simply to place themselves under that of France,
he was probably prepared to forego all territorial
aggrandisement beyond the Alps.

Henry IV. had fully made up his mind that when
he was prepared for war and an opportunity offered
he would attack Spain and Austria, but the time and
manner of the attack were to be determined by circumstances.

The death of Queen Elizabeth (1603) was most

sincerely mourned by her old ally. " She was," he said, " my second self, the irreconcilable enemy of our enemies." * Sully was at once sent to persuade her successor to embark on an anti-Spanish policy, and to conclude a yet closer alliance with France. James I. was at first eager for peace with Spain and spoke of the Dutch as rebels who deserved no help. But the discovery of a plot for his assassination changed his mood, and he listened to the advice of his wiser ministers, especially of Cecil, who, though unwilling either to engage England in a struggle which might overtax her resources, or to assist France to acquire the sovereignty of the Netherlands, was averse to any peace which should not effectually limit the power of Spain. Olden Barneveld also came to England to plead in person the cause of his countrymen, and impressed the British Solomon by the vigour of his genius and the cogency of his arguments. James listened complacently to proposals for a double marriage between the Dauphin and his only daughter, the Lady Elizabeth, and between Prince Henry and Elizabeth of France. In the treaty which was finally signed there was no mention of these betrothals, but the English King promised to allow soldiers to be levied in England and Scotland for the defence of Ostend besieged by the Spaniards, while Henry IV. engaged

---

* The expression occurs in a letter given by Sully in the *Économies Royales*, of doubtful authenticity, since it purports to have been written by the King on the day before that on which we know that he heard of Elizabeth's death, and bears other traces of Sully's workshop for manufacturing documents. But Henry says very much the same thing in a letter written to his ambassador in England shortly after.

to defray the expenses of this force, a third part of what he spent being deducted from the debt he owed to the English Government. Accordingly a reinforcement of 6,000 men joined the contingent, which, under Sir Francis Vere, was assisting Maurice to resist Spinola.

In Germany, French diplomacy was active, endeavouring to unite the Protestant princes divided by dynastic quarrels and theological hatred, and to prepare the way for the elevation of a non-Austrian prince to the Imperial throne. In order to distract the attention of the Hapsburgs, Henry IV. endeavoured to prevent the conclusion of peace in 1602 between Turkey and the Emperor. In 1603 the French ambassador urged the new Sultan, Achmet, an energetic and ambitious prince, to conclude peace with Persia and to turn his arms against Hungary. The capture of Pesth by the Moslem was thus to some extent the consequence of the diplomacy of the Most Christian King to whom the inventor of the "Grand Design" attributes the intention of turning the Turk bag and baggage out of Europe.

French agents also sought to turn the sufferings of the Moriscos, the half converted descendants of the Spanish Moors, to account, by inciting them to defend themselves by arms against their fanatical and foolish oppressors.

But nowhere was Henry's diplomacy more successful than in Italy. He remained on good terms with the Pope and influential at Rome, while refusing to permit the promulgation in France of the decrees of the Council of Trent, and maintaining his right to appoint to vacant bishoprics and benefices, and that of his parliaments to receive appeals from the ecclesiastical courts and even to deprive bishops of their sees, an abomination in the eyes of the High Church and Ultramontane party.

On the death of Clement VIII. (March, 1605) French influence and gold brought about the election of the Cardinal Alexander de' Medici (Leo XI.), and on his death within less than a month after his elevation, of the Cardinal Camillo Borghese (Paul V.), a prelate who, at any rate, was no friend of Spain.

But nothing did more to raise the French King's reputation and influence in Italy than his successful mediation in a quarrel concerning ecclesiastical immunities between the Pope and Venice (1606). Spain hoped as the champion of the Church to obtain a pretext for attacking and humbling the Republic, which had been the persevering and dangerous, though cautious opponent of her Italian policy.   Henry IV., on the other hand, owed a debt of gratitude to Venice, which had been the first Roman Catholic power publicly to acknowledge his title, and he more than repaid that debt by enabling the Senate to conclude an arrangement with the Holy See by which Paul V. virtually surrendered all disputed points, and thereby abandoned that claim of the spiritual power to pre-eminence over the temporal, which Rome had struggled during so many centuries to establish.   But the Italians were less impressed by a concession, which marks an epoch

in the history of the Church, than by the victory won by French over Spanish diplomacy. The
Duke of Savoy, who had gained nothing from his
connection with Spain, abandoned the dream of a
Burgundian kingdom extending to the Rhone, and
hoped by allying himself with France to obtain
Lombardy or some equivalent accession of territory
at the expense of his former allies.

But the French King was not always the aggressor
in the contest of intrigue, nor was the advantage
always on his side. Just as the Spanish army was
still the army of Pedro Navarro and of Gonsalvo of
Cordova, of Alva, and Farnese, still the most perfect
instrument of warfare in Europe, surpassing other
troops in organisation, professional pride and discipline, so Spanish diplomacy still displayed the
Machiavellian arts, the restless activity it had learnt
when directed by the untiring vigilance of the recluse
of the Escurial. Scarcely a day passed but Henry
was reminded that Spain retained both the power
and the will to do him an injury.

Soon after Biron's conspiracy it was discovered
that the secretary of Villeroy was in the pay of
the Spaniards and communicated to them all the
secrets of the French foreign office. The Count of
Auvergne, who had cunningly secured an opportunity to continue his treasonable correspondence
by affecting a wish to make his relations with the
Court of Madrid the means of obtaining information
for the French Government, disclosed only what was
unimportant or untrue and persisted in conspiring
against his King and country.

27

The domestic life of Henry IV. was very much
what his extraordinary disregard of decency and
dignity deserved, and it was never more stormy and
uncomfortable than about this time (1604). He was
tormented by the reproaches and by the mutual abuse
of his wife and mistress. Mary of Medici complained
that Madame de Verneuil dared to insinuate that she
was the King's true wife, her son the legitimate
heir.   If the King were to die, she, his widow, and
the Dauphin would be exposed to great danger.
The domestic and foreign enemies of the Government would be eager to support the claim of Henriette's boy as a pretext for troubling the kingdom.
Henriette, on the other hand, maintained that, even
during her lover's life, she had reason to dread the
jealous hostility of the Florentine ; while if anything
were to happen to Henry, who could protect her and
her poor orphans against the Queen Regent?   The
least the King could do was to give her some strong
castles and towns in which they might seek a
refuge.   As he refused to entertain such a proposal,
she spoke in such terms of his wife and so tauntingly
to her lover, that he was nearly provoked into boxing
her ears.   But so great was her power over him, so
delightful and amusing her society, so alluring, as it
would seem, even her devilry and malice, that on the
next day he would again be at her feet and lamenting her coldness.   For she scarcely deigned to conceal her indifference ; were he not a King, she used
to say, no one would tolerate him as a lover, and he
had good reason to believe, that there were others
whom she regarded with more favour.

In the middle of June (1604) the English ambassador handed to the King a letter, in which James I. advised him to seize the person and papers of one Morgan, a Spanish spy and agent, then in Paris. It appeared from documents in Morgan's possession that the Count of Auvergne and the Entragues were seeking not only to secure the support of Spain for Henriette and her children in the event of the King's death, but also intended to attempt some treason during his lifetime.

Auvergne was in his county; the King sent for Entragues, but he and his daughter stoutly denied that there had been more than vague talk between them and the Spanish ambassador as to whether the King of Spain would promise Henriette a refuge in his dominions. Entragues was not immediately arrested, and hurried to his Castle of Marcoussis, where three moats and drawbridges always raised would secure him against a surprise. He was therefore not a little astonished when early one morning his curtains were drawn by a royal officer, and he saw his room filled with archers of the Guard ; four of whom had passed the triple moats and bridges, in the dress of country women bringing butter and eggs for their lord's breakfast, overpowered the sentinels and admitted their comrades.

Entragues was carried off to the Bastille, and with him a voluminous correspondence between the conspirators and the Spanish Court, containing proposals for the assassination of the King and a promise signed by Philip III. to recognise the son of Madame de Verneuil as heir to the French throne on the decease of Henry IV. The only thing wanting was the celebrated promise of marriage. On a hint that he might thus buy his pardon, Entragues told where it might be found hidden in a hole in the wall. The prisoner signed a declaration that this was the authentic promise, and that no other to the same effect existed. There had been a popular rumour of one written by the King with his blood, which Henriette was said to keep in her own possession.

In the meantime Auvergne had been arrested. Madame de Verneuil also was placed in confinement. The culprits were brought to trial before the Parliament. Entragues and Auvergne were convicted of high treason and sentenced to death. Henriette was remanded until further evidence could be procured. The lives of her father, an inveterate and unscrupulous intriguer, and of her half-brother, who, under a not unpleasing exterior and a dignified grace of manner, such as few of his father's house were wholly unable to assume, had the soul of a swindling lacquey, were justly forfeited. The King's advisers were urgent that the law should be allowed to take its course. The execution of a King's son for treason, and for conspiring with foreign powers would have been an even more useful warning to high-born traitors than the death of Marshal Biron. Henry had done his best to overcome his passion for Henriette d'Entragues. At first he turned for assistance and sympathy to his wife. But, he complained to Sully, she received his advances coldly and, when he would have caressed her, assumed a repellent air. There was nothing about her which could make it easy to forget the graceful vivacity, the nimble wit of his perfidious mistress. But perhaps fire might drive out fire. The Princess of Condé had about her a young relation Jacqueline de Beuil, conspicuous among the beauties of the Court for her golden hair and brilliant complexion, her infantile yet voluptuous grace. The King determined to make her his mistress. Perhaps he hoped to find in her more placid nature some of the repose he had lost with his Gabrielle. The Princess of Condé did not properly appreciate the advancement in store for her cousin, but the King gave her very roughly to understand that she, at any rate, was not the person to affect scruples of honour. The young lady herself regarded the matter more simply as a business transaction. She bargained for a title, an estate, a pension, a large sum of ready money and a husband.

The King was in no hurry to discard a toy so costly as the new mistress, yet he did not find that she enabled him to forget the old. The corrupt perversity, the fiery temper, the biting tongue of Madame de Verneuil were more stimulating to his jaded taste, than the cloying sweetness of a more beautiful but soulless courtesan. He felt that he must have his Henriette back, and all the more because she affected to scorn him and would not sue for mercy. But if he cut off the father's head, even he, dead as he was to all sense of seemliness, felt that he could scarcely again be the daughter's lover. Entrague's life, therefore, must be spared. The Count of Auvergne, he argued, was too weak in character, too blasted in reputation to be dangerous,

and it might seem unworthy of his magnanimity to
send the last scion of the House of Valois to the
scaffold.  Instead, therefore, of being led out to
execution, the Count was locked up in the Bastille,
while Entragues and his daughter were released.

Early in the new year (1605) the King was again
in amorous correspondence with Henriette, begging
her to love him, to whom all the rest of the world
compared with her was as nothing.  Mlle. de Beuil,
now Countess of Moret, was indeed retained, as a
refuge when the mistress was spiteful and the wife
sulky.  Before long the resources of the royal harem
were further extended by the addition of a third
publicly acknowledged mistress.  Mary of Medici
appeared to resent her husband's infidelities less
violently, now, when she shared his affections with
many, than when she dreaded the dangerous influence of Henriette d'Entragues alone.  The irregularity of the King's conduct was perhaps the less
displeasing to her, because it compelled him to buy
her complaisance by shutting his eyes to the scandalous favour and unbounded influence of Concini
and his wife, Leonora.

Shortly after the conspiracy of the Entragues,
discovery was made of a plot to betray Marseilles,
Beziers and other towns in the South to the Spaniards.  In the North they were again treating with
Bouillon, who was disappointed by the refusal of
the Huguenot Assembly which met in 1605 at
Châtelleraut, to countenance his opposition to the
King.  Henry at length lost patience with this
troublesome intriguer.  He advanced upon Sedan

with a small army and a powerful battering train.
When the Duke saw that neither Protestants nor
Spaniards would stir a finger to help him, he capitulated. The terms he obtained were favourable in
the extreme. No punishment was inflicted on him
except the occupation of Sedan during four years
by a royal garrison under a Huguenot commander.
The leniency of the King is perhaps to be excused
by his desire to conciliate the Protestants and the
neighbouring German princes, who interceded for
Bouillon, yet that ruler bears the sword in vain who
encourages by impunity plots dangerous to the
security of his country and to the lives of his
subjects.

On September 20, 1604, Ostend, a mere heap of
ruins, capitulated after a siege of three years. In
the next campaigns nothing that military genius
could effect against an adversary scarcely less able
was left undone by Spinola. He freely spent the
greater part of his vast wealth, 14,000,000 gold
crowns, in the service he had entered as a volunteer,
yet, although he won some battles and took some
fortresses, no real progress was made towards the
conquest of the revolted provinces, while every part
of the Spanish Empire was suffering from the persistent and successful maritime war waged by the
Dutch. The state of the Spanish Netherlands was
deplorable. On the northern frontier the land was
desolate for miles; grass grew in the streets of
Ghent and Bruges, the quays of Antwerp were
deserted. Nor were the Dutch unwilling to treat.
The load of taxation borne by the country was very

heavy, and if the prosperity of the traders and of the maritime population increased, the sufferings of the agricultural population were great. Moreover, a powerful party desired peace, because they were jealous of the almost regal authority of Prince Maurice, to which, while the war lasted, they must needs submit.

Some overtures were made by Archduke Albert as early as 1603, but it was not till four years later that negotiations for peace were opened in regular form. After the great preliminary difficulty, the recognition of the United Provinces as free and sovereign States had been overcome, and a truce for eight months concluded, it was very unlikely that hostilities would again be resumed. Henry IV. would have preferred the war to drag on till the time was ripe for him to avenge himself and Europe on the House of Austria. But if the Dutch would not continue the struggle without more help than it was convenient for him to give, then the best he could do was to secure their gratitude by taking an active and friendly part in the negotiations, and by protecting them against any treachery or double dealing intended by the common enemy. He accordingly sent President Jeannin to attend the Conference at the Hague as his representative, and concluded a defensive alliance with the United Provinces, which was to come into force immediately after the conclusion of peace (January, 1608).

The Nuncio and some of the Jesuits about the French Court assured the Spanish Government, that Henry IV. might be induced not only to abandon the Dutch but even to turn his arms against them, if his daughter were betrothed to the second son of Philip III. and the sovereignty of a re-united and Catholic Netherlands secured to them after the death of Archduke Albert. Encouraged by the Pope, Philip III. sent Don Pedro of Toledo, a grandee of the highest rank and a cousin of Mary of Medici, as his ambassador to Paris, to propose a close alliance between the two Courts, cemented by a double marriage between the royal children. Such an arrangement would have been as acceptable to the Catholic party, the former Leaguers, in the Council, as to the Queen. They saw that the nearer the time drew for the accomplishment of the King's anti-Spanish designs the more he inclined to the Protestants. Old Huguenots like Aubigné, began to be seen about the Court ; and it was felt that when once Henry, as the head of a Protestant coalition, had drawn the sword against the dynasty, whose cause was identified with that of Romanism, he must, of necessity, be led farther in the same direction. The situation, was not unlike that before the massacre of Bartholomew, when the adoption by Charles IX. of the policy of Coligny, the declaration of war against Spain, would have been followed by the triumph of the Protestants and of their friends in the royal council.

But Henry IV. could not be tempted, by a bait more glittering than substantial, to change the whole of his policy : to abandon his cherished hope of so humbling the Hapsburgs that their ambition should never again be dangerous to France or Europe. He was asked forthwith to abandon and attack his allies, but the price of his dishonour was future and contingent.   When Don Pedro at his first audience said that his master would gladly negotiate on the basis of the proposals made to him for a double marriage, Henry indignantly interrupted him.   " What proposals?" he had made none himself and would sooner lose his hand than be false to his allies!

It was in vain that the Castilian bent his pride to flattery.   Taking the King's sword from a page he kissed it, saying that he now was a happy man, since he had held in his hands the sword of the bravest King in the world : threats availed even less.   When Don Pedro exclaimed, in the heat of dispute, that the King, by helping the Dutch, might provoke Philip III. to assist French malcontents, Henry burst forth : " Let your master have a care, I should be in the saddle before his foot touched the stirrup."

Don Pedro remained eight months in France courted by the Queen and doing his best to fan once more the old embers of the League into a blaze.   Again the drum ecclesiastic was beaten in the Parisian pulpits and again the piety of the mob made the streets unsafe to the Huguenots.   Again the Guises began to cabal and to complain of the harshness with which the King exacted the price of Mercœur's pardon, the hand of his daughter for the Duke of Vendôme.   Nothing availed to force the Spanish alliance on Henry, or to save Spain from the humiliation of recognising the independence of the little country which for forty years had successfully defied the efforts of the greatest and wealthiest empire the world had seen since the first barbarian hordes crossed the Roman frontiers. Owing in great measure to the skilful diplomacy of Jeannin, supported by the English envoys, a treaty was signed (April 9, 1609) between Philip III. and the Dutch, which recognised the independence of the United Provinces and secured to them the right of trading to all parts of the Indies not actually occupied by the Spaniards. It was an empty concession to Spanish pride that the treaty took the form of a twelve year's truce and not of a perpetual peace.

# CHAPTER XI.

COMPLICATIONS IN GERMANY—PREPARATIONS FOR
WAR—ASSASSINATION OF THE KING.

### 1609–1610.

VEN before peace had been concluded
at The Hague it had become clear
that the outbreak of hostilities in
Germany could not be long delayed.
The Peace of Augsburg (1555) had
been nothing more than a temporary
acquiescence on the part of both sides in the *status
quo*, a truce which could not be lasting. The
struggle had been too equal. Both sides were
irritated, neither convinced that in a second trial of
strength they might not be able to overwhelm their
opponents. Hardly any circumstance likely to provoke and embitter the conflict was wanting. There
were dynastic jealousies and feuds, a universal sense
of uneasiness and insecurity, theological odium. On
both sides the confident assurance of foreign support;
on both violations or evasions of the terms of a compromise purposely ambiguous, and pregnant with

disputes more dangerous than those which it was supposed to settle.

The Protestants, who, during the tolerant reign of Maximilian II. had appeared likely to become as predominant in Hungary and Bohemia and southern Germany as in the north, were alarmed by the rapid progress of the Counter Reformation. The Jesuits —*Viscera magnarum domuum dominique futuri*—were all powerful in the Courts of Vienna and Munich. In the Austrian and Bavarian dominions, in most of the ecclesiastical principalities of southern and in many of those of northwestern Germany the Lutherans were obliged either to submit to persecution or to conceal their dissent. The Imperial law courts, the only remaining centre of national unity, became violently orthodox and partial.

The threatening attitude of the Emperor Rudolph convinced the Protestant Princes that it was absolutely necessary that they should unite for their common defence. In 1601 a first defensive alliance was concluded between the Elector Palatine, the Elector of Brandenburg, the Landgrave of Hesse and some others.

In 1605 the Protestants of Hungary and Transylvania allied themselves with the Turks against their persecuting sovereign. The revolt spread into the hereditary dominions of the Hapsburgs. Compelled by necessity and by the unanimous wish of his family, the Emperor, whose character was an unhappy mixture of obstinacy and weakness, of unbridled sensuality, degrading superstition and despondent apathy, allowed his far more able and

tolerant brother Matthias to exercise a temporary
dictatorship and to save his empire by well-timed
concessions.  It was agreed that Matthias should be
elected King of the Romans.  But the Ultramon-
tanes induced the Archduke Ferdinand, a man of
great ambition and a zealous Catholic, to come forward as a rival candidate to his cousin.  Rudolph
also refused to perform the engagements entered into
in his name by Matthias, who thereupon with an
Austrian, Hungarian and Moravian army, marched
upon Prague where the Emperor was and extorted
the cession of half of his dominions and a promise
of the reversion of the remainder.  Since Matthias
owed his success to the support of the Protestants,
he was compelled to grant them toleration in the
countries of which he became the ruler (summer of
1608).

At the diet held in the beginning of 1608, the
Protestants demanded the reform of the Imperial
courts, and an explicit renewal of the Religious
Peace to be promulgated in a more comprehensive
form ; and when their demands were rejected they
left the diet in a body.

After so open a schism the outbreak of war sooner
or later was certain, and a new and larger Union of
Protestant Princes was at once formed.  The leading spirit of this confederation was Prince Christian
of Anhalt, a former officer and friend of Henry IV.
Saxony stood aloof, but all the other Protestant
Princes and many of the Free Cities joined the Union.

The domestic dissensions of the Hapsburgs ; the
imbecility of the Emperor, who was sinking into a

state of furious melancholy; the Protestant reaction in the Austrian provinces and Hungary; the alliance of the Protestant States of the Empire, were circumstances which could not but suggest to Henry IV. that the time had come when a fatal blow might be struck at the Austro-Spanish power. In the next year (March 25, 1609) an event happened certain to precipitate the struggle for which both sides were now more or less prepared. John William, Duke of Cleves, Juliers and Berg, died childless. The Elector of Brandenburg and the Count Palatine of Neuburg were the nearest heirs, claiming through the two eldest sisters of the late Duke. But the Emperor maintained that the Duchies were male fiefs, which could only descend in the direct male line, while the Saxon princes appealed to old instruments, confirmed by the Imperial courts, which secured to them the reversion of the possessions of the House of Cleves.

The question of the succession to the dominions of the Duke of Cleves was one of vital importance. Lying as they did along the lower Rhine and close to Belgium and Holland, in the hands of a Catholic like the late Duke, they connected the bishoprics of Munster, Paderborn and Hildesheim with the ecclesiastical electorates and the Spanish Netherlands thus interrupting the communications of the Protestants of Central Germany with the Dutch. That they should pass into the hands of a Protestant would be a fatal blow to the Catholics of northern Germany and would threaten the security of the Spanish Netherlands.

Aware of the advantages of possession, the Elector of Brandenburg and the Count Palatine of Neuburg had at once endeavoured to occupy the Duchies. They would have come to blows in the process, had not the Landgrave of Hesse persuaded them to govern the country jointly until their claims could be submitted to arbitration or otherwise decided. The Emperor cited the claimants to appear before his Court, and, since the "Possessioners," as they were called, paid no attention to the summons, he put them under the ban of the Empire and ordered the Archduke Leopold to take possession of the territory as Imperial Commissioner.

On the very day on which Henry IV. heard of the death of the Duke of Cleves, he wrote to Jeannin, then at The Hague, that the Emperor would without doubt try to seize the fortresses of the Duchies and to possess himself of at least the better part of the territory, but that he was determined not to allow any such addition to the power of the House of Austria; and that if war came he would wage it in no half-hearted fashion. Jeannin in reply told him that Barneveld, the leader of the peace-party in the United Provinces, had assured him that if the King of France took up the cause of the Elector of Brandenburg, the claimant whose title appeared strongest, the Dutch would stand by him against no matter whom. Neither France nor Holland could permit Spain and Austria to establish themselves at their gates in a position which commanded the Rhine.

Archduke Albert desirous of peace, and well aware

that Henry IV. and his allies, if victorious, were likely to seek an indemnity at his expense, proposed that the Germans should be left to fight out their own quarrels. He would not interfere, and he would also persuade his brother-in-law Philip III. to remain neutral. Henry replied, the Archdukes might please themselves, but that whatever happened he was determined to help his friends. Even the pacific James I. announced his intention of joining with France and Holland in defence of Protestant Germany against Austria and Spain; but since the continental powers were more directly interested than England, it was for them to make the first move. In Italy, Charles Emmanuel was now the zealous ally of France. He had made up his mind that the hereditary ambition of his family could not be satisfied west of the Alps. As the reward of his help in driving the Spaniards out of Italy he hoped to receive the Duchy of Milan, and the title of a King of Lombardy. It was thought that the prospect of annexing Naples to the patrimony of St. Peter might induce the Pope to join the league against Spain. The island of Sicily was to be the price of the active co-operation of Venice.

Henry had wisely abandoned the idea of any territorial aggrandisement in Italy, but there was an understanding that Charles Emmanuel, if he received Lombardy, should cede Savoy and Nice to France. The King was very far from intending to go to war for an idea, as some of the panegyrists of his disinterested policy would have us believe, or if for an idea, it was for that idea of nationality which has since

28

his time so often provided a useful excuse for dynastic ambition. " I am well content," he said, " that every place where Spanish is spoken should belong to Spain, where German is spoken to Germany. But every land where the French tongue is used, ought to be mine." No doubt he hoped ultimately to overcome the objections of England to the annexation of the Walloon Provinces, and of the Swiss to that of Franche-Comté, and to secure the possession of Lorraine by the projected marriage of the Dauphin to the daughter and heiress of the Duke.

Meantime (August, 1609), by the connivance of the commander of the garrison, Archduke Leopold had obtained possession of the strongly fortified town of Juliers, and began to carry on desultory hostilities with the Possessioners. But with a few troops supplied by the Ecclesiastical Electors and some other Catholic Princes he could effect little. The Austrian Princes were engrossed by their family dissensions, and the Spaniards were fully occupied by the expulsions of the Moriscos, the most costly and suicidal act of bigotry and folly ever perpetrated even by that fanatical and shortsighted Government. There was therefore abundant time for Henry to complete his negotiations and preparations before he began the war.

It had been arranged that a congress of the Princes of the Protestant Union to be attended by the envoys of France should meet at Hall in Swabia at the beginning of the next year (January, 1610). Until then nothing was decided. Many about the King were averse to war and in favour of a compromise,

some because war increased the influence of their
rivals, others because they believed that under existing circumstances the King of Spain and the
Emperor would be found ready to grant everything
that could reasonably be demanded.

Spanish influence was in the ascendant at the
Court of Florence, and the Tuscan ambassador confirmed Mary of Medici in her opposition to her
husband's policy. Nor were his allies as forward as
he had hoped. Venice displayed her usual caution.
The Pope could hardly fail to see that the success
of Henry IV. would mean a check to the future progress of orthodoxy, possibly the total ruin of the
German church. In short the only certain allies of
France in Italy were Savoy and Mantua. James I.,
the Dutch and the German Princes were unwilling
to do more than defend the rights of the Possessioners. It was therefore believed that a peaceable
solution was not impossible when an event occurred
which has been said to have determined Henry to
draw the sword.

It has pleased those writers who are attracted by
the romantic in history or who love to deduce great
events from the trivial accidents of our physical existence, to expatiate at length on the story of Henry
IV's unseemly passion for Charlotte de Montmorency, and although it may not have materially
affected the course of events, we cannot well pass it
by in silence. It discredited the King's policy by
enabling his enemies to represent it as swayed by
personal and unworthy motives, and it affords an
impressive warning that if we indulge our pleasant

vices we may become their unhappy and degraded slaves

As Henry grew older, the private history of his life became neither more edifying nor less eventful. Henriette d'Entragues, notwithstanding her infidelities, her treasonable intrigues, her bitter tongue,— she spoke to the King, it was said, not as to an equal, but as to her footman,—and her scarcely concealed aversion, continued the reigning favourite. The Duke of Guise and the Prince of Joinville were among her admirers and she was not without hopes of terminating a distasteful connection by a splendid marriage. There are few things more pitiable than the letters in which the King by mingling threats and cajolery seeks to overcome the coldness of his mistress. Nor were his relations with the other ladies who shared his favour more dignified. Not one of them seems to have felt any real affection for him. They laughed at him behind his back with the young courtiers and nobles who were his fortunate rivals. He complained that his married life was a hell upon earth; that his wife was entirely ruled by Concini and Leonora, who in everything incited her to oppose his wishes. But conscious of his own shortcomings he did not dare to insist that the mischievous couple should be sent back to Italy.

In one respect only, Mary de' Medici fulfilled his expectations. In nine years she bore him six children. There was no longer any danger that a direct heir to the Crown would not be forthcoming. Henry IV. playing with his children is a familiar figure in popular history, and no doubt he was in his way an affectionate father. But there was a marvellous absence of decorum and discipline in the royal nursery at St. Germains, where his legitimate and illegitimate offspring were brought up under the supervision of a Mme. de Monglat, a respectable but not overwise woman.

One afternoon towards the beginning of 1609, the King passing through a gallery of the Louvre found a bevy of young ladies practising for a ballet, nymphs of Diana armed for the chase. As he came by, one of these, a girl of fifteen, raised her javelin as if in act to strike. Such was her grace, her beauty and the magic of her eyes that Henry seemed to himself to be pierced to the heart and about to faint.

The nymph was Charlotte de Montmorency, one of the two children born to the Constable by his second wife, a woman of middling birth, who, it was whispered, owed to some supernatural agency her wondrous loveliness and the splendid marriage it enabled her to make. She died young, some said the demon had been an impatient creditor, leaving two children the inheritors of her charms, Charlotte, and a boy whose death on the scaffold was to be the most impressive object lesson given to the French nobility before the Revolution.

Mlle. de Montmorency was betrothed, with the King's approval, to Francis de Bassompierre, a young noble of Lorraine whose graces and good looks had acquired the King's favour, and who, though barely twenty, was the gayest gallant and most accomplished lady-killer of the Court.

Shortly after this passing encounter the King was

laid up by an attack of gout.  By day he meditated
on the incomparable charms of Charlotte de Montmorency, who more than once accompanied her
aunt, the Duchess of Angoulême, on a visit to his
sick room.  By night his attendants endeavoured to
soothe his pain by reading aloud the romances which
were then thrilling the polite world.  The intermina-
ble rhapsodies of the lovesick shepherds and shep-
herdesses, the quintessential sentiment, the Platonic
gallantries of the *Astrée*, weigh like the drowsiest of
opiates on the eyelids of the few who now open
the dusty volumes of M. d'Urfé.  But they pro-
foundly stirred the fancy of the King.  Perhaps just
because there could be no greater contrast than that
between his own life of active adventure, varied by
realistic amours, and the ideal world of vaporous
sentiment and alembicated passion to which he was
introduced.  Thus two centuries later the Corsican
ogre sympathised with the sorrows of Werther and
the perplexities of Pamela.

As the paroxysm of his gout abated Henry felt
that a new and delightful sensation might be found
in a pure and romantic, but not unrequited passion
for the girlish bride of his favourite.  Bassompierre
was summoned, and as he knelt by the royal bedside listened with surprised dismay to the communication made to him.  His master confessed that he
was desperately in love with the Constable's daughter and therefore asked him to give up the projected
marriage.  If the fair Charlotte became Bassompierre's wife and loved him, he, the King, would hate
the happy husband ; if she loved the King, her hus-

band would hate the King.   In either case there
would be enmity between them.   Henry said he intended to marry her to the Prince of Condé, who
scarcely cared for anything but hunting, and for
nothing less than ladies' society.   He would keep
her about the Court and find in a tender and mutual,
but pure, attachment the delight and solace of that
old age which he felt to be creeping on him.   Bassompierre informs us in his memoirs that his love
was as warm as the chilling prospect of marriage
would allow, and the connection with the Montmorencys was too flattering and advantageous to be
foregone without regret.   But he saw at once that
the King was determined, that unless he yielded
with a good grace he would lose both his bride and
the royal favour.   In short the lover sighed, but the
courtier obeyed, and had his reward in the embraces
and flattering promises of the King.   But on this
occasion at least we heartily sympathise with Charlotte, who when informed of the change that had
been made in the disposition of her hand, passed by
her too facile lover with a shrug and a glance that
sent him in grief and mortification to his room
where, he assures us, he spent three days without
food or sleep.

The plan arranged by the King was far from an-
swering his expectations.   Condé, it is true, gratefully accepted the King's pension and appeared to
be far more interested in his wife's dowry than in
her person.   But when he clearly understood the
part it was intended that he should play, when he saw
the King who was usually plain in dress and pain-

fully neglectful of his person, powdered and scented
and vying in silks and satins with his courtiers, when
he found that his wife was not only receiving but
replying to the passionate elegies and sonnets composed for their master's use by Malherbe and other
rhymesters of the Court, then, in the King's phrase
he began "to play the devil," and after some angry
scenes in which Henry entirely lost all sense of dignity and decorum, as well as his temper, carried off
the Princess to a castle not far from the Flemish
frontier. The King followed his mistress, and
dressed as one of his own huntsmen stood with a
patch over his eye by the roadside to see her pass.
He penetrated in the same disguise into the courtyard of a house where she was dining and when she
appeared at a window kissed one hand to her, while
he pressed the other to his heart. The extravagance
of such behaviour must have delighted the malice
of his enemies, but we almost forget it in our disgust
at the baseness of the dowager Princess of Condé,
and of the Constable, Duke of Montmorency, who
were willing to gain the royal favour at the price of
their daughter's honour.

At length (30th November, 1609) Condé finding
himself betrayed by those who had most reason to
be true to him, fled hastily with his wife across the
frontier, apparently intending, as he professed, to
place her in the care of his sister, the Princess of
Orange at Breda. When Henry heard of his cousin's
flight his dismay and confusion were extreme. He
at once summoned his most trusted advisers, the
Chancellor (Brulart de Sillery), Villeroy, Jeannin.

One had proposed this, another that, when Sully reached the scene of the discussion, the bedroom of Mary de' Medici, whose last child, the ill-starred Henrietta Maria, had been born a few days previously. As soon as the King saw Sully he went up to him: "M. de Sully, the Prince is gone and has taken his wife with him."—"Well, Sire, if you had followed my advice and locked him up in the Bastille, you would know where to find him."—"The thing is done; it is no use talking like that. The question is, what am I to do now?"—"Let me go back to the Arsenal, sup and sleep upon it, and then I shall perhaps have some good advice to give you."—"No, no, I want it at once." Upon this the Duke turned away, and after drumming some time on the window turned round and came towards the King. "Well, have you thought of something?"—"Yes." —"What then ought we to do?"—"Nothing." "What, nothing?"—"Yes, nothing. If you do nothing at all and appear quite indifferent, no one will think anything of the Prince, or help him, and in three months he will be reduced to sue for terms. But if you show your anxiety and your eagerness to get him back, he will be thought much of, and assisted with money. Many will be ready to support him to spite you, who, if you disregard him, will take no notice of him."

Sully's good advice did not suit the excited mood of the King. Messengers were despatched in every direction to intercept the Prince if possible, and as there was no doubt that he must at least pass through the Netherlands, a special envoy was sent

denouncing him as a traitor and enemy to the public
peace and asking the Archdukes to permit his arrest,
or at least not to grant him a refuge in their dominions.  No incident could have been less to the taste
of the Infanta and her husband.  They were sincerely
desirous of peace and anxious to give no offence to
their powerful neighbour, and it must be allowed
that their conduct in the whole affair was conciliatory
as well as dignified and honourable.  Archduke
Albert said that Condé had asked his permission to
travel through his dominions with his wife, in order
that they might visit their sister the Princess of
Orange, that he could not violate the safe conduct
he had given, but that the Prince would not be
allowed to remain in the country.

Condé thought it more prudent to send his wife
on alone to Brussels, where she lived in the palace
of the Prince of Orange, while he himself hurried to
Cologne.  It was only after Henry had asked the
Archduke to use his influence to persuade his cousin
to return to France, that he was permitted to come
to Brussels, where his hosts did their utmost to effect
a reconciliation between him and the King.  Spinola
and the Spanish ambassador were less nervous about
offending the King of France, more desirous of retaining such an instrument of annoyance against him
as Condé was likely to prove.  For although his
personal qualities were below mediocrity, he was the
first Prince of the Blood and next in the succession
to the King's children, and he bore a name which
could not but endear him to the Protestants.  If
Henry persisted in his hostile projects against Spain,

Condé might be used to excite troubles in France, while in the event of negotiations his extradition was a concession which costing little might be dearly sold. He was accordingly encouraged to hurry secretly to Milan, where he was sumptuously entertained in the Ducal palace.

Before leaving Brussels the Prince had seen his wife safely lodged under the roof of the Archdukes. A plot for her escape concerted before his departure between her and the emissaries of her royal lover had been betrayed by Henry's inability to conceal his joyous anticipations. His disappointment when, after leaving Paris with four coaches, he met on the road from Flanders (February 15, 1610), not his nymph, but a messenger who brought the news of failure, was even greater and more open. "I am so shrunk with my worries," he wrote to one of his agents at Brussels, "that I am nothing but skin and bones. Everything disgusts me. I fly society, and if out of civility I allow myself to be led into any company my wretchedness is completed."

Although she was treated with extreme kindness by the Infanta neither Spanish devotion nor etiquette were to the taste of Charlotte de Montmorency. Her French attendants were gained by the King and enlarged on the triumph and glories of which she was deprived by her husband's jealousy. She stimulated the impatience and passion of her royal lover by her complaints and by the tenderness of her replies to his letters. The Constable repeatedly wrote, as he was instructed, to the Archdukes, begging them to allow his daughter to return to him.

They replied that they had promised the Prince to watch over his wife until he could return to claim her, and that they might not with honour break their word. They refused to entertain Father Cotton's suggestion that they might connive at her escape,— a persistence most creditable to them, for Condé had not impressed them favourably and they were unfeignedly anxious to do nothing which might lead to a war with France. Henry IV. and his ministers did their utmost to persuade them that peace was impossible unless Charlotte de Montmorency was given up to her father. " The repose of Europe rests in your master's hands," said President Jeannin to the ambassador of the Archduke. " Peace and war depend on whether the Princess is or is not given up. Everything else is immaterial " ; while the King reminded him that Troy fell because Priam would not send Helen back.

It would be a dark blot on the fame of Henry of Bourbon were it true that he was prepared to begin a war which was likely to extend its ravages into every part of Europe, not in order that he might humble a power which had persistently pursued the ruin of France, which had incited her nobles to treason, her mobs to revolution, which had placed the dagger in the hands of numberless assassins, a power whose policy was identified with intolerance and persecution ; not in order that he might roll back the wave of bigotry and oppression that threatened to sweep over Germany ; not in order that he might consolidate the power of France by uniting under his sceptre the whole French-speaking race ;

but only in order that he might gratify a senile and adulterous passion. But we are glad to know that twelve years of persevering negotiations and carefully prepared alliances prove that this was not so. The episode of the Princess of Condé discredited the King, disturbed his serenity of mind, distracted his judgment at a time when the great enterprise, which he was about to take in hand, required that he should be in full possession of all the powers of his intellect, but it had little influence on the course of events. The King and his ministers used the large forces assembled for quite a different purpose, as a bugbear to frighten the Archdukes. But when they refused to purchase security by a compliance inconsistent with their honour, it was not on Brussels that the French armies prepared to march. On the contrary, four days before his death (May 10, 1610), the King in the most friendly terms asked the Archduke Albert's permission to lead his army across his territory to the assistance of his German allies; a permission granted by the Archduke, notwithstanding the opposition of Spinola and of the Spanish party in his Council.

On the 1st April (1610) the Spanish ambassador, Don Inigo de Cardenas, demanded an audience of the King to inquire into the object of his armaments and warlike preparation; since they were far more extensive than was consistent with their avowed object, the expulsion of the Archduke Leopold from Juliers. If they were directed against the Netherlands, his master considered the interests of his sister his own. Henry in reply commended the loving care of Philip III. for one so near him in blood ; but added that it was a pity the King of Spain had so much superfluous charity left to bestow on other people's relatives. If such a rebel as Condé had fled from Spain into France, he would soon have sent him back. Then warming to his theme, he complained of the part played by Spain in the conspiracies of Biron, of the Entragues, and whenever else there was an opportunity of doing him an injury. As for the Archdukes, it was true they had at first appeared willing to act the part of friendly neighbours, but they too had changed their tone in obedience to orders received from the Escurial. Don Inigo after pointing out in reply that Henry had helped the Dutch and shown his ill-will to the Spaniards in many other ways, asked categorically whether it was against the King his master that so powerful an army was assembled. " I arm myself and my country," said the King, " to protect myself, and I have taken my sword in hand to strike those who shall give me cause."—" What then shall I tell my master ? "—" Whatever you please."

Thirty thousand infantry, six thousand cavalry were collecting at Châlons and the King had proclaimed his intention of himself leading them to the Rhine, where, according to a treaty concluded at Hall (January, 1610), the Princes of the Protestant Union had promised to place 10,000 men under his orders. The Dutch and the King of England were now, as has been noticed, disposed to hang back, but it was hoped that the persuasion of Prince Henry of Wales, who dreamt of laurels to be gathered under the auspices of the victor of Coutras and Ivry, and the authority of Maurice of Nassau would prevail. Fifteen thousand men under Lesdiguières were waiting in Dauphiny to join the army of the Marshal's old opponent, the Duke of Savoy, in the invasion of Lombardy, and although the Marquis of Mantua was the only other Italian Prince who had promised active co-operation, it was expected that certainly Venice, and possibly the Pope, would be tempted by the prospect of large and easy territorial aggrandisement to join in the attack on Spain. The avowed intention of the French King to procure the election of the zealously orthodox Duke of Bavaria as King of the Romans, might convince the Holy Father that he did not aim at the ruin of the Church either in Germany or elsewhere.

Ten thousand men commanded by the Marquis of La Force were expecting orders to cross the Pyrenees and to assist the Moriscos of Aragon and Catalonia, who were being driven towards the frontier, to recover and defend their homes. It was thought that the Spanish nobility who loudly protested against the persecution of their vassals, would, if they did not help, at least not resist the invaders. If this diversion did not suffice to prevent Philip III. from sending reinforcements to Italy and assisting his Austrian cousins, a larger army under the Duke of Montbazon might invade Spain by St. Sebastian and the west.

Henry IV. and his advisers had left little undone which might command success against enemies already half overthrown by their own errors and divi-

sions, yet he appeared to have lost his joyous elasticity
of spirits. He, whose cheerful countenance, whose
serene and gay intrepidity and hopeful self-reliance
had inspired his followers with confidence whatever
the odds they faced, did not himself now share the
enthusiasm with which his officers and soldiers were
preparing for a campaign in which victory seemed
easy. Those about him complained that he had
become morose and irritable, and lamented that he
should be thus changed by the violence of his passion for the Princess of Condé. He himself, as we
have seen, attributed his melancholy to this cause.
But he had other and juster reasons for disquiet.
He was too humane and had too deep a sense of the
value of peace to begin so great a war with a light
heart. When he had drawn the sword before, it had
been in self-defence; but now he was the aggressor,
it was he that would have to render an account for
the bloodshed and misery to come. Besides he had
too much experience not to know that the most careful precautions, the most artful combinations avail
nothing against the insolent caprice of fortune. The
success of his plans, everything, depended on his life.
The thrust of a lance, a stray bullet might, at the
very moment of victory, prove more disastrous to
the cause than the most ruinous defeat. He had
dark forebodings that his life might be cut short
even before he had met the enemy. The conviction
was very general that Spain would not forego the
use of her wonted weapon against so dangerous an
opponent. The murder of the King of France was
reported in several parts of Europe before it had

actually taken place. The Jesuit preachers and others had again begun their incendiary sermons. Popular alarm and indignation were excited by the usual lies. The Huguenots had plotted a general rising and massacre of the Catholics. The conspiracy had been detected, but the King would not allow the guilty to be punished. He was himself about to attack the Pope and to bring him in chains to Paris, to help the German heretics to root out the orthodox remnant in the Empire. Why else were all his armies commanded by Huguenots, Lesdiguières, Bouillon, La Force, Créqui, Rohan?

These were the methods, so Henry IV. remarked on a previous occasion, by which the day of the barricades and the assassination of the late King had been brought about, yet he treated such direct incentives to sedition with a leniency which under the circumstances was certainly culpable. Meeting one day a Jesuit who had preached in his presence with the utmost violence against heretics, and their scarcely less guilty protectors, who, he protested, ought not to be permitted to live, Henry said, " Well, Father, won't you pray to God for us?"—" How can we pray to God for you, Sire, when you are going into an heretical country to exterminate the handful of Catholics left." Instead of being angry the King turned away and laughed, " Zeal has turned the poor man's head." It was zeal such as this which placed the knife in Ravaillac's hand.

The misgivings of the King were intensified by the warnings of Villeroy and Jeannin and of others of his Council, who were either honestly averse to a war with Spain or opposed to a policy supported by their rivals. In addition to these causes of disquiet he was plagued by the lamentations and importunities of his wife. Her disappointment that the King would not entertain the project of an alliance with Spain, the soreness which, however accustomed to his ostentatious infidelity, she could not but feel at his preposterous passion for the Princess of Condé, scarcely needed to be inflamed by the malice of Leonora Galigai, and Concini, to produce domestic storms very displeasing to Henry, who wished to be surrounded by contented faces. He tried to propitiate his wife by appointing her Regent during his absence, and by granting her desire to be solemnly anointed and crowned Queen of France. A ceremony which would add to the security and dignity of her position and make her claim to the Regency in the event of the King's death more indisputable. Henry did not make this last concession very readily. The Queen's coronation delayed his departure to the army and the opening of the campaign three weeks (till May 19th), and cost much money at a time when there were more serious demands on the treasury. Moreover he could not shake off the foreboding of some evil which might happen to himself, intensified by an impression that he would die in a carriage and at some public ceremony.

On the 20th March the King signed the ordinance which appointed the Queen Regent and nominated the Council of Fifteen by whose advice she was to act. The most important members were the Cardinals Joyeuse and Du Perron, the Duke of Mayenne, and Marshal Brissac, of the Barricades. By placing the leaders of the Catholic party in the Council of Regency, Henry apparently sought to remove the bad impression made on the orthodox by the high military commands bestowed on heretics. He was no doubt confident that the dread of displeasing a victorious sovereign would secure the co-operation of the Council in his policy, however distasteful to them. Mayenne, moreover, had given repeated proofs of loyalty and did not appear to be implicated in the intrigues, by which the younger members of his family had lately annoyed the King.

On May 13th the Queen was crowned with great splendour at St. Denis. On the 16th she was to make a state progress through the streets of Paris. On the 19th her husband was to leave the capital to take the command of the well-equipped army of 35,000 men assembled since April at Châlons.

It was not yet known whether the Archdukes would allow the French to cross their territory as friends. Henry perhaps hoped that they would not. Whatever its discipline and valour, the small army under the orders of Spinola at Namur could scarcely be a match for his superior forces, and if it were defeated the Netherlands would be at his mercy. A few thousand men would suffice to drive the Archduke Leopold out of Juliers, and it is uncertain what use he intended to make of his army if Archduke Albert gave him no pretext for commencing hostilities. Perhaps he himself hardly knew in what direction the most decisive blow might be struck,

and meant to be guided by events and by the action
of his opponents.

On the morning after the Queen's coronation
Henry was restless and anxious. " When I am no
more," he said to the Duke of Guise and others
standing by, "you will know what you have lost."
After dinner he threw himself on his bed, but could
not sleep. He then thought he would visit Sully,
who was unwell at the Arsenal. Once or twice he
left the room, but came back, saying to the Queen,
" My dear, shall I go?" She, seeing him so undecided, begged him to stay, but at last he made up
his mind, kissed her and went.

He got into his coach with the Dukes of Épernon
and Montbazon, the Marquis of La Force, and four
other gentlemen. Dismissing the captain of his
guards he started for the Arsenal escorted only by
some footmen, who ran or walked with the carriage,
one of the clumsy conveyances then used, something
between a cart and a four-post bed with leather curtains on wheels. As they turned out of the Rue St.
Honoré into the Rue de la Ferronerie, a narrow lane
running along one of the sides of the Cemetery of
the Innocents, the footmen made a cut across the
cemetery to meet the carriage at the other end of
the street. A little way down the Rue de la Ferronerie the King's coach was obliged to draw close
up to the side and then to stop in passing two carts.
As it stopped a man jumped on one of the hind
wheels, leant over into the carriage and plunged a
knife twice into the breast of the King who was
leaning forward with his arm round Épernon's

shoulder. Henry scarcely uttered a cry ; the second blow severed one of the large arteries close to the heart. A gentleman was about to run his sword into the assassin, who stood, knife in hand, as if astonished at what he had done and making no attempt to escape, but Épernon forbade him on his life to hurt the man, whom the King's attendants protected from the fury of the collecting crowd. The curtains of the coach were drawn, the people were told that the King was only wounded and his lifeless body was carried back to the Louvre.

In a second the knife of a mad fanatic had altered the course of the world's history. Had Henry IV. prospered in the undertaking he meditated, and assuredly the chances were much in his favour, Germany would have been spared the horrors of the Thirty Years' War, the ruin of her material prosperity, the paralysis for a time of all intellectual energy and growth. Protestantism would have become predominant, or at least would not have been crushed, in Hungary and Bohemia and other Austrian dominions. The House of Savoy would have founded an Italian kingdom two centuries and a half before the time when an allied French and Piedmontese army drove the Austrians out of Lombardy. Yet we must not forget that the triumph of Henry IV. would have raised France to a pre-eminence such as that to which she attained during the first years of the present century. Henry of Bourbon, no doubt, would not have used his power in the same fashion as Napoleon Buonaparte. But who could answer for his successors? Would it have been well for the independence of European nationalities, for progress and liberty, had the ambitious egotism of a Lewis XIV. been able without fear of resistance to determine the destinies of Europe. France herself might have perished like Spain, exhausted by the despotism which drew from her the strength to enslave others. But it is as unprofitable as it is easy to speculate on what might have been, had things not been as they were.

No French king was ever more deeply and generally lamented than "the Bearnese." Eye-witnesses wrote that it was impossible to describe the grief and tears of the Parisians. "What will become of you?" men were heard to say to their children, "you have lost your father!"

In the provinces the country-people gathered along the highways in anxious crowds to ask travellers whether the King indeed was dead? When assured that this was so they dispersed grief-stricken and with frantic lamentations to their houses. Some of the educated classes, like De Vic, the Governor of Dieppe, took to their beds and died of grief. A touching tribute to the King's memory was offered by the mob, who received the Protestants on their way to service at Charenton not with the usual insults, but with demonstrations of affection and respect.

The Queen, who by the loss of her faithless husband, had become the first person in the State, and who could now indulge unchecked her fondness for her unworthy favourites, those favourites themselves, the partisans of Spain, the great nobles who looked

DEATH MASK TAKEN FROM FACE OF HENRY IV.

forward with joyful anticipation to a weak and divided Regency,—all these had gained too much by the King's death for it to be believed that they sincerely lamented him.   It was natural, therefore, that in an age fertile in such crimes, it should have been reported that his murderer was merely the tool of others, a weapon wrought and fashioned to take a life like Jacques Clément and Balthazar Gérard.

The Queen and the Concinis, the Jesuits and Spain, Épernon and Madame de Verneuil have been severally accused of having at least been privy to the murder of Henry IV.   Some historians like M. Michelet appear to think that all the powers of darkness were leagued together to quench the light of France.   Yet it seems scarcely possible to condemn the mistress and not to absolve the wife, and if, as Voltaire remarks, Ravaillac was incited to kill the King by the Spaniards at Naples, he was not suborned by Épernon at Angoulême.

But all such suppositions are at variance with the account which the assassin gave of himself and of his motives ; an account which was plain and consistent, corroborated by independent evidence, never shaken by the most painful bodily and mental tortures, and which entirely negatives the assumption that Ravaillac was the instrument of others or even that he had accomplices.

Francis Ravaillac had entered a convent of Bernardins, but at the end of his noviciate was rejected on account of his fantastic and extravagant conduct. He next attempted to gain his living as a schoolmaster at his native Angoulême, but a gloomy and forbidding exterior, a visionary and disordered intellect were not likely to recommend him as an instructor of youth; and he was more than once imprisoned for debt.

The shrill hysterical rhetoric of the preachers who continued the traditions of the League, their fierce denunciations of heresy and of the King who allowed the accursed thing to remain in the midst of his people to draw down God's judgment upon them, the casuistic subtleties of the books, which justified means by ends, and taught that it was better that one man should suffer than the people perish, wrought upon the distempered imagination of the starving enthusiast. His existence was perhaps wretched, yet life is life, and that devotion is respectable, however mistaken, which is prepared to sacrifice existence for the supposed good of others. Nor did Ravaillac wish to shed blood unnecessarily. Before he killed the King he determined to warn him of the errors of his ways, to give him room for amendment. If he could persuade him to abandon his heretical allies and to exterminate his heretical subjects, all would be well. For a whole month the fanatic sought in vain to obtain an interview (Christmas, 1609). Then he left Paris and returned to Angoulême. Before Easter he was back again in the capital, so poor that he was obliged to steal the knife with which he hoped to slay the enemy of true religion.

Yet again doubts and scruples arose. He broke off the point of his knife and set out once more for Angoulême. As he knelt at Étampes before a crucifix, the wounds and sorrow of the Redeemer seemed to reproach him for indifference to the sufferings of Christ's Church. He heard moreover that the King was about to attack God in the person of his Vicar. Hesitation now gave place to a firm resolve; he repointed his knife upon a stone, turned his face towards Paris and watched with dogged determination for an opportunity to kill the tyrant, for he had learnt in his books, that the prince is a tyrant who refuses obedience to the Church and leagues himself with the unrighteous against God's people.

That he had no accomplices he persisted in asserting under the most horrible torments and at the moment of his death, when his confessor threatened him, unless he spoke the truth, with the most certain pains of hell. And if he had accomplices would he have been reduced to stealing the knife wherewith to execute his purpose? He was equally positive that he had not been encouraged or instigated to murder the King by anybody or anything, except the sermons he had heard and the books he had read. He had expected all good Catholics to sympathise with him and to bless him for what he had done. Perhaps he remembered the images of Jacques Clément, exalted on the altars and venerated with honours almost divine. He was amazed and distressed by the howls of execration with which his appearance was greeted, by the frantic efforts of the mob to snatch him from his guards and to tear him limb from limb, by the yells and curses which answered the request of his confessor, that the people should pray for him while he suffered his barbarous doom.

The despair of all patriots, the scarcely dissembled satisfaction of the domestic and foreign enemies of France at the King's death are a convincing proof of his greatness. We may find another in the almost enthusiastic admiration felt for him by many of those who lived in his intimacy, even when they were severe censors of his failings. Aubigné was a caustic, often an ungenerous critic of a prince who, he believed, had failed fully to appreciate his own transcendant merits, but after relating an instance of Henry's frank magnanimity, he exclaims in a tone of the sincerest conviction: "Such was the King our master, if he had his faults he had also sublime virtues." And this evidence has all the more weight because many of Henry's weaknesses and shortcomings were of the kind which most prevent a man from appearing heroic to those about him. He inherited from his spendthrift father Antony of Bourbon, whose attendants sent back each evening the articles he had pilfered during the day, that unreasoning delight in small gains of which such kleptomania appears to be the exaggeration. This tendency made him mean in small matters, greedy of winning in the games of chance to which he was addicted, and out of temper when he lost.

His sensuality was, as we have seen, unbridled and not over nice in the gratification it demanded. A liking for coarse food highly spiced and redolent of garlic, for heavy perfumes and full-bodied wines, a neglect of personal cleanliness, remarkable even in the 17th century, may be explained by the circumstances of a life spent in the saddle and under arms, but contrasted with the more refined luxury of his predecessor, and indicate a coarseness of material and moral perception, which sometimes betrayed itself in a want of tact, remarkable in a man of ready sympathy and of warm, though superficial and transient, emotions.

Yet it is not strange that, in spite of all, he should have exercised great personal fascination over those who approached him, since even we, who are uninfluenced by personal contact with so rich and vigorous a nature, fall to some extent under the charm of his unflagging energy, his boundless good temper, his unfeigned humanity. He gained much popularity by the frankness with which he treated his friends and his enemies, by the ostentatious openness of his dealings both public and private. He was not, he boasted, one of those princes who had not sufficient virtue to be relieved from the necessity of concealing their faults.

Insensible to adulation himself, he excelled in the art of flattering others. Whether writing with his own hand to the newly chosen mayor of some provincial town, or begging Beza to continue his fatherly admonitions; or assuring the old Marshal that young Biron is as dear to him as a brother, and that it may be said of them like master, like man; or addressing some companion in arms in a tone of military comradeship, his letters are models of skilful flattery. He never forgets to court his friends by small and cheap attentions. He offers his own doctor to Ségur, and regrets that his many affairs prevent him from coming himself to help in nursing him ; he will bring one or two cheerful companions to dine with another invalid. When he thinks that it will be acceptable, the dose of compliment is open and undisguised ; he seems to be ever on his knees before Queen Elizabeth, "kissing humbly," as he says, "the fair and fortunate hands which hold for him the keys of good and evil fate." He is unsparing of protestations of affection : " Be assured that I am your best friend, the best master you could ever have." He is prodigal of expressions of gratitude and vague promises. Often full of regrets when, like the brother of Du Plessis-Mornay, his servants die at the very moment when he was going to do something great for them. Mornay himself must not imagine that he will permit him to be ruined in his service—" I am too good a master." If he is told that his friends are discontented, he assures them that he closes his ears to such calumnies.

How far was he consciously insincere? It is not easy to answer this question in the case of a man of such vivacity, so susceptible of the feeling of the moment. He probably felt at the time what he expressed so warmly and so naturally. Yet he himself allowed that he often meant to deceive. " Necessity," he said, " compels me to say now this, now that." It is certain that he hated Épernon, and with good reason, yet he writes to him in a tone of cordial friendship, and he assures Matignon that he had never made any complaint of his conduct, a few days after filling a letter to Henry III. with charges against him. Nevertheless, tried by the standard of those times—compared, for instance, with Philip II. or Elizabeth of England—we must allow Henry the praise of having been straightforward and honourable in word and deed. Much of the impression of insincerity and double-dealing often left upon us, is perhaps due to the contrast presented by his violent though fleeting passions and emotions, to his cold heart and patient, persevering ambition.

His apparent incapacity to conceal his feelings—he often turned pale and showed great agitation, his tears flowed readily—was of service to him. Few suspected how cool and calculating a politician was hidden under the exterior of the blunt, outspoken soldier and sportsman, of the genial man of pleasure. And when occasion required, Henry was not incapable of self-control. J. A. De Thou tells in his memoirs how, when during the siege of Rouen, Marshal Biron had complained of some mistake made by Crillon, the "brave Crillon," a gallant officer, but a licenced and extravagant braggart, came to the King's quarters to excuse himself. His excuses soon became argumentative, then passion and blasphemies took the place of argument. At length the King told him to leave the room, yet he constantly reappeared, while Biron, sitting on a chest, pretended to be asleep and not to hear the insults, "mangy hound" and the like, shouted into his ear. Henry changed colour with impatience and anger, yet restrained himself. After Crillon at length was gone, he turned to De Thou and others who were marvelling at his patience. " Nature," he said, "made me hot-tempered, but anger is a bad counsellor, and since I have known myself I have always been on my guard against so dangerous a passion."

Passionate he may have been by nature, but certainly no man was ever less resentful. Michelet perhaps is partly right when he speaks of the unfathomable depth of indifference to all things, which lay at the root of Henry's character. Such indifference would account for the fact that he does not appear to have been jealous of even his best loved mistresses. Bellegarde was more than suspected of having been the lover both of Gabrielle and of Henriette, and of even having dared to court the Queen, yet he never lost his master's favour. The same indifference may explain his extraordinary placability, "his patience in bearing reproof and his invincible hardness of heart." Not only during the earlier part of his life did he bear the rebukes of the Calvinist ministers, and even do public penance at their bidding, but when King of France he listened not less patiently to the admonitions of more orthodox preachers. No solicitations of Madame de Verneuil could induce him to punish a Jesuit, who had reproached him for coming to hear God's word surrounded by his harem. Next day he went to hear the same Father and thanked him for his reproofs, only begging him to administer them more privately in future.

It is perhaps not fanciful to trace some of the features of the character of Henry IV. in that of his grandson, Charles II. of England. In both we find the same profligacy, the same low estimate of men, the same dislike of seeing what is unpleasant, the same desire to be surrounded by contented faces, the same physical good nature which since it expected nothing was incapable of righteous indignation on finding nothing. Yet Henry's readiness to forgive, may more charitably be deduced from what was perhaps his most excellent quality, his unaffected humanity. No commander of the time was more anxious to provide for the comfort of his men, to mitigate the sufferings of his enemies. No King was more sincerely anxious to make the life of his poorer subjects less miserable. Again and again he warns magistrates not to inflict unduly severe punishments. Twice he flogged the Dauphin with his own hand, once for cutting off the head of a sparrow, and again for wishing that some one would kill an attendant who had displeased him. No faults were so unpardonable in his eyes as cruelty and vindictiveness.

Though experience had taught him to expect little from mankind he was not incapable of recognising and admiring merit and virtue. He was not, wrote Du Plessis-Mornay, one of those princes born in the purple and cradled in a Court, the predestined prey of sycophants, who can know of men only what they are told, but on the contrary was as well able as any in his kingdom to judge of the character and of the deserts of those about him. He used to say, that though shamefully betrayed by many he had been deceived by few.

But we must beware lest in the endeavour to enumerate and to balance the failings and frailties, the merits and virtues of such a man, we lose all true appreciation of him as a whole, and so form a judgment less just than that embodied in the traditional view of his character.

There was that about him which, whatever he did, prevented him from appearing mean or hateful, and it is not without reason that of all the Kings who have occupied the French throne, Henry of Navarre still retains the first place in the memory and affection of his people.

There have been many better men than Henry IV., greater statesmen, more consummate generals, but few men have appeared on the stage of history better equipped for their allotted part. The defects in his character were numerous and patent. He was no Cæsar—not a man whose very failings bear the impress of greatness, of something above the ordinary standard of humanity—still less was he a flawless hero, a Marcus Aurelius, an Alfred, or a St. Lewis. The life of such men, like a Greek tragedy, maintains throughout the same lofty and measured dignity. The life of Henry of Bourbon may rather be likened to an Elizabethan drama, interspersed with incongruities, with scenes of comedy, and even of low buffoonery, but perhaps for that very reason touching more nearly our human sympathies.

**THE END.**

# HOUSE OF LORRAINE.

Ferri II. of Lorraine, count of Vaudemont, Guise, etc., d. 1470
m. Yolande of Anjou, daughter of René of Anjou and Isabella of Lorraine, daughter and heiress
of Charles, duke of Lorraine etc., Bar, etc.

René II, duke of Lorraine and Bar, etc., d. 1508
m. Philippa of Egmont

---

Antony, duke of Lorraine and Bar, etc., d. 1544
m. Renée of Bourbon, daughter of Gilbert,
Ct. of Montpensier

Francis, duke of Lorraine and Bar, b. 1517, m. Christina of Denmark, d. 1545

Nicholas, duke of Mercœur, b. 1524, d. 1577

Charles, duke of Lorraine, etc., b. 1543, d. 1608, m. Claude, daughter of Henry II.

Henry, duke of Lorraine, b. 1563, d. 1624, m. Catherine of Bourbon, sister of Henry IV.

Louisa of Lorraine, b. 1553, d. 1601, m. Henry III

Henry, Count of Chaligny

Philip Emanuel, duke of Mercœur, b. 1558, d. 1602, m. Mary of Luxemburg, duchess of Penthièvre

Frances, duchess of Mercœur and Penthièvre, etc., b. 1592, d. 1669, m. Cæsar, duke of Vendôme

---

Claude, duke of Guise, etc., b. 1496, d. 1550
m. Antoinette of Bourbon, d. of Francis,
Count of Vendôme, d. 1583, æt. 89

John, Cardinal of Lorraine, d. 1550

Francis, duke of Guise, b. 1519, d. 1563, m. Anne of Este, daughter of Hercules, duke of Ferrara and of Renée of France. She afterwards m. the duke of Nemours and d. 1607

Charles, Cardinal of Lorraine, b. 1524, d. 1574

Claude, duke of Aumale, d. 1573

Mary, m. James V. of Scotland, d. 1560

Mary, Q. of Scots, m. Francis II., d. 1587

Charles, duke of Aumale, d. 1631

Henry, duke of Guise, b. 1550, d. 1588, m. Catherine of Cleves, who d. 1633, æt. 85

Charles, Cardinal of Lorraine, b. 1524, d. 1574

Charles, duke of Mayenne, b. 1554, d. 1611

Lewis, Cardinal of Lorraine, d. 1588

Catherine, b. 1552, d. 1596, m. Lewis of Bourbon, duke of Montpensier

Charles, duke of Guise, b. 1571, d. 1640

# HOUSE OF BOURBON–VENDÔME.

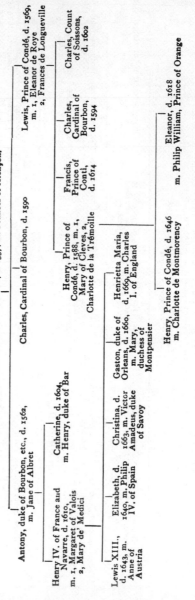

Charles, duke of Vendôme and Bourbon, d. 1537, m. Frances of Alençon.

Antony, duke of Bourbon, etc., d. 1562, m. Jane of Albret

Charles, Cardinal of Bourbon, d. 1590

Lewis, Prince of Condé, d. 1569, m. 1, Eleanor de Roye 2, Frances de Longueville

Charles, Count of Soissons, d. 1602

Henry IV. of France and Navarre, d. 1610, m. 1, Margaret of Valois 2, Mary de' Medici

Catherine, d. 1604, m. Henry, duke of Bar

Henry, Prince of Condé, d. 1588, m. 1, Mary of Cleves 2, Charlotte de la Trémoille

Francis, Prince of Conti, d. 1614

Charles, Cardinal of Bourbon, d. 1594

Lewis XIII., d. 1643, m. Anne of Austria

Elizabeth, d. 1640, m. Philip IV. of Spain

Christina, d. 1663, m. Victor Amadeus, duke of Savoy

Gaston, duke of Orleans, d. 1660, m. Mary, duchess of Montpensier

Henrietta Maria, d. 1669, m. Charles I. of England

Henry, Prince of Condé, d. 1646 m. Charlotte de Montmorency

Eleanor, d. 1618, m. Philip William, Prince of Orange

# INDEX.

## A

Acadia, 358
Achmet, Sultan, 415
Agen, 118, 379
Aix, Parliament of, 27
Alava, 61
Albert, the Cardinal-Archduke, 310, 322 *et seq.*, 326, 424, 432, 442 *et seq.*, 451
Albret, see Henry of, and Jane of.
Alençon, 108
Alençon, Francis, Duke of (afterwards Duke of Anjou), his character, 92 ; watched by his mother, 101 ; escapes and heads the rebels, 105, 108 ; concludes peace with the Court, 109 ; opinion of the Protestants, 117 ; mischief making at Pau, 133 ; death, 138 ; gave Cambray to Balagny, 304
Amiens, 286, 287, 317 ; siege of, 319 *et seq.*
Amyot, 377
Angoulême, 455
Angoulême, Duke of, 79
Anhalt, Prince Christian of, 236, 430
Anjou, Duke of, see Henry III., and Alençon.
Anjou, House of, 16
Antony of Bourbon, King of Navarre, in the power of the Guises, 21 ; his influence at Court, 29 ; changes sides, 33 ; reproaches Beza, 35 ; killed before Rouen, 41 ; his character, 44 ; married to Jane of Albret, 48 ; a Protestant, 51 ; reverts to Catholicism, 52
Antwerp, 150, 423
Arbaleste, Charlotte, Mme. Du Plessis-Mornay, 121
Arques, battle of, 199
Armada, the Invincible, 163, 224
Arnauld, Antoine, 296
Arras, 317
Artois, 190, 299, 413
Aubigné, 90, 106, 107, 133, 135, 136, 157, 175, 200, 221, 259, 330, 377, 382, 410, 425
Auch, 129
Augsburg, Peace of, 428
Aumâle, Duke of, 90
Aumont, Marshal, 195, 197, 200, 209
Auneau, 159
Auvergne, 216, 379
Auvergne, Count of, 389, 403, 407, 409, 417, 419 *et seq.*
Avignon, 105

## B

Balagny, 304
Balzac, Francis de, Lord of Entragues, 389, 419 *et seq.*
Barneveld, Olden, 414, 432

Barrière, 267, 284
Bassompierre, 437 *et seq.*
Béarn, 336
Beaufort, Duchess of, see Gabrielle.
Beda, 4
Belin, Count of, 201, 256, 277
Bellegarde, 229, 231, 462
Bergerac, Peace of, 127
Berquin, Lewis de, 4, 5
Beuil, Jacqueline de, 421
Beza, 35, 51, 55, 145, 259, 459
Birago, 77
Biron, Marshal (the elder), 187, 210, 212, 221, 237, 238, 241, 244, 246, 461
Biron, Duke of (the younger), 244, 299, 300, 319, 322, 374, 401 *et seq.*
Blavet, 327
Bouillon, see Turenne.
Bourbon, Family of, 44
Bourbon, Peter, Duke of, 44
Bourbon, Charles, Constable of, *ib.*
Bourbon, Charles, Cardinal of, 138, 141, 145, 191, 204, 217
Bourbon, the younger Cardinal of, 226
Brandenburg, Elector of, 432
Brantôme, 81
Brissac, 180, 277, 280 *et seq.*, 451
Brittany, 203, 224, 327
Burgundian kingdom, 225, 417
Burgundy, 286, 297, 299, 402, 405
Bussy d'Amboise, 374

C

Caëtano, 225
Cahors, storm of, 130
Calais, 196, 233, 311 *et seq.*, 326, 327
Calvin, his book dedicated to Francis I., 5 ; his doctrine, 6 ; favourable to political liberty, 8 ; advocates non-resistance, 19 ; his opinion of Antony of Bourbon, 45

Cambray, 304, 327
Canada, 358
Canaillac, 380
Cardenas, Don Inigo de, 445
Casaubon, 348, 372
Câteau-Cambresis, Peace of, 12
Catherine de' Medici, Regent, 21 ; favours the Reformers, 29 ; her character, 30; accepts L'Hôpital's policy of conciliation, 31 ; urges Condé to protect her against the Guises, 36 ; keeps Henry of Navarre at Court, 53 ; her ladies, 54 ; dread of Spanish interference, 58, 61 ; alarmed at the influence of Coligny over Charles IX., 73 ; determines his death, 75 ; wishes to continue opposition to Spain, 94 ; secures the succession of Henry III., 101 ; visits the Court of Navarre, 128 ; to make mischief, 129 ; opposed to the Huguenots, 140 ; advises Henry III. to yield to the League, 145 ; intercedes for Guise, 164 ; dying, 170 ; trusted La Noue, 237 ; her books, 372
Catherine of Navarre, 51, 125, 134, 227, 229, 387
Caudebec, 243, 244
Cecil, 71, 74, 83, 94, 105
Chaligny, Count of, 90, 241
Châlons, 286
Champagne, 286, 287
Champlain, 357
Charenton, 218 ; "Temple" of, 342, 454
Charles IX., besieges St. Jean d'Angely, 57 ; disposed to peace, 58 ; his hatred of Spain, 64 ; wishes to marry his sister to Henry of Navarre, 69 ; influenced by Coligny, 73 ; desires Queen of England to help Orange, 74 ; anger at the attempt against Coligny, 76 ; visits him, 77 ; consent to

the massacre extorted by his mother, 78 ; his character, 91 ; his Government, 99 ; miserable death, 100

Charles II. of England, 463

Charolais, 327

Chastel, 296

Châteauneuf, Mme. de, 90

Châtillon, 126, 159, 176, 178, 199, 203, 238

Cherbourg, 107

Chicot, 90, 241

Chrestien, Florent, 56, 373

Clement VIII., 268, 305, 324, 416

Clément, Jacques, 182, 457

Clèves, question of succession to, 431

Clovis, 274

Cognac, 59

Colbert, 125

Coligny, presents petition from Reformers, 20 ; powerful after the death of Francis II., 21 ; reluctant to begin the war, 36 ; Condé under his influence, 41 ; at Jarnac, 42 ; defeated at Montcontour, 57 ; collects an army in the south, *ib.* ; anxious for peace, 59 ; invited to Court, 62 ; reception there, *ib.* ; at Henry of Navarre's wedding, 70 ; influence over Charles IX., 74 ; attempt on his life, 76 ; death and character, 79 ; patron of Du Plessis-Mornay, 120

Commines, 113

Concini, 394, 422, 436, 451, 455

Condé, Lewis, Prince of, rival of the Guises, 20 ; in their power, 21 ; leader of the Huguenots, 33 ; offers to raise 50,000 men against the Guises, 35 ; abandons Paris and the King, 36 ; his character, 40 ; death at Jarnac, 42

Condé, Henry, Prince of, 43, 87, 98, 101, 108 110, 128, 150, 174, 369

Condé, Henry II., Prince of, 333, 378, 439, 440, 442, 443

Condé, Charlotte de la Trémoille, Princess of, 174

Condé, Charlotte de Montmorency, Princess of, 437 *et seq.*

Corbeil, 223

Corisande, see Grammont.

Cossé, 62, 101, 109

Cotton, 410

Council, the Royal, its composition, 63 ; decides against war with Spain, 74

Coutras, battle of, 155

Crillon, 164, 461

## D

D'Amours, 157, 259

Damville, Duke of, 100, 118, 126 (after 1579, see Montmorency).

Dauphin, the (Lewis XIII.), 50, 397, 414, 434, 463

Dauphiny, 14, 27, 344

De Monts, 357

De Thou, J. A., 56, 121, 139, 334, 363, 369, 372, 461

Dieppe, 26, 196

Dijon, 14, 286, 299, 300

D'O, Francis, 185, 258, 272, 309, 351

Dohna, Fabian of, 158

Dolet, Stephen, 11

Dombes, Prince of, 224

Dominicans, 306

Doria, Carlo, 288

D'Ossat, Cardinal, 306, 325

Douai, 322

Dreux, 206, 255

Du Bourg, 15

Du Châtel, Bishop of Macon, 11

Duelling, 89, 369

Du Perron, 259, 306, 372, 451

Du Plessis-Mornay, valor at Eausse, 119 ; birth, education, character, 120 *et seq.* ; mission to Henry III., 136 ; satisfaction at death of Guise, advice to Henry of Navarre, 176 ; at

Ivry, 207 ; Villeroy attempts to convince him that Henry IV. must conform, 213 ; mission to Queen Elizabeth, 239 ; believes that Henry IV. will not change his religion, 256 ; disappointed, 260 ; summoned repeatedly to Court, 261 ; ill rewarded, 271 ; distrusts the King, 329 ; yet approves of his policy in regard to the Protestants, 381 ; and of the Edict of Nantes, 343 ; urges Henry IV. to marry again, 380

Duprat, 4

D'Urfé, 438

Dutch, 73, 97, 140, 142, 150, 195, 239, 246, 290, 299, 312, 313, 321, 326, 414, 424, 427, 432, 435, 446

E

Eausse, 119

Edict of Fontainebleau (1540), 14

Edict of Châteaubriand (1551), 10

Edict of Compiègne (1557), *ib.*

Edict of January (1561), 31

Edict of Bergerac (1577), 127

Edict of Nantes (1598), 335

Egmont, Count of, 206, 211

Elizabeth of England, supported by Philip II., 16 ; her vacillation a cause of the massacre of St. Bartholomew, 72 ; dares not quarrel with the French, 94 ; plots for her assassination, 139 ; urges Henry III. not to submit to the League, 146 ; he desires her advice, 161 ; Jezebel, 162 ; vigorously helps Henry IV., 196 ; blames his humanity during siege of Paris, 220 ; sends an army into Brittany, 224 ; admired by Sixtus V., 225 ; sends Essex and 6,000 men to Normandy, 233 ; angry at loss of her men before Rouen, 239 ; yet sends rein-forcements, 242 ; rebukes Henry IV. for apostasy, 265 ; delays to relieve Calais, 312 ; offensive and defensive treaty between her and Henry IV., 313 ; not very forward in helping to retake Amiens, 320 ; warned by Henry IV. that she must make peace, 326 ; recalls her troops from Brittany, 327 ; warns Biron, 404 ; her death lamented by Henry IV., 413 ; his flattery of her, 460

English, assist La Rochelle, 97 ; volunteers, 321

Entragues, see Balzac.

Épernon, Duke of, 90, 138, 140, 144, 165, 188, 286, 309, 403, 405, 407, 452, 460

Erasmus, 4

Ernest, Archduke, 253, 299

Essex, Earl of, 233, 236, 239, 311, 404, 407

Errard, 364

F

Farnese, Alexander, Duke of Parma, 140, 141, 149, 163, 189, 217, 219, 220, 237, 240, 242 *et seq.*, 250

Ferdinand, Archduke, 430

Feria, Duke of, 253 *et seq.*, 278, 280, 283

Fleix, Peace of, 132

Fleurance, 129

Fontainebleau, 368, 386

Fontaine Française, engagement at, 301

Franche Comté, 190, 290, 297, 299, 413

Francis I., 3, 5, 46, 372

Francis II., 18, 21, 50

Fuentes, Count of, 303, 311

G

Gabrielle d'Estrées, 229 *et seq.*, 263, 290, 307, 379 *et seq.*

Geneva, 9, 400

Germany, 155, 233, 413, 423, 428 *et seq.*, 434, 435

Givry, 186, 287

Gondi, Bishop of Paris, 219

Gondi, Count of Retz, 77

Grammont, Corisande, Countess of, 134, 138, 156, 175, 227

Gregory XIV., 225

Guise, Francis, Duke of, 17, 35, 36, 41

Guise, Henry, Duke of, privy to plot against Coligny, 76, 78; superintends his murder, 79; affects humanity, 83; his character, 92; offers to protect Du Plessis-Mornay, 120; Lieutenant-General of the League, 144; surprises Germans at Auneau, 159; hated by Henry III., 160; enters Paris in defiance of the King, 164; at the barricades, 165; objects of his ambition, 166; despises Henry III., 169: assassinated, 170; blood calls for blood, 339

Guise, Charles, Duke of, 190, 243, 248, 254, 286, 288, 436, 451

Guise, Charles of, Cardinal of Lorraine, 17 *et seq.*, 105

Guise, Lewis, Cardinal of, 171

Guise, Mademoiselle de, 397

Guises, their policy and ambition, 16; summon the States-General, 20; their toleration, 34; provoke the outbreak of war, 35; distrusted by Philip II., 137; ally themselves with Spain, 141; distrust Catherine de' Medici, 154; their party, 183; claims on Provence, 288; their intrigues, 451

### H

Hall, conference at, 434

Hall, Treaty of, 446

Harlay, 363, 372

Hâvre, 203, 234

Henriette d'Entragues, 389 *et seq.*, 396 *et seq.*, 418 *et seq.*, 436, 455

Henry of Albret, King of Navarre, 46, 48, 49

Henry II., persecutes the Protestants, 10; killed, 15; introduces Jesuits into France, 293

Henry III., suspected of death of Condé, 42; victorious at Montcontour, 57; at his sister Margaret's wedding, 70; the accomplice of his mother in the plot against Coligny, 75, and in persuading Charles IX. to consent to the massacre, 77; his account of the massacre, 79; his effeminate dress and character, 91, 116; King of Poland, 98; compelled to leave France, 100; flies from Poland yet loiters on his way to France, 102; progress in the South, 104; his foolish profusion and superstition, 105; his policy and errors, 114; etiquette at his Court, 115; offers fair terms to the Huguenots, 127; concludes Peace of Fleix, 132; his misgovernment, *ib.*; insults his sister Margaret, 136; wishes Navarre to conform, 139; recognises him as his heir and accepts the Garter, 141; dares not resist the League, 144; yet warns Navarre to be on his guard, 146; surrenders to the League, 148; hates Guise, 160; perplexity, 161; defied by Guise, 164; compelled to fly from Paris, 166; tries to conciliate the League and the Estates at Blois, 168; determines to get rid of Guise, 169; assassination of Guise and consequences to the King, 171 *et seq.*; he shows favour to

Châtillon, 178 ; interview with Navarre, 179 ; besieges Paris, 181 ; assassinated, 182 ; names Henry of Navarre his successor, 185

Henry IV., swears fidelity to the Protestant cause, 43 ; his birth and early education, 49 ; at the French Court, 52 *et seq.* ; with his mother at Nérac, 55 ; the source of his versatility, 56 ; accompanies Coligny in the campaign of Montcontour and afterwards, 59 ; his domains, 61 ; proposed husband of Margaret of Valois, 62, 63 ; arrangements for the wedding, 68 ; the ceremony, 69 ; spared after massacre of St. Bartholomew, 87 ; difficulty of his position, 88 ; serves at siege of La Rochelle, 97 ; carefully guarded by the Queen-Mother after death of Charles IX.; determines to escape, 105 ; and does so, 107 ; awaits events, 109 ; readmitted into Calvinist Communion, 117 ; protector of the churches, *ib.* ; receives a deputation from the Estates, 118 ; his valour at Eausse, 119 ; agrees to Peace of Bergerac, 126 ; visited by the Queen-Mother, 128 ; engages in a futile war, 129 ; storms Cahors, 130; concludes Peace of Fleix, 132 ; quarrels with his wife, 133 ; wishes to marry the Countess of Grammont, 135 ; rejects the offers of Philip II., 137 ; invited to Court by Henry III., 138 ; offers to help the King against the League, 145 ; his stirring letters, 151 ; his manifesto, 152 ; answer to Papal excommunication, 153 ; wins battle of Coutras, 155 ; his troubles in 1587-8, 173 ; grieves for

Condé, 175 ; rejoices at the death of Guise, 176 : convenient illness, *ib.* ; his interview with Henry III. and appearance, 179 ; his accession, 183 ; his title to the throne based on indefeasible hereditary right, 184 ; reply to demands of Catholic courtiers, 186 ; recognised by a large part of the army and by the Swiss, 187 ; his army melts away, 188 ; his opponents divided, 190 ; his difficulties 192 *et seq.* ; retires into Normandy, 195 ; refuses to buy Elizabeth's help by surrender of Calais, 196 ; takes up a strong position before Dieppe, 197 ; defeats Mayenne, 199 ; recognised by Venetian Senate, 202 ; attacks suburbs of Paris, *ib.* ; marches to the west, 203 ; attacks the towns around Paris, 206 ; defeats Mayenne at Ivry, 209 *et seq.* ; prevented from advancing on Paris by Biron, 212 ; general desire for his conversion, 213 ; his own feelings in regard to this, 214 ; determines to blockade Paris, 216 ; advised by Biron to raise the siege and meet Parma, 221 ; who eludes him, 222 ; his army disperses, 222 ; discontent and intrigues among his supporters, 225 *et seq.* ; quarrels with Corisande, 228 ; having made the acquaintance of Gabrielle d'Estrées, 229 ; promises to " receive instruction " and confirms the edicts protecting the Huguenots, 232 ; collects a Protestant army, 233 ; with which he besieges Rouen, 236 ; meets Parma at Aumâle and is wounded, 240 ; his energy, 241 ; continues the siege of

Rouen on Parma's retreat, 242; obliged to raise the siege by Parma, *ib.*; baffled by ill will of Biron and skill of Parma, 244; obliged to disband his army, 246; announces to envoys of the Estates that he will " receive instruction within two months," 254; his conversion, 256 *et seq.*; effects of his conversion, 266; attempts against his life, 267; the Pope will not absolve him, 268; he grants very favourable terms to rebels, 270 *et seq.*; importance of coronation ceremony, 272; coronation at Chartres, 274; negotiates surrender of Paris, 276; pays Brissac liberally for opening the gates, 279; enters Paris, 281; his clemency, 287; makes Guise Governor of Provence, 288; determines to attack Spain, 290; his attempted assassination by Jacques Clément, 295; banishes the Jesuits, *ib.*; rebukes the delays of Parliament and Chambre des Comtes, 298; joins Biron in Burgundy, 300; wins skirmish of Fontaine Française, 301; hurries north on hearing of siege of Cambray, 304; besieges La Fère, 305; absolved by Clement VIII., 306; his policy of conciliation not unsuccessful, 309; his destitution, 310; unable to save Calais, 311; takes La Fère, 312; treaty with Elizabeth and Dutch, 313; summons an Assembly of Notables, 314; his frank eloquence, 316; hears of the surprise of Amiens, 318; begs for supplies, 319; defeats Archduke Albert's attempt to relieve Amiens, 322; refuses to abandon his allies, 325; yet opens negotiations with Spain, 326; and concludes peace (of Vervins), 327; grants favourable terms to Mercœur, 328; secures toleration and civil rights to the Huguenots by the Edict of Nantes, 329 *et seq.*; insists that the Edict shall not be a dead letter, 338 *et seq.*; continues to watch over the interests of the Protestants, 342 *et seq.*; endeavours to reform the finances, 347; the public distress and its causes, 350 *et seq.*; he fosters manufactures in opposition to Sully, 354; also maritime and colonial enterprise, 356 *et seq.*; interested in agriculture, 358; reorganises the army, 364; pardons 7,000 gentlemen for killing their adversaries in duels, 369; did more for the material welfare than for the intellectual and moral progress of his subjects, 371 *et seq.*; careless of literature, 373; a greater patron of painting and sculpture, 375; coarseness of manners at his Court, 376; anxiety about his life, 378; his growing devotion to Gabrielle d'Estrées, 379; wishes to marry her, 382, this marriage unpopular, 385; his grief at Gabrielle's death, 387; resigns himself to marry Mary de' Medici, 388; but falls in love with Henriette d'Entragues, 389 *et seq.*; meets his wife at Lyons, 394; introduces mistress and wife, 396; pleased by birth of a Dauphin, 397; rapid successes against Savoy, 400; his generous treatment of Biron, 401; who confesses something of his intrigues with the Duke of Savoy, 402; and is sent to England, 404; he takes pre-

Henry IV.—(*Continued.*)
cautions against the conspiracy, 405 ; and summons Biron to Fontainebleau, 406 ; would have pardoned him even at the last, *ib.* ; determines to readmit the Jesuits, 411 ; waits for a favourable opportunity to attack Spain and Austria, 413; negotiations with James I., 414 ; and the Turks, 416 ; mediates between Paul V. and Venice, 416 ; discovers conspiracy of the Entragues with Spain, 419 ; tries to break with Henriette, 420 ; but can not and therefore pardons her father and brother, 421 ; compels Bouillon to surrender Sedan, 423 ; helps the Dutch to negotiate a peace with Spain, 424 ; rejects overtures for marriage treaty with Spain, 425 ; and determined to interfere in affairs of Juliers-Cleves, 432 ; hopes for alliance of England and Italian powers, 433 ; aspires to rule wherever French is spoken, 434 ; disappointed by backwardness of his allies, 435 ; merited unhappiness of his private life, 436 ; falls in love with Charlotte de Montmorency, 437 ; marries her to the Prince of Condé, 439 ; follows her in disguise, 440 ; indignant that Condé should carry her out of the country, 441 ; threatens the Archdukes with war unless they give up the Princess, 444; the threat not seriously meant, 445 ; angry interview with the Spanish ambassador, *ib.* ; prepares to open the campaign with overwhelming forces, 447; yet unusually anxious, 448 ; opposition to his policy by the Queen and his Catholic advisers, 449 ; tries to propitiate the Queen by allowing her to be crowned, 450 ; gloomy forebodings, 452 ; his assassination, 453 ; his character, 458 *et seq.*

Henry, Prince of Wales, 415, 446

Holland, see Dutch

Hugh Capet, 273

Huguenots, see Protestants

Hulst, 312

Humières, 112

### I

Ibarra, 280, 283

Isabella the Infanta, 253 *et seq.*; 310, 324, 399, 442 *et seq.*

Ivry, battle of, 208, 331

### J

Jane of Albret, Queen of Navarre, presents her son to the army, 43 ; married to Antony of Bourbon, 48 ; death of her children, *ib.* ; hurries to Pau for the birth of her son Henry, 49 ; slowly converted but faithful to Protestantism, 51 ; educates her son, 55 ; comes to Court to arrange his marriage, 64 ; her opinion of Margaret of Valois, 65 ; fears for her son, 66 ; her death, 69 ; zeal for learning, 373

James I. of England, 414, 433, 435, 446

Jarnac, battle of, 42

Jeannin, 121, 205, 235, 283, 424, 427, 432, 440, 444, 449

Jesuits, 138, 143, 267, 284, 292 *et seq.* ; 305, 345, 410, 424, 429, 449, 455

Joan of Arc, 273

John Casimir, Count Palatine, 110, 158

Joyeuse, Duke of, 140, 145, 155

Joyeuse, Cardinal, 450

## L

La Charité, 59
La Fére, 286, 305, 311, 312
La Fin, 401, 405, 409
La Force, Marquis of, 447, 452
La Gaucherie, 51, 54, 55
Languedoc, 19, 100, 102, 150, 225, 286, 344
La Noue, 29, 117, 118, 120, 130, 200, 212, 221, 223, 237, 271, 374
Laon, 286, 287
La Réole, 129
La Rochefoucauld, Count of, 42, 69
La Rochelle, 26, 59, 62 ; siege of, 97, 117, 130, 175
La Trémoille, Duke of Thouars, 150, 188, 212, 261, 335
League, The, supplied with principles by Protestant writers, 97 ; neither patriotic nor popular, 104 ; its formation, 112 ; organisation in Paris, 142 ; its manifesto, 143 ; new ultimatum to Henry III., 162 ; its unpopularity, 169 ; atrocities of its defenders, 177, 213 ; more and more Spanish, 180, 189 ; yet not all Leaguers subservient to Philip II., 204 ; Mayenne dissolves the Council General, 205 ; condemned by Villeroy, 214 | its army annihilated at Ivry, 216 ; on bad terms with Sixtus V., 225 ; the extreme party wish that Philip II. might rule over them, 234 ; can only continue to exist by his assistance, 246
Le Fevre, 1
Le Mans, 107, 203, 216
Leo XI., 415
Leonora, Dosi or Galigai, 374, 422, 436, 451
Leopold, Archduke, 434, 451
Le Pollet, 198, 199
Lepsius, 373

Lerma, Duke of, 402
Lesdiguières, 286, 374, 400, 447
L'Estoile, 89, 121, 162, 193, 368
Lewis VI., 274
Lewis X., 273
Lewis XI., 276
Lewis XIV., 266, 454
L'Hôpital, 31 *et seq.*
L'Huillier, 281
Liancourt, 230
Longpré, 322
Longueville, Duke of, 195, 197, 200, 299, 302
Lorraine, Duke of, 144, 289
Lorraine, Claude, Duchess of, 85, 145
Louvre, 57, 166, 282, 368
Lover's War, 129
Low Countries, see Dutch.
Loyola, 292
Luther, 3
Luxembourg, 297, 299

## M

Machiavelli, 30, 64, 113
Malesherbes, castle of, 389
Malherbe, 377, 392, 440
Marcoussis, 419
Margaret of Angoulême, 3, 46, 47
Margaret of Valois, her infant orthodoxy, 29 ; negotiations for her marriage to King of Portugal, 61 ; her hand offered to Henry of Navarre, 62 ; her character, 67 ; marriage, 69 ; her account of the night of St. Bartholomew, 85 ; a friend to her husband, 88 ; rejoins him, 128 ; her Court at Pau, 133 ; returns to her mother, 181 ; insulted by Henry III., *ib.* ; a prisoner in Auvergne, 379 ; agrees to a divorce, 381 ; writes to Gabrielle d'Estrées, 385
Mariana, 409
Marmoustier, 274
Marot, 11, 377
Marseilles, 288, 357

Mary de' Medici, her birth, 388 ; married by proxy to Henry IV., 392 ; her journey to Lyons, 393 ; appearance and character, 394 ; her favourites, *ib.* ; complains of the pretensions of Henriette d'Entragues, 418 ; less jealous of three rivals than of one, 422 ; desires alliance with Spain, 435 ; her children, 436 ; appointed Regent during the King's absence, 430 ; suspected of being privy to her husband's murder, 454

Mary, Queen of Scots, 16, 143

Matthias, Archduke, 430

Maurevert, 90

Maximilian II., 429

Mayenne, Charles of Loriaine, Duke of, 90, 141 ; recognised as head of the League, 173 ; subservient to Philip II., 180 ; jealous of his nephew, Guise, 190 ; his character, 191 ; defeated at Arques, 199 ; negotiates with Philip II., 204 ; appoints a Council of State, 205 ; flight at Ivry, 212 ; humiliated by Parma, 222 ; summons the States-General, 234 ; wishes to prevent the marriage of Guise and the Infanta Isabella, 235 ; Urged by Jeannin to come to terms with the King, *ib.* ; joins Parma to relieve Rouen, 240 ; which he hopes to hold without Spanish help, 241 ; but is mistaken, 242 ; ousts the "Sixteen," 248 ; his unpopularity, 249 ; summons the States-General to Paris, 250 ; takes Noyon, 255 ; accepts an armistice, but sends his son-in-law to Madrid, 268 ; re-establishes the Council of Sixteen, 277 ; leaves Paris, 278 ; pertinacious in disloyalty, 289 ; joins the Constable of Castile in Franche-Comté, 300 ; retires to Châlons,

302 ; submits to the King, 307, his character, 308 ; before Amiens, 309 ; where he does good service, 323 ; appointed a member of the Council of Regency, 451

Meaux, 270

Mendoza, 139, 141, 180, 216, 241

Mercœur, Duke of, 224, 289, 327

Meulan, 206

Miossans, Mme. de, 49

Monluc, 29, 304

Montauban, 61, 97

Montbazon, Duke of, 447, 452

Montcontour, battle of, 57

Montgomery, Count of, 15, 83, 99, 100

Montmorency, Constable, 4, 16, 21, 25, 61

Montmorency, Duke of, 99, 100, 109, 126, 146, 150, 225, 309, 317, 403, 405, 443

Montpensier, Duchess of, 162, 182, 218, 283, 284

Montpensier, Duke of, 210, 312

Moriscos, 415, 434, 447

Mornay, see Du Plessis.

N

Nançay, M. de, 86

Naples, 433

Napoleon, 45, 156, 454

Nassau, 94 ; see Orange.

Navarre, kingdom of, 45

Nemours, Duke of, 210

Nemours, Duchess of, 284, 396

Nérac, 51, 52, 55, 133, 379

Neuburg, Count Palatine of, 431

Nevers, Duke of, 77, 268, 303

Nîmes, 105

Normandy, 20, 180, 203, 236, 344

Noyon, 255

O

Orange, William, Prince of, 74, 94, 120

Orange, Maurice, Prince of, 195, 224, 415, 424, 447
Orange, Princess of, 387
Ostend, 415, 423

**P**

Palissy, Bernard, 84
Paré, Ambrose, 79
Paris, centre of orthodoxy, 28 ; its religious houses there, *ib* ; ferocity of inhabitants, 83 ; the barricades, 165 ; expels Henry III., 166 ; grief for death of Guise, 172 ; besieged by Henry III., 181 ; rejoicings at his murder, 182 ; suburbs attacked by Henry IV., 203 ; blockaded after Ivry, 217 ; reliance on Philip II., 217 ; famine, 218 ; peace or bread, 219 ; relieved by Parma, 222 ; garrisoned by Spaniards, 224 ; famine again, 234 ; detestation of the League, 236 ; the Sixteen attempt a reign of terror in Paris, 248 ; Moderates insist on negotiations, 249 ; surrender only prevented by Spaniards, 277 ; terms of surrender, 279 ; changes hands peaceably, 280 ; filthy squalor of the streets, 365 ; improved by Henry IV., 366 *et seq.*
Parliament of Paris, hesitates to punish heretics, 15 ; hostile to the Reformers, 24 ; opposes the League, 154 ; declares the Salic law inviolable, 255 ; annuls everything done to the prejudice of the Crown, 285 ; scolded by Henry IV., 298 ; remonstrates against lenient treatment of Mayenne, 307 ; compelled by the King to register the Edict of Nantes, 339 ; effect on it of system of pur-

chase, 362 ; sentences Biron, 407 ; protests against the return of the Jesuits, 411
Parliament, Protestant judges in, 338
Parma, see Farnese.
Pau, 49, 52, 57 ; Court of, 133
Paul V., 416, 433, 435, 447
Pazzi, 393
Petrucci, 61
Philip II., enemy of the House of Guise, 16 ; proposed as husband to Jane of Albret, 47 ; would have liked to burn her, 54 ; expects a high price for helping French Catholics, 58 ; common enemy of Protestantism, 71 ; overtures to Henry of Navarre, 137 ; allies himself with the Guises, 142 ; claim of his daughter to French Crown, 146 ; promises to help the League, 189 ; expects the title of the Infanta Isabella to be recognised, 205, 234 ; more ready to send men than money to France, 214 ; neglects Netherlands for France, 224 ; sends 4,000 men to Brittany, 234 ; cruel treatment of La Noue, 237 ; determines to send Parma to impose his will on the Estates at Paris, 250 ; instructions to Feria, 254 ; treats with Épernon, 286 ; everywhere active against Henry IV., 289 ; not to be bearded with impunity, 291 ; ally of the Jesuits, 292 ; sends great reinforcements to the Low Countries, 303 ; quarrels with the Jesuits, 305 ; formidable though bankrupt, 310 ; wishes to leave peace to his successors, 324
Philip III., 402, 419, 425, 427, 433, 446, 447
Picardy, 303
Pignerol, 102

Place Royale, 367
Poirson, 372
Poissy, 206
Poitou, 344
Politicians (Moderate party), 61, 72, 99, 116, 153, 180, 249, 315
Portocarrero, 317, 322
Protestants, in France, opponents of despotism, 8 ; organised by Calvin, 9 ; sufferings under Francis I. and Henry II., 10 *et seq.* ; their organisation and numbers, 13 ; of all ranks, 14 ; rejoice at death of Henry II., 16 ; called Huguenots, 19 ; conspire against the Guises, 20 ; their policy at Estates of 1561, 22 ; their numbers at beginning of religious wars, 25 ; unequally distributed 26 ; believed to be in the ascendant, 29 ; attacked by the mob and refused justice in the courts, 33 ; challenged by the Guises, 35 ; were they right to begin the war ? 37 : their strength and weakness, 39 *et seq.* ; effect on the Protestant cause of the first eight years of war, 60 ; close connection of their fortunes with those of Protestants elsewhere, 71 ; massacred unresistingly, 82 ; a more popular party after St. Bartholomew's day, 96 ; encouraged by successful resistance of La Rochelle, 98 ; assisted by Politicians, 99 ; form a confederation with them in Languedoc, 102 ; more and more confined to certain provinces, 103 ; obtain favourable terms by the Peace of "Monsieur," 109 ; consequent reaction, 111, 113 ; hold aloof from the States-General of 1576, 116 ; obtained reasonable terms in the Peace of

Bergerac, 127 ; the League excite the people against heresy, 143 ; Edict of Toleration revoked (1586), 148 ; prospects of the Huguenots in the struggle, 149 *et seq.* ; joint manifesto of Protestants and Politicians, 152 ; assembly at La Rochelle, 175 ; treaty with the Royalists, 177 ; their policy, 183 ; Huguenot valour, decisive at Arques, 200 ; careless of constitutional reforms, 315 ; the discontented majority refuse to help the King to retake Amiens, 321 ; their grievances against the King unfounded, 330 *et seq.* ; he did all that he could for them by the Edict of Nantes, 337 ; their organisation and power, 343 ; their distribution, numbers, and unpopularity, 344 *et seq.* ; refuse to support Bouillon against the King, 422 ; popular feeling excited against them, 449
Provence, 27, 286, 288, 344
Provins, 223, 356
Pyrenees, 45.

## Q

Quebec, 358
Quercy, 130

## R

Rabelais, 377
Ravaillac, 455 *et seq.*
Renée of France, Duchess of Ferrara, 11
Rheims, 205, 234, 273
Richelieu, 265
Ronsard, 91, 377
Rose, Bishop of Senlis, 255
Rosne, Marshal de, 311, 312
Rosny, Maximilian de Béthune, Baron of (Duke of Sully), his education and character, 122,

*cf.* 348; reputation, 125; advises Henry IV. to conform, 258; negotiates surrender of Rouen, 276; vainly attempts financial reforms, 309; finds funds necessary for siege of Amiens, 320; reorganises the finances, 348; his dignities and rewards, 349; exposes peculation, 350; not a revolutionist, 352; improves roads and plans canals, 353; a free-trader, 354; believes in sumptuary laws, 355; improves incidence of tallage, 358; tries to make publicans disgorge, 360; systematises the sale of legal appointments, 362; financial result achieved, 363; his memoirs not to be trusted, 383; hated Gabrielle d'Estrées, *ib.*; fails to induce Biron to confess, 406; opposes the readmission of the Jesuits, 411; the inventor of the "Grand Design," 412; sent as ambassador to James I., 414; his good advice after flight of Condé, 441

Roucy, Count of, 374

Rouen, 26, 62, 173, 203, 234, 236, 238 (siege of), 241 *et seq.*, 275, 315, 338, 356

Rudolf, Emperor, 429

**S**

Sadolet, 11

Saluzzo, 399

Sancy, 187, 290, 383

Saumur, 108, 177

Sauves, Madame de, 128

Savoy, Charles Emmanuel, Duke of, 102, 225, 364, 399 *et seq.*, 417, 433, 435

Saxony, 430

Scaliger, Joseph, 56, 348, 358, 372

Schomberg, Count of, 207

Schomberg, Count of Nanteuil, 334

Sebastian of Portugal, 61

Sedan, 409, 423

Ségur, 459

Senlis, 107

Serres, Olivier de, 358

Sforza, Francis, 276

"Sixteen," the, 162, 234, 248, 277

Sixtus V., 153, 225

Smith, Adam, 359

Spinola, 415, 423, 442, 451

Soissons, Charles of Bourbon, Count of, 125, 156, 387

Sorbonne, see University of Paris

Stafford, Sir E., 161

States-General of 1561, 22; of 1576, 116, 126; of 1588, 168; abortive meeting at Rheims, 234; of 1593, 251, 269; unpopularity of States-General, 314

St. André, Marshal, 25, 33, 41

St. Bartholomew, massacre of, 78 *et seq.*; account given by French Court, 93

St. Denis, battle of, 41, 218, 264, 451

St. Germains, Peace of, 59

St. Germains, Palace of, 368

St. Jean d'Angeli, siege of, 57

St. Luc, 278

St. Pol, Count of, 303, 311, 317

Sully, see Rosny

Suresne, 254

Swiss, 155, 180, 208, 211, 227, 236, 245, 302

**T**

Tassis, 241

Tavannes, 74, 77

Teligny, 73, 76

Thouars, Duchess of, 397

Thouars, Duke of, see La Trémoille

Toledo, Don Pedro of, 426

Toleto, Cardinal, 269, 305

Touchet, Marie, 389

Toulouse, 27, 131, 173, 225, 286 ; Parliament of, 341
Tournon, Cardinal, 11
Tours, 285
Trent, Council of, 269, 416
Turenne, Viscount of, Duke of Bouillon, 128, 150, 212, 221, 233, 236, 261, 290, 297, 299, 303, 335, 369, 376, 402, 403, 409
Tuscany, Grand Duke of, 310, 388

### U

University of Paris, the judge of orthodoxy, 2, 3, 6 ; declares that incompetent princes may be deposed, 162 ; that Henry III. has forfeited the Crown, 172 ; that Henry IV. is incapable of reigning even though absolved by the Pope, 217; no students, 224 ; recants, 285 ; quarrel with the Jesuits, 293 ; reformed, 372
Usson, castle of, 380

### V

Vassy, massacre of, 34

Velasco, Don Fernan de, 299 *et seq.*
Vendôme, Cardinal of, 138
Vendôme, Cæsar, Duke of, 297, 308, 328, 382
Vendôme, Charles, Count of, 44
Venice, 202, 305, 416, 433, 435, 447
Vere, Sir Francis, 415
Verneuil, Marchioness of, see Henriette
Vervins, Peace of, 327, 399, 412
Vielleville, Marshal, 41
Villars, 238, 241, 270, 275, 303, 304
Villeroy, 121, 189, 194, 205, 213, 221, 235, 252, 266, 383, 417, 440, 449
Vitry, 270

### W

Walsingham, 61, 71, 74, 120, 233
Wurtemberg, Christopher, Duke of, 34

### Z

Zamet, 386
Zwingli, 4